This is a study of rural social structure in the English county of Essex between 1350 and 1525. It seeks to understand how, in the population collapse after the Black Death (1348–1349), a particular economic environment affected ordinary people's lives in the areas of migration, marriage and employment, and also contributed to patterns of religious nonconformity, agrarian riots and unrest, and even rural housing. The period under scrutiny is often seen as a transitional era between 'medieval' and 'early-modern' England, but in the light of recent advances in English historical demography this study suggests that there was more continuity than change in some critically important aspects of social structure in the region in question. Among the most important contributions of *A rural society after the Black Death* are its use of an unprecedentedly wide range of original manuscript records (estate and manorial records, taxation and criminal-court records, royal tenurial records, and the records of church courts, wills etc.) and its application of current quantitative and comparative demographic methods.

A rural society
after the Black Death

Cambridge Studies in Population, Economy and Society in Past Time 18

Series editors

PETER LASLETT, ROGER SCHOFIELD and E. A. WRIGLEY

ESRC Cambridge Group for the History of Population and Social Structure

and DANIEL SCOTT SMITH

University of Illinois at Chicago

Recent work in social, economic and demographic history has revealed much that was previously obscure about societal stability and change in the past. It has also suggested that crossing the conventional boundaries between these branches of history can be very rewarding.

This series will exemplify the value of interdisciplinary work of this kind, and will include books on topics such as family, kinship and neighbourhood; welfare provision and social control; work and leisure; migration; urban growth; and legal structures and procedures, as well as more familiar matters. It will demonstrate that, for example, anthropology and economics have become as close intellectual neighbours to history as have political philosophy or biography.

For a full list of titles in the series, please see end of book

A rural society after the Black Death: Essex 1350–1525

L. R. POOS

Associate Professor in the Department of History,
The Catholic University of America,
Washington DC

CAMBRIDGE UNIVERSITY PRESS

Cambridge
New York Port Chester Melbourne Sydney

PUBLISHED BY THE PRESS SYNDICATE OF THE UNIVERSITY OF CAMBRIDGE
The Pitt Building, Trumpington Street, Cambridge, United Kingdom

CAMBRIDGE UNIVERSITY PRESS
The Edinburgh Building, Cambridge CB2 2RU, UK
40 West 20th Street, New York NY 10011–4211, USA
477 Williamstown Road, Port Melbourne, VIC 3207, Australia
Ruiz de Alarcón 13, 28014 Madrid, Spain
Dock House, The Waterfront, Cape Town 8001, South Africa

http://www.cambridge.org

First published 1991
First paperback edition 2004

A catalogue record for this book is available from the British Library

Library of Congress cataloguing in publication data

Poos, Lawrence R. (Lawrence Raymond)
A rural society after the black death: Essex 1350–1525. / Larry Poos.
p. cm. – (Cambridge studies in population, economy and society in past time, 18).
Includes bibliographical references (pp.308–25) and index.
ISBN 0 521 38260 2 hardback
1. Essex. (England) – History. 2. Essex (England) – Social conditions.
3. England – Social conditions – Medieval period. 1066–1485.
4. England – Social conditions – 16th century. 5.
Black death – England – Essex – History. I. Title. II. Series.
DA670.E7P66 1991
942.6′7 – dc20 90–2692 CIP

ISBN 0 521 38260 2 hardback
ISBN 0 521 53127 6 paperback

Contents

Figures

Tables

Preface

The work represented in this book has spanned many years and two hemispheres, and my indebtedness for help and advice is correspondingly wide-ranging. Two institutions have provided complementary, equally congenial atmospheres to work in. My friends at the Cambridge Group for the History of Population and Social Structure laid the foundations for my understanding of social-science history and unfailingly welcome my annual return. My students and colleagues at The Catholic University of America continue to point out that I always have more to learn.

I owe even greater debts to many individuals who have helped my Essex research along. Richard Smith first started me out on this path, and spent much time commenting on my research and text. Roger Schofield's keen editorial scrutiny likewise helped me avoid running aground upon many shoals. The book would have been less than it is without information and specialist insights generously provided by Jeremy Boulton, Bruce Campbell, Richard Helmholz, Anne Hudson, Ray Powell, Andrew Prescott, Steve Rappaport, Michael Sheehan, David Souden and M. C. Wadhams. The text has greatly benefited from close reading and commentary by Richard Britnell, Elaine Clark, Barrie Dobson, Christopher Dyer, Michael Gervers, Jo Ann Hoeppner Moran, Jon Wakelyn and Richard Wall. My mistakes remain my own.

Financial support for portions of my research came from the British Academy, the Ellen McArthur Fund of the Cambridge University Faculty of History, and the American Bar Foundation. Catholic University's special projects fund contributed to the costs of preparing illustrations. I am grateful to Ann Padfield and Adrian Gibson for permission to adapt the illustrations in Chapter 4 from their publications. Grateful thanks are also due to people at the various record repositories I have haunted, in particular the Essex Record Office, the Public Record Office, Westminster Abbey, and New College, Oxford.

Citations from the archives of New College, Oxford, are made by kind permission of the Warden and Fellows; similarly, citation of St John's College, Cambridge, Archives D57.170 is made by kind permission of the Master, Fellows and Scholars. Portions of Chapters 5, 7 and 8 will have appeared in print in preliminary form already, and I am grateful to the *Economic History Review* and to Basil Blackwell Ltd for permission to reproduce them here.

Abbreviations

BL	British Library, London
Bodl.	Bodleian Library, Oxford
CALC	Cathedral Archives and Library, Canterbury
CCR	*Calendar of Close Rolls*
CPR	*Calendar of Patent Rolls*
ERO	Essex Record Office, Chelmsford
GL	Guildhall Library, London
GLRO	Greater London Record Office
JRL	Joseph Regenstein Library, Chicago
LAO	Lincolnshire Archives Office, Lincoln
LPL	Lambeth Palace Library
NCO	New College, Oxford
PRO	Public Record Office, London
SJCC	St John's College, Cambridge
SRO	Suffolk Record Office
UCO	University College, Oxford
VCH	*Victoria County History*
WAM	Westminster Abbey Muniments
WRO	Wiltshire Record Office, Trowbridge

PART I

Reflections on a transitional era

In 1502 in the Essex parish of Walthamstow, a labourer named Richard Gamone drew up his last will and testament. As did virtually every other testator of his time and place, Gamone began by commending his soul to God and all the saints, and his body to Walthamstow churchyard. He went on to leave a cow to the churchwardens for them to rent out to parishioners, and he asked them to apply the proceeds to various 'lights' in the church: lamps to Our Lady, St Katherine, the Trinity, and others. Hopeful of the lasting nature of his gift, he added, 'This money to be payde to the seid ligchts yerly whylys the Worlde last'.[1] Gamone could not know that, in one very important way, the world he was speaking of would last barely a generation after his death, when the English Reformation would render unacceptable these conventional Catholic pieties. But it is less easy to speak with confidence about how long the rest of the world Gamone knew as his would last.

English history from the late fourteenth to the early sixteenth century has often been regarded as a transitional era, a phrase historians commonly employ to indicate that they understand what had gone before and what came after much better than what was going on in between. If a recent survey of British history can claim that 'the later Middle Ages now appear as an age of turbulence and complexity',[2] the social, economic and demographic characteristics and evolutions that the era witnessed are particularly difficult to schematise. And yet, buried somewhere within that cluster of characteristics and evolutions, there was much that lies at the very core of what most historians understand to have divided the 'medieval' from the '(early) modern'. It is little wonder, then, that few social historians are bold, or foolhardy, enough to try to span this era. But evolutionary

[1] ERO D/AER 2/6. [2] Morgan, *Oxford history of Britain*, p. 193.

schemes to explain that transition are not altogether lacking in recent historiography.

Probably the most influential model of change within England during this period is a cyclical model, arising from renewed attention in the post-war years to quantitative economic history and first adumbrated by M. M. Postan.[3] This understanding of late-medieval society places prime emphasis upon the long-term relationship between aggregate population and agrarian resources as chief determinant of prices, wages, living standards and land utilisation. Pressures of people upon land as the English population reached its medieval peak in the decades around 1300, the extermination of roughly one-third of the country's people in the Black Death of 1348–9, and more than a century of demographic stagnation and agrarian contraction thereafter: all these had far-reaching effects not only upon England's economy but also upon the structure of rural society, effects which in some, though by no means all, cases would be reversed in the next wave of demographic expansion in the 1500s.

Somewhat counterpoised to cyclical models of this sort are unilinear schemes, the most vehemently expressed being that posed by Marxist historiography.[4] Under such views a complex of political, legal, social and economic power relationships approached crisis point by the later fourteenth century. Out of the trauma of that crisis a different social order eventually emerged: a fundamentally 'feudal' order gave way to a fundamentally 'capitalist' one. Other unilinear schemes of different ideological stripes, whether concerned with the transformation of state power and the establishment of a more modern apparatus of monarchical or parliamentary rule, or of ecclesiastical settlement and the institutional and religious implications of the Protestant Reformation, none the less emphasise those aspects of English society that were irreversibly broken off from their late-medieval antecedents.

Putting these schemes and theories into such uncompromisingly foreshortened forms does, of course, risk caricaturing them. What is more noteworthy, though, is that all these schemes tend to presuppose that such wide-ranging changes must have been accompanied by

[3] These arguments find their classic expression in Postan, *The medieval economy and society*; more recent mainstream writers of medieval English economic history follow Postan's lead to a large extent, e.g. Miller and Hatcher, *Medieval England*; Bolton, *The medieval English economy*; Hatcher, *Plague, population and the English economy*.

[4] The classic exposition to this 'crisis' debate on the European-wide scale is contained in Hilton, ed., *The transition from feudalism to capitalism*; a more recent synthetic statement is Martin, *Feudalism to capitalism*. The unease with which Marxist historiography still contemplates demography is exemplified by the essays in Aston and Philpin, eds., *The Brenner debate*. Some perceptive critical remarks are made concerning the meaning of these changes by Glennie, 'In search of agrarian capitalism'.

transformations in English society at its most basic levels: those of family, household, neighbourhood and parish, and of individual English men's and women's experiences of them. A recent polemical debate concerning the origins of English 'individualism' demonstrated, if nothing else, how self-evident it is to most historians of the period that these basic levels of English society must have been fundamentally affected by all that was going on around them.[5]

This book is an attempt to disentangle one small piece of this large puzzle. It is a study of rural social structure – that much-bandied-about term being taken here to mean, broadly, patterns of common people's migration, settlement, marriage and work, along with associated patterns of material and mental culture. Each of these experiences is comprehensible only within the matrix of all the others. This study takes as one of its points of departure the immense body of knowledge that has been gained over the last twenty years or so – much more, alas, than can ever be recovered about previous centuries – about England's early-modern social structure. Recent studies have concluded beyond reasonable doubt that from the mid-sixteenth until well into the eighteenth century, English rural society was characterised by a cluster of features at some odds with traditional depictions of its medieval precursors. In early-modern English rural society, men and women were highly mobile, married late and resided mostly in small nuclear households, and their behaviour in all these respects was keenly sensitive to their economic environment and its changes across time and space.[6] And so this study deliberately sets up what is known empirically about these later centuries as a benchmark against which to gauge late-medieval England's 'medievality', and seeks to find ways to measure the similarities and differences.

This book is also a local study of rural life in a particular corner of England at the end of the middle ages: a district in the northern and central areas of the county of Essex, little more than 500 square miles, and probably containing no more than 20,000 people at any point in the fifteenth century. 'The district', as this study's shorthand for it will often be, can be formally defined as the Hundreds – administrative divisions larger than townships but smaller than counties – of Chelmsford, Dunmow, Freshwell, Hinckford and Uttlesford (see Figure I.1).

[5] The debate referred to here is that ensuing from Macfarlane, *Origins of English individualism*. See, in particular, Hilton, 'Individualism and the English peasantry'; White and Vann, 'The invention of English individualism'; Poos and Bonfield, 'Law and individualism'.

[6] The most recent literature at time of writing this is cited in the appropriate chapters below. The single most important study in this context is Wrigley and Schofield, *Population history of England*.

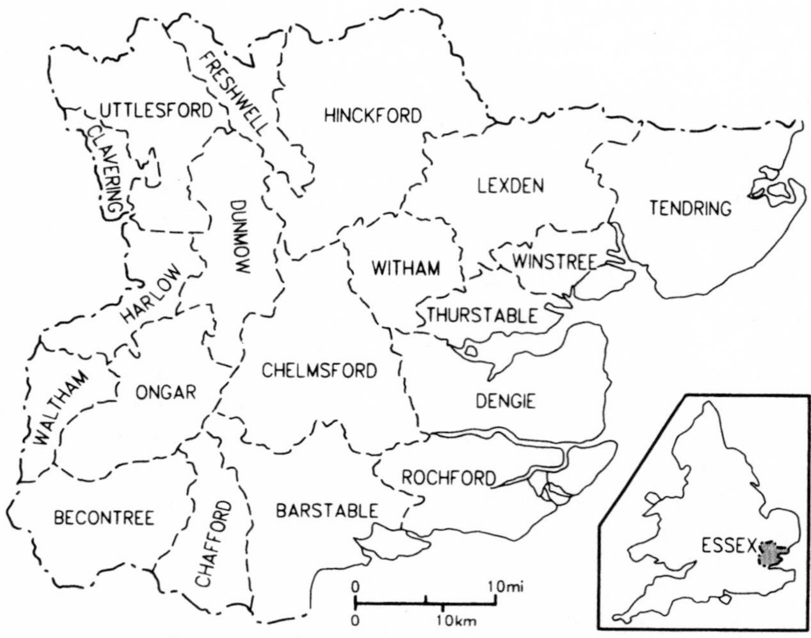

Figure I.1 The hundreds of medieval Essex

But what distinguished this district as a unit was a handful of measurable features of its local economy and social structure: among others, a high density of population, an unusually marked development of rural industry (especially textiles), a large degree of social and economic differentiation, and a propensity toward religious nonconformity and violent agrarian unrest.

This district was by no means, then, a 'typical' corner of England at the time, if there were such a thing. In fact, in many ways its social structure exhibited features (as much of this book will be taken up with showing) usually regarded as characteristic of England well after the middle ages closed. It was, in that sense, more complex than English society in this period has conventionally been regarded. Whether its social structure was indeed so precocious as all this would imply would become clear only after much study of other places, and such a claim need not be pressed here. But case studies of places on the sharp end of change, if such this district was, are often useful test cases of the limits of chronological evolution, for to understand the limiting case is to appreciate better the factors contributing to that very same change.

To propose a district as the subject of local study of social structure in medieval England is something of a departure from recent norms. Studies of individual villages or communities, both in the middle ages and in the early-modern period, have been among the most illuminating recent contributions to social history.[7] Village studies offer many advantages, not least in their offering a scale of enquiry that allows individuals and families to be reconstituted through painstaking linkage of their many appearances in different documentary contexts. Village studies also mesh well with the geographical limits of the manor, the institution that generated some of the most useful records of medieval rural life. But village studies also pose difficulties. Manorial-court records, so rich for some aspects of village society, have their limits, and fall some way short of substitutes for complete registers of demographic events.[8] Moreover, they become rather less informative in precisely this period, because most manors' jurisdictional powers were irrevocably ebbing away in the later fourteenth century with the eclipse of serfdom and the seigneurial order it entailed. On the other hand, there are many other sources – church- and royal-court records, tax lists, central-government tenurial records and wills, for example – that may cover particular communities sparsely or not at all, but when taken in the aggregate present meaningfully large bodies of evidence at larger geographical levels. And despite the variations of local economy and society even at the sub-county level, it will still be necessary to treat some bodies of evidence in this study at the county level, and to go to other portions of Essex or even just outside the county's borders for evidence entirely lacking within the strictly defined district.

The nature of the evidence also makes it necessary to pretend at times that 1350–1525 is a period of some characteristic coherence. That is to say, where only one body of evidence from some specific point within the period is available for a particular analytical problem, one can do little more than cautiously take that evidence as somehow generally representative of the period as a whole, with informed speculation about the changes that lay on either side of that point. For changes there of course were; and if the following chapters appear in places to treat the period as an undifferentiated block of time, that

7 Some noteworthy examples of such studies include Wrightson and Levine, *Poverty and piety*; McIntosh, *Autonomy and community*; and several of the essays included in Smith, ed., *Land, kinship and life-cycle*.

8 These issues are discussed in Poos and Smith, 'Legal windows onto historical populations?'; Razi, 'The use of manorial court rolls'; Poos and Smith, 'Shades still on the window'; Razi, 'The demographic transparency of manorial court rolls'.

must not be taken to imply that the era lacked its own internal rhythms.

Ultimately, the documents that medieval England has left exposed to the scrutiny of social-structural historians will never be as satisfactory as the parish registers, household listings, settlement examinations and diaries with which students of post-medieval England have been blessed. This book must, then, seek to recreate a district by combining as many different bodies of evidence as are available. And it turns out that north-central Essex is unusually well provided with material for the reconstruction of demography and social structures in this period. Even so, for only some aspects of local economy and society will this evidence be anything like unequivocal. All the more necessary, therefore, does this fact make it to construct a holistic picture. If a number of patterns that individually are less than conclusive still point in one direction, that direction must surely be the more credible. Many of these sources are oblique, in the sense that they were generated for purposes even further removed from the interests of twentieth-century historians than is usually the case with social-history sources. Extra effort is required, then, to transform their data to forms even generally comparable with later material.

It is one of the primary assumptions of this book that in historical research which is oriented towards the social sciences, scrutiny of both raw materials and the processes required to extract meaningful patterns from them must be rigorous, systematic, explicitly articulated, and replicable. Concern with the process of derivation is part of the telling, even at the risk of intruding into the story itself. The chapters that follow address many problems that only quantitative data can meaningfully illuminate, and it is inherent in the nature of the evidence from this period that calculations from records like the later-fourteenth-century poll-tax returns or manorial rentals demand especially careful explication.

On the other hand, manorial-court cases, depositions rendered before ecclesiastical courts, and evidence taken before royal tenurial inquests have left much in the way of narrative or anecdotal accounts. The present study also uses these accounts extensively. But the Essex countryfolk who made their fleeting appearances on the historical stage in these contexts almost all remain just names, and to understand administrative context is vital for assessing the meaning of their stories. In fact, the importance of evidence of a legal nature for the chapters that follow is a recurrent theme. Discourses upon the nature of evidence and upon how one must work with it have been kept to a minimum in the following pages, and where possible they are relegated to footnotes or appendices.[9] To separate such matters entirely from the analysis, though, would be to risk damage to the analysis itself.

What follows does not aspire to total reconstruction of the district in the period, for such is impossible. To state merely one of the most obvious limitations, the experiences of rural women in this as in most preindustrial societies – experiences that were critical to the demographic makeup of this society, to say nothing of their claim to a commensurate share in its material and mental culture – are perforce more difficult to recover, though necessary to infer. The following chapters can be read, rather, as a series of interlocking essays, each confronting a specific knot of problems but all contributing to an edifice. What runs through them is a concern to see each knot as part of a larger web. That is, in fact, what this world was.

[9] It has been unavoidable to exclude from the main text some lengthy discussions, for example of calculations from the poll-tax returns (Chapter 7), consistory-court depositions (Chapter 8), or testimony rendered at proof-of-age hearings (Chapter 9). Appropriate cross-references are given elsewhere when these bodies of material are referred to. Appendices at the end of this study discuss in more detail the poll-tax data, derivations of time-series data for land rents, prices and wages, and evidence for fulling mills as an index of the rural cloth industry.

PART II

'Country-dwellers, common folk and craftsmen'

A chronicler's description of a rural mob at Pleshey, 1400[1]

The central and northern district of Essex during the later middle ages contained a quite distinctive configuration of social, economic and occupational groups, and of local economic and settlement geography. By the early fourteenth century, at least half of local households were smallholders or landless, drawn into wage labour or artisanal by-employment. Unlike what may have happened in other regions of England, this situation did not change appreciably after the Black Death of 1348–9 extinguished one-third or more of the district's residents. To the contrary, marked disparity of landholding and occupation continued to characterise the area well beyond the close of the medieval period. Hence much of the following chapters will address the factors contributing to this situation, their ultimate implications for local social structure, and the differences in experiences that different groups within the local population underwent.

The district was very densely populated during the period. Besides helping to account for economic disparity, two further corollaries of population density were market dependence and occupational complexity, both probably stemming from local circumstances rather than the influence of external urban centres such as London. In fact, the economic typology of local communities did not make for sharp demarcations between 'urban' and 'rural'. Craftsmen and retailers permeated the smallest villages and the smallest satellite hamlets of larger settlements.

As in most of England, the post-Black Death period witnessed shifts

1 Thompson, ed., *Chronicon Adae de Usk*, p. 42, describing how the Earl of Huntingdon, imprisoned at Pleshey after an abortive *coup* attempt, was taken and beheaded by a mob: '... per pagances captus ... per plebeyos et mecanicos decapitatur ...'. See also below, Chapter 11.

in local agriculture and land use as animals gained in relative importance to grain. The district's settlement and field systems did, however, mitigate against disruptive transformations of the rural landscape, which in this district has remained remarkably unchanged over the centuries. At the same time as agriculture contracted, however, rural-based clothmaking expanded rapidly in importance here, absorbing significant numbers of people from the countryside. Rural industry in the district comprised a loose network of individuals, working part-time in different phases of the production process, instead of a classic putting-out or cottage industry. Local economy and social structure thus complemented one another, as many of the land-poor were absorbed into clothmaking and other artisanal work.

One of the most tangible artefacts of economic differentiation in the district was the rural houses that locals occupied, still standing in surprisingly large numbers. Houses grew in size and in the variegation of their living spaces, though this was primarily the experience of better-off agriculturalists. Local houses were thus flexible enough to accommodate a variety of household sizes and types. They were, in that sense, a microcosmic mirror of the social structure that fitted into them.

1

People, land and occupations

There are many ways to approach the study of an historical rural society. One of the most revealing is to begin by inspecting cross-sections of its economic composition, for doing so can lead to many insights into the nature of that society that are not necessarily obvious at the outset. In this respect the two most revealing indices that late-medieval Essex sources can provide are landholding profiles and occupational structures.

The rural economy of northern and central Essex in the later middle ages was a mixture of farming, crafts or industry, and trading, and the basic unit of production in this economy was the household, with family labour inputs supplemented, at times heavily, with hired workers. And yet households differed widely in their endowments of land or other capital, and at least half of all the families in the district during the later fourteenth and fifteenth centuries derived much or most of their income from wages earned from others. Landholding and occupation were therefore intricately intertwined. Later sections of this study will observe that many demographic and other aspects of life in late-medieval Essex differed considerably between different occupational groups, so a first step towards understanding the significance of these experiences is to be quite precise about how the groups were configured.

Within any traditional agrarian society the landholding profile – the distribution of landholdings of different sizes among its population – bears much influence upon the nature of social relationships and economic development. It is unlikely that any such society could be found in which every household, family or individual enjoyed an absolutely equal share in land.[1] But although distributions of landholding sizes are only an imperfect measure of economic inequality in any

[1] Hilton, 'Reasons for inequality'.

rural society, and a host of other factors also influence economic complexity, land distributions are revealing of the extent to which many within that society will be forced to seek employment in non-agricultural activity or in working on other people's land, or will find themselves entering market transactions to obtain basic subsistence commodities. In medieval England, several historians have argued, a tenement of ten to fifteen acres in size would probably have been the minimum (depending, of course, on the levels of rent, taxes and so on owed) for a 'typical' villager's family to subsist upon agriculture alone.[2]

Many factors influenced how unequally landed resources were distributed among families in medieval England.[3] The profile of holding sizes at any given time in a particular community reflected, first of all, cyclical and non-cyclical effects of a previous generation's micro-demography, most specifically the range of inheritance and devolution patterns among families with varying numbers of offspring surviving to assume parents' endowments in real property and chattels. Depending upon both a manor's formal inheritance customs and, probably rather more importantly, the ways and degrees to which parents made use of alternative means of transmitting their property to the next generation outside the formal 'custom of the manor', each generation might reconstitute itself in a potentially different landholding configuration, simply because some parents had no children to succeed them, while others had a few, and still others had many.[4]

But inheritance or devolution was by no means the only way, or even the most common way, for land to change hands in later-medieval Essex. By the later thirteenth century at the latest, as in much of England, the customary law of most Essex manors (which set the

[2] E.g. Postan, *The medieval economy and society*, pp. 132–4; Titow, *English rural society*, pp. 89–90; Hilton, *A medieval society*, pp. 121–3.

[3] Some historians of medieval English agrarian society have been much influenced in their treatment of this subject by models first proposed in analysis of Russian peasant society by A.V. Chayanov and V.I. Lenin. These models, respectively and put very crudely, proposed either that tenurial differentiation stemmed mainly from cyclical forces relating landed resources to the labour supply and consumption needs of the 'peasant' family over its generational life cycle, or alternatively that divisions among 'rich and poor peasants', while ubiquitous in traditional rural societies, were exacerbated by market-influenced capital accumulation. These models are discussed by Smith, 'Some issues concerning families and their property', pp. 6–21; the general influence of Russian studies upon earlier generations of English medievalists is discussed in Gattrell, 'Historians and peasants'. Smith demonstrates the general inapplicability of Chayanovian theory to the medieval English context. The present study similarly regards it as unhelpful to import such theories to this local setting.

[4] These points are summarised in Smith, 'Some issues concerning families and their property', esp. pp. 38–68; cf. Hilton, 'Reasons for inequality', p. 279.

legal terms under which most property was held by villagers) had come to recognise such a firm claim to title that individuals could buy, sell, or lease land among themselves quite readily, so long as transfer was effected in the manorial lords' court and followed prescribed terms. Village land markets were especially active in southeastern England by the fourteenth century, and this was certainly the case in Essex.[5] In the Essex manors of Great Waltham and High Easter from 1351 to 1389, transfers recorded in the surviving manorial-court records imply that an area of land approximately equal to the total acreage of all tenant holdings in the two manors changed hands roughly every fourteen years, with *inter vivos* transactions accounting for a greater acreage transferred than inheritance or other post mortem devolution.[6] With such an active land market present, competition among individuals and families already of unequal economic standing would also be reflected in each new generation's landholding profile. Seigneurial interest or policy might work to constrain land markets, for example to forestall fragmentation of some holdings below a viable minimum size, but this is less apparently the case in southeastern England than elsewhere.[7]

Finally, the long-term relationship between aggregate population and land obviously had a critical effect in setting both mean holding sizes per person or household and, potentially, the degree of inequality among holding sizes. It is generally agreed that as England's population reached its high-medieval zenith some time in the decades around 1300, in more densely peopled parts of the country (such as north-central Essex, as Chapter 2 will show) land hunger was becoming acute. Many more people were forced out of landholding altogether or at least were relegated to smallholder ranks. Under the circumstances, short-term harvest fluctuations could be devastating to those whose landholdings fell beneath a threshold size sufficient to provide a margin of safety for riding out a year's deficient yields. In the agrarian crisis of 1315–17 caused by disastrously bad weather, for

5 The literature on this subject is voluminous. General discussions, references to other recent research, and useful case studies are contained in Smith, ed., *Land, kinship and life-cycle*, and Harvey, ed., *The peasant land market*.

6 Poos, 'Population and resources', pp. 219–20; cf. Dyer, *Lords and peasants in a changing society*, p. 301, where it is estimated that at one West Midlands manor in the fifteenth century, one-tenth of the manor's holdings changed hands every year.

7 Such a seigneurial policy is inferred by Harvey, *Westminster Abbey*, esp. pp. 299–314. That such a policy was not universal, especially in areas of Essex and East Anglia where classic common-field systems of the Midlands type were largely absent, has been argued by Smith, ' "Hereditary" and "proprietary" rights', esp. pp. 114–23.

example, many smallholders were forced to sell out, presumably to those higher up in the tenancy echelons.[8] On the other hand, in the wake of the Black Death, with many fewer hands to hold the available land, historians have tended to presume that a kind of 'promotion' process took place, by which previously modest tenants who survived might buy into a larger share.[9] On this last point, however, there have in fact been surprisingly few systematic empirical studies, especially at the regional or supra-community level. A community's landholding profile at any point in time thus also reflected recent and longer-term aggregate demography.

The only systematic evidence for observing landholding profiles empirically in later-medieval England comes from manorial rentals, documents drawn up irregularly by manorial officials and listing all the manor's tenants, with descriptions of the lands they held and rents and other services that they owed for it, at the time of compilation.[10] These sources are not without their problems. They differ widely in degrees of detail given and in their susceptibility to quantification. The tenurial units they record may in some cases be standardised abstractions rather than tangible physical units of area, and local definitions of an 'acre's' dimensions varied.[11]

Moreover, rentals were primarily concerned to record rents and services owed by persons holding land directly from the manorial lord and so were likely to be unconcerned with subtenants, though the actual occupation of the land resulting from subletting might differ from the notional distribution of direct tenancies.[12] The idiosyncrasies of individual rentals' compilation and contents must be examined closely before their evidence can be accepted at face value. Finally, it should be reiterated that, because rentals expose to the historian's gaze only those persons who actually held land directly of the manor, undertenants and the wholly landless were not recorded in these documents, and so one is able to view only the manor's tenants and not the community's entire population or even all its heads of households. Still, medieval agrarian historians have long viewed

[8] Kershaw, 'Agrarian crisis', pp. 118–29; Razi, *Life, marriage and death in a medieval parish*, pp. 39–41, 94–8.

[9] The classic statement of this premise is Postan, 'Agrarian evidence of a declining population', pp. 208–11.

[10] Harvey, *Manorial records*, pp. 15–24.

[11] Harvey, ed., *Manorial records of Cuxham*, pp. 76–9; Jones, 'Land measurement in England'.

[12] An especially revealing example of this, taken from an Essex manor, is discussed in McIntosh, 'Land, tenure and population'.

these sources as the best means of observing degrees of tenurial inequality and making conjectures about rural living standards.[13]

Tables 1.1 and 1.2 present data for landholding profiles from twelve rentals drawn from central and northern Essex both before and after the Black Death. Though at least three dozen rentals survive from manors in this district during the period, the sample presented here was selected because these rentals met minimum criteria for quantifiability, most importantly reasonably clear definitions of the physical dimensions of tenurial units and some indication that undertenants had not been entirely omitted. Such a relatively small number of suitably quantifiable rentals may in part be a function of the district's field systems and tenement forms, because in the absence of open-field or common-field arrangements typical of Midland England at the time, landholdings were more likely to be expressed as irregular, enclosed parcels without stated acreages.[14] The manors in question varied widely in size and number of tenants, as well as economic types of community represented. In the case of one, Thaxted, the central settlement was a sizeable market town surrounded by outlying agricultural hamlets,[15] and tabulated here are only those agricultural holdings not in the possession of persons who also had burgage tenures within the town itself, in order to minimise the urban nature of the tenantry represented in the data. Taken collectively these data yield a broadly based impression of landholding profiles within the district at large.

For each rental, all of a given individual's different properties, of different legal or tenurial statuses, were aggregated to form a 'tenancy'. In the tables are compiled tenancy sizes, in terms of acreages of arable land (omitting meadow, pasture and other forms of non-arable property that in practice were not always listed among tenants' possessions).[16] Separate categories were allotted for those persons who held only messuages, cottages, or other types of residential property, and for those who held 'unquantifiable' property of miscellaneous types (typically properties described as a 'piece'

[13] E.g. Miller and Hatcher, *Medieval England*, pp. 134–64; Hilton, *A medieval society*, pp. 88–133; Titow, *English rural society*, pp. 64–96.

[14] See below, Chapter 2.

[15] Newton, *Thaxted*.

[16] In the enclosed field system prevailing in this district common grazing land was rare and, with few exceptions, limited in size. Most grazing took place on fallowed arable land within enclosed tenements: see below, Chapter 2. This is emphasised here because it means that to omit non-arable land in the distributions of Tables 1.1 and 1.2 is not necessarily to distort the agrarian value of the tenements in question, as might first appear.

Table 1.1. *Distribution of tenancy sizes, seven Essex manorial rentals before the Black Death (1288–1340)*

	Number of tenancies in each size category							
	Matching 1288	Stebbing 1294	Borley 1308	Middleton 1309	High Easter 1328	Great Waltham 1328	Margaretting 1340	Total
House-site etc. only	0	4	2	2	23	26	10	67
Unquantifiable	2	12	2	4	13	27	7	67
>0–5 acres	20	21	13	17	47	122	22	262
>5–10 acres	2	6	15	6	30	45	7	111
>10–15 acres	4	8	1	3	37	27	3	83
>15–20 acres	0	0	5	0	11	11	1	28
>20–25 acres	1	1	2	1	4	4	1	14
>25–30 acres	0	0	0	1	3	7	1	12
>30–35 acres	0	0	0	1	1	3	0	5
>35–40 acres	1	0	1	1	1	5	0	9
>40 acres	0	2	1	2	2	7	0	14
Total	30	54	42	38	172	284	52	672

Sources: Matching (Househam Hall), 1288: PRO. SC12.7.44.
Stebbing, 1294: BL Add. Roll 66041.
Borley, 1308: BL MS Harley 1006 fos. 13–20.
Middleton, 1309: BL MS Harley 1006 fos. 20–29v.
High Easter, 1328: PRO.DL43.2.32.
Great Waltham, 1328: BL Cotton Ch. XIII.5.
Margaretting (Fristling Hall), 1340: ERO D/DP M1411.

[*peciam*] of land or a 'corner' [*angulum*], for example)[17] that may generally be taken as implying in most cases very small holdings.

Table 1.1 presents seven rentals from the sixty years before 1348, at the culmination of centuries of aggregate demographic growth in England at large. Although tenancy-size distributions were not absolutely uniform from manor to manor there was in fact a remarkably similar landholding profile in all these communities, from the quite small to the quite large. If a definitive criterion for smallholders in these places is taken as those possessing no more than five acres of arable land, then virtually one-half (48.7 per cent) of all tenancies expressed in arable acreages fell into this category in the seven manors aggregated together. Under a broader criterion – tenancies of no more than five acres, plus those consisting solely of residential property or unquantifiable, miscellaneous but probably mostly quite small pieces of land – nearly three-fifths (58.9 per cent) of all the manors' tenants would be classified as smallholders. And, once again, the wholly landless are excluded from these data.

Such an extreme degree of polarisation in landed resources should be placed into comparative perspective. Though direct comparisons are by no means straightforward, smallholders in this Essex district were proportionately far more numerous than in other communities or regions of England in the last generations before the Black Death.[18] Examples can certainly be found of more severe tenurial fragmen-

[17] Examples of such miscellaneous units are PRO.DL43.2.5 (Barnston rental, 1435): '... unam peciam terre cum sepibus & fossatis inclusam ... unum cotland' vocatum Bakeres ... '; PRO.DL43.2.32 (High Easter rental, 1328): ' ... quamdam placeam unius curtilagie ... quoddam angulum apud Hobbetranebredg ... '; BL Cotton Ch. XIII.5 (Great Waltham rental, 1328): ' ... j purpresturam iuxta portam Johannis Burdayn ...'. As noted below (Chapter 4), *tenementum* in north-central Essex usually denoted a messuage-site, plus outbuildings and attached gardens, though this probably cannot be presumed in all cases, so property described as such has also been classified 'unquantifiable' here. The rentals represented in Tables 1.1 and 1.2 all permit larger standardised holdings like virgates to be expressed in acreages, thus further making it likely that these 'unquantifiable' units are mostly small. Classification of tenancies in Tables 1.1 and 1.2 follows the guidelines in Poos, 'Population and resources', pp. 200–5.

[18] E.g. Kosminsky, *Studies in agrarian history*, pp. 216–23 (29 per cent of villeins and 47 per cent of free tenants in six Midlands counties were recorded in the 1279 Hundred Rolls as holding less than five acres); Postan, *The medieval economy and society*, pp. 127–9 (at 104 manors in the home counties and southern England in the mid- and later thirteenth century, approximately 45 per cent of tenants held less than a quarter-virgate); Dyer, *Lords and peasants in a changing society*, pp. 299–301 (at four West Midlands manors in 1299, tenants holding less than a half-yardland ranged from 26 to 42 per cent of all tenants); Titow, *English rural society*, p. 79 (at Bishop's Waltham, Hants, 51.5 per cent of all tenants held less than ten acres in 1332). Even in other, less densely populated parts of Essex, tenurial fragmentation was less marked: cf. McIntosh, 'Land, tenure and population', pp. 18–24 (at Havering in southwestern Essex in 1352/3, about 38 per cent of tenancies totalled less than five acres).

Table 1.2. *Distribution of tenancy sizes, five Essex manorial rentals after the Black Death (1383–1444)*

	Number of tenancies in each size category					
	Stebbing 1383	Thaxted 1393	Great Leighs *c.*1400	Barnston 1435	Stebbing 1444	Total
House-site etc. only	6	6	0	1	10	23
Unquantifiable	14	17	18	9	18	76
>0–5 acres	29	33	7	10	27	106
>5–10 acres	11	9	4	7	14	45
>10–15 acres	7	5	3	2	9	26
>15–20 acres	2	4	1	1	3	11
>20–25 acres	1	4	0	0	1	6
>25–30 acres	1	1	2	1	1	6
>30–35 acres	1	1	2	1	1	6
>35–40 acres	0	0	0	0	0	0
>40 acres	1	7	0	0	3	11
Total	73	87	37	32	87	316

Sources: Stebbing, 1383: BL Add. Roll 65957.
Thaxted, 1393: ERO D/DHu M58 (only tenancies not containing burgage property included here).
Great Leighs, *c.*1400: PRO.DL43.3.8.
Barnston, 1435: PRO.DL43.2.5.
Stebbing, 1444: BL Add. Roll 66046.

tation, though mostly in other parts of eastern or southeastern England and especially in places characterised by extensive pastoral husbandry or partible inheritance.[19] The landholding profile of northern and central Essex, as later sections of this study will show, was a corollary of both a very high population density in the district and a local economy in which more than half its rural dwellers were substantially dependent upon wage labour in agriculture or work in industrial, artisanal, or trading activities as early as the first half of the fourteenth century.

Manorial rentals with usable data are scarcer in this district from the later fourteenth and fifteenth centuries, and unfortunately none has

[19] E.g. Smith, 'Kin and neighbours', pp. 20–2 (nearly half the tenancies in Redgrave, Suffolk, in the later thirteenth century were less than two acres); Campbell, 'Population change and the genesis of commonfields', pp. 176–82 (for a similar situation at Martham, Norfolk); Hallam, *Settlement and society*, pp. 197–222.

been discovered that dates from the later 1400s and that lends itself to this form of quantitative analysis. Table 1.2 presents material from only five rentals (two of them from the same manor) during the hundred years after 1350. Though the sample size is smaller than that of the earlier rentals, the patterns are again fairly consistent among the communities in question. Here too, virtually one-half (48.8 per cent) of all tenancies expressed in arable acreages consisted of no more than five acres, while by the broader definition of smallholding nearly two-thirds (64.9 per cent) of all tenancies ranked among the humblest levels of propertyholders. This, in short, looks remarkably similar to the pre-1348 sample, and indeed there is no statistically significant difference between the earlier and later aggregations.[20] And although the earlier and later samples are composed of different groups of manors and so the representative nature of their aggregative data would be difficult to prove conclusively, in the one case where a single manor – Stebbing – can be followed through three sequential compilations extending over 150 years, a similar statistical perdurance of tenurial fragmentation was certainly part of that community's later-medieval history.[21]

To trace in detail the workings of local land markets and devolution, in order to show the incremental steps through which tenancy distributions were maintained so persistently, would require going beyond the boundaries of this study and would perhaps strain the available evidence. In the short run – that is, in the decade or two after the Black Death and the vacating of a sizeable fraction of Essex tenements – some property fell vacant for years, some was taken up immediately by surviving heirs, and some found ready takers among persons well equipped with the money and other wherewithal to assume it. Lords used a carrot-and-stick approach to try to maintain

[20] A chi-square test classifying the data from the last columns of Tables 1.1 and 1.2 into two columns, and subdividing tenancy sizes into four rows (>0–5 acres plus residential property only plus unquantifiable property only, >5–20 acres, >20–35 acres, and >35 acres) yields a chi-square statistic of 5.267, not significant at the .05 level (3 degrees of freedom).

[21] Aggregating as above for Stebbing's three rentals yields a chi-square statistic of 1.688, not significant at the .05 level (6 degrees of freedom). The superficially puzzling fact that there were so many more tenancies (73 and 87) after the Black Death than before (54) at Stebbing is a salutary reminder that numbers of tenants recorded in manorial rentals do not necessarily bear any meaningful relationship to resident population. The later Stebbing rentals include farms (cash rents) of land, almost certainly (though not explicitly) mostly former demesne land, with the result that the 1444 rental pertains to more than double the total arable acreage in tenants' hands encapsulated in the 1294 rental. In short, to compare absolute tenant *numbers* over this period is not necessarily to compare apples with apples, but distributions of land *within* each cohort of tenants are more meaningfully comparable.

their rent rolls. In a few places, hints survive of coercive pressures brought by lords to force suitable tenants, usually men already among the ranks of well-to-do agriculturalists, to take up unclaimed properties. At Great Waltham in 1355, thirteen villeins were ordered distrained to take possession of unclaimed land because 'they are able both in body and in goods to assume vacant tenements'.[22] Something similar is implied at Birdbrook a few years later.[23] But over the longer run such a policy was simply untenable, and lords were forced to make concessions. Already in the last quarter of the fourteenth century the per-acre lease rates of arable land paid in manors in this district of Essex were dropping quickly.[24]

The broader implication of these data is clear. There was no wholesale promotion of smallholders, proportionately speaking, in this district of Essex in the century after the Black Death. Unlike, for example, the estates of the Bishopric of Worcester in the West Midlands over a similar period, there was no proportional growth of numbers of large tenancies and no corresponding decrease in the ranks of middling and lesser tenants.[25] Even in Cheshunt, just over the Essex border in neighbouring Hertfordshire, landholding in the later fifteenth century did not begin to approach such a degree of polarisation.[26] Clearly the situation reflected in the tables above was specific to a quite localised set of circumstances. Put more bluntly, the long-term persistence of a smallholding or near-landless stratum in rural society would appear to have been an integral feature of this district of Essex, where an essentially identical land distribution in the decades around 1600 was merely a continuation of an already long-entrenched phenomenon.[27]

This being so, an equally distinctive occupational composition was likely for the district's rural population, and such was indeed the case.

22 PRO.DL30.64.812 (Great Waltham court, 11 Nov 1355): ' . . . nativi domini et potentes tam in corpore quam in catallis accipere et tenere tenementa vacua etc Et ideo preceptum est ipsos omnes attachiare contra diem dominicam proximam sequentem . . . '. In each case the tenant accepted the land but paid no entry fine 'because he took it against his will [quia illam cepit contra voluntatem]'. Cf. Poos, 'Population and resources', pp. 248–50.

23 ERO D/DU 267/29 (Birdbrook leet, 20 Jul 1364): [Chief pledges] 'presentant quod Willelmus filius Johannis Balleye nativus domini est sufficiens etatis ad tenendum terram domini Et dominus concessit eidem Willelmo mesuagium & terram quondam Paternoster . . .' [no entry fine recorded].

24 See below, Chapter 2.

25 Dyer, *Lords and peasants in a changing society*, pp. 298–301.

26 Glennie, 'In search of agrarian capitalism', pp. 18–19.

27 Hunt, *The Puritan moment*, pp. 16–19, citing unpublished research by F. Hull, notes that in the late sixteenth and early seventeenth centuries in Essex as a whole, 46.0 per cent of the holdings for which acreages are available in a sample of manorial rentals totalled five acres or less; in northern Essex the figure was 56.7 per cent.

For the purposes of this study, lay Essex rural dwellers below the social level of the gentry have been broadly classified into three major occupational categories, based upon the terms used to describe them in contemporary documents. These groupings are 'agriculturalists'[28] (for example, *liber tenens, nativus tenens, firmarius, cultor, frankeleyn, husbandman* and the like), 'labourers' (*laborator, laborarius, famulus*[29]), and 'craftsmen and retailers' (virtually anyone else given an artisanal or trading description). Historians have in fact long recognised that Essex, along with certain portions of East Anglia, had unusually high proportions of wage labourers and rural craftsmen residing in its late-medieval countryside, compared to other regions of England.[30]

But, especially since these broad occupational groupings will form the basis by which demographic and other differences are examined within the district's population in the following chapters, it should be emphasised that the ostensible precision with which contemporary sources subdivided people by means of these appellations masks a more complex reality. The same person or members of the same household, at different times of a given year or at different stages of their life cycles, could be successively a wage-earner on another's land, a small-scale farmer, and a cloth-weaver or ale-brewer. It must be presumed – and it can and will be tested, below – that when these terms were employed in tax returns or other documents, they bore some realistic relationship to the principal means by which livelihoods were gained or social status recognised.

And in fact there is evidence that English society generally was evolving a more complex and precise terminology to denote social ranks in the later fourteenth and fifteenth centuries: in short, that contemporary conceptualisations of social and occupational strata were sharpening. Successive sumptuary statutes in 1363, 1463 and 1483 forbidding different classes of person wearing overly costly apparel – in itself betokening keen sensitivity to shiftings among ranks and degrees – placed servants in husbandry, common labourers, and servants to rural artisans at the bottom of a finely graded social ladder.[31] Coleman and Hilton have shown that literature of social commentary in the same period drew distinctions between the

[28] This admittedly inelegant word has been deliberately chosen to avoid somewhat value-laden terms like 'peasant', or terms like 'farmer' that carry a specialised connotation among medieval agrarian historians.

[29] *Famulus* is a somewhat ambiguous term, which can also mean 'servant'. Its meaning is discussed below, Chapter 9.

[30] E.g. Hilton, *Bond men made free*, pp. 171–5.

[31] 37 Edw. III cc. 8–15, 3 Edw. IV c. 5, 22 Edw. IV c. 1; printed in *Statutes of the realm* vol. i, p. 380; vol. ii, pp. 399–401, 468–70.

generally virtuous 'ploughmen' (or in present terminology, agriculturalists) and the less trustworthy, perhaps even less human labourers – 'like beasts', one author affirmed.[32]

The only source yielding anything like a systematic impression of the relative size of these three occupational groupings in late-medieval Essex is the returns from the 1381 poll-tax collection. This means that at only one fixed point during the later middle ages can even an approximate occupational composition be glimpsed; significant later changes in this composition are conceivable, but unlikely to have altered things entirely. The poll-tax returns also pose considerable difficulties of analysis, and these are considered in more detail elsewhere.[33] These records are the closest approximation to a census enumeration that survives from the later-medieval period in England, but they fall well short of a census in that, for example, it is impossible to gauge household size and structure from them. Though in theory the returns constitute listings of all lay persons, male and female, aged 15 years and older and falling above the ranks of the very poor, the Essex listings in particular are a serious underenumeration of this age group. Moreover, they were less likely to exclude, and so over-emphasise the relative numbers of, the better-off agriculturalists at the expense of labourers and possibly poorer artisans as well.

The ways in which the tax collectors at the village level recorded occupational information also make this analysis less than straightforward. Collectors, or those who recorded the tax lists for them, varied greatly from community to community in their apparent interest in recording taxpayers' occupations in the first place. Many communities' returns lack this information entirely, and in very few returns are all heads of households given occupations. There are also wide variations among Essex townships in the degrees to which the occupational designations given were elaborated beyond a very few basic types.

One further difficulty is that of defining the unit for comparison. In cases like this entry from the 1381 Bocking return:

Fuller – John Robyn
Agnes his wife
Alice his daughter[34]

[32] John Gower, in his *Vox clamantis*, discussed by Coleman, *English literature in history*, pp. 148–9; cf. Hilton, *English peasantry in the later middle ages*, pp. 21–4.

[33] See Appendix A.

[34] PRO.E179.107.68:

Fuller' Johannes Robyn – ijs.
Agnes uxor ejus
Alicia fillia ejus – xijd.

or in other words where a (virtually always male) 'ego' with occupational designation is immediately followed in the list by persons whose identities are defined solely in relationship to that 'ego' (spouses, children or other relatives, or servants), it seems reasonable to consider this a household in the normally accepted sense: a co-resident group sharing functions of production and consumption.[35] But residential demarcations are in fact never explicitly given in these sources. The example given above shows the format almost universally employed in these tax returns. And since only the apparent heads of these units, the 'egos', were given occupations, the practice adopted here is to term these units 'households' (being careful always to employ the inverted commas to show the hypothetical nature of the groups, as distinct from households normally construed). Table 1.3 displays the occupational data by 'household' from the three hundreds, Chelmsford, Dunmow and Hinckford, that lay at the core of the north-central district of Essex and whose returns consistently contain occupational information.

Of those 'households' in the communities in question whose heads were given occupations – slightly more than half the total 'households' in these townships – approximately one-quarter were agriculturalists, one-quarter were craftsmen and retailers, and rather more than half were labourers.[36] It should be reiterated, though, that the latter figure is undoubtedly an underestimate of the true prevalence of labourers in rural Essex society, while agriculturalists are conversely overrepresented here.

The poll-tax data and the tenurial patterns are, however, strikingly consistent. No more than one-quarter, and in practice probably rather fewer, of the families in north-central Essex derived their livelihoods from agriculture on their own properties to such a degree that their

[35] Social scientists and historians have applied different shadings of meaning to the concept of households; these are helpfully discussed in Netting, Wilk and Arnould, eds., *Households*, esp. pp. xiii-xxxiv.

[36] In the sample given in Table 1.3, 1,695 of 3,132 (54.1 per cent) 'households' were given occupations. It is an open question whether 'households' not designated with occupations were of a different social or economic composition from those that were: in other words, whether the likelihood of being designated with an occupation was independent of occupation itself. Some perspective is thrown upon this by considering the Hinckford Hundred returns alone, because in these sources a higher proportion of all 'households' (1,332 out of 2,013, or 66.2 per cent) than in this larger sample were given occupational designations. Here, occupational composition was little different from the larger sample presented in Table 1.3: agriculturalists 371 (27.9 per cent), labourers 765 (57.4 per cent), craftsmen and retailers 196 (14.7 per cent). The possible error factor caused by this is undoubtedly less significant than that caused by differential tendencies to pay this tax in the first place; for further discussion see Appendix A.

Table 1.3. *Occupational data, 1381 poll-tax returns: Chelmsford, Dunmow and Hinckford Hundreds*

	'Households'	
Agriculturalists	426	(25.1%)
Labourers	884	(52.2%)
Craftsmen/retailers	385	(22.7%)
Total (70 townships represented)	1,695	

Of craftsmen/retailers:	
Clothworkers	110
Construction workers	76
Smiths	53
Bakers/brewers	45
Cobblers	27
Butchers	21
Other	53

Note: Townships whose returns entirely lack occupational data are omitted from this tabulation. Number of townships represented from each hundred: Chelmsford 12, Dunmow 13, Hinckford 45.
Sources: PRO.E179.107.49; E179.107.63; E179.107.68; E179.123.44; E179.240.308.

contemporaries regarded them primarily in these terms; a similarly small proportion of tenants in the Essex rentals of the period possessed more than 10 or 15 acres of arable land. At the other extreme, the much larger ranks of smallholders (plus the completely landless, excluded from the tenurial evidence) furnished the half or more of families in the district who were substantially dependent upon wages earned through working for others, in itself tantamount to the contemporary understanding of the word 'labourer'.

Table 1.3 also provides some general clues to the nature of the non-agricultural sector of the district's local economy, in the form of major subdivisions within the craftsmen/retailers group. In some cases, especially those of clothworkers or bakers and brewers,[37] these pursuits were often by-employments complementing other forms of agricultural and non-agricultural work. The relative importance of

[37] The position of clothworkers is discussed below, Chapter 3; for brewers and bakers, see especially Bennett, 'The village ale-wife'.

these activities is thus likely to have been larger even than is implied by those taxpayers denoted by – as if to indicate more exclusive employment in – the occupations in question. Of these crafts, cloth-workers (weavers, fullers, dyers, tailors and the like) stand out as most prominent by a considerable margin, and the rural cloth industry was of sufficient importance within the local economy of the district to warrant closer examination of its structures (below, Chapter 3). Next in importance were construction workers: mostly carpenters, plus some tilers, thatchers, sawyers and so on. These were followed in importance by smiths, and by the bakers and brewers who represented a significant provisioning trade in the district. Finally, cobblers and butchers found extensive employment with the products of the district's expanding production of farm animals.

Occupation and tenure of land in rural Essex were, as might be expected, closely related at the individual as well as the aggregate level. Though many persons in all three major occupational groupings possessed real property in the later middle ages, to be designated by one of the terms grouped under the heading 'agriculturalists' clearly meant having substantial property, while both labourers and, to a slightly lesser extent, craftsmen and retailers were generally involved in propertyholding on a much more modest level, if at all. While this may seem tautological, in practice it is seldom possible to demonstrate empirically. But through nominal linkage of persons who appeared in both the 1381 poll-tax listings and in near-contemporary rentals from manors in Stebbing (1383) and Thaxted (1393), some data are available on tenancy sizes by occupation.

Table 1.4 presents these data, once more in the case of Thaxted including only those tenants who did not include among their holdings properties held by burgage tenure in order to minimise the urban nature of the group.[38] Again, these average data are approximate, for reasons already discussed and several more besides. Nominal linkage in sources like these is sometimes difficult, and in the time lapse between tax lists and rentals circumstances may have altered substantially for some of these individuals. Since the rentals record only direct tenants, some, especially among the labourers, of those who did appear in tenurial records may be unrepresentative of their contemporaries by that very fact. Nevertheless, the differences among the groups are clear. On average agriculturalists in this sample

[38] In these calculations, the arable acreage of tenancies consisting solely of residential property or of unquantifiable units has been taken as zero. While in the latter case this potentially risks underestimating tenancy sizes, in practice this is unlikely to be very significant, since only 8 of the 65 tenancies represented in Table 1.4 were of this category.

Table 1.4. *Landholding sizes by occupation, Stebbing and Thaxted, 1381–93*

	Agriculturalists	Craftsmen/ retailers	Labourers
N	19[a]	36[b]	10[c]
Median acreage	12.00	3.00	2.25
Mean acreage	27.97	6.59	4.20
Standard deviation	36.89	8.00	5.47
Number of tenancies comprising only residential property	0	2	1

Notes: [a] 10 from Stebbing, 9 from Thaxted.
[b] 9 from Stebbing, 27 from Thaxted.
[c] 6 from Stebbing, 4 from Thaxted.

Sources: PRO.E179.107.49 m.24; PRO E179.107.68; BL Add. Roll 65957; ERO D/DHu M58.

possessed not much less than thirty acres, though their acreages ranged from less than five to more than a hundred. The mean holdings of both other groups in this sample put them definitively into the smallholder category, though here again in a few exceptional cases tenancies were rather larger. Differences in holding sizes between labourers and agriculturalists, and between craftsmen or retailers and agriculturalists, are statistically significant, but those between labourers and craftsmen or retailers are not.[39]

A few examples will help to illustrate the range of situations concealed beneath these rudimentary statistics. At Stebbing in 1381, William Pounfreyt *laborarius* was listed with his wife in the tax return, and two years later held a messuage (house-site) and two and a half acres of land.[40] In the same community John Lytle, another *laborarius* appearing without spouse in the tax listing, possessed a cottage and eleven acres.[41] At the other end of the landholding scale Nicholas Richmond, a *liber tenens* in the 1381 Thaxted tax return, held more than 130 acres of arable land plus other property at one of Thaxted's outlying hamlets in 1393.[42] The circumstances of craftsmen and retailers were rather more varied, doubtless depending upon both the nature of their occupations and the extent to which agriculture was a

39 A Mann-Whitney nonparametric test between arrays of holding sizes is significant at the 0.05 level between labourers and agriculturalists and between craftsmen/retailers and agriculturalists, but not between labourers and craftsmen/retailers.

40 PRO.E179.107.68; BL Add. Roll 65957.

41 *Ibid.*

42 PRO.E179.107.49 m.24; ERO D/DHu M58.

supplement to their other work. Richard Wyseden, a Stebbing weaver, had a modest three acres in 1383, whereas a carpenter in the same community, Nicholas Page, possessed a more substantial tenement with a messuage and twenty acres.[43]

The multi-faceted nature of some craftsmen's activities in this period is illustrated more clearly by the occasional anecdotal or episodic careers that can be pieced together from manorial and other local evidence. John Holeman of Great Waltham was heavily fined by royal justices in 1352 for (unspecified) breaches of the Statute of Labourers, probably for taking excessive profits in the course of one or more of his local trades: he was also cited by Waltham's manorial court throughout the 1350s and 1360s for offences related to his work as a butcher, and on at least one occasion as an ale-brewer as well. He possessed a cottage and attached land at about the same time.[44] At the other end of the tenurial scale and in the same community John Tanner, who was indicted under the Statute in 1389 for excessive profits from tanning and whose two servants were indicted at the same time for receiving excessive wages, had acquired at least 50 acres of land in the previous few years.[45]

Several points emerge from all this. On the one hand, there were no absolutely rigid demarcations in terms of property tenure among the three major occupational groupings. Some labourers in late-medieval Essex, like English farm labourers for centuries to follow, also raised grain and animals on their own small properties; each sphere of their work supplemented the other. Artisans also had agricultural interests on a variety of scales. Both groups thus shaded off into agriculturalists, rather than being in all cases completely set apart from them.

[43] PRO.E179.107.68; BL Add. Roll 65957.

[44] PRO.E137.11.2 (Essex estreat roll, 1352), for John Holeman's fine of 10s.; PRO.DL30.64.807 (Waltham and Easter leet, 9 Jun 1351), PRO.DL30.64.814 (Waltham leet, 24 May 1358), PRO.DL30.64.816 (Waltham leet, 28 May 1360), and PRO.DL30.66.827 (Waltham leet, 29 May 1371), examples of amercements of John Holeman for illegal butchering; PRO.DL30.64.807 (Waltham and Easter leet, 9 Jun 1351), John Holeman amerced for assize of ale infraction; PRO.DL30.64.811 (Waltham court, 16 Dec 1354), John Holeman and wife lease a cottage and curtilage.

[45] PRO.KB9.25 m.6 (King's Bench indictment file, Essex, 1389), John Tanner indicted for excessive profits; *ibid.* m.7, his servants also indicted for excessive wages; PRO.DL30.64.817 (Waltham leet, 20 May 1361), PRO.DL30.65.826 (Waltham leet, 6 Jun 1370), and PRO.DL30.66.835 (Waltham leet, 14 May 1383), examples of John Tanner amerced in local courts for illegal tanning; PRO.DL30.65.825 (Waltham court, 12 Jul 1369), PRO.DL30.66.829 (Waltham courts, 19 Feb 1376 and 30 Jun 1376), PRO.DL30.67.838 (Waltham court, 21 Feb 1386), and PRO.DL30.67.839 (Waltham court, 15 May 1387), John Tanner's land acquisitions. Tanner was also at various times a local official in this community, serving as constable and chief pledge in the 1370s and 1380s: PRO.DL30.66.829 (Waltham leet, 14 Jun 1375), PRO.DL30.66.834 (Waltham leet, 29 May 1382).

Nevertheless, on the other hand the property endowments of those persons termed in the documents by one or more variant of agriculturalist were typically of a wholly different order of magnitude. Definitive movement between groupings within the space of a lifetime there certainly was (though no evidence survives to gauge its frequency), but the tax collectors at the village level were being far from capricious in assigning occupational labels to their neighbours when they listed them.[46]

Such is the picture that emerges from a variety of evidence from the fourteenth and early-to-mid-fifteenth centuries. To trace occupational or tenurial structure on through to the chronological end point of this study is more difficult. The very nature of many of the most commonly used sources for English local history changes considerably from the late 1300s to the mid-1500s, a genuine barrier to perceiving the transition from 'medieval' to 'early-modern'. But one further body of material – the subsidy returns of 1524 and 1525 – suggests that in the early sixteenth century, central and northern Essex was little changed from the more immediately post-Black Death period in all these respects.

These tax collections of the 1520s were assessed on a basis quite different from previous subsidies: taxpayers paid (and were recorded individually as such) on the basis of either the wages they earned, the land they held, or the goods they owned.[47] Though once again local practices varied widely, it appears likely from several counties' returns that taxpayers assessed on wages, and those assessed on goods worth less than 40s., together constitute a reasonable approximation to the group of labourers in the localities in question (minus some unknown, non-negligible percentage of the latter excused entirely from the tax because their goods or wages fell below the minimum level of 20s.).[48]

[46] One unique example among the 1381 poll-tax returns makes this somewhat more explicit. The listing for Chelmsford (PRO.E179.107.63 m.4) gives, in addition to taxpayers' names, occupations and tax assessments, brief notes indicating the basis upon which the assessors set the tax, in the form of notations about tenure of land or value of moveable goods. Most craftsmen and retailers were noted as having no tenure or tenure worth very modest sums per annum.

[47] The most recent and exhaustive study of these taxation returns is that by Cornwall, *Wealth and society*.

[48] Dyer, *Standards of living*, p. 214; cf. Cornwall, *Wealth and society*, pp. 200–1, noting that in Rutland in 1524 well over 90 per cent of taxpayers listed as labourers were assessed at 20s. in wages or 40s. or less in goods, while in the 1522 Suffolk muster returns the corresponding figure was about 84 per cent. The exact form in which a hundred's tax returns were recorded was quite variable, but in at least one Essex return in 1524, several townships' lists specifically record labourers separately as those assessed on 'ernyngs' (PRO.E179.108.154: Witham Hundred); assessed earnings among 275 men ranged from 20s. (218 taxpayers) to 40s. (8) and 50s. (2) (15 townships). See also below, Chapter 10.

Table 1.5. *Taxation in three central-Essex hundreds in 1524*

Hundred	Number of townships	Taxpayers taxed				Total
		on wages	on goods (<40s.)	on goods (40s.+)	on land	
Chelmsford[a]	19	173	182	462	94	911
Dunmow[b]	19	14	379	445	48	886
Witham[c]	15	275	49	323	25	672
Total	53	462	610	1,230	167	2,469

Note: Only townships whose returns are completely legible are included in this dataset.

Sources: [a] PRO.E179.108.151.
[b] PRO.E179.108.161.
[c] PRO.E179.108.154.

The statute by which Parliament granted this subsidy singled out taxpayers liable at the lowest rate in the following terms:

And of every maner person borne under the Kynges obeysaunce beyng of thage of xvj yeres or above and beyng of the value of xls. in goodes or takyng any dayely wekely or yerely wages or other profettes for wages to the yerly value of xxs. or above and havyng none other substaunce wherby the same person shuld or ought to be set accordyng to this acte as is a foresaid at higher or gretter somme iiijd. yerely duryng the said twoo yeres.[49]

By this measure, Essex in the 1520s did not necessarily possess a distinctively higher complement of wage-earners than a number of other counties in southern or eastern England, but its level of wage dependence was (on the basis of this evidence) demonstrably higher than in areas of the country further north or west.[50] In three central-Essex hundreds in 1524 taxpayers assessed upon wages, and upon goods worth less than 40s., comprised roughly 43 per cent of all taxpayers (see table 1.5).[51]

Moreover, these data show that although the proportion of all taxpayers who were assessed on wages varied greatly from hundred to hundred (in this dataset 19.0, 1.6 and 40.9 per cent respectively), the corresponding proportion assessed at goods under 40s. varied inversely, so that the two categories combined represented a much more consistent proportion (39.0, 44.4 and 48.2 per cent). In other words, in the view of the tax collectors the two may well have been alternative classifications for the same social class, the wage-dependent. At any rate, when due allowance is made for the rather different bases of this and the later-medieval poll-tax collections, the impression lent by the 1524 returns is entirely compatible with the earlier scenario of something around or over one-half of the district's households being heavily reliant upon earnings.

From such a perspective it is all the clearer that this district's society was one marked, from high-medieval on into Tudor times, by a very

[49] 14 & 15 Henry VIII c.16, printed in *Statutes of the realm* vol. 3, p. 231. The terms of this grant, then, made both annually employed servants and day labourers liable under the 'wages' heading, unlike the 1514 subsidy, for which only wages received 'by the yere' were made liable: Schofield, 'Taxation and the Tudor state', pp. 234–5. Data from rural hundreds in five counties, when compared with the muster rolls of 1522, suggest that 'about 6 per cent of the eligible population escaped notice in the tax assessments': Wrigley and Schofield, *Population history of England*, p. 567. It should be noted that the subsidies' base was (largely male) household heads.

[50] Cornwall, *Wealth and society*, pp. 201–3, 268–9: solely on the basis of proportions of all taxpayers assessed at 'nil' or £1, Essex ranked roughly equal with Sussex, Suffolk and Buckinghamshire, slightly higher than Rutland, Lincolnshire and Leicestershire, but much higher than Cornwall, Shropshire, or more northerly counties.

[51] These lists are used here because they are especially scrupulous in distinguishing the basis of taxation (wages, goods, or land) for each taxpayer.

pronounced imbalance of landed resources and wage dependency. And although the concept of 'occupation' at the time was perhaps more fluid than its modern connotations would imply, by contemporary definitions wage-earners with little or no land comprised the majority of the district's rural population from the fourteenth century onward. The remarkable continuity of landholding profiles in the district, throughout the period of this study, was a basic structure of long standing rather than a peculiar conjunction of convergent shorter-term circumstances.

2

Geography of a local economy

To examine its people in terms of occupational structures or economic layers is to consider only one dimension of the district. It is also necessary to examine how people fitted into the spaces they inhabited. The great majority of Essex people in the later middle ages lived in small rural communities, containing no more than 200 souls, and the great majority worked in agriculture for part or all of the year. But even within the fairly close confines of a single county, there were wide variations in the density of settlement and the sizes, forms and functions of communities. These patterns in turn hold clues to understanding spatial variations in agriculture, influences of markets (including the largest market in all of England, the city of London), and the distribution of industrial and other non-agricultural activities. Industry – specifically, the district's most important rural industry, clothmaking – and its geography will be considered in more detail in the next chapter. But the district's general human and economic geography must first be examined.

In 1377, when the returns of the first poll tax permit a reasonably reliable picture to be sketched of relative population densities in different parts of the country, Essex ranked roughly only at the median among English counties in recorded settlement density.[1] But county-wide averages can conceal many contrasts at more local levels. Figure 2.1 maps densities of taxpayers per square mile on a township-by-township basis from the 1377 taxation in Essex in order to demonstrate this point.

[1] Enrolled county totals are published in Russell, *British medieval population*, pp. 132–3, correcting Oman, *The great revolt of 1381*, pp. 162–5. Calculation from these data indicates that of 37 counties for which enrolled returns survive, Essex ranked 18th. Recorded lay poll-tax payers per square mile in 1377 ranged from a low of 9.83 (Northumberland) to 141.78 (Middlesex and London). The median was 32.57 (Berk-

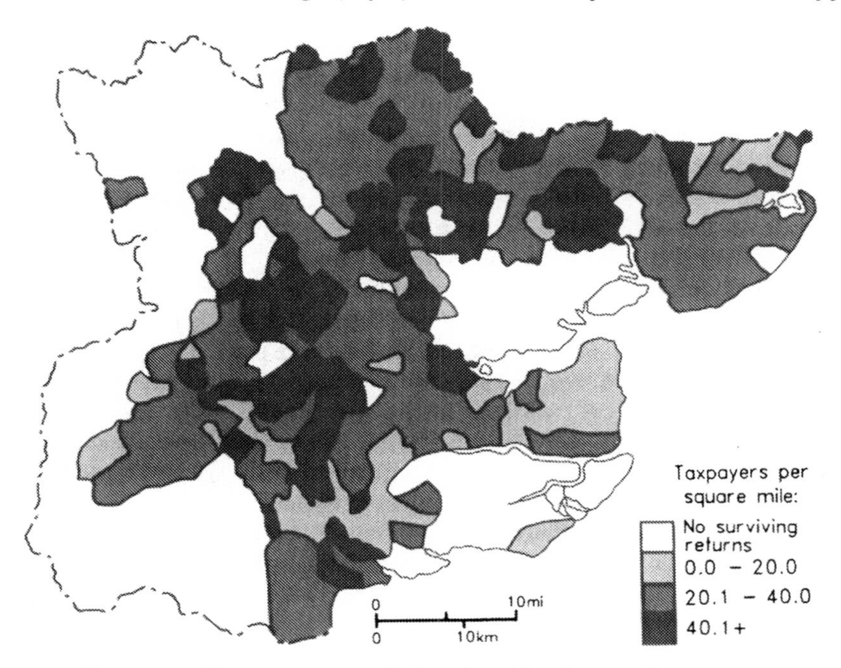

Figure 2.1. Essex 1377: population densities from poll-tax returns

Though the surviving data do not cover the entire county, when they are examined in this way they uncover a revealing picture. Population density was relatively low in the southeastern coastal marshes and in the wooded and heavy-clayland region in the south of the county. But it is also apparent that there was a thickly peopled band of townships running through the central and into the northern areas, covering much of the district at the heart of this study and extending northward into East Anglia. In 25 townships in Chelmsford Hundred at the centre of the county (excluding the county town of Chelmsford itself), backward extrapolation from the poll taxes on the basis of tithing data indicates that density of settlement approached or exceeded 100 persons per square mile at the peak of the medieval population expansion in the years around 1300, and hence did not fall far short of the population density of this same area at the time of the first English census in 1801.[2] Such a density of settlement undoubtedly

shire); the figure for Essex was 33.14. Cf. Baker, 'Changes in the later middle ages', pp. 190–2; Smith, 'Human resources', pp. 198–202.

[2] PRO.E179.107.46; *1851 Census, Great Britain* vol. 6, pp. 628–32. In all of Chelmsford Hundred except the townships of Chelmsford, Moulsham (aggregated with Chelmsford in the census) and Sandon (1377 return missing), 3,767 paid tax in 1377 (implying

helps to explain the persistence of a large stratum of near-landless labourers and craftsmen in the district throughout the later middle ages.

Just as the southeast of England gradually came to claim a greater proportional share of the nation's aggregate wealth from the fourteenth to the early sixteenth century, so too did these same densely populated areas of Essex figure prominently in the rising economic weight that this corner of the country boasted. In part, of course, concentration of aggregate (not necessarily *per capita*) wealth was a corollary of concentration of people. Comparisons of the changing geographical distribution of wealth in England over this period rest upon comparisons of the lay subsidy of 1334, a levy of one-fifteenth and one-tenth of the value of moveable goods, with the 1524–5 subsidies upon land, goods and wages. When data from these two taxes are compared on a hundred-by-hundred basis, all five hundreds in the central-northern district of Essex rank well above the national median; Dunmow Hundred, near the centre of the county, ranks well into the national top quintile.[3] In aggregate, then, this district possessed a concentration of wealth that was not exceptionally high in the early fourteenth century, but that was growing quite rapidly *vis-à-vis* the nation at large during the period of this study. It was a wealth, however, that was very unevenly distributed among local countryfolk.

A densely settled, occupationally diverse and economically differentiated population has certain implications for the geography of local settlement. A population of this sort implies a degree of commerciali-

a total population of about 4,983 to 5,476, without allowing for tax evasion or clergy, who were exempt; for the basis employed here for estimating total population from poll-tax-paying numbers, see below, Appendix A). The tithing data from several Essex communities (see below, Chapter 5) imply that in the years around 1300 resident population was two to two and a half times that of 1377. In 1801, 14,676 dwelt in the same townships, in an area of 117.4 square miles.

[3] Since the bases for these taxes were different, no simple comparisons can be made of assessed wealth as such. Instead, the comparison must be based upon tax paid in 1524–5 as a fraction of assessed wealth in 1334. Darby, Glasscock *et al.*, 'The changing distribution of wealth in England', discuss these comparisons and (p. 258) map the resulting statistics by hundred for the entire country. The median score (1524–5 tax divided by 1334 assessed wealth) was 9.21 per cent, and the threshold for highest quintile was 16.65 per cent. Essex hundredal data have been taken from Glasscock, ed., *The lay subsidy of 1334*, pp. 79–89, and from Sheail, 'Regional wealth in England' vol. 2. The data for 1524 have been used here for Essex; those for 1525 differed only very marginally. For the county at large, 1524–5 tax divided by 1334 assessed wealth was 19.99 per cent; Dunmow Hundred, 20.34; Uttlesford and Freshwell Hundreds together, 15.41; Chelmsford Hundred, 13.01; Hinckford Hundred, 11.71. The coastal and northeastern hundreds of Essex also scored very high in this comparison. In 1334, Essex ranked only 26th, out of 39 counties with usable data, in assessed wealth per square mile: Glasscock, 'England *circa* 1334', p. 141.

sation, in the buying and selling of basic foodstuffs and clothing especially, since few had land enough to live in the self-sufficiency of an idealised peasant economy. Commercialisation in turn implies an institutional framework for exchange. In the medieval English countryside a charter of licence was required for a weekly open market, proprietary interests in which had compelled Essex landlords in the expansionary economy of the 1200s to found many new markets in hopes of profit from rents and tolls.[4] Not all these new markets took root, or ever transcended the size or sophistication of mere villages, and in fact most lapsed into desuetude in the later middle ages.[5] Where they did take root, and assumed a redistributive role for the agricultural surplus production of the surrounding countryside, communities might grow up to support provisioning or other services and secondary industries, with people coming to market from surrounding villages or further afield as their clientele.[6] Pleas of debt entered in manorial courts can occasionally reveal the extent of goods and services exchanged and networks of credit relationships erected in places of this sort. In the large market community of Writtle between 1382 and 1490, the extant records of 967 court sessions included 948 pleas involving 1,189 debts, more than half of which arose from hiring, leasing, or other transactions distinct from simple sale and purchase of commodities.[7] Density of market communities, then, is one index of economic complexity.

Figure 2.2 maps the sites of Essex markets known to have existed before 1350.[8] The geographical distribution of these market centres was influenced by several factors. Many were situated along the Thames estuary to the south, by the sea coast, or upon major roads linking the largest urban centres of the greater region. These factors apart, in a very general way the concentration of markets in Essex parallels population densities, being relatively sparse in the eastern and southwestern sectors of the county but rather more dense in mid- and northern Essex. And in a broader comparative perspective, Essex as a whole in the fourteenth century does appear to have possessed a

4 Britnell, 'The proliferation of markets in England'; Britnell, 'Essex markets before 1350'.

5 Of 78 markets known in the county before 1350, only 27 were apparently still in operation in the sixteenth century. Those likeliest to survive were those founded earliest, in the largest communities, and closest to major roads or the coast. Everitt, 'Marketing of agricultural produce', p. 474; Britnell, 'Essex markets before 1350', p. 19.

6 The early development of one such market community, Newland in Witham, is described in Britnell, 'The making of Witham'.

7 Clark, 'Debt litigation', pp. 251, 254.

8 Identification of Essex markets here follows Britnell, 'Essex markets before 1350'.

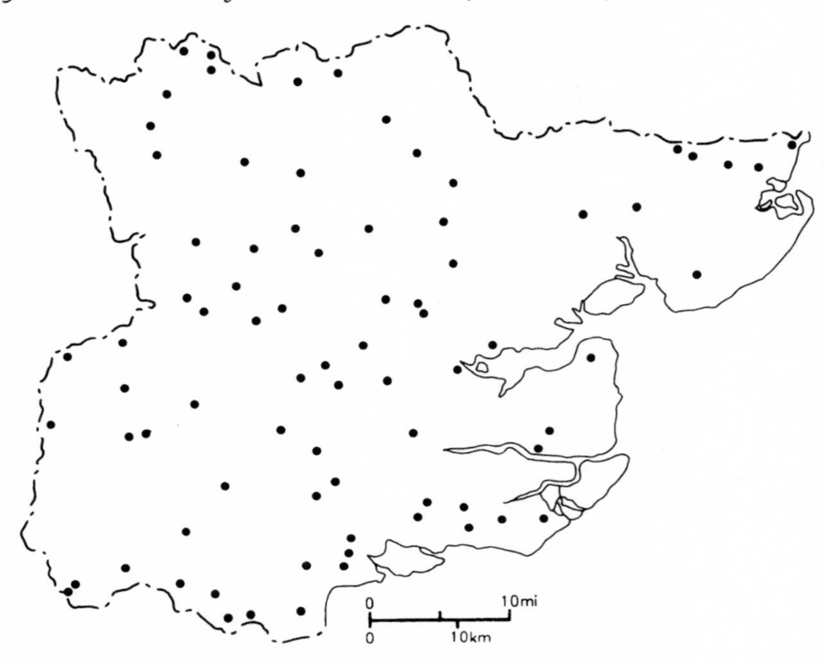

Figure 2.2. Market towns in medieval Essex

somewhat higher density of markets than, for example, the Midlands counties of Nottinghamshire and Staffordshire.[9]

But the relationships in medieval England between market centres and the rural economy in which they existed could take many different functional forms. At one extreme, redistributive, service and secondary industrial activities might cluster very tightly into market centres. It has in fact long and widely been thought that this was the manner in which a commercialised economy grew out of the feudal agrarian European middle ages.[10] But medieval villages from quite early on

[9] This is based upon a comparison of Essex's 78 known markets (Britnell, 'Essex markets before 1350') with Nottinghamshire's 32 (Unwin, 'Rural marketing in medieval Nottinghamshire') and Staffordshire's 45 (Palliser and Pinnock, 'The markets of medieval Staffordshire'). Staffordshire had roughly three-quarters the geographical area of Essex; Nottinghamshire was about three-fifths Essex's size. Both of these Midlands counties had lower population densities, and higher proportions of non-inhabitable territory, than Essex.

[10] Though traditionally concerned with larger corporate urban centres, rather than smaller market communities, the model of an urban/commercial/industrial sector 'external' to the feudal agrarian economy and gradually growing up to influence it has been a particular debating-point among Marxist historians. Positions are summarised in the introduction to Hilton, ed., *The transition from feudalism to capitalism*, esp. pp. 17–19; Martin, *Feudalism to capitalism*, esp. pp. 46–54. In recent years Hilton has

were likely to contain at least a few artisans whose work was ancillary to agriculture.[11] At the other extreme, service, industrial and generally non-agricultural economic activity might be more widely dispersed, bringing economic variegation into villages themselves. Whether it was a result of the particular features of its local setting, or was merely a more developed harbinger of a trend taking place everywhere, Essex by the later 1300s has long been recognised as being closer to the latter than the former alternative, and the chief symptom of this is the occupational complexity of its rural communities.[12]

Table 2.1 depicts the hierarchy of occupational complexities in 38 northern Essex townships in the later fourteenth century.[13] Occupational data presented here are taken from the 1381 poll-tax returns for Hinckford Hundred, plus the listing for the contiguous township of Thaxted (in Dunmow Hundred).[14] These particular returns have been chosen because they are especially detailed for occupational analysis.[15] The data are still far from perfect, especially as it is by no means clear that the tax subcollectors in every township were equally prone to draw detailed distinctions between occupational groups. But taken as a group these patterns can reveal something of the features of economic complexity in the district.

The table ranks townships down the vertical axis in probable order of population size from largest to smallest, on the basis of the 1377 returns, which are more reliable than the 1381 records for aggregate population estimates. Township sizes in the sample ranged from Thaxted, with 668 taxpayers in 1377 (probable total population roughly 880–970) to Rayne and Ovington, with 23 and 14 taxpayers (30–33 and 19–20 total populations?) respectively.[16] This group of places was in fact heavily skewed towards smaller settlements, one-half of the 38 having fewer than 110 taxpayers in 1377. Along the

given much attention to the importance of small market centres, which – with some acknowledged exceptions, of which Essex was one – he sees as sharply distinguished occupationally and functionally from agrarian communities. Cf. Hilton, 'Small town society in England', esp. pp. 56–7, and 'Medieval market towns', esp. pp. 21–3.

11 Cf. Hilton, *The English peasantry in the later middle ages*, p. 13: Hilton's influential definition of the peasantry as a class includes as a central element 'labourers, artisans, building workers' who are derived from and form part of the peasantry.

12 E.g. Hilton, *Bond men made free*, pp. 169–72.

13 This tabulation follows in form the analysis of early-sixteenth-century Suffolk tax returns in Patten, 'Village and town'. The author is grateful to Roger Schofield for suggesting this approach to him.

14 Sources: PRO.E179.107.68; E179.123.44; E179.240.308; E179.107.49.

15 1,558 (78.4 per cent) of the 1,986 'households' in these listings were given occupational designations.

16 For the basis of these estimates of total resident populations in 1377, see below, Appendix A.

Table 2.1. *Township rank-orders by size and occupational complexity, Dunmow and Hinckford Hundreds, 1381*

Community, by size	Free tenant	Labourer	Carpenter	Tailor	Smith	Weaver	Cobbler	Butcher	Fuller	Franklin	Brewer	Draper	Shepherd	Tiler	Skinner	Baker	Villein tenant	Cowherd	Ploughman
Thaxted [M]	X	X	X	X	X		X	X			X	X		X	X	X	X		X
Bocking	X	X	X	X	X	X	X	X	X	X	X	X	X	X	X				X
Finchingfield	X	X	X	X	X		X						X			X			
Felsted [M]	X	X	X	X	X	X	X	X	X	X	X	X					X		
Sible Hedingham	X	X	X	X	X				X			X		X					
Stebbing [M]	X	X	X	X	X	X	X	X	X			X	X	X	X		X		
Steeple Bumpstead [M]	X	X		X	X														
Toppesfield	X	X	X	X									X						
Braintree [M]	X	X	X	X	X	X	X	X			X				X	X			
Wethersfield	X	X	X			X												X	
Alphamstone & Bures	X	X			X	X													
Sturmer	X	X	X	X	X		X		X										X
Shalford	X	X																X	
Ridgewell [M]	X	X																	
Belchamp St Paul	X	X																	
Belchamp Walter	X	X																	
Gestingthorpe	X	X	X					X											
Birdbrook	X	X		X						X									
Bulmer	X	X			X														
Stambourne	X	X	X					X			X								
Stisted	X	X		X			X												
Gosfield	X	X								X									
Belchamp Otten	X	X		X															
Pentlow	X	X				X													
Lamarsh	X	X	X						X										
Brundon & Ballingdon	X	X																	
Great Yeldham	X	X			X														
Great Maplestead	X	X	X																
Pebmarsh	X	X		X					X										
Tilbury-iuxta-Clare	X	X																	
Little Yeldham	X	X																	
Panfield	X	X	X													X			
Ashen	X	X																	
Middleton	X																		
Great Saling		X	X	X						X									
Twinstead	X	X		X															
Rayne	X		X			X				X			X					X	
Ovington		X																	

Vills known to have possessed markets before 1350 are marked [M]. Only occupations appearing in the tax returns of at least three of the listed vills are tabulated here.
Sources: For poll-tax returns, see notes to text. For market status, Britnell, 'Essex markets'.

horizontal axis are listed the occupations given in the poll-tax returns, in order from those listed in the largest number of townships to the smallest, or from the nearly ubiquitous 'free tenants' (*liberi tenentes*) and 'labourers' (*laborarii*) to cowherds and ploughmen, who were much less frequently singled out for specific mention. The body of the table simply indicates whether a given occupational designation appears in each township's listing.[17]

In general, the larger a township's population, the more diverse were its occupational complexion and the range of non-agricultural activities it supported.[18] This is hardly startling in itself, but some qualifications are necessary. Table 2.1 ranks places in order of township population, but in a region of dispersed settlement like Essex this figure is not the population of a compact village community or concentrated settlement site. Felsted, to take one example, while ranking quite high in township population (263 taxpayers in 1377, or perhaps a total of about 350 to 380), had a rather small market centre that probably accounted for fewer than half of these inhabitants, surrounded by a number of scattered hamlets and isolated farmsteads.[19] Some anomalies are also apparent in the table. For instance, the listing of the relatively large vill of Belchamp St Paul contains only 'free tenants' and 'labourers', and the infrequent appearance in these returns of brewers (a by-employment that manorial evidence implies would be found in virtually every rural settlement of any size in medieval England)[20] is noteworthy. Both of these anomalies are probably due to the tax subcollectors' disinclination in some places to elaborate their descriptive terminology beyond a few basic social types, or to bother to recognise artisanal activity that may have been of a part-time or secondary nature.

If anything, the poll-tax evidence by itself would appear to understate considerably the scope and diversity of non-agricultural pursuits, including those of industrial artisans as well as victuallers and others processing the products of local agriculture, that were typically found in a smaller Essex community. A couple of examples can be drawn from the regulatory infractions that filled the membranes of

17 Due to constraints of space, and also to simplify analysis, occupations that appear in the returns for only one or two townships in this sample are omitted, as are servants.

18 Linear regression between a township's 1377 taxpayer total and the number of occupations appearing in its 1381 listing yields a correlation coefficient of 0.757 (when only the occupations listed in Table 2.1 are included) or 0.876 (when all occupations in the tax listings are included); N = 38.

19 This township's local settlement topography is discussed further later in this chapter. For the basis of this estimate of its total resident population in 1377, see below, Appendix A.

20 Cf. Clark, *The English alehouse*, pp. 20–34.

most leet-court records in Essex during the period. At Boreham, a small market centre where no more than about 140 people dwelt in 1441, the leet court of that year mentioned in connection with such infractions two butchers, a fishmonger, a baker, and eight brewers and four regrators (retail sellers) of ale, all the latter twelve being females. At Great Waltham, a large, complex township lacking a market, and having roughly 400 to 440 inhabitants in the later 1350s, a typical year's leet court during that decade registered the presence of one fuller, two whittawers and two tanners, at least one butcher, and ten brewers of ale (again, the latter almost all female). And like the poll-tax returns, these curial records are only selective and incomplete registers of such activities.[21]

But several points are clear. The presence or absence of a market in a rural Essex settlement is a poor predictor of a community's economic complexity. A wide range of commercial transactions and industrial activities, in the clothmaking, victualling, apparel, and construction areas especially, characterised larger and middling-sized places even where formal market institutions were not present within the vill. Rather than clear-cut urban/rural dichotomies of function, a hierarchy of economic typologies is apparent. Communities in the district ranged from a very few places that can be regarded as unambiguously urban centres – Thaxted certainly,[22] Braintree (plus its virtual suburb, Rayne) probably, and perhaps Bocking – through a broad band of middling-sized communities containing 150 to 250 inhabitants but still a variety of non-agricultural activities. Even quite small villages were capable of supporting more than just the most basic functions. Access to a variety of goods and services or access, at least potentially, to employment in a similarly broad spectrum of production, need not have required a very long journey for dwellers in the late medieval Essex countryside.

This is in sharp contrast to Hilton's arguments concerning the southern West Midlands at the same period, where he found 'a sharp functional differentiation from the agricultural hinterland' displayed by small market centres; in Essex and East Anglia, he noted, penetration of commercial and artisanal activity into rural communities 'reduced the distinction between town and country'.[23] Essex in this respect more closely resembled rural Suffolk in the early sixteenth

[21] PRO.SC2.171.33 (Boreham leet, 30 Jun 1441); PRO.DL30.64.813 (Great Waltham leet, 1 Jun 1357). Resident populations have been estimated from these communities' tithing data; see below, Chapter 5 and Appendix A.
[22] Cf. Newton, *Thaxted*.
[23] Hilton, *The English peasantry in the later middle ages*, p. 85.

century, where a similar exercise has examined occupational complexity from the early-Tudor subsidy and muster rolls.[24]

As for genuinely large urban centres, there was only one in the county. Colchester, with perhaps 5,000 to 6,000 residents in the later fourteenth century, though only just ranking within the ten most populous towns in England then, still dwarfed the next-largest Essex communities by a factor of five or six.[25] Throughout the later middle ages, Colchester's demands for foodstuffs and for raw wool for its cloth industry resulted in purchases of these products from surrounding villages and from places further away that could be reached by water. Yet, as Britnell's careful research has shown, the effective reach of Colchester's demands for grain from its immediate rural hinterland did not extend much beyond eight miles, and its urban consumption is unlikely to have absorbed all the surplus agricultural production even within this radius. Nor was the flow of migrants to the town in the decades around 1400 from smaller communities in Essex and East Anglia of such dimensions as to affect the hinterland's population noticeably.[26] The diversified and commercialised nature of the central-northern Essex economy can hardly be ascribed, then, to the tentacles of market forces emanating from the nearest large town.

Essex did, however, lie partly within the shadow of a much larger town. During the fourteenth and fifteenth centuries the city of London outdistanced provincial English towns in its concentration of economic influence. On a much larger scale it too made its presence felt in the surrounding countryside, affecting in particular the markets for agricultural surplus, the demand for land, and the magnetic lure of the capital for migrants. By the early 1500s, southwestern Essex in particular sent to London produce, especially the products of pastoral husbandry, as well as providing staging-posts and fattening grounds for drovers bringing cattle from further north. The county also sent human resources, in the form of persons taking up apprenticeships and other less structured employment positions in the city.[27]

It is difficult to measure the geographical scope of London's market influences in a satisfactory or systematic manner. But since part of Essex at least lay within the immediate environs of the metropolis, it is

24 Patten, 'Village and town'.

25 Russell, *British medieval population*, pp. 142–3, for 1377 poll-tax figures; Baker, 'Changes in the later middle ages', pp. 293–5; Britnell, *Growth and decline in Colchester*, pp. 22, 93–6, 262.

26 Britnell, *Growth and decline in Colchester*, pp. 35–47, 96–7, 141–58, 246–57.

27 Baker, 'Changes in the later middle ages', pp. 245–7; Bolton, *The medieval English economy*, p. 229; Thirsk, 'The farming regions of England', pp. 53–5; Wareing, 'Geographical distribution of the recruitment of apprentices'.

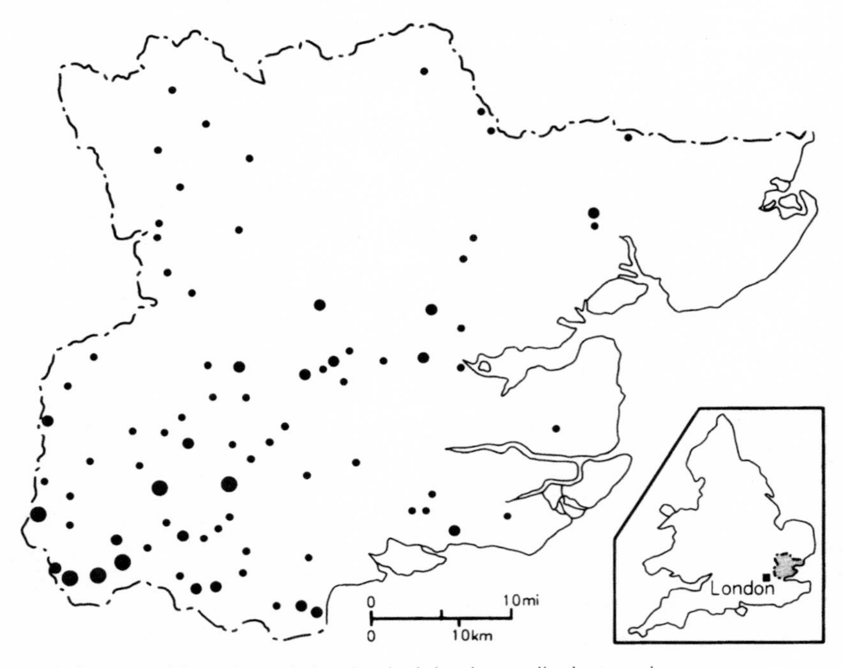

Figure 2.3. Essex properties in Londoners' wills 1374–1488

necessary to gain some sense of the length of its economic reach into the countryside. One indirect but tangible way of doing so is to consider London's effects upon property immediately outside the city. A number of local studies have recently shown that wealthier Londoners, especially towards the end of the fifteenth century, actively sought to acquire land and houses within a radius of ten to fifteen miles of the capital. In the Lea Valley in southern Hertfordshire, in the manor of Havering in southwestern Essex, and in northwestern Kent, Londoners were acquiring property to sublet to others, as targets of investment for surplus liquidity, and as secondary residences.[28]

Figure 2.3 depicts the involvement of Londoners in Essex property, taking as its source the wills of 94 citizens of London enrolled in the London Commissary Court from 1374 to 1488. Londoners' wills

[28] Glennie, 'In search of agrarian capitalism', pp. 23–30; McIntosh, *Autonomy and community*, pp. 221–3; Brown, 'London and north-west Kent'.

during the period frequently made references to real property outside the city. Figure 2.3 simply plots the locations appearing in all those wills mentioning Essex property, with an indication also of how many testators during the years in question made reference to property in any given place.[29]

This spatial distribution undoubtedly reflects at least two different patterns. Persons originating in the countryside who subsequently established themselves in the city might retain property (or retain kinship or other social ties and eventually inherit or otherwise acquire property) in their home parishes. Alternatively, financially successful Londoners, whatever their origins, might acquire Essex property in places with which they had no previous ties, for reasons already stated. Figure 2.3's distribution none the less seems a reasonable measure of the intensity of Londoners' property involvement at successive distances from the capital into the countryside.

The figure confirms that this involvement was quite intensive in the southwestern quarter of the county. Beyond a radius of twenty miles from the city, however, the intensity of this involvement tails off quite sharply, and for most of the north-central district of the county it seems rather insubstantial. The pull of London's influence was demonstrably long, though an increasing part of London's supplies were channelled not overland but by water from coastal sources in southeastern England. An effective radius of fifteen to eighteen miles or so within which market influences were keenly felt in the Essex countryside seems to accord well in proportional comparison with Colchester's experience. Direct involvement in the rural property market is admittedly only an imperfect index of this pull. On the basis of this evidence, however, the commercialisation and economic complexity of northern Essex seems likely to have been generated more from within its own local circumstances of settlement density and economic differentiation than it was through the direct effects of London's influence.

Despite all these characteristics of economic complexity, however, agriculture remained the dominant factor in the local economy, and all other economic activity in the countryside fitted into the interstices of agricultural production. As anywhere else in medieval England, Essex agriculture was both influenced by and in turn influenced population density, occupational complexity and marketing networks. More profoundly, though, agriculture was shaped by the physical terrain in which it was rooted and by many previous centuries' legacies of settlement, clearance, field systems and manorial organisation.

[29] Fitch, ed., *Index to testamentary records in the Commissary Court*.

Medieval Essex agriculture has not been investigated so closely as that of other English regions, and in the absence of more detailed local studies only a brief sketch of general patterns can be given here.[30] Like other features of its geography, the county's agriculture varied a great deal within a small area.

Everywhere in the county and throughout the medieval period, agriculture combined arable production – grain and legumes, especially wheat and barley in the north-central district – with pastoral husbandry – cattle, sheep, swine and horses. But the fertility and workability of soils were the chief influences upon how pastoral and arable were mixed at any given point in time, while longer-term economic cycles also affected the balance over time. John Norden, the Elizabethan 'chorographer', wrote of Essex, 'It is to be noted how the perticuler comodeties are, as it were, quartered out, and possess seuerall places w^th^in the Shire'.[31] Along much of the coastline, extensive low-lying marshlands combined with terrace sands and gravels, ideal for cattle and sheep but poor for grain. These thinly peopled areas, which sent fleeces to Colchester and other Essex clothmaking centres and which were noted for the quality and quantities of cheeses they sent to market in London and elsewhere in the later middle ages, were also notably unhealthy. Malaria persisted here through the early-modern era and, Norden complained, the place 'gave me a moste cruell quarterne feuer'.[32] Most of the remainder of southern and southwestern Essex sat upon London Clay, a heavy and also fairly infertile soil. Woodland was especially abundant here, with some areas remaining of earlier medieval royal forests. The north and northwestern areas of the county, by contrast, formed a plateau of chalky boulder clay, cut through by many streams and accompanying loessal soils. This district was the best suited for grain, which dominated its agriculture throughout the middle ages and whose fertility was able to support a much denser population.

One simple way of illustrating these contrasts over space, and also of showing some changes over time, is set out in Tables 2.2 and 2.3. These data come from inquisitions post mortem, legal proceedings required at the death of any lay persons holding property directly

[30] The following discussion is based mainly upon Allen and Sturdy, 'The environmental background'; Rackham, 'The medieval landscape'; McIntosh, *Autonomy and community*, pp. 137–52; Mate, 'The estates of Canterbury Cathedral Priory'; Mate, 'Pastoral farming in south-east England'; Britnell, *Growth and decline in Colchester*, pp. 35–47, 141–68, 246–57; Britnell, 'Utilisation of the land'; Britnell, 'Agriculture in a region of ancient enclosure'; Britnell, 'Agricultural technology and the margin of cultivation'.

[31] Norden, *Speculum Britanniae pars*, p. 7.

[32] *Ibid*. Cf. Dobson, 'Marsh fever'.

from the Crown.[33] Among other information rendered by local juries, the records of inquisitions post mortem often included extents, or summary descriptions and valuations of the property in question. These properties ranged in size from small freeholdings to entire manors (in which case the data tabulated here pertain to the manorial demesnes, the lands theoretically in the possession of manorial lords rather than their tenants, though many demesnes had in fact been leased out to tenants by 1400).

These data, skewed as they are toward demesne land, thus do not in all cases directly reflect the agrarian practices of husbandmen and other lesser countryfolk. But land-use and cropping patterns on manorial demesnes, as several medieval agrarian historians have recently argued, are none the less likely to reflect agricultural practices prevailing locally among all cultivators, large or small, in broad terms.[34] Some confirmation of this point – though too sparse to be susceptible to systematic quantitative treatment – is afforded by occasional proceedings in Essex manorial courts where a tenement's complement of stock and crops is recorded. In 1369 at Great Waltham, John Tanner assumed a six-year lease of property from Humphrey Clerk. The property in that year was sown with 40 acres of wheat and 38 acres of spring grain, and its stock included two horses, one bull, six cows, twenty ewes and a ram, plus ten quarters of seed wheat and ten of seed oats and a plough.[35] This landholding, then, accords well with

33 Cf. Raftis, *Assart data and land values*, esp. pp. 12–22. The data tabulated here are taken from every extent surviving for Essex property among the original manuscript inquisitions post mortem at the Public Record Office. For convenience's sake, the periods into which they have been divided here are delimited by kings' reigns – those of Edward I, of Richard II, and of Edward IV and Richard III – to produce roughly quarter-century-long datasets approximately a century apart. The sources are thus taken from PRO document classes C134, C136 and C140–141 respectively. Systematic study of these extents for agrarian history will appear in important forthcoming work by B. M. S. Campbell; a foretaste of this work in Norfolk appears in Campbell, 'The complexity of manorial structure', esp. pp. 228–32 and 253–4, n.19, where it is noted that the inquisitions post mortem, though less reliable than manorial accounts, tell essentially the same story with regard to land forms and uses as the manorial material and moreover provide a better cross-section of lay estates. The author is extremely grateful to Dr Campbell for providing data from the Essex extents of Edward I's reign, and for discussing the sources and the Essex results with him.

34 Campbell, 'Arable productivity in medieval England', esp. pp. 397–8, and Mate, 'Medieval agrarian practices', esp. p. 31, have recently argued that medieval demesnes tended to follow prevailing local practices.

35 PRO.DL30.65.825 (Great Waltham court, 12 Jul 1369): '. . . Item predictus Humfridus per licenciam domini tradidit predicto Johanni cum firma predicta ij equos . . . j bovem . . . vj vaccas . . . xx oves matrices et j hurtardum . . . x quarteria frumenti pro semine et x quarteria avene pro semine cum toto stramine et tota palea xl acrarum frumenti et xxxviij acrarum bladi quadragesimi unam carucam cum ij vomeribus ij culteriis et j spanneschakel ferri . . .'.

the grain-producing orientation mixed with subsidiary animal-raising that was typical of the county's central district.

These sources have other drawbacks. The reliability of their valuations of each type of land, expressed as expected profit per acre per annum, has been questioned by historians,[36] and the numbers of properties appearing in these documents (especially properties for which valuations are given) grow rather smaller later in the period. A different group of properties comprises the sample for each period, so the respective samples are not strictly comparable in terms of absolute acreages. But relative levels of land use for different purposes, which are the focus here, are not obscured by this. When considered in the aggregate these extents – like the property descriptions of freehold land transferred by the legal devices known as feet of fines, which Dyer has used in a similar way to investigate late-medieval Warwickshire[37] – yield credible impressions of contrasts in local agriculture over the period.

Table 2.2 considers the basic question of land use, or the mean acreage per property made up of arable land, meadow, pasture and woodland. The large standard deviations of absolute acreages apparent in this table confirm the wide variability in size of property in the dataset; what is of interest here is the relative areas of different land types. A crude measure of the balance between arable and pastoral land use is given by including in the last column the ratio of meadow plus pasture to arable land. Table 2.3 presents the mean valuation in pence per acre of each category of land. In both tables the data are divided into three periods of roughly a quarter-century each: the late thirteenth century near the apogee of the medieval demographic expansion, the transitional period in the late fourteenth century, and the later 1400s near the nadir of the economic contraction at the end of the middle ages. Also in both cases, figures are given for the entire county, and then are subdivided into three regional groups, comprising the hundreds of the north-central district, the coastal hundreds along the eastern and southeastern edges of the county, and the southwestern district.[38]

When the county's subregions are compared, the north-central

[36] Cf. Raftis, *Assart data and land values*, pp. 12–15.

[37] Dyer, *Warwickshire farming*, pp. 9–10.

[38] These 'subregions' have been defined here as the Hundreds of Chelmsford, Dunmow, Freshwell, Hinckford and Uttlesford for the 'north-central'; Dengie, Rochford, Tendring, Thurstable and Winstree for 'coastal'; and Barstaple, Becontree, Chafford, Harlow, Ongar and Waltham for 'southwest'. This is doubtless rather crude, since hundred boundaries hardly followed geological boundaries, but as a rough division it works reasonably well. It should be noted here that the three 'subregions' taken together cover less than the entire county.

Table 2.2. *Land use (acreages) in medieval Essex: inquisitions post mortem data*

	Arable			Meadow			Pasture[a]			Wood			
	mean acres	standard deviation	N	mean acres	standard deviation	N	mean acres	standard deviation	N	mean acres	standard deviation	N	$\frac{m+p}{a}$[b]
1272–1307													
County	242.9	203.8	221	8.5	11.2	221	11.2	26.2	221	6.8	15.5	221	0.08
'North'	271.4	247.5	95	9.8	12.0	95	10.0	26.0	95	8.0	15.7	95	0.07
'Coastal'	214.2	126.9	50	4.7	5.7	50	12.6	32.9	50	7.2	18.3	50	0.08
'Southwest'	188.6	119.8	42	11.4	15.3	42	14.1	25.5	42	3.2	9.6	42	0.14
1377–99													
County	164.5	144.0	77	9.7	14.6	77	27.9	59.8	77	14.1	34.9	77	0.23
'North'	210.2	169.7	27	10.4	11.0	27	11.0	14.4	27	22.8	52.5	27	0.10
'Coastal'	107.4	104.6	26	4.4	8.0	26	32.8	69.5	26	13.1	21.2	26	0.35
'Southwest'	221.4	133.3	14	17.3	24.0	14	35.8	56.7	14	3.7	9.4	14	0.24
1461–85													
County	143.0	171.8	80	15.8	23.0	80	30.5	66.0	80	19.9	41.9	80	0.32
'North'	152.3	208.9	21	13.6	22.8	21	31.2	63.4	21	19.4	51.5	21	0.29
'Coastal'	137.2	82.6	11	7.3	8.0	11	75.8	112.5	11	16.7	15.4	11	0.61
'Southwest'	152.8	192.7	34	19.4	25.2	34	23.6	51.9	34	22.9	47.3	34	0.28

[a] Includes pasture in marshland and heath as well as *pastura*.
[b] Represents ratio of mean area of meadow plus pasture to arable.
Sources: See notes to text.

Table 2.3. *Land values in medieval Essex: inquisitions post mortem data*

	Arable			Meadow			Pasture[a]			Wood		
	mean d./acre	standard deviation	N	mean d./acre	standard deviation	N	mean d./acre	standard deviation	N	mean d./acre	standard deviation	N
1272–1307												
County	4.6	1.9	221	23.0	6.3	172	10.3	4.7	124	–	–	–
'North'	4.3	1.1	95	24.1	6.4	81	10.8	3.8	65	–	–	–
'Coastal'	4.9	2.6	50	22.8	7.1	30	7.4	3.8	17	–	–	–
'Southwest'	5.0	1.9	42	20.3	4.9	32	9.8	3.3	22	–	–	–
1377–99												
County	3.1	0.9	51	21.1	8.5	38	9.7	5.0	34	23.0	15.1	8
'North'	3.1	0.6	19	22.9	8.0	17	10.0	5.8	18	15.8	14.3	5
'Coastal'	3.1	0.9	14	14.3	5.1	8	6.0	2.0	4	–	–	–
'Southwest'	3.3	1.1	11	20.7	3.0	9	10.9	3.5	9	–	–	–
1461–85												
County	2.6	1.4	20	16.2	6.0	13	4.0	4.1	5	–	–	–
'North'	2.8	1.6	9	21.3	3.8	3	–	–	–	–	–	–
'Coastal'	–	–	–	–	–	–	–	–	–	–	–	–
'Southwest'	2.0	0.6	5	14.8	4.7	5	–	–	–	–	–	–

[a] Includes valuations only of *pastura* and excludes marshland and heath.
Sources: See notes to text.

district's stronger orientation toward arable agriculture is readily apparent in the two earlier samples. Conversely, by the later fifteenth century this district shifted proportionately rather more away from grain and towards animal production than the southwestern area. The coastal district's data reflect the large tracts of marshland there, which gained even more relative prominence after the Black Death.

Considering both the county-wide figures and those for individual areas over time underscores the fact that Essex as a whole mirrored to a considerable extent the agrarian history of England at large over the later middle ages. The earliest figures confirm the pressure of people upon resources that Essex agriculture experienced in the decades around 1300: land use was tilted sharply toward the more calorific-efficient grain production and away from grazing, and (although one must be more cautious in drawing firm conclusions about this) land values also appear quite high compared with 200 years later. By both measures the later fourteenth century was a time when these pressures had eased substantially, with an enhancement of the pastoral at the expense of the arable and with a notable decline in arable land values, though the declines in values for meadow and pasture are less marked. But by the later fifteenth century these changes had progressed even further. Pastoral husbandry had gained ground more broadly throughout the county, and arable land values had dropped by nearly one-half from their high-medieval peaks. Though to different degrees and with somewhat different chronologies, these different sectors of the county followed country-wide trends that witnessed former croplands lapsing permanently to grass or even woodland, or at least to intermediate status which allowed them to be switched back and forth irregularly between arable and pastoral use over the years.[39] This evolution of land use also had important implications for the demand and forms of agricultural labour, to which discussion will return later.[40]

At least when taken in the aggregate in this manner, the data for land values found in the inquisitions post mortem extents are not likely to be wholly misleading. They can be compared with the annual prices per acre of arable land farmed out (in the medieval sense, of being leased on strictly cash terms) at eight manors plus three other estates in central and northern Essex from the 1340s into the 1450s.

[39] Cf. Britnell, 'Agricultural technology and the margin of cultivation'; Britnell, 'Utilisation of the land'. For broader patterns across England, cf. Bolton, *The medieval English economy*, pp. 207–45; Baker, 'Changes in the later middle ages', pp. 197–217.

[40] See below, Chapters 9–10.

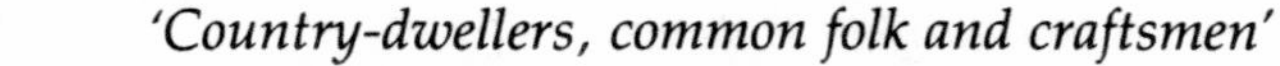

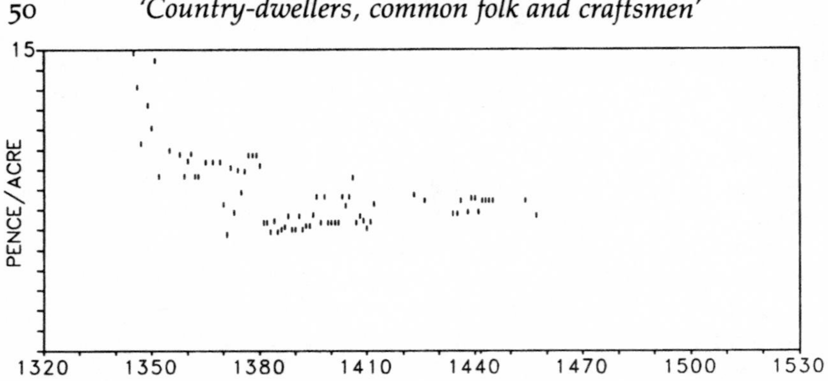

Figure 2.4. Land farms (cash rents per acre) of arable land in Essex 1345–1457

Appendix B at the end of this study discusses the derivation of these data, which are graphed in Figure 2.4.

From a pre-Black Death level usually ranging between 12d. and 15d. per acre, annual farms in the north-central district varied between 6d. and 9d. in the later 1300s before coming to rest in a more narrow band around 6d.–7d. per acre by the mid-fifteenth century. Unfortunately usable data are lacking for later periods. So, however suspect might be the absolute level of land valuations in individual inquisitions post mortem, their aggregate movement over the period seems quite consistent with the manorial evidence: a slackening demand for arable land in the later fourteenth century which settled at a low equilibrium point by the second or third quarter of the next century.

Here, as elsewhere in the country, drastically reduced population and relatively abundant land drove down rents, despite an intricate and rearguard attempt by landlords to forestall this.[41] Grain prices also settled to new, lower levels, but in this case the pattern was less straightforward. Aggregated series of prices for wheat and barley in the same group of Essex manors during the fourteenth and fifteenth centuries are displayed in Figures 2.5 and 2.6. Again, Appendix B discusses the derivation of these price data.

It is inherent in the nature of preindustrial grain-price behaviour that year-on-year price fluctuations were often erratic, reflecting most immediately the state of individual harvests. This is obvious in Figures 2.5 and 2.6. But the broader trends display peaks in the mean prices of both grains in the quarter-century after 1350, and thereafter a more steady price level, roughly equivalent to that of 1326–50 but with

[41] See below, Chapter 11.

less variability.[42] That the price of land fell more, proportionately, than the price of grain reflects both lower demand and greater flexibility of land use.

One more aspect, and the most fundamental, of the district's economic geography is its local level, that of the community. As everywhere in pre-modern England, patterns of settlement forms and field systems were critically important ingredients of rural society. Once more, compared with other regions of the country, these features of local geography have been little studied in Essex until quite recently.[43] And yet they present some distinctive patterns. Most of Essex lay outside the region of the English common-field system, with its interspersed strips of tenants' lands and its communal cropping and grazing regimes. Instead, in north-central Essex a landholding of moderate or larger size consisted of one or more fields enclosed by hedges and ditches, and an adjacent messuage containing a house and other buildings. Fields and tenements described in these terms are ubiquitous throughout the district.[44] The impenetrability of Essex hedges was such that William Heyward, fleeing from an altercation in a field near Maldon in 1372 and finding himself backed against its hedge, claimed to have had no alternative but to kill his pursuer in self-defence.[45] Landholdings of this sort often bore names

42 With such broken series, moving averages are not too meaningful. But the quarter-century means of these two grains were as follows:

Grain	Period	Number of years in observation	Mean price (shillings/quarter)	Standard deviation
Wheat	1326–50	15	5.207	2.091
	1351–75	11	6.341	1.046
	1376–1400	21	4.852	1.400
	1401–25	5	4.469	1.150
Barley	1326–50	14	4.429	1.765
	1351–75	18	6.613	1.716
	1376–1400	25	4.502	1.100
	1401–25	7	4.774	0.887

43 The following discussion is derived largely from Poos, 'Population and resources', pp. 190–6, and Britnell, 'Agriculture in a region of ancient enclosure'.

44 E.g. Gervers, ed., *Cartulary of St John*, pp. lxxiii–iv; PRO.DL30.63.795 (Great Waltham and High Easter court, 28 Feb 1335): a croft 'sicut sepibus et fossatis includitur vocato Schergotisland'. In one land transaction at Great Waltham in 1366, a half-virgate was divided between two tenants, and the enrolled agreement specified that the tenement's 'capitalis domus, grangia, gardinium', six separate pieces of land in named 'crofts' or 'fields', one parcel of meadow and one of moor were each to be divided in half: PRO.DL30.65.822 (Great Waltham court, 22 Jan 1366).

45 PRO.JUST2.35.5 m.3 (coroner's inquest, 31 Mar 1372): '. . . Ricardus ate Brok iam mortuus & Willelmus Heyward de Maldon predicta contendebant verbis in quoddam

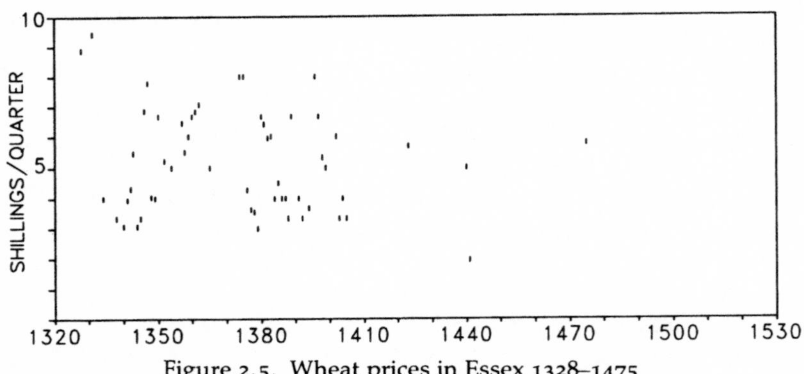

Figure 2.5. Wheat prices in Essex 1328–1475

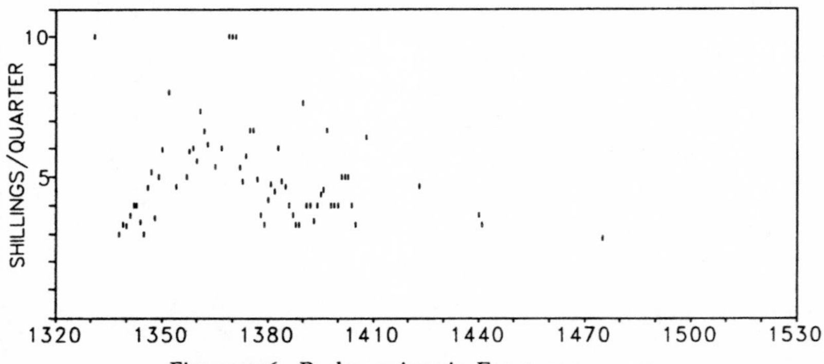

Figure 2.6. Barley prices in Essex 1331–1475

associated with previous tenants and persisting many generations despite changes of occupants. Dispersed settlement was a corollary of this enclosed-field system. In many parishes, scattered hamlets and isolated farmsteads were common, instead of the nucleated core of the Midlands-type village. And so the 'community' of this area resided less in compact propinquity than in its institutional framework and social relationships.

campo eiusdem ville & predictus Willelmus fugiebat usque ad quendam sepem crescentem in campo predicto quem nullo modo perterire poterat et predictus Ricardus ita ferventissime prosequebatur ad interficiendum predictum Willelmum quod idem Willelmus nullo modo potuisset salvasse vitam suam nisi cum defendisset et sic idem Willelmus tractavit cultellum suum & se ipsum defendit & vulneravit predictum Ricardum sub mamilla eius dextera unde moriebatur . . .'.

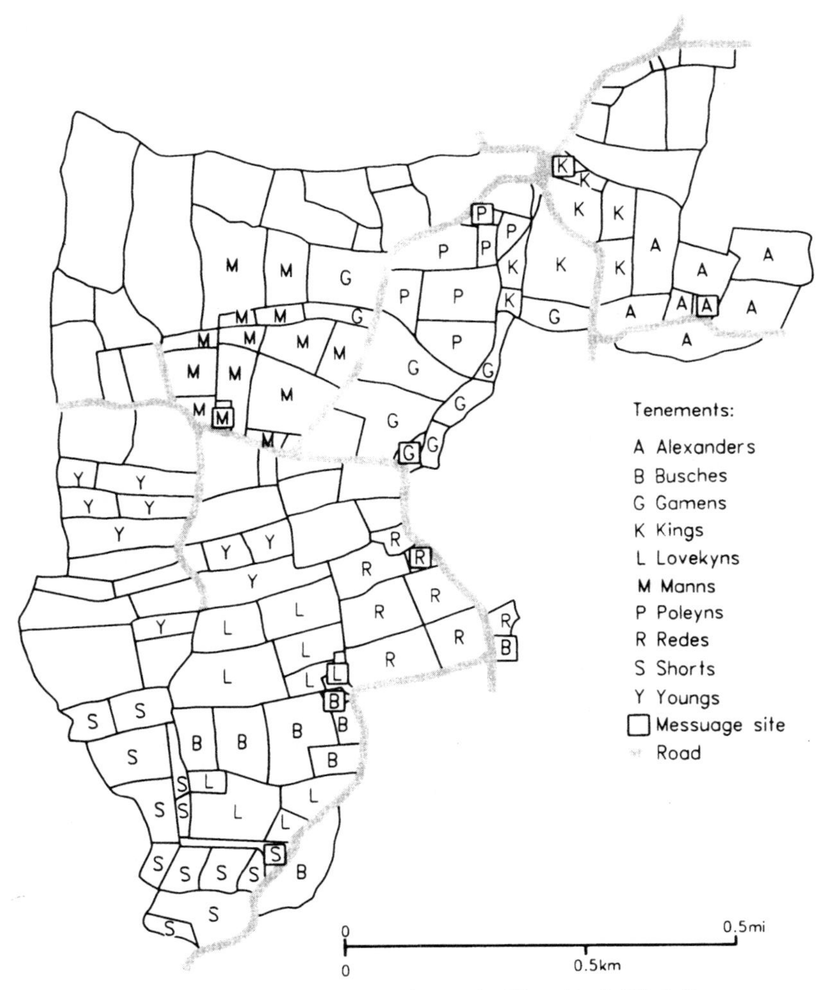

Figure 2.7. Some tenement forms in West End, High Easter

As a tangible illustration, Figure 2.7 reproduces a section of a remarkably detailed map of High Easter, made in 1654 and depicting ten tenements in the hamlet of West End with their constituent fields and messuages.[46] Though it would obviously be cavalier to presume that this map represents the exact forms of the tenements in question

[46] Figure 2.7 is based upon ERO D/DWv P2, re-drawn to scale from the second edition of the Ordnance Survey six-inch map of the later nineteenth century, at which time virtually all the field boundaries of the 1654 map were still intact.

two or three centuries earlier, in fact they all can be identified (in some cases with corroborating topographical details) from late-medieval manorial sources.[47] It is thus quite likely that this was essentially the way these tenements were arranged in the fourteenth and fifteenth centuries.

Until recently, this distinctive Essex local topography has been conventionally regarded as a product of enclosure directly from woodland in the late Anglo-Saxon or early Norman era. But recent work by landscape archaeologists has pushed its origins considerably further back in time. Fieldwork indicates that the rectilinear nature of field forms here stems ultimately from Roman or even earlier land divisions. Recently developed dating techniques imply that the hedgerows dividing these fields, and often still surviving, are at least as old as the high middle ages.[48] As a result, with the exception of some incidents involving heath, woodland, or other grazing grounds, mid-Essex by and large escaped post-medieval enclosure movements typical of common-field England, with their concomitant social dislocations, often violent protests, and wide-ranging alterations of local landscapes.[49] The countryside's physical face here changed strikingly little from the later middle ages to the twentieth century.

Such a distinctive local topography bore further implications for local social structure. Outside the northwestern corner of the county, where common fields did exist, one rarely encounters echoes of communal land management, in the form for instance of bylaws regulating boundaries between adjacent strips of arable land or punishments for enclosing land that should have been open to common grazing.[50] In the north-central district, in the absence of

[47] Cf. Poos, 'Population and resources', pp. 194–5. For example, in 1328 Cristina Kyng and Geoffrey Alisaundre were recorded as holding one customary virgate together (PRO.DL43.2.32: High Easter rental, 1328). The juxtaposition of Kings' and Alexanders' tenements in the 1654 map implies that these were the constituents of the original virgate.

[48] Rodwell, 'Relict landscapes in Essex'; Williamson, 'The Roman countryside'; Drury, *Excavations at Little Waltham*; Rackham, 'The medieval landscape'.

[49] Hunt, *The Puritan moment*, pp. 34–5, discusses a few sixteenth-century Essex enclosure riots.

[50] Cromarty, *Fields of Saffron Walden*, discusses the common fields of one northwestern Essex parish. A few references to common-field regimes survive from manorial courts of this corner of Essex: e.g. NCO 3595 (Priors Hall in Birchanger leet, 28 Sep 1402): '... Prior de Thremenale inclusit quendam campum vocatum Lilho unde pastura esset communis ad grave nocumentum ...'; NCO 3599 (Priors Hall in Birchanger leet, 6 Jun 1551): 'Et ad hanc curiam ordinatum est quod omnes tenentes huius manerij qui subverterent aratris suis aut aliter aliquas metas vocatas Balks' ponent easdem ut ex antiquo iacere solebant ...'. Other references elsewhere in the county to ploughing out divisions between tenants' land may refer to divided areas within enclosed property, as opposed to common fields as such: e.g. NCO 3657 (Priors Hall in

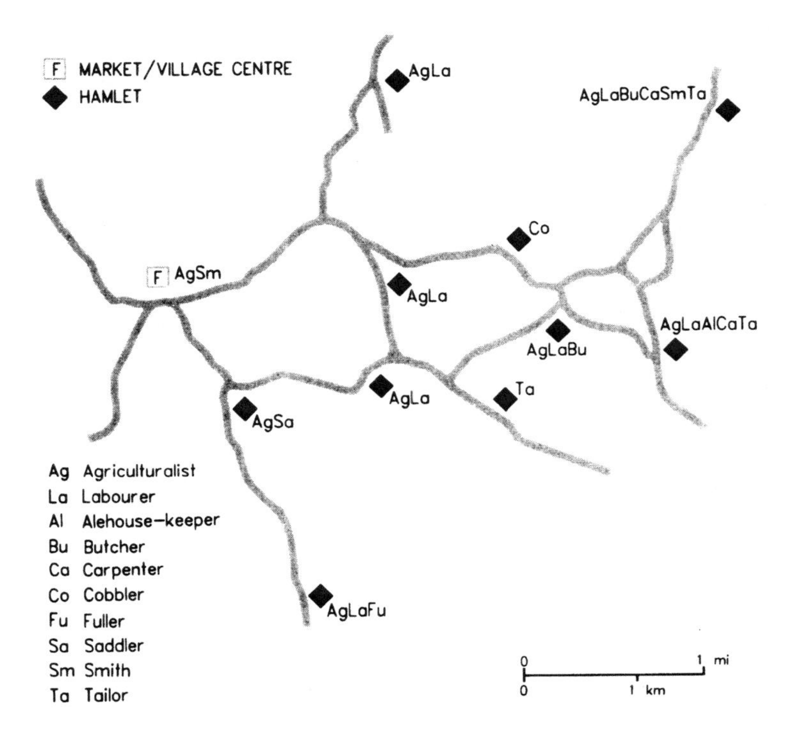

Figure 2.8. Felsted in the later fourteenth century

common pasture upon fallow-course land within common fields, such communal pasturage as was available was usually restricted to roadside and other waste land or dispersed 'greens', or occasional tracts of heathland, or else grazing was available for a fee in lords' parks.[51] The cushion against subsistence crises that common grazing resources afforded the poorer in other English field systems was thus more limited here. At the same time, by its very nature such a field system leaves few recorded traces of the ways tenants rotated crops or otherwise managed their own individual, enclosed properties.[52] What

Lindsell leet, 8 Jun 1420): 'Johannes Templer amovit unam dolam cum caruca sua positam inter terram ipsius Johannis & terram Mordow' Pyk . . .'.

51 Rackham, 'The medieval landscape', pp. 104–6; Britnell, 'Agriculture in a region of ancient enclosure', pp. 52–5; cf. BL Maps 199.d.24, an early-nineteenth-century map of Felsted depicting the enclosure of a few roadside wastes and greens.

52 For example, a three-course crop rotation among the constituent parts of an enclosed half-virgate at High Easter in 1336 is implied by a land transaction in which Isabel atte

evidence does exist implies that enclosed tenements in Essex could be managed, like many East Anglian field systems, quite flexibly; individual tenants could vary crop rotations and convert land from arable to pastoral use and back, especially in the fifteenth century when land use became more mixed, with none of the wholesale disruption to the community's land at large that would be entailed in a common-field system.

Dispersed settlement also helped to blur further the distinction between 'urban' and 'rural' economic spheres in the mid-Essex countryside. Just as artisanal, industrial, or commercial occupations were not restricted merely to the larger market communities in the district, so too were craftsmen and retailers broadly dispersed among hamlets or other small settlements outside the cores of the communities' village centres. Felsted, a large parish with a market centre surrounded by at least eight hamlets (some as far as three miles away from the village centre), is a good example. This community's 1381 poll-tax return records an especially diverse occupational profile, including ten different categories of craftsmen and retailers. Of 165 taxpayers listed, in 109 'households', it is possible to cross-link 45 with their appearances in a near-contemporary rental of Felsted manor, and so to plot the residential pattern of different occupational groups among the village centre and its satellite hamlets.[53] The result is illustrated in Figure 2.8.

As with any such exercise in cross-linkage, there are inevitably ambiguities.[54] Figure 2.8 shows the presence of cross-linked taxpayers/tenants in different occupational categories, not the number of persons in each category. It is a minimal distribution, in the sense that

Bregg surrendered her property to her son but retained during her lifetime 'tres acras terre videlicet de qualibet seisona unam acram': PRO.DL30.63.796 (Great Waltham and High Easter leet, 23 May 1336). Most evidence for crop rotations in this district comes from demesne property: Britnell, 'Agriculture in a region of ancient enclosure'; Britnell, 'Agricultural technology and the margin of cultivation'.

[53] PRO.E179.107.68 (1381 poll tax); PRO.SC11.188 (Felsted rental, 1367); additional topographical detail from ERO D/DCw M158/1 (Felsted rental, 1576).

[54] Straightforward nominal linkage of this sort always bears an element of imprecision, but here the 14-year lag between rental and tax return means that intervening changes of property or individual circumstances add a further source of possible identification error. But in this case it at least appears safe to infer residence, rather than simply some elements of these individuals' property-holding. The 1367 rental is arranged under the headings of Felsted's various hamlets. In most cases (33 of 45), persons cross-linked between rental and poll-tax return were listed in 1367 as holding residential property: for example, 'domus (Thomas Skynner . . . pro domo in quo manet)', messuage ('Johannes Drane pro mesuagio suo'), or 'tenementum', usually in Essex documents of this period (see below, Chapter 4) meaning house-site ('Johannes Cook pro tenemento Dany'). Moreover, all but 4 of these 45 cross-linked individuals held all their property in one hamlet.

only cross-linked individuals can be plotted; it is hardly likely, for instance, that Felsted's market centre contained only agriculturalists and smiths.[55] None the less, the implications are clear. Economic variegation and commercial or industrial activity permeated the mid-Essex countryside and were integral features of its rural society, spilling well beyond the boundaries of primary settlement nucleations.

The district's countryside in the later middle ages, then, was extremely complex. But its human geography – especially its persistently high density of people upon land – meshed with its physical and spatial configurations, especially its field and settlement patterns, to produce the market-oriented and industrialised local economy that this chapter has sketched out. It was the combination of these factors, rather than urban or market influences external to rural society, that helped to ensure continuing economic and occupational differentiation. And despite the stagnation of grain prices after the later 1300s, the nature of local land forms and underlying factors of soil and geology allowed the north-central district's agriculture to evolve flexibly towards a shifted equilibrium of land use. The district thus presents a paradox: even in the century and a half after 1350, when labour was relatively scarce, there were still many land-poor and seasonally underemployed people, a necessary precondition for expanding rural industry. And it is to the area's most important rural industry, woollen clothmaking, that the next chapter turns.

55 The 1367 rental lists 29 residential or commercial properties in Church End, the community's market centre.

3

The rural cloth industry

The industrial component of the district's rural economy, as has already been shown, was large and diverse enough to employ a significant fraction of the local population. In most respects this industrial sector and its participants are documented only fleetingly and tangentially, and much remains to be discovered about its organisation. But one industry was large and important enough to lend some critical insights into more general questions of the area's economy and social structure.

Northern Essex, along with districts of southern Suffolk just across the River Stour, was among the premier clothmaking regions of England in the later middle ages, although the fortunes, organisation and geography of the local industry were by no means static throughout the period. By the last decade of the fourteenth century, the only other English region of comparable geographical size, to which Essex and Suffolk ranked second in production of cloths of assise, was the southwestern area of Wiltshire, Somerset and Bristol with its hinterland.[1] But by contrast with this latter region, the rise to prominence of Essex and Suffolk was relatively late, and the second half of the fourteenth century was a time of fairly rapid development of local textile production.

Within Essex during this period manufacturing cloth, mainly cheaper, medium- to lightweight grades of woollens, achieved an importance within the local rural economy second only to agriculture, at least in terms of relative numbers of persons employed. Such is indicated by the 1381 poll-tax returns: among 'households' whose heads were recorded with occupational designations in all listings

[1] This statement is based upon aulnage data; this evidence is discussed below. Cf. Baker, 'Changes in the later middle ages', pp. 222–8; Bolton, *The medieval English economy*, pp. 267–73.

surviving for the entire county, textile workers (weavers, fullers, dyers, tailors, or drapers) were outnumbered only by agriculturalists and labourers.

This prominence is all the more marked in view of the fact that, whereas 'households' engaged in clothmaking were as numerous as this in the Essex returns as a whole, the industry was in fact heavily concentrated in the northern portion of the county. In Hinckford Hundred, which was in the very centre of the Essex textile district and whose poll-tax returns contain especially detailed occupational data, clothmakers' 'households' represented 5.5 per cent of those given occupational designations, or 3.6 per cent of all 'households' generally.[2] It is likely that these figures are, if anything, minima: in particular, small-scale agriculturalists, labourers, or other types of artisans who themselves, or members of whose households, worked on a part-time or secondary basis in cloth production may not have been classed as clothworkers in the returns. One need not dismiss entirely as a fabrication in support of special-interest pleading, then, the statement in a Parliamentary petition of 1393 on behalf of Essex and East Anglian clothworkers, that 'many and the greater part of the people of the said districts ... are able to do nothing else but work in that craft'.[3]

Figure 3.1 maps geographical patterns of cloth production in Essex between the late fourteenth and early sixteenth centuries. The map combines vills in which clothworkers were recorded in the 1381 taxation, parishes of residence for pre-1526 testators identified in surviving wills as clothworkers, places of cloth marketing recorded in accounts for collection of aulnage (a duty imposed upon cloth offered for sale) in Essex in 1395–7, 1398–9 and 1467–8, and localities of known fulling mills. Each of these indices poses its own problems of interpretation, and in several cases is arguably uneven in geographical provenance. There was considerable variation from hundred to hundred in the poll-tax returns' inclusion of occupational data, for example, and archival losses have resulted in a quite small number of wills surviving for the county at large before 1500.[4] On the other hand aulnage

[2] In Hinckford Hundred, 73 'households' were headed by clothworkers, out of 1,332 given occupational designations and a total of 2,013 'households', whether occupationally designated or not. It is an open question whether those 'households' not given any such designation might represent an occupationally unrepresentative subset of the entire population.

[3] *Rotuli Parliamentorum* vol. iii, p. 320: '... considerantz, que la substance & greindre partie des gentz des ditz pays d'Essex', Suff', & partie de Norff', ne savont autre chose faire sinoun de laborer sur la dite mestiere; & sont menuz gentz, que serroit grant pite pur destruire lour vivre'.

[4] Emmison, ed., *Wills at Chelmsford* vol. i; Fitch, ed., *Index to testamentary records in the Commissary Court* vol. i. Eleven clothmakers' wills, from seven parishes, are included

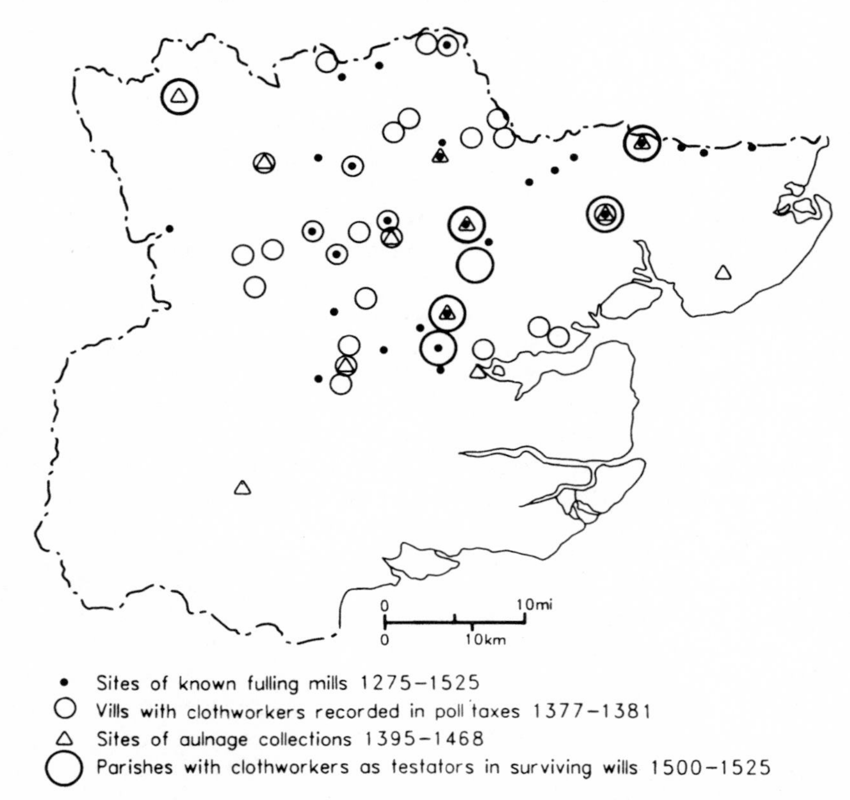

Figure 3.1. The cloth industry in later-medieval Essex

accounts, especially the three collections employed here, which are generally regarded as the most reliable available for Essex, are much more likely to reflect production centres throughout the county, without any obvious reason for omitting places in one geographical area or another.[5]

in this distribution: ERO D/ACR 1/182, D/ACR 2/28, D/ACR 2/145(Coggeshall); D/ACR 1/138, D/ACR 2/74 (Colchester); D/ACR 2/183 (Dedham); D/ACR 1/173, D/ACR 2/4 (Kelvedon); D/ACR 2/83 (Ulting); D/ACR 1/38 (Walden); D/ACR 2/174 (Witham).

[5] PRO.E101.342.9 (1395–7); E101.342.13 (1398–9); E101.343.4 (1467–8). The accuracy of aulnage accounts, especially those of the fifteenth century, has been questioned by some, especially Carus-Wilson, 'Aulnage accounts'; Bridbury, *Medieval English cloth-making*, pp. 56–9. But the accounts of the 1390s for Essex used here are generally reckoned to be fairly free of more serious errors, at least for the purpose of identifying individual markets: Bridbury, *Economic growth*, p. 34. The Essex account for 1467–8 was the product of administrative reforms in collection and is therefore likely to be more accurate than most fifteenth-century accounts: Britnell, *Growth and decline in Colchester*, pp. 187–9. In Figure 3.1, only places where cloths were sealed for sale are

Carus-Wilson's well-known essay on the importance of the fulling mill argued that harnessing water power for clothmaking marked a significant technological innovation for the industry – in fact, a medieval 'industrial revolution' – and moreover helped to accelerate the flight of the industry from town to countryside, particularly in the more hilly regions of southwestern, western and northern England where fast-running streams were available for mill construction by forward-looking seigneurial investment.[6] Pelham subsequently expanded this argument, augmented Carus-Wilson's list of known mills and extended it to the end of the fourteenth century, and mapped the resulting distribution.[7] In his recent discussion of medieval English clothmaking Bridbury, reproducing Pelham's map, was highly sceptical of Carus-Wilson's arguments, in large measure because of the relative paucity in Pelham's mapped distribution of fulling mills in lowland and eastern England, where both direct evidence and indirect inference imply a well-established rural industry by the 1300s.[8]

It is immediately obvious that, whatever the general validity of Carus-Wilson's arguments may prove to be, her own and Pelham's compilations of fulling mills are grossly inadequate for Essex, based as they appear to have been largely upon more easily available printed sources. For the purposes of the present study a further search has been made for mills within the county, primarily in unprinted extents contained within inquisitions post mortem, miscellaneous royal inquisitions, feet of fines, and manorial-court rolls and accounts. Whereas Pelham's map appears to contain no more than a half-dozen fulling mills in Essex before 1400, in fact 31 have been documented into the early 1500s, and extended search might well eventually bring more to light.[9] Approximately half of these fulling mills are documented in sources, such as inquisitions post mortem, that are unlikely to pose any biases of unequal coverage over different parts of the county, although evidence for other mills is taken from an admittedly more random sampling of surviving estate records.[10]

plotted, while other place-names occasionally mentioned as homes of individual vendors are omitted; see below for more on this.

6 Carus-Wilson, 'An industrial revolution of the thirteenth century'.

7 Pelham, 'Distribution of early fulling mills'; Pelham, *Fulling mills*.

8 Bridbury, *Medieval English clothmaking*, pp. 16–25; cf. Bolton, *The medieval English economy*, pp. 157–8; Holt, *Mills of medieval England*, pp. 155–6.

9 Documentary references to these mills are provided in Appendix C at the end of this study.

10 It should be noted that water mills were sometimes converted from grain milling to fulling in the later middle ages: Britnell, *Growth and decline in Colchester*, pp. 76–7 cites examples from later-fourteenth-century Colchester. Cf. Holt, *Mills of medieval*

Thus, although each of these four indices of the geographical dimensions of late-medieval Essex cloth production may be incomplete in itself, taken together the broader pattern is remarkably consistent. Almost without exception, the clothmaking centres shown in Figure 3.1 lay north of a line running from Chelmsford to Maldon and east of a line running from Chelmsford to Walden. And although the better-known centres with large-scale production – Colchester, Halstead, Coggeshall and Bocking, most notably – are all represented on this mapped distribution, the great majority of these places were quite small rural communities.

This should not, of course, be taken to mean that cloth production, especially of a smaller-scale or mostly non-commercial nature, was unknown elsewhere in the county; from other evidence, examples to the contrary can certainly be found.[11] Equally importantly, it must not be inferred that any individual place plotted on this map as a 'clothmaking centre' necessarily was greatly dependent upon the industry or that cloth manufacture went on there continually throughout the middle ages: inclusion of one or two weavers in a 1381 tax return for a vill need scarcely betoken production of major dimensions, either then or a half-century or century later, while new fulling mills were erected, and old ones decayed into disuse, throughout the fourteenth and fifteenth centuries.[12] Britnell, who has recently expressed some doubt that the 'concept of industrial development as a regional phenomenon' is usefully applicable to this area, has also argued that only a minority of villages here actually possessed a cloth industry of significant proportions in the later middle ages.[13]

But the geographical boundaries of clothmaking in Essex do seem to have been fairly sharp, and the reasons for this pattern fit within a larger continuing debate concerning rural industry or 'protoindustrialisation', not just in late-medieval England but also in preindustrial Europe at large. Carus-Wilson's arguments about the importance of water-driven fulling, though cast into doubt by some historians, seem with certain qualifications more substantiated in view of the extensive use for fulling to which the slow-running, small Essex waterways are now shown to have been put. Perhaps not an 'industrial revolution', and certainly with a somewhat different geographical provenance

England, pp. 132, 156, 160. Since many extents in inquisitions post mortem often mention only *molendina aquatica* ('water mills'), some of these terse phrases may conceal fulling mills.

[11] E.g. McIntosh, *Autonomy and community*, pp. 155, 229, 286, shows that for much of the fifteenth century the manor of Havering (in southwestern Essex) contained at least a few weavers and fullers.

[12] See Appendix C.

[13] Britnell, *Growth and decline in Colchester*, p. 85.

from that which she inferred, the recorded presence of many Essex mills is still a sensitive barometer for the existence, chronology and spatial distribution of the local industry.

In an equally influential essay Thirsk, dealing primarily with the sixteenth century, argued that places marked by dense concentrations of population and by primarily pastoral agrarian production, and therefore by large numbers of rural households experiencing underemployment or seasonal unemployment, were expecially likely to develop rural industries of significant scale.[14] These arguments have been echoed more recently in connection with post-Black Death England.[15] At the same time, lines of argument similar to Thirsk's have been incorporated into more ambitious theories of protoindustrialisation, specifically in generalisations concerning ecological zones in which protoindustrial development was most likely to occur. Equally important in the arguments that have been made for the significance of protoindustrialisation were its effects upon demography: some historians have argued that, by providing work for the otherwise underemployed, it encouraged earlier marriages and boosted fertility and population growth. Recent critics of these theories have cast considerable doubt upon their empirical validity, though most of this debate has centred upon periods no earlier than the seventeenth century.[16]

At a very local level this district in the later fourteenth and fifteenth centuries fits only rather imperfectly within such posited agrarian preconditions and demographic consequences of rural industrial development. For one thing, although it has been shown that northern Essex did experience a marked shift toward pastoral production in the 150 years after the Black Death, a large part of this shift came in the 1400s (after the Essex industry had already achieved its full medieval development) and the local agrarian regime remained markedly more arable in nature than other parts of the county. Thus one of the central preconditions of protoindustrial theory would seem to apply only partially here. Moreover, what is available in the way of nuptiality data for central Essex runs counter to the notion that the district's artisans married earlier than agriculturalists in the later fourteenth century.[17]

[14] Thirsk, 'Industries in the countryside'.

[15] E.g. Baker, 'Changes in the later middle ages', p. 225; Bolton, *The medieval English economy*, pp. 269–70.

[16] The most comprehensive statement of these theories is Kriedte, Medick and Schlumbohm, *Industrialization before industrialization*, esp. pp. 12–37; see the criticisms by, among others, Houston and Snell, 'Proto-industrialization?', esp. pp. 477–9; Clarkson, *Proto-industrialization*, esp. pp. 15–27.

[17] This evidence is discussed in Chapter 7.

On the other hand, this district continued to possess a high population density (relative to other portions of the county and region) and a high proportion of cottagers and smallholders highly dependent upon wage labour and by-employments. Thus while doubtless only very imperfectly proletarianised (itself another tenet of protoindustrialisation theory), the requisite underemployed workforce was certainly there. Moreover a well-developed network of small market centres, and also larger exporting sites like Colchester, Maldon and Ipswich, further facilitated marketing opportunities, while the extensive if relatively late development of water-driven fulling met no apparent technical bars from the district's terrain. It would be misconceived to posit one comprehensive set of circumstances influencing the development of clothmaking regions in late-medieval England as a whole. In this district, it was the locally particular combination of technical enablement, marketing opportunity, and an amenable social structure which helped to bring about the development that occurred.

One reason for caution is that remarkably little is known about the structure, organisation and participants in the cloth industry in rural and small-town Essex in the later middle ages. Only a cursory sketch can be pieced together, from isolated litigation among individuals involved in different stages of production, from occasional indictments against weavers and fullers for excessive profits under the fourteenth-century economic legislation, and from aulnage accounts. The situation is rather different, then, from the more highly regulated environment of larger towns like Colchester, whose industry has recently been studied exhaustively by Britnell.[18]

But the evidence, fragmentary as it is, indicates that in the later fourteenth and early fifteenth centuries, when the industry expanded rapidly in rural Essex, there was little in the way of 'capitalist' or entrepreneurial enterprise or of a classic putting-out system at the heart of cloth production in the countryside. Instead, many people worked on a small-scale basis, often on only one or two stages of the manufacturing process (from spinning and weaving to fulling and marketing the finished product),[19] and sometimes in tandem with other petty crafts or agricultural labour. In this respect the countryside was similar to Colchester itself.[20] The aulnage accounts' lists of individual cloth vendors occasionally included occupational desig-

[18] Britnell, *Growth and decline in Colchester*, esp. pp. 53–85, 163–92.

[19] An excellent short account of the stages of clothmaking, and its archaeological remains hitherto unearthed, is given in Clarke, *Archaeology of medieval England*, pp. 129–37.

[20] Britnell, *Growth and decline in Colchester*, pp. 77–9.

nations in addition to surnames: in the account for 1395–7, at Colchester and other marketing centres, and also in the smaller communities nearby from which vendors brought finished cloths to sell, craftsmen or retailers such as smiths, bakers, tailors and merchants were included. Even more prominent were fullers, who were drawn from several villages and who were, it appears, especially likely to buy cloths after weaving, finish them, and market them afterwards.[21]

For poorer individuals or households, the earlier, probably less technically demanding stages of production – particularly spinning and weaving – were by-employments fairly easy to enter and leave. Capital costs were likely to have been within reach, for example, of persons exiting a few years of servanthood. In later-fourteenth-century Colchester, a loom and a pair of shuttles typically cost £1 or so.[22] It would thus be possible to gain some extra income from weaving at seasons of slack demand for agricultural labour. The rare surviving wills of weavers in the region reinforce the impression that such people typically possessed only rather humble endowments. In 1511 at Coggeshall, for instance, a weaver named John Sponer bequeathed (besides 8d. to the parish church's high altar) merely his 'brode lome w^{t} all thyngs therto' and his house to his elder son after a life-interest to his widow, and 'the litil cham[ber] in the towne' (perhaps a workshop?) to his younger son.[23] And in 1389, two Essex weavers were listed among the (probably agricultural) labourers indicted for taking excessive daily wages at Little Chesterford and Hatfield Heath.[24]

But even in a fairly unstructured industry, artisans still required initial capital and some training, especially in the more skilled production stages. Chance references to formal apprenticeships, in clothmaking as in other industries, turn up occasionally in testimony at inquests to prove the ages of feudal heirs, though these apprenticeships were most common in larger towns. In 1404 Edmund Brid sent his son to

[21] PRO.E101.342.9 mm. 1v, 2, 5v, 13; the latter membrane, listing vendors of cloth at Maldon, includes 'John Fayrstede, fuller, of Maldon', 'John Seman, fuller, of Woodham Walter', 'Thomas Rouge, fuller, of Southminster', and 'Thomas Dunnyng, fuller, of Heybridge', as well as a sufficiently large number of persons with one variation or another upon 'Fuller' given as a surname to imply that these were in many cases occupationally derived rather than patronymics.

[22] Britnell, *Growth and decline in Colchester*. pp. 75–6. [23] ERO D/ACR 1/182.

[24] PRO.KB9.25.m.10: 'Item presentant quod ... Johannes Spryngold Webbe de eadem [i.e. Springwell in Little Chesterford, from previous name in list] [and many others] ... sunt communes laboratores ... per diem pro excessivo lucro capiendo videlicet quolibet die tempore yemale ijd. & prandium & in autumpnale iiijd. & prandium & aliquo vd...'; *ibid.*, m24v: 'Item dicunt quod ... Johannes Yonge Webbe senior [identification in Hatfield Heath perhaps doubtful, inferred from previous name in list] [and many others] ... sunt communes laboratores ... [etc.]'.

Colchester from a village approximately 15 miles away to be apprenticed as a sawyer;[25] nine years later Thomas Graunger, a Colchester man, took an apprentice weaver.[26] Even in the countryside, however, establishment in an industrial craft was not achieved without costs or, necessarily, entirely individualistically. In 1351, at the age of 19 years, at the village of Benington (Herts.) a few miles west of the Essex border, William Founde 'was put by his friends to his craft [as a dyer]'.[27]

In the absence of guild or other types of corporate regulation found in large urban industries, when disputes arose over contractual obligations between individuals at various stages of production or over agreements about quality or price, manorial or other local courts were usually the only venues available for litigation in rural Essex. The only exceptions to this, generally, were occasional attempts in criminal-court jurisdictions to indict middlemen who engaged in deceptive practices or overpricing. For example, in 1380 an Essex King's Bench indictment file included a charge against John Baronn of West Hanningfield for buying cloths and stretching them out to a greater width, 'in deception of the people'.[28] It is therefore to the occasional litigation concerning such matters that one must turn to gain more insight into the nature of the industry and its participants. The relatively few surviving cases with full circumstantial details from Essex courts reinforce the impression that there was an extensive network in these communities of contractual agreements to weave, dye, or finish, with one party providing materials and the other the expertise and work, the quantities involved usually being quite small.[29]

At Writtle in 1401 one man sued another for detention of two 'dozens' or *duodene* (cloths characteristic of this region, half the length and taxed for aulnage purposes at half the rate of a standard-sized 'cloth of assise'), which the defendant was to have woven with materials supplied by the plaintiff.[30] At Great Dunmow in 1389 one

[25] PRO.C139.31.69 (inquest, 13 Mar 1427): '... posuit Johannem filium suum apprenticium cuidam Johanni Weles in Colcestr' in arte alutarij erudienda ...'. The village was 'Notley' (sic). On the uses of proof-of-age inquests as evidence for social history, see below, Chapter 9.

[26] PRO.C.139.31.73 (inquest, 17 Jul 1427): '... cepit Johannem Balde tanquam apprenticium suum in arte textoris ...'.

[27] PRO.C135.259.9 (inquest, 21 Mar 1376): '... Willelmus Founde dyer ... ipse positus fuit per amicos suos ad artificium suum predictum ...'.

[28] PRO.JUST2.36.3 m.5.: '...Johannes Baronn de Westhanyfeld draper emit pannos de latitudine virgate & ponit dictos pannos super tectorem & facit pannos de latitudine unius virgate & unius quarterij virgate in deceptione populi ...'.

[29] Cf. Clark, 'Debt litigation', pp. 255–8.

[30] ERO D/DP M204 m.8 (Writtle court, 20 Aug 1401); 'Thomas Seveyn queritur de Henrico Barneby de placito detentionis duarum duodenarum de Blanketto ...

woman sued another, from Little Easton (a small village about two miles away), for 14d. for weaving and fulling eight ells of cloth.[31] Similarly, at Hatfield Broadoak in 1384 one man sued another for 18d. for dyeing six ells of cloth.[32] And at Bocking in the same year, a weaver had been furnished with yarn for weaving 'blanket' cloth (a cheap grade of woollen cloth) by a woman who was subsequently indicted and imprisoned for an unspecified felony; this emerged in the Bocking court rolls only because the cloth was confiscated as felon's chattels.[33] In Bocking, in fact, clothmaking crafts were sufficiently widely practised that a recalcitrant defendant in a suit of debt in 1389 found his cloth, yarn, dyestuffs and garments seized by court officials as distraints.[34] In another suit at Writtle in 1405, a woman claimed that she had been the servant of another for a year and a quarter and that her ex-mistress still owed her, in addition to her servant's stipend, 1s. 5½d. for spinning at least 13 pounds of wool.[35] Finally, in the 1389 indictment file of economic offences, six weavers from five different Essex communities were charged with excessive profits, and the

queritur quod predictus Henricus ei iniuste detinet predictas duas duodenas quas deliberavit ad texandum quas postquam textate fuissent eidem Thome deliberasset & nondum deliberavit . . .'.

31 ERO D/DMg M39 (Great Dunmow court, 9 Jul 1389): 'Margeria Wysman queritur de Alicia Sarden de Eyston parva de placito debiti Et dicit quod ei debet . . . xiiijd. pro textura & fulleratura viij ulnarum panni albi Et predicta Alicia solempniter exacta non venit et ballivus retornat quod predicta Alicia districta est per viij ulnas panni albi precij xld. et dictus pannus in plena curia deliberata dicte Margerie ad salvo custodiendum . . .'.

32 ERO D/DGe M251 (Hatfield Broadoak court, 3 Dec 1384): 'Mattheus Chall . . . optulit se versus Johannem Webbe de placito debiti et dicit quod ei debet xviijd. pro tinctura vj ulnarum panni . . .'.

33 CALC U15.11.4 (Bocking court, 26 Jul 1384): ' . . .Thomas Bocher Webbe . . . habuit filum laneum & lyneum de catallis Alicie Forster felone incarcate apud Colcestr' & indictate pro diversis feloniis <quas fecit> ad textandum in duobus Blankettis ad opus predicte Alicie Forster Et unde predictus Thomas textravit unum Blankettum ex longitudine sex ulnarum Et postea predictus Thomas Bocher Webbe liberavit Ricardo Boone uni constabulariorum ville de Bockyng predictum Blankettum textratum & filum lineum pro alio Blanketto . . . ad opus domini tanquam catalla felone . . .'.

34 CALC U15.11.12 (Bocking court, 12 Jul 1389): 'Agnes que fuit uxor Petri Taylor queritur de Ricardo Cook & Katerina uxore eius de duobus placitis debiti . . . & ad respondendum summoniti &c Et nichilominus x ulne panni largi de blueto j quarterio ulne minus . . . j gonna bipartata de rubeo panno & panno strangulato cum j capitio nigro ad idem non concusso . . . iij manutergia debilia . . . filum de russeto pro coverlyttis faciendis xvj libre . . . quod liberatur ad textando & fullando . . . diversa lignea pro bracina . . . remanent Ideo preceptum est premunire contra proximam quod tunc sint ibidem ad ostendum vel dicendum quare predicta catalla predicte Agneti liberari non debeant . . .'.

35 ERO D/DP M209 (Writtle court, 25 Jul 1405): 'Johannes Yewen & Agnes uxor eius queruntur de Emma atte Lee de placito debiti Et unde . . . queruntur quod predicta Emma eis iniuste detinet vs. pro stipendio ipsius Agnetis deservientis eidem Emme per unum annum & unam quartam partem anni . . . ixd. pro filacione ix librarum lane vjd. pro filacione iiij librarum lane ijd. obulum pro filacione lane . . .'.

terminology of these cases again implies that they were working on a fairly small scale. These indictments were for weaving a few cloths over a period of one or two years for a number of clients, though since the charge in these cases was for taking excessive sums of money for the transactions in question this evidence does not necessarily reflect the weavers' total output over that time.[36]

During the century and a half after the Black Death virtually the only people (apart from a very few genuine entrepreneurs, discernible mainly from the later 1400s) who might qualify as large-scale capital investors and traders within the rural Essex cloth industry were fullers. Fulling mills were major constructions, usually built by manorial lords: the best-known Essex example is that of Bocking, where the prior of Christ Church, Canterbury, spent £28. 0s. 8d. to erect one in 1303.[37] But from the mid-fourteenth century onward, most Essex lords capitalised upon their investment in fulling mills by letting them out at farm, usually for lengthy periods.[38] For the fuller who took upon himself one of these arrangements, the financial scale of the operation was considerable, in part because a cottage or tenement and a yard for drying and stretching cloths after fulling usually accompanied the mill in the leasing arrangement.[39]

In 1403 John Aspelonn took the fulling mill at Birdbrook, plus a tenement and attached lands, for a term of 20 years at £2. 6s. 8d. per year.[40] Aspelonn was responsible for maintenance and repairs to the mill, with the lord providing timber; in fact, in one or two cases suits in manorial court between fullers and carpenters over agreements to make repairs to mills constitute virtually the only surviving evidence

[36] PRO.KB9.25 mm.3,4,13,14v,16v. From m.14v: 'Item dicunt quod Thomas Barbour de Stanford [-le-Hope] cepit de Cristiana atte Hill & diversis hominibus in hundredo predicto [i.e. Barstaple Hundred] pro una duodena texanda panni lani stricti & latitudinis quarteriorum xd. apud Stanford in annis xij & xiij domini Regis Ricardi secundi et [one or two words illegible] extorcionem per annum ijs.'.

[37] BL MS Cotton Galba E.iv.fo.106: 'Anno Mccciij Novo molendino fullonico xxviij[li] viijd'.

[38] See Appendix C for documentary references to this. Holt, *Mills of medieval England*, pp. 156–8, doubts that fulling mills normally proved very profitable to lords.

[39] E.g. *Calendar of inquisitions miscellaneous* vol. v., p. 133; cf. Clarke, *Archaeology of medieval England*, p. 134.

[40] ERO D/DU 267/31 (Birdbrook court, 24 Sep 1403): 'Ad istam curiam dominus concessit ad firmam Johanni Aspelonn fuller' molendium suum fullonicum & unum tenementum vocatum Wythelardes cum terra & prato pertinentibus ad eundem ... a vigilia Sancti Michaelis proxima futura usque ad finem & terminum xx annorum ... Reddendo inde domino per annum ... quatuor marcas sterlingorum ... Et dictus Johannes sustinebit manutenebit domum molendini in tegulando & daubando domino inveniente grossum meremum ... & firmarius furrabit & legabit instrumenta dicti molendini ... [etc.]'.

for the presence of a fulling mill in a given place.[41] Other lords continued to pay maintenance costs for mills they leased out, in which case manorial accounts are good guides to the mills' continuing operation.

But the returns to a fuller might also be high; in 1389 three fullers, two at Bocking and one at Halstead, were each indicted for charging 4s. for fulling a 'dozen'.[42] This is one-third higher than Britnell's estimate of the normal rate in Colchester at about the same time,[43] but even at the lower 'normal' rate the potential for profits was doubtless considerable, so long as market demand and local supply were both buoyant. Once again, although surviving fullers' wills from Essex before the mid-sixteenth century are so few as to make any systematic assessments of assets untenable, this evidence also implies that considerable wealth and wide-ranging interests were typical of fullers. At Ulting in 1518, John Nele bequeathed substantial sums of money, various pieces of real property, and cattle to his widow and sons. In addition Nele left the remaining years of his lease, in partnership with two other men, of a fulling mill, with 'all my toles & instruments belongyng to myn occupacon ... a shoppe to work in and a chamber in the house that I bought ... [and] the Residue of my wole to helpe to pay my detts'.[44] And, as already shown, rural fullers were also prominent vendors of cloth, at least some of which they probably purchased from others after weaving.

It is unfortunately quite difficult to chart quantitatively the rises and falls in production or the degree of participation of smaller rural communities in the Essex cloth industry in this period in any systematic fashion from the aulnage accounts. The accounts were concerned with places where cloths were offered for sale, and only infrequently noted the villages of origin from which vendors brought cloths to market. In 1395–7, for example, cloths sealed at Maldon were brought to market by persons from eleven other communities within a 15-mile

41 ERO D/DP M209 (Writtle court, 17 Jul 1406): 'Johannes Friday fullere & Johannes Fullere junior optulent se versus Johannem Herry ... Et unde ... queruntur quod predictus Johannes Herry eis iniuste infregit convencionem de factura cuiusdam molendini vocati Pacchingmelle Et ideo iniuste quia certis die & anno predictus Johannes Herry convenit cum predictis Johanne Friday & Johanne Fullere ad reficiendum ac reparandum molendinum predictum sufficienter ut predicti Johannes Friday & Johannes Fullere possent fullere pannum in predicto molendino per ix annos quam convencionem eis infregit ...'.

42 PRO.KB9.25 m.16v: e.g. 'Item presentant quod Johannes Russell de Halsted fuller die Jovis proximo post festum sancti Michaelis regni regis nunc xj de Thoma Sewale [rest of line torn off] unius duodene panni lanei fullatura recepit iiijs. per extorcionem & sic de aliis & continuit a festo Michaelis anno xj usque festum Sancti Michaelis [rest of line torn off]'.

43 Britnell, *Growth and decline in Colchester*, pp. 60–2.

44 ERO D/ACR 2/83.

radius around the town in addition to the cloths sold by Maldon residents, and it is conceivable that many of the latter had themselves purchased the cloths in finished or unfinished state from producers elsewhere.[45] In 1467–8, of the 96 cloths recorded as having been sealed at 'Chelmsford and Maldon', only 43 (44.8 per cent) were sold by residents of those towns; the other vendors were listed as residents of four other, small rural communities and five were sold by (unnamed) 'various inhabitants dwelling in vills near the said town' (i.e. Maldon).[46] Thus while it is relatively simple to gauge the fortunes of cloth *markets* over the later middle ages, as Britnell has done, the relative importance of rural and urban production must remain unclear.

The raw aulnage data, imprecise though they are, imply that between the middle and last decades of the fourteenth century Essex clothmaking centres increased their output by a factor of at least five.[47] One factor sometimes cited as aiding in this expansion is the influx of Flemish workers, especially into the region's largest towns, in the early and middle decades of the fourteenth century.[48] But these immigrants are rather difficult to detect in the smaller production centres of the region; they surface only in miscellaneous contexts, like the manslaughter accusation made at Castle Hedingham in 1374 against 'Peter le Walsshe, flemyng, webbe',[49] and it would appear difficult to ascribe much importance to their presence in the region's industry as a whole.

Britnell has shown that the Colchester market assumed an increasingly dominant role within the region during this era of expansion, with traders bringing cloths to the town's fairs from a broad hinterland. In turn, the fortunes of the town's cloth market were tied, above all, to export opportunities. And the same influence was decisive when, by the second quarter of the fifteenth century, the cloth production of the region at large had peaked. Whereas Suffolk's industry continued to expand into the later 1400s, that of Essex maintained a more or less constant output in the middle and latter

[45] PRO.E101.342.9 m.13.

[46] PRO.E101.343.4 m.3. The places were 'Bekyrley' (unidentified), 'Woodham' (Woodham Walter, Mortimer, or Ferrers?), Springfield, 'Waltham' (probably Great Waltham, six miles north of Chelmsford), and 'diversis inhabitantibus in villatis iuxta predictam villam comorantibus'.

[47] Regional aulnage data are tabulated in Bridbury, *Medieval English clothmaking*, p. 114. The strengths and weaknesses of these data for the purposes of comparing different regions' production, and of each region's production over time, are discussed *ibid.*, pp. 56–9, and by Britnell, *Growth and decline in Colchester*, pp. 79–81.

[48] Britnell, *Growth and decline in Colchester*, pp. 20, 72; cf. Bolton, *The medieval English economy*, pp. 267–8.

[49] PRO.JUST2.35.5 m.3.

parts of the century. Meanwhile, the share of this output marketed at Colchester continued to rise relative to other, smaller marketing centres.[50] And at the same time the organisation of the industry also evolved, with more production dominated by larger, more truly entrepreneurial figures like the much-storied Paycockes of Coggeshall,[51] employing their own ranks of workers, as opposed to the earlier, more widely based production of relatively independent artisans.

Within this later period of general stagnation in the rural Essex industry, the fortunes of smaller communities involved in textile production varied widely. Dedham's experience, for example, closely mirrored that of Colchester, with remarkable prosperity in the early 1400s being reversed after midcentury.[52] Still smaller communities, with smaller cohorts of workers, were doubtless even more volatile. The records in manorial accounts of fulling-mill farming constitute a surrogate measure of the strength of local production, and these again varied in fortunes and chronology. It seems reasonable to infer that Birdbrook's fulling mill, described as in disrepair in 1360, was reconstructed in response to local demand, since it was farmed out continually from the 1380s to the 1440s, when it was 'totally destroyed' and not farmed out again in the medieval period.[53] At Claret Hall in Ashen, by contrast, local activity appears to have come later: this manor's surviving accounts contain no mention of the mill or its farming-out until 1391/2. The price which a fulling-mill farm commanded is another sign of the varied fortunes of local industry: Felsted's mill, for example, was farmed for 63s. 4d. per annum in the 1390s, but commanded £4 by the 1420s.

Despite the shortcomings of the evidence, then, the general implications of the Essex rural cloth industry for the local economy and social structure seem clear. At a time of abrupt depopulation and agrarian contraction, the local cloth industry expanded remarkably quickly, drawing into its orbit an increasing number of workers who were otherwise economically marginal. The continuing, large proportion of cottagers and smallholders in the region during the century after the Black Death was thus at the same time an enabling factor and a consequence of local industrial output, for as long as there remained a buoyant demand (fuelled chiefly, it would appear, by exports). For these people the various stages of clothmaking provided at least a

50 Britnell, *Growth and decline in Colchester*, pp. 53–85, 163–92.

51 Power, *The Paycockes of Coggeshall*.

52 Britnell, *Growth and decline in Colchester*, pp. 251–2.

53 For documentary references to this and other mills referred to below, see Appendix C.

supplemental means of income, though one that was variable and that meshed with other forms of employment. The industry's organisation remained broadly based among many small-scale or part-time workers, loosely welded into a production network rather than being more rigidly organised into an archetypal putting-out system. Such a system, if present at all, was only in its infancy towards the end of the fifteenth century.

4

Houses

The houses in which rural people dwelt at the end of the middle ages, and the other buildings that they constructed and used, shed some unexpected light upon a number of aspects of the society of their inhabitants. In the tangible structures within which these people passed much of their lives, economic change intersected with social structures. Comparative levels of construction expense, complexity and sophistication reflected living standards and economic stratification, while household arrangements meshed with physical spaces. In short, the various permutations of housing in the district embodied both the layered economic and social strata and the co-resident units of local people's lives.

In Essex during the later fourteenth and fifteenth centuries, the houses of the better-off in rural society gradually evolved more numerous and varied rooms, serving to underscore in a very tangible manner the gulf in modes of life between wealthier agriculturalists and poorer labourers. Yet it has been only relatively recently that historians have combined archaeological and documentary evidence to produce a clearer picture of the physical structures of medieval rural houses from social strata below the gentry.

Evidence for the century or so after 1350 is especially full for England as a whole. In this period manorial lords, facing declining rent-rolls and concerned by the physical deterioration of their customary tenements, registered their anxieties in the manorial-court records in the form of constant orders to their tenants to repair houses and other buildings, and also in recorded agreements with new tenants assuming holdings to undertake substantial repairs or rebuilding, at times with the lord contributing materials.[1] In a valuable study Field analysed some remarkably detailed court-roll entries of this sort from

[1] Dyer, 'English peasant buildings'.

Worcestershire, yielding quite full information for house and room sizes in particular.[2] Unfortunately such detailed evidence is rare for most regions of England, Essex included. At the same time, residential and other social arrangements within houses have been even less fully investigated, and documentary evidence for these matters must be pieced together from tangential and fleeting references in manorial records, ecclesiastical-court depositions, and coroners' inquests.[3]

Essex is an especially apt place for such study, since here, and in southeastern England generally, pre-1500 houses from even relatively humble social levels have survived in impressive numbers.[4] In this part of the country stone is scarce, so sub-gentry houses were almost without exception entirely timber-framed, with wattle-and-daub walls. Many early Essex houses have been identified in recent years by architectural historians, beneath the veneers of subsequent refurbishing.[5] These discoveries have been due in no small part to the work of Hewett, who painstakingly assembled a chronological framework for carpentry techniques, permitting a fairly precise set of criteria for dating existing structures.[6] In the process, layouts of rooms and chronology of construction, alterations and enlargements have been established for many early Essex houses.

Essex tenurial documents usually used the term 'messuage' (*mesuagium*) or 'tenement' (*tenementum*) to describe the dwelling-house and outbuildings, plus the site or farmyard in which they stood. In the relatively rare instances when the outbuildings within a messuage were enumerated or described in contemporary documents, there were typically two to five structures including the house itself. At Widdington in 1419, the manor-court jurors cited Richard Perye for allowing his tenement to fall into disrepair, 'which same tenement is built with five buildings, viz. two granges [*grangiis*], one hall [*aula*, or dwelling-house], one kitchen [*coquina*] and one stable [*stabulo*]'.[7] In

[2] Field, 'Worcestershire peasant buildings'.

[3] Smith, 'Rooms, relatives and residential arrangements'.

[4] A survey currently being conducted to identify buildings of historical importance has to date listed approximately 15,000 structures in Essex, of which more than half are either pre-1500 or contain pre-1500 portions. The author is extremely grateful to Mr M. C. Wadhams, who has been working on this survey for the Essex County Council, for this information and for generally discussing domestic architecture in late-medieval Essex with him.

[5] E.g. Wadhams, 'Historic building surveys'; Carrick, Richards and Wadhams, 'Historic building surveys'.

[6] E.g. Hewett, *The development of English carpentry*; Hewett, 'Aisled timber halls'; Hewett, 'The smaller medieval house'.

[7] NCO 3620 m.10 (Priors Hall in Widdington court, 24 Oct 1419): '. . . quod quidem tenementum est quinque domibus edificatum videlicet duobus grangiis una aula una coquina & uno stabulo . . . '.

1443 at Barnston, a father and son took over 'one tenement built with one principal house [*principale domo*], one grange and one kitchen'.[8] Similarly, a 'cottage' (*cotagium*), used here to mean not a small, humble house but rather a tenement of a particular status at customary manorial law, might contain two, three, or four structures, as in the '*cotagium* built with two buildings, parcel of a certain tenement called Godwynestenement' which Margery widow of John Smalpece held at her death in 1419 at Widdington.[9]

Neither documents nor surviving structures reveal much about outbuildings in these tenements. Separately standing kitchen structures for cooking were commonplace (though not universal), whether termed *coquina* or *pistrina* (bakehouse), and several of these structures are known to have survived in Essex, most however from tenements of higher social status than ordinary villagers'.[10] It is known from later evidence that some of these buildings still stood at least into the early Stuart years, by which time they had often been converted to other uses when cooking had moved into the main house with the insertion of brick chimneys.[11] Less is known about other types of structures found within Essex tenements, such as the 'barn [*horreum*] in Pyes tenement . . . and the house called Insethous' which John atte Wode of Barnston was ordered to repair in 1453.[12]

One of the most revealing contemporary descriptions of a messuage and its buildings to survive from this region was drawn up at Witham in 1359, when two sisters divided a tenement called Gosselyns equally between themselves as co-heiresses. This was a quite substantial holding, with more than 33 acres of arable land, 8 of meadow, nearly 7 of pasture, and 2 of wood. Within the messuage one sister and her husband received a 'grange called le Whatberne' and a cowshed (*boveria*); the other sister and her husband received 'a certain building called le Chesehous', another called 'le Larderhous', a 'grange called le Otberne' and the 'Heyhous', while the two couples were to share the

8 PRO.DL30.58.720 (Barnston leet, 24 Apr 1443): ' . . . unum tenementum una principale domo una grangea & una coquina edificatum . . . '.

9 NCO 3620 m.10 (Priors Hall in Widdington court, 24 Oct 1419): ' . . . unum cotagium ij domibus edificatum parcellam cuiusdam tenementi vocati Godwynestenement . . . '.

10 Hewett, 'A medieval timber kitchen'; Wadhams, 'Historic building surveys', p. 85. Mr Wadhams has informed the author that five more detached kitchens have since been discovered in addition to these examples already published, three of them probably submanorial.

11 Edwards and Newton, *The Walkers of Hanningfield*, pp. 95–6 n. 24.

12 PRO.DL30.58.721 (Barnston court, 26 Nov 1453): ' . . . ad reparandum horreum in tenemento Pyes ruinosum . . . & similiter domum vocatam Insethous . . . '.

bakehouse.[13] They also divided between them several gardens and curtilages within the messuage.

Houses themselves were also described by a range of terms: 'principal house', 'dwelling-hall' (*aula habitacionis*),[14] 'the tenement's principal house called le Fyrehous',[15] or the 'principal house called le Hallehous'.[16] The simplest floor-plan, indeed almost archetypal among earliest houses at many social levels, was the hall (*aula*), a single room open to the roof-timbers and containing an open hearth. Essex halls were typically between 12 and 16 feet wide and two or more 'bays' long, a bay being the roughly square space between pairs of major upright timbers in the side walls. But by the later fourteenth or early fifteenth century, even houses of relatively lowly status in Essex were increasingly likely to have cross-wings or at least bays demarcated by separating walls, at one or both ends. These end-sections might contain one-story 'chambers' (*camere*) or, more rarely, a lower chamber or parlour and an upper 'solar' (*solarium*).

The construction histories of individual Essex houses have been investigated in sufficient numbers by architectural historians to demonstrate these general patterns in surviving structures. Two nearly 'textbook examples' of the H-plan house built in the fifteenth century – with one-story open hall flanked by one cross-wing with parlour below and solar above, and at the other end service or storage rooms topped with another upper chamber – have recently been studied at Hill Farm in Moreton (illustrated in Figure 4.1) and Rolls Farm in Magdalen Laver, both in western Essex, and many more could be cited.[17] Even more intriguing – since they demonstrate the gradual upgrading of older buildings during the period – are cases where pre-existing houses were enlarged or expanded in the fifteenth century. Examples include Petches Farm in Finchingfield, where a three-bayed hall plus partitioned-off end bay of the late thirteenth or early fourteenth century was enlarged with a two-storied, three-bay cross-wing in the early 1400s. Another is 'Tudor Cottage' in Stebbing,

[13] ERO D/DCm Z 18/5: ' . . . quadam grangia vocata le Whatberne & boveria . . . quadam domo vocata le Larderhous & quadam grangia vocata le Otberne & Heyhous una cum . . . quadam domo vocata le Cheshous . . . '.

[14] GLRO DL/C/205 fo. 86v.

[15] PRO.DL30.58.721 (Barnston court, 9 Jul 1454): tenant cited for disrepairs 'in tenemento suo vocato Rowhayes ut in daubura le Fyrehous & coquine ibidem . . . '.

[16] ERO D/DTu M244 (Great Waltham court, 16 Jun 1463): 'Ad ultimam curiam precedentem Ricardus Stable habuit in preceptis ad reparandum bene & sufficienter unam principalem domum vocatam le Hallehous unam coquinam & unam parvam domum porcorum situatas infra tenementum suum nativum vocatum Rammes . . . '.

[17] Padfield, 'Two mediaeval houses'; cf. Brown, *English farmhouses*, p. 60 (Bream's Farm, Great Leighs); more generally, Forrester, *Timber-framed houses of Essex*, pp. 1–6.

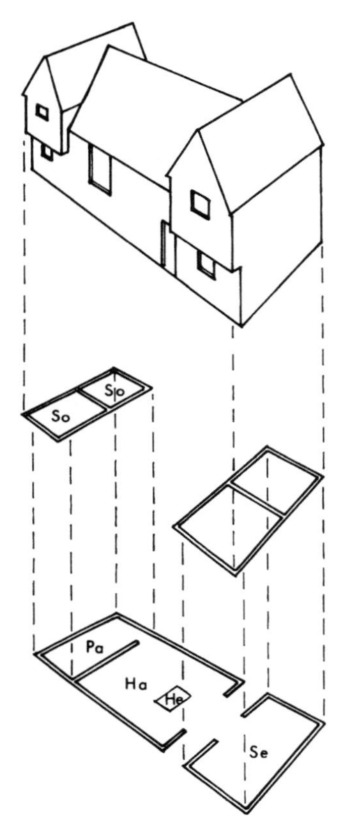

Figure 4.1. Hill Farm, Moreton, fifteenth century
Source: Adapted from Padfield, 'Two mediaeval houses', p. 3.

a fourteenth-century hall to which a storied cross-wing was added in the first quarter of the fifteenth century.[18]

For the most part, manorial evidence by itself is uninformative about rooms within Essex houses, though some brief glimpses come from orders for tenants to rebuild or repair. At Barnston in 1445, Richard Bragge was ordered to repair 'one chamber at the northern end of the principal house in his villein tenement called Celeres';[19] at High Easter in 1366, Matilda Marhach was similarly ordered regarding her 'solar

[18] Carrick, Richards and Wadhams, 'Historic building surveys', p. 88; Hewett, *The development of carpentry*, pp. 82, 118; cf. Hewett, 'The smaller medieval house', pp. 172–4 (Songers, Boxted).

[19] PRO.DL30.58.720 (Barnston leet, 31 Mar 1445): ' . . . unam cameram ad finem borialem principalis domus tenementi sui nativi vocati Celeres . . . '.

with a chamber . . . which are ruinous'.[20] Again, the 1359 division of Gosselyns tenement is somewhat more revealing in this regard. One sister was to occupy 'the entire hall, from the western solar-wall, with the chambers adjoining the east end of the said hall', while the other sister received 'the other solar with gardrobe [privy] and other chambers adjoining under them, at the western end of the said hall'.[21]

The impression that emerges from Essex in the century and a half after the Black Death, then, is one of increasingly elaborate and subdivided living spaces becoming general in the county by the later fifteenth century, while Hewett's work has underscored the remarkable sophistication and carpentry skills employed in these structures. It is only logical to presume that this meant more expensive housing also, but that is difficult to demonstrate. Dyer estimated that *de novo* construction of a substantial West Midlands villager's house in the fifteenth century might cost between £2 and £4 for labour and materials, certainly a consequential sum.[22] In Essex, though manorial accounts are filled with records of construction and repairs to lords' buildings and mills and the hiring of carpenters, usually at 5d. or 6d. per day by the 1400s, virtually no direct evidence survives to indicate the costs to a 'typical' villager of the construction of a house at this date, let alone to compare these costs with those of earlier periods. That villagers entered formal agreements with skilled carpenters for house construction is clear from occasional litigation for broken agreements. In 1390, John Ays of Stisted sued John Seburugh, carpenter, of Bocking (about four miles away), claiming that he had hired Seburugh to construct a house which he then intended to lease out, but that the carpenter failed to do the work, and other workers had to be hired; Seburugh countered that Ays had not provided proper materials or prepared the work-site. But other than the 40s. damages Ays claimed, no indication of labour costs for the house is given.[23]

20 PRO.DL30.65.826 (High Easter court, 13 Sep 1369): ' . . . solarium suum cum una camera . . . que sunt ruinose et discooperte . . . '.

21 ERO D/DCm Z 18/5: ' . . . tota aula a pariete solarij transversi versus occidentalem cum cameris in fine orientale dicte aule annexatis . . . alterum solarium cum garderoba & omnibus cameris annexatis & appendentibus tam sub predicto solario quam sub garderoba predicta . . . '.

22 Dyer, 'English peasant buildings', pp. 28–31.

23 CALC U15.11.11 (Bocking court, 19 May 1390): ' . . . fecit convencionem cum ipso Johanne Seburugh carpentario quod ipse faceret sibi de novo in villa de Stisted & eciam quod ipse faceret similiter unam domum longiorem de longitudine viij^to ceperularum & latitudine xvj pedum . . . ita quod ipse Johannes Ays posset illos dimittere firmariis suis pro certa firma &c Predictus Johannes Seburugh predictam convencionem non implenit nec tenuit nec implenere & perficere noluit set semper se retraxit Ita quod conduxit alios operarios ad perficiendum opus predictum . . . & meremum domorum stetit nudum & putrescebat . . . Et predictus Johannes [Sebu-

But the general pattern of gradual improvement is clear, and the temptation is strong to view this amelioration of housing as symptomatic of a widespread bettering of living standards among rural dwellers in general, consonant with the rising daily wage rates and relatively low prices and rent levels of the period. To an extent this is undoubtedly true, but it must also be qualified. Dyer, for one, has cautioned against looking for a sudden, dramatic improvement in housing in this era, or for a foreshadowing of the later 'great rebuilding' which was once believed by historians to have taken place in England in the later sixteenth and early seventeenth centuries; he prefers to view 'the late medieval "rebuildings" in terms of trends and processes rather than revolutions'.[24]

During the late-medieval population depression many pre-existing messuages and dwellings obviously became redundant, and several consequences might follow. Tenants who managed to accumulate much land might find themselves with several messuages and considerable temptation to remove timbers and other materials from buildings for which they no longer had any need, to use in repairing or expanding their own houses or outbuildings.[25] At High Easter in 1382 Richard Gamen had two quarter-virgates with tenements and was cited by the manor court because he 'took and removed two ruined buildings from the tenement called Wakemannes in order to repair various houses upon his other villein tenement'.[26] Landlords might concede the inevitable and allow this, for a price. At Barnston in 1456, Richard Olyver paid his lord 13s. 4d. to dismantle 'two old and ruined buildings' from his customary tenement called Huntes, 'because nobody has lived there for many years, nor does anyone want to live there'.[27] And in 1352 at High Easter the reeve accounted for the sale of at least twelve ruined buildings, undoubtedly for the sake of their building materials rather than as viable edifices, from tenements left in

rugh] dicit . . . per defaltam eiusdem Johannis Ays non fecit venire meremum nec paruit locum ubi operasse debuisset set per pluras vices quo ipse & sui venerunt ad perficiendum opus predictum carebant de meremo & aliis necessariis . . . '.

24 Dyer, 'English peasant buildings', p. 40.

25 Harvey, *Westminster Abbey*, p. 308.

26 PRO.DL30.66.834 (High Easter court, 23 Apr 1382): Richard Gamen had two quarter-virgates and 'super quod quarterium vocatum Wakemannes fuerunt duo domus debiles et ruinose quas dictus Ricardus cepit et asportavit a dicto tenemento vocato Wakemannes ad faciendas et emendandas diversas domos super aliud tenementum nativum . . . '.

27 PRO.DL30.58.721 (Barnston court, 2 Dec 1456): ' . . . optulit domino de fine . . . pro licencia habenda ad deponendas dictas veteres & debiles domos dicti tenementi . . . eo quod nullus ibidem commoravit per quampluros annos elapsos nec quisque ibidem manere cupit . . . '; cf. PRO.DL30.58.720 (Barnston leet, 11 Apr 1436), for another example.

the lord's hands in the wake of the Black Death.[28] It is likely that this pattern of redundant housing stock also helps to account for the proliferation in the later middle ages of messuage or tenement sites that contained only non-residential buildings, or that had been subdivided and whose buildings had been parcelled between different subtenants, such as the 'messuage built with one grange' at Barnston in 1420,[29] or the 'grange and bakehouse within a customary tenement' which one couple leased to John Newman at Takeley in 1393.[30]

But opportunities to consolidate buildings from several tenements in order to upgrade structures upon one's principal dwelling-site were likely to fall only to those tenants who managed to engross large holdings, and it has already been shown that in later-medieval Essex only relatively few individuals enjoyed such fortunate circumstances. For the less fortunate, and especially for those labourers and petty craftsmen who had no need for an entire complement of agricultural outbuildings, inexpensive housing was available among the cottages that had escaped falling into ruin, or even subleased rooms within larger houses belonging to manorial tenants. In the former case, most series of Essex manorial accounts contain a scattering of farmed-out cottages, rarely for lease-rates greater than 6d. or 12d. per annum, as in the '6d. for one cottage once Ralph at Cros's' collected at Borley in 1408/9.[31] But at most manors there was no compelling need at customary law to register in court short-term subleases between villagers, so it was only seldom and usually in extraordinary circumstances that these arrangements left any trace in the records. At Great Waltham in the early 1360s, John Hamond had 'a certain chamber which he was accustomed to lease out annually for 3s.', but this detail emerged only in the form of a somewhat puzzling trespass suit Hamond brought in 1366 against someone who, he claimed, was scaring off potential lodgers.[32] At Writtle in 1449, John Folkes sued

[28] PRO.DL30.64.808 (Great Waltham and High Easter court, 30 Jun 1352): ' . . . Ricardus Kenston praepositus de Alta Estre vendidit diversas domos existentes in tenementis diversorum nativorum existentibus in manibus domini videlicet ad tenementum quondam Agnetis le Yonge iiij domos debiles pro vs. vjd. . . . Item vendidit ad tenementum Ade Kyng j domum ruinosam pro xiiijd. . . . [etc.]'. Christopher Dyer has pointed out that some medieval houses were virtually 'prefabricated', in that timber frames removed from one building could have been re-erected elsewhere and so should not always be envisaged as simply scrap material.

[29] PRO.DL30.58.719 (Barnston leet, 10 Apr 1420): ' . . . unum mesuagium una grangia edificatum . . . '.

[30] NCO 3697 m.22 (St Valery's or Warish Hall in Takeley court, 17 Dec 1393): ' . . . quasdam grangiam & pistrinam existentes in tenemento customario . . . '.

[31] CALC beadles' rolls, Borley: ' . . . de vjd. de cotagio quondam Radulphi at Cros . . . '.

[32] PRO.DL30.65.822 (Great Waltham court, 23 Jun 1366): ' . . . habet quamdam cameram quam solebat dimittere annuatim pro iijs. Item quod Saierus [Kyng] tam oppress-

Stephen Reve, to whom he had leased a *tenementum* called Laurencemondes, charging that Stephen had kept two horses in the 'chamber at the upper end of the said tenement's main house', and the horses had damaged the chamber's walls, windows and doors.[33] Scattered cases like these doubtless point to a much more widespread letting-out of rooms or parts of houses to humbler rural dwellers in the area.

Both Dyer and Hewett have warned against presuming too readily that all smaller cottages were necessarily of less durable or skilful construction, or cost less on a per-size basis, than the larger houses of the better-off at the village level in the fifteenth century, though Dyer points out that costs of cottage constructions (in the few cases where evidence survives) could range widely.[34] Nevertheless it remains likely that, as in early-modern England, the enlargements and improvements that have been observed in later-medieval Essex were experienced rather unevenly by different layers of local rural society. While the poorer and the non-agriculturalists might have leased vacant cottages or sublet rooms, the more substantial agriculturalists and craftsmen were the most direct and earliest beneficiaries of upgraded housing.

To demonstrate this social selectivity conclusively would require that a number of standing houses with recoverable construction histories be linked with tenurial documents revealing their tenants at or near the time when the houses were built or expanded, but it is only rarely possible to do so. The local settlement topography of much of Essex does make linkage of this sort more feasible than is often the case in other parts of England. In this area of dispersed settlement, with many hamlets and isolated farmsteads, the messuage with its house and outbuildings typically by the later fourteenth century had acquired a farm-name (often demonstrably the surname of an earlier tenant) that persisted over long periods and despite later changes of tenancy.[35] But even so, only a few houses in this district can be linked with medieval occupants.

iones et gravaminia tenentibus eiusdem Johannis camere predicte de die in diem fecit et per suos fieri permisit per quod tenentes eiusdem Johannis dictam cameram tenere recusaverunt . . . '.

33 ERO D/DP M253 m.7 (Writtle court, 10 May 1449): ' . . . ipse Stephanus tenuit de eodem Johanne ad firmam unum tenementum suum vocatum Laurencemondes . . . duos equos ipsius Stephani in camera existentes ad superiorem finem capitalis domus dicti tenementi inclusit & hospitavit quiquidem equi sic in dicta camera inclusi & hospitati parietes eiusdem camere fregerunt & eciam fenestras portas & hostia dicti tenementi . . . '.

34 Dyer, 'English peasant buildings', p. 40; Hewett, 'The smaller medieval house', p. 172.

35 Poos, 'Population and resources', pp. 195–6.

One example is a house at an isolated hamlet within the parish of Felsted, now known as Gatehouse Farm and one of the best-known medieval timber houses of modest proportions in the county. Originally a two-bay hall with a cross-wing at each end (though the solar wing has been demolished), Hewett dates the hall to the early fourteenth century at the latest, and regards the surviving service wing as an addition made later in the same century.[36] In 1367 this house and messuage were part of a landholding comprising two half-virgates, a second messuage, and other (unquantified) land, thus placing its tenant within the uppermost ranks of post-Black Death Essex manorial tenants.[37]

Much the same is true for another house in the same parish, Bridge House Farm. The core of the present house is a large open hall of the early fifteenth century; within its messuage also stands a much smaller building, of late-thirteenth- or early-fourteenth-century construction and possibly the original dwelling-house which was demoted to other uses when the larger house was built.[38] This messuage was attached to a half-virgate of land bearing the same name as the house, and in 1367 its tenant also possessed two further parcels of land (again, unquantified).[39] This house thus also belonged to one of the substantially better-off of local tenants.

In some contrast to these two examples is a quite small house at Hatfield Broadoak, now called 'Oak Cottage' (illustrated in Figure 4.2).

[36] Hewett, *English historic carpentry*, p. 131; cf. Forrester, *Timber-framed houses of Essex*, p. 4; Brown, *English farmhouses*, p. 56.

[37] The name 'Gatehouse Farm' is relatively recent. A detailed manorial survey of Felsted from 1576 (ERO D/DCw M158/1; unnumbered folios), which describes abuttals of one property upon the next and so allows tenements to be located precisely within the parish's topography, makes it clear that this property was known as 'Wades halfe yarde' in the Elizabethan era. It bore the name 'Wades' in much earlier surveys of *circa* 1170 (Chibnall, ed., *Charters and custumals of Holy Trinity Caen*, p. 41), *circa* 1223 (*ibid.*, p. 93), when it was described as a virgate, and 1367 (PRO.SC11.188). In 1367 its (unnamed) tenant held 'dimidia virgata terre Wadis', 'tenemento Wode', 'terra Kyronn', 'uno alio mesuagio' and 'terra Letekoc' (Lutcock's, described in 1576 as another 'half-yardland' and known today as Sparling's Farm, was doubtless carved out of the original Wades virgate, as the Elizabethan abuttals imply).

[38] The author is grateful to the present owner of Bridge House Farm, Mr John Hartgill, and to Mr Wadhams, who has inspected the smaller house for the Department of the Environment, for discussing this chronology with him; cf. Brown, *English farmhouses*, p. 67. According to Mr Wadhams, it is uncertain whether the earlier building is the original house or a detached kitchen.

[39] 'Bridgehowse halfe yarde' in 1576 (ERO D/DCw M158/1) can be identified with 'Breggehous' or the 'dimidia virgata de Ponte' of *circa* 1223 (Chibnall, ed., *Charters and custumals of Holy Trinity Caen*, p. 93; Reaney, *Place-names of Essex*, p. 423). Though not named as such in the 1367 rental (PRO.SC11.188), despite the dangers of equating surnames with farm-names, the rental's description of tenements' locations within hamlets implies that this tenement belonged then to a Robert atte Bregge, along with 'terra Holde' and 'dimidio crofto iacente sub gardinium Helpiston'.

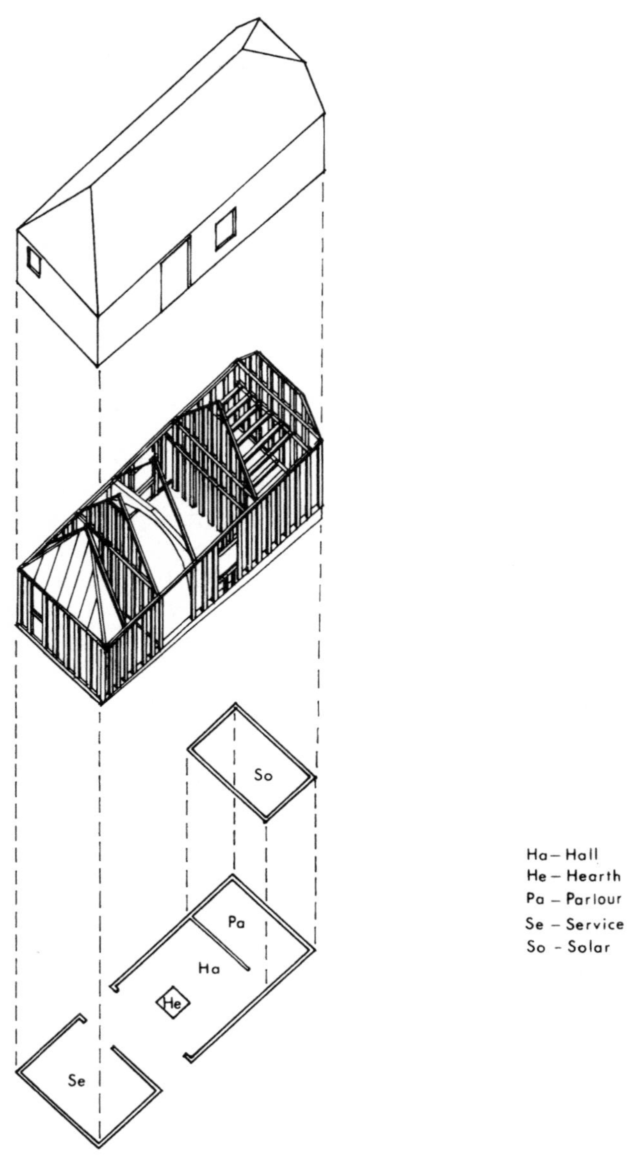

Figure 4.2. Oak Cottage, Hatfield Broadoak, fifteenth century
Source: Adapted from Gibson, 'Small medieval houses in Essex', p. 23.

It is approximately 12 feet by 30 feet in size, with a small hall, one-storied service end-bay and two-storied solar/chamber end-bay, and datable to the fifteenth century.[40] Precise identification of this tenement in the local manorial records is more problematic than with the Felsted examples, but none of the tenants holding messuages in this location in the Hatfield Broadoak manorial survey of *circa* 1450 held agricultural land elsewhere in the manor at that time.[41] This house, then, located on the fringe of the parish's main settlement area and about a quarter-mile away from Hatfield Broadoak's market and commercial centre, more probably belonged to a retailer or craftsman of moderately prosperous standing, but unfortunately little more can be said about its place within local social structure.[42]

Some, and especially the better-off, of Essex rural people, then, lived in more complex and diversified houses towards the end of the middle ages, and this was undoubtedly related at least in part to the continued economic differentiation at large in local society. At the same time, it is just possible to gain some fleeting glimpses of how types of social arrangements within and between households fit into physical living spaces. The hall, with its open hearth and eating table, remained the most public of rooms at this social level, and friends and neighbours gathered there. Ironically, one of the contexts in which these meetings left traces in the records was in defamation suits before the ecclesiastical courts. In 1495 Ralph Tilborn of Stratford testified that

> on last All Saints' Day, between the fourth and fifth hour after noon, this deponent was in the hall inside Christopher Smyth's house, along with John Mundon, Thomas Waren, Christopher Smyth, Thomas Austen and Thomas Loveson, when and where, after various conversations between Thomas [Austen] and Thomas [Loveson], the said Thomas [Austen] said to Thomas Lowson . . . 'Thow callyst me fals mann byhynd my bakke, why doth se ye soo?'. And the other Thomas replied . . . 'Nay I cald you nott fals butt ye be a fals mane to me in your delyng'.[43]

[40] The house, now known as 'Oak Cottage', is described by Gibson, 'Small medieval houses in Essex', pp. 24–6; cf. *VCH Essex* vol. 8, pp. 163–4.

[41] ERO D/DBa M3 fo. 122. The house was located at the subsettlement called *Brodestrete* (Broad Street Green), where eight tenants were listed in *circa* 1450.

[42] In the middle of the fourteenth century, a charter of 1346 indicates, the messuage immediately to the north of the site of Oak Cottage contained a bakehouse (the terms of its lease indicating that it was likely a commercial establishment), and a tanner occupied the one to the north of that: BL Add. Ch. 28598.

[43] GL MS 9065 fo. 243: ' . . . in festo omnium sanctorum ultimo preterito post vesperas inter horas iiij & v post meridiem eiusdem diei presens fuit iste juratus in aula infra domum habitacionis Christopheri Smyth situata una cum Johanne Mundon Thoma Waren Christophero Smyth Thoma Austen & Thoma Loveson ubi & quando post diversa communicata inter eosdem Thomam & Thomam dictus Thomas dixit eidem Thome Lowson in anglice hec verba . . . [etc.]'.

Five years earlier at Buttsbury, a deponent said that he and four other persons had been present 'in the house of John Stoner junior at Buttsbury ... that is, within and near the door toward the public street' when John Ponder accused Margaret Samer of having said that 'Johanna, to whom John's wife had given birth, was not John's daughter but the daughter of a certain friar'.[44]

But in contrast to these un-neighbourly interludes, friends were also gathered in halls when couples exchanged vows or pre-contracts of marriage. In 1471, John Dyx recalled in the course of a matrimonial-suit deposition, he and three others

> were present in the dwelling-hall [*aula habitacionis*] of Margery [Mylsent] in the parish of Great Holland ... and William Laykyn, standing, said to Margaret, also standing in the said hall near the doorway toward the highway ... 'Margaret, do you want to have me as your husband?', and she replied 'freely she wanted to have him as her husband, more than ever any woman loved any man ... '.

All those present later 'went to a table in the same hall and there ate bread and cheese and drank ale'.[45]

But these matrimonial exchanges also took place in the more intimate lower chambers or parlours of Essex houses. In 1476 a witness recalled having heard vows of marriage between a couple 'in a certain lower parlour' of a house in Chingford.[46] Heads of household or other family members ordinarily had their beds in these chambers or solars; in 1475, another deponent remembered, a couple exchanged vows in a house in East Ham, 'both of them sitting on the side of the bed situated in the chamber of the said house'.[47] But servants in these houses

[44] *Ibid.* fo. 70: ' ... presens fuit iste juratus in domo Johannis Stoner junioris infra Buttisbury predicta situata videlicet infra et prope ostium eiusdem domus versus publicam stratam ubi et quando dictus Johannes Ponder recitavit eidem Margarete si ipsa prius dixisset quod Johanna quam uxor dicti Johannis peperit constante matrimonio inter eosdem non erat filia dicti Johannis sed quod ipsa fuit filia cuiusdam fratris ... '.

[45] GLRO DL/C/205 fos. 86v–87: ' ... presens fuit iste juratus una cum Thoma Bogeys Willelmo Laykyn & Margareta Mylsent & non pluris in aula habitacionis dicte Margarete infra parochiam de Holond Magna situata ubi & quando ... Willelmus Laykyn stando dixit eidem Margarete eciam stanti in dicta aula prope ostium eiusdem ex parte alte vie ... vultis habere me in maritum vestrum que respondit quod libente voluit habere ipsum in maritum suum eo quod numquam mulier dilexit aliquem virum quam ipsum Thomam [mistake for William?] citra mortem mariti sui permortui ... accesserunt ad mensam in eadem aula & ibidem comedebant panem & caseum ac potabant cervisiam ... '. See Chapter 7 for discussion of exchanges of matrimonial vows in settings like this.

[46] *Ibid.* fo. 271: ' ... in domo Thome Manninge situata infra parochiam de Chyngeford London' diocesis videlicet in quadam bassa parlura eiusdem domus presens fuit iste juratus ... '.

[47] *Ibid.* fo. 272v: ' ... dicta verba erant prolata utroque sedente super latus lecti situati in camera dicte domus ... '.

probably slept elsewhere, in the hall itself, the service-bay chambers or even in another building. A coroner's jury reported in 1370 at Great Tey that Sarra Pyk, 'lying ill and infirm in her bed, lit a candle for light, and afterward the servants of the house went away to their beds, and so for lack of care the candle fell into straw and burnt Sarra's bed, and she, lying in it, unable to save herself, was burnt dead'.[48] Beds in these subsidiary rooms were also the scenes of other major events in the life cycles of individuals: earlier in the fourteenth century (though this may well pertain to a slightly higher social level) a man recalled the birth of an heiress 'in the great chamber in the higher end of the hall' of a house at Great Leighs.[49]

Perhaps the most revealing insights into residential arrangements, though, come from retirement agreements recorded in manorial courts, in which an elderly tenant or couple transferred their property to offspring or others, with formal, often quite detailed arrangements by which the transfer was conditional upon the new tenants' providing room, board and other things to the grantor during the latter's lifetime.[50] In a brief survey of cases like this where explicit divisions of living space were enrolled within the agreement, Smith points out that quasi-independent household arrangements were often embodied in the assignment of respective rooms within the tenement.[51] Drawing attention to the distinction between a 'houseful' – simply the group living under one roof – and the 'household' – the group sharing functions of production and consumption, such as cooking – he warns against drawing too simplistic connections between household structure and house space. Houses and other buildings within tenements could be subdivided in a number of ways to support more than one residential unit. One looks in vain in this district for any sign of the exclusive identification by the extended representatives of one lineage with one *domus* epitomised by the residents of early-fourteenth-century Montaillou in southern France.[52]

Some retirement agreements recorded in Essex manor courts simply divided the rooms of a house, as was done at Gosselyns in the division already considered. At Lindsell in 1392 a woman reserved for herself

[48] PRO.JUST2.35.5 m.1v (inquest, 15 Sep 1370): ' . . . iacens in lecto suo infirma & valde debilis percepit illuminare candelam pro lumine habendo & postea famuli domus exiverunt ad lecta sua et sic ob defectum custodie dicta candela cecidit in straminem & arsit lectum dicte Sarre & dicta Sarra iacens in eodem lecto impotens & debilis non se adimare conbusta fuit mortua . . . '.

[49] PRO.C135.13.9 (inquest, 12 Apr 1328): ' . . . apud Lyes in magna camera in superiore parte aule . . . nata . . . '.

[50] Clark, 'Some aspects of social security'; Hanawalt, *The ties that bound*, pp. 229–34.

[51] Smith, 'Rooms, relatives and residential arrangements'.

[52] Le Roy Ladurie, *Montaillou*, esp. pp. 24–52.

'two chambers under one house for her dwelling-space [*mancione*]'.[53] At Ingatestone in 1344 another woman received 'one chamber with the solar above'.[54] Other agreements were more precise about the sharing of space. At Fyfield in 1402, Richard Colford was to have 'the lower chamber at the north end of the said tenement for making his bed, and the right to sit beside the hearth in the hall'.[55] At Great Waltham in 1379 Agnes Croucheman reserved for herself 'a chamber with the solar above . . . right of entry to the main house . . . and right of entry to the kitchen-building with the pot and mill whenever it pleases her'.[56] At the same community sixteen years later, another woman was to have 'the whole house called le Ferhous [i.e. the principal house] except the lower chamber to the west, and also entry to the kitchen-building'.[57] In one of the most involved of these arrangements, at Ingatestone in 1471, William Morce surrendered two cottages with gardens and six acres of land, for which he was to receive 21 marks over the next few years, and he retained 'two chambers at the upper end of the hall . . . and a small kitchen-building . . . [and] one parcel of land to build a shop beside the highway'.[58]

A similar concern for subdividing living space occasionally appeared in late-medieval Essex wills. Two clothworkers' wills cited in the previous chapter are pertinent in this regard also. The Ulting fuller, John Nele, in 1518 left his house to his widow for her lifetime; to his eldest son John, who also received his fuller's tools, he willed 'a shoppe to work in and a chamber in the house . . . duryng his mothers liff so that he be good & gentill to his mother or els she to put hym frome that same duryng her liff'.[59] The Coggeshall weaver cited earlier

53 NCO 3655 m.14 (Priors Hall in Lindsell court, 12 Dec 1392): ' . . . duas cameras sub una domo pro mancione dicte Margerie . . . '.

54 ERO D/DP M15 (Ingatestone court, 24 Sep 1344): ' . . . una camera cum solario superedificato . . . '.

55 ERO D/DCw M99 (Fyfield court, 29 Mar 1402): ' . . . aisiamentum pro lecto suo faciendo & habendo in bassa camera in fine boriali aule tenementi predicti et eciam aisiamentum sedendi iuxta focum in aula predicta cum liberis ingressu & egressu tempore rationabili & competenti . . . '.

56 ERO D/DTu 239 (Great Waltham court, 20 Dec 1379): ' . . . unam cameram cum quodam solario superpendente . . . aysiamentum in capitale domo et libero introitu & exitu . . . aysiamentum in coquina cum plumbo & molario quoadcumque eidem Agneti placuerit . . . '.

57 *Ibid.* (Great Waltham court, 14 May 1395): ' . . . domum vocatam le Ferhous integram preter cameram inferiorem versus occidentem et eciam aisiamentum in coquina dicti tenementi . . . '.

58 ERO D/DP M54 (Ingatestone court, 11 Jun 1471): ' . . . duas cameras ad superiorem finem aule tenementi supradicti . . . ac unam parvam coquinam in curtilagio . . . unam parcellam soli ad edificandum ibidem unam shopam iuxta regiam stratam . . . '.

59 ERO D/ACR 2/83.

left his son 'the litill cham[ber] in the towne' and his widow 'the howse that Y do dwel in' in 1511.[60]

Both wills and formally recorded retirement agreements are weighted bodies of evidence, in that the better-off in village society were disproportionately more likely to have been authors of these legal instruments. This sort of person was also the most likely to have possessed the variegated living spaces which have been discussed here. Evidence for the social selectivity of these evolving house forms and living arrangements thus remains suggestive rather than conclusive, and it is an open question whether it points to a purely economic matter or one in which style or taste was a contributing factor.

But in this most tangible form, in surprisingly many cases still standing today, lie embodied artefacts of many of the social structures and economic changes that rural Essex society experienced in the century and a half after the Black Death. Houses and other buildings, the physical spaces that surrounded people's important life-cycle events and household configurations, themselves evolved along trajectories that resulted from the changes of the times: demographic stagnation, rural artisanal and occupational articulation, and uneven economic promotion. The ways in which different strata in the Essex countryside, the better-off agriculturalists and the less well-off labourers, fared in this regard are one dimension of the divergent paths – economic, demographic, cultural – which these groups took in the waning decades of the middle ages and which constitute much of the focus of the chapters that follow.

[60] ERO D/ACR 1/182.

PART III

'The total sum of all persons'

Township subcollectors' return of poll-tax payers, Great Dunmow, 1381[1]

The course and causes of aggregate population change were intimately interwoven into the fabric of society and economy of later-medieval Essex. And yet it is precisely these demographic patterns that have proved most elusive to historians of the period. Sources affording reliable estimates of the scale and chronology of local population change and the factors that influenced it, let alone estimates that bear comparison with the historical demography of other times and places, are exceedingly scarce and opaque in England before the mid-sixteenth century. But the central and northern district of Essex has left records pertaining to demographic measures that, cumulatively, are unique for England as a whole. It is by no means the case that these sources can unequivocally answer all the questions one might wish to ask about the demographic system of the later middle ages. Within the limits imposed by their very nature and that of derivations made from them, however, their answers are remarkably consistent.

In many Essex communities during the period the system of frankpledge required that resident adolescent and adult males be enrolled into groups called tithings. From sixteen communities in the district, the numbers of males in tithing can be reconstructed on a year-to-year basis, in some cases from the late thirteenth to the late sixteenth century, constituting an index of aggregate population change. With minor variations there is substantial agreement among the series. From a high point around 1300, demographic decline began

[1] PRO.E179.107.49 m.7: 'Summa totalis omnium personarum in villata de Dunmawe Magna'.

in the district with severe famines in the second decade of the fourteenth century and continued to 1349. The Black Death here was especially severe, with 40 per cent mortality or higher. Population continued to contract until the early 1400s. From then on until the 1520s it was essentially stationary.

It is more difficult to disentangle the relative importance of fertility and mortality in causing such a prolonged period of demographic equilibrium. Combining records of tithing entry and of tenant deaths contained in the manorial court rolls of three local communities yields a very approximate measure of life expectancy. Records of women's 'churching' (purification after childbirth) constitute a rough measure of annual births in the parish of Walden. Taken together, these three datasets imply that the period from the late 1300s to the early 1500s was another in a series of cyclical phases of population history, consonant with England's post-medieval national experience. Through this period the rural population of Essex came to rest at a level roughly one-half of its apogee around 1300, and (by extrapolation from England's national pattern) also roughly one-half of its next historical demographic crest in the mid-seventeenth century. Demographic equilibrium was probably the product both of mortality somewhat higher, and of fertility markedly lower, than was typical in the England of Elizabeth I.

5

Population aggregates over time

The central and northern district of Essex is unique in that it affords a large volume of data for aggregate population change between the late 1200s and the sixteenth century. This evidence comes from the annual totals of resident adolescent and adult males in sixteen communities, provided by the frankpledge system administered through leet and manorial courts. The tithing data have the advantages of being based explicitly upon residence, rather than the tenure or tax payment that forms the basis of the great majority of medieval documents upon which population estimates are usually based, and of extending over a lengthy period and over a number of communities of varying sizes, types and administrative lordships. The near-unanimity of the patterns that these data reveal, and the ways in which the data can be cross-checked at various points with other local sources to verify their credibility as accurate reflections of local populations, indicate that for this district at least the course of aggregate change can be recovered with considerable confidence.

Legal and administrative aspects of frankpledge as a basic element of local jurisdiction in medieval England have been studied reasonably fully. As early as the tenth or eleventh century, rudimentary functions of policing and providing surety for good conduct were vested in small groups, or tithings, within townships. After the Norman Conquest, certain local jurisdictional franchises came into the hands of baronial or lesser landlords; in many townships, annual or semi-annual 'views' of frankpledge (where the memberships of tithings were reviewed and new members enrolled) were thereby fused with jurisdiction over minor criminal offences, public nuisances, and infractions against the assises of bread and ale exercised by manorial lords in leet courts, whereas elsewhere these matters might remain within the purview of the sheriff's tourn. In the case of these 'private views', frankpledge administration was therefore closely linked with the operations of the manorial courts, and it is from the later thirteenth century onward, when it became common practice to produce regular series of detailed records from manorial-court proceedings, that sufficient material survives to illustrate fully the tithing system's features.[1]

By the later 1200s, rather different arrangements prevailed in eastern England from those found in the western and northern regions of the country.[2] In Essex a frankpledge jurisdiction typically possessed several tithings, each consisting of one or two chief pledges and a number (usually ranging from five to twelve) of tithingmen. All males aged 12 years and older and resident within the jurisdiction for at least a year and a day were required to be sworn into tithing; women, clerics and wealthy freemen (in practice, apparently restricted to men of gentry or higher status) were the only residents excepted. In some places lists of all members of a jurisdiction's tithings were written down periodically, and surviving examples imply some element of kinship or residential propinquity among the memberships of individual tithings. The chief pledges of all the jurisdiction's tithings comprised the jury responsible for answering the articles of the view, presenting offenders at the leet, and in certain circumstances rendering evidence or verdicts to higher judicial bodies such as gaol-delivery hearings. The tithing in turn assumed a degree of corporate responsibility for ensuring attendance by, and especially for producing delinquents from among, its members.

During the century after the Black Death the tithing systems of different communities underwent a variety of experiences. In some places, leet and tithings became moribund, whether owing to divided or indifferent lordship, population decline or rapid turnover of residents through migration, or competition from other legal institutions such as peace sessions. But in other communities the institution remained a vital organ of local administration well into the early-modern period. In fact, at least one late Tudor Essex landlord attempted to resurrect the medieval tithing system wholesale after it had earlier fallen into disuse.[3] Evidence of the tithing system's administration permits several different types of insights into the dynamics of local communities in late-medieval Essex; this study will

[1] Morris, *The frankpledge system*; Crowley, 'Later history of frankpledge'; Cam, *The hundred and the hundred rolls*, pp. 124–8.

[2] The discussion of the following two paragraphs is derived chiefly from Crowley, 'Later history of frankpledge'; Poos, 'Population and resources', pp. 45–8, 64–7; Clark, 'Tithing lists from Essex'; Newton and McIntosh, 'Leet jurisdiction in Essex manor courts'.

[3] Newton and McIntosh, 'Leet jurisdiction in Essex manor courts', p. 9.

return to this evidence in later chapters, using records of tithing entrants or lists of tithing members for inferences about mortality and migration.[4] But for present purposes it is the data for totals of resident adolescent and adult males, as an index of total local population, which make the tithing material critically important.

Among other obligations, the tithings were liable to render a cash payment to the franchise's lordship each year at the leet.[5] This apparently evolved from the 'custom' or hundredpenny, owed to the Crown by many Essex tenants, that was mentioned in Domesday Book and that included a *per capita* payment in Colchester in 1086.[6] By the early fourteenth century, in many places this 'common fine' or 'tithingpenny' payment was a fixed sum, paid annually by the community as a whole, but in certain communities it represented a payment of a halfpenny or penny from each chief pledge and tithingman and fluctuated from year to year in proportion to the tithings' membership and therefore, at least in theory, to the resident population of males aged 12 years and older.

Series of annually fluctuating tithingpenny data survive from fifteen Essex communities (all but two in the central and northern portion of the county), extending in some instances over lengthy periods before and after the Black Death, although in other cases incomplete survival of documents means much fewer data over shorter periods of time. Data survive from the large, complex rural communities of High Easter and Great Waltham, the smaller rural lordships of Berden, Birchanger, Little Canfield, Chatham Hall (in Great Waltham township), Margaret Roding and Stebbing, the market communities of Boreham, Hatfield Broadoak and Writtle, and the older of the two market centres at Witham along with Cressing, a rural dependency of Witham manor.[7]

4 See below, Chapters 6, 8 and 9.

5 E.g. PRO.DL43.2.32 (High Easter rental, 1328): ' . . . Et est ibidem queddam consuetudo ad dictum visum franciplegj tentum annuatim die Jovis in Septimania Pentecostie quod quilibet xij annorum dabit jd. pro capite suo . . . '; BL Add. Roll 65926 (Stebbing leet, 31 Mar 1434): 'Omnes capitales plegij quorum nomina patent supra presentant quod dant de commune fine ad hunc diem tam pro quolibet capite eorum quam decennariorum suorum obulum unde summa hoc anno patet in capite . . . '.

6 E.g. Domesday Book II, 106b: 'Sueno I domum quam tenuit Goda tempore Regis Edwardi ad Elmesteda et tunc reddebant consuetudinem Regis modo reddunt nisi caput hominis' (quoted from Rumble, ed., *Domesday Book* B3m).

7 Sources: High Easter: PRO.DL30.63.750 – DL30.72.891. Great Waltham: PRO.DL30.63.750 – DL30.68.850; ERO D/DTu M239–42; ERO D/DHh M151. Berden: ERO D/DU M565/1–4. Birchanger: NCO 3595–8. Little Canfield: BL Add. Roll 19108. Chatham Hall: ERO D/DTu M257–9. Margaret Roding: UCO Pyx G–H. Stebbing: BL Add. Rolls 65926, 65929, 65933, 65936, and 65937; BL Add. MS 40632A fos. 53–67v; PRO.DL30.77.979; PRO.SC2.173.89. Boreham: PRO.SC2.171.25, 171.30, 171.32, 171.33. Hatfield Broadoak: ERO D/DGe M251; ERO D/DK M1; BL Add. Roll 28555. Writtle: ERO D/DP M189–92 (cf. Newton, 'Medieval population statistics'). Witham

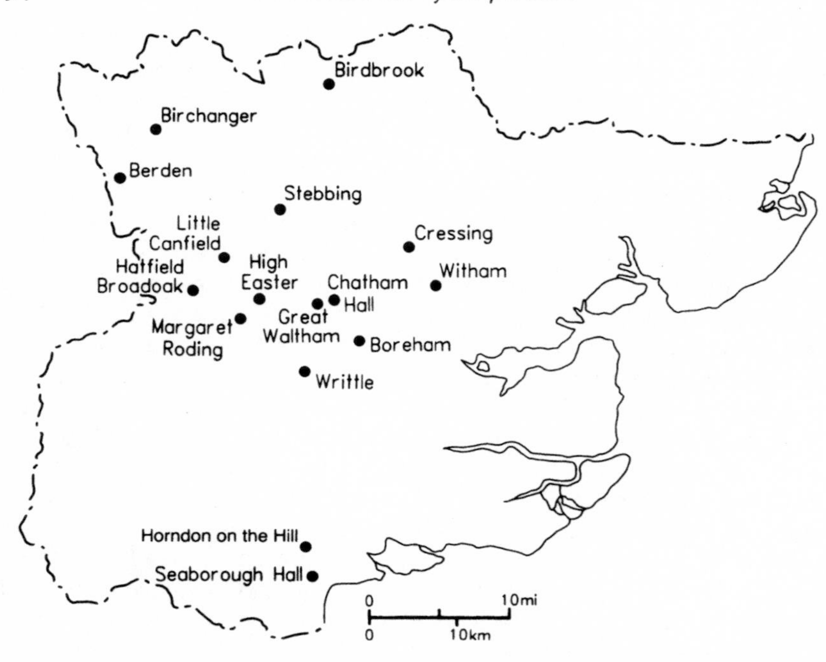

Figure 5.1. Sources of tithing data in medieval Essex

Two quite small rural jurisdictions near the Thames estuary, Horndon on the Hill and Seaborough Hall (in Mucking township), furnish a few data from the southern portion of the county.[8] For Birdbrook, another small rural community in northern Essex, the common fine was fixed but three lists of tithing members' names survive from before and after the Black Death, allowing comparison with the fuller tithingpenny data.[9] As Figure 5.1 shows, with the exception of the two southern Essex communities, all these places lie within approximately 30 miles of one another.

and Cressing: ERO D/DBw M98–100 (the Witham figures refer to the 'old market' settlement at Witham, whereas the later-founded 'Newland' market with its associated settlement had a separate leet jurisdiction and a fixed common fine: cf. Britnell, 'The making of Witham').

8 PRO.SC2.173.6; cf. Russell, *British medieval population*, pp. 226–7.

9 ERO D/DU 267/85–7. Unfortunately these lists can be dated only approximately, to (respectively) *circa* 1325, *circa* 1340 and *circa* 1425. There are several other Essex communities from which occasional lists of tithings' memberships survive and which might therefore be cited for occasional population estimates, but these have been omitted here as none has more than three or four surviving lists and none (besides Birdbrook) has surviving lists of both pre- and post-Black Death date: cf. Crowley, 'Later history of frankpledge'.

Internal evidence from the court records of these manors reveals minor variations in tithing administration from place to place, and these differences have some bearing upon how the raw data of tithingpenny payments are to be interpreted. In each case the value of the payment must be converted to numbers of halfpennies or pennies, depending upon the *per capita* payment customary for that manor, in order to yield totals of males in tithing and present at the leet. Certain adjustments must be made to these raw totals, however. At some manors, tithingmen failing to appear at the leet could be 'bailed': that is, their absence was noted but excused on their pledges' undertaking to ensure their attendance at the next court. Similarly, at some leets tithingmen absent without permission were also noted and amerced, while at other manors circumstantial evidence suggests that the chief pledges paid their tithings' full obligation whether all their tithingmen were present or not. In most years several males would be named and ordered sworn into tithing by the court, either because the son of a resident had reached the age of 12 or because a newcomer had settled within the community, and so those recorded as being out of tithing must be added to the total in tithing, in order to estimate resident population. The number of absentees, newly sworn tithingmen, and males ordered into tithing have therefore been summed with the raw tithingpenny data, as appropriate to the particular jurisdiction in question.[10] The resulting datasets are graphed in Figure 5.2.

As the graphed series indicate, there is a wide variety of community sizes, degrees of completeness in surviving data, and periods covered by these series. Moreover, relatively small local populations such as these, as may be expected, exhibit noticeable short-term fluctuations around underlying trends. But although these datasets reflect the administrative apparatus of a number of different manorial lordships, there is sufficient agreement among long-term trends to suggest that the series register demographic reality rather than idiosyncratic artefacts of individual manors' jurisdictions. The only likely exception was Chatham Hall, where internal evidence implies an especially weakened seigneurial authority, conceivably reflected in the particularly marked decline over the latter portion of this series.[11]

It has been shown elsewhere[12] that several of these series can be compared at various points in time with other sources for local population, and that when an estimate for total local population in a

10 For discussion of variations in administration, and therefore in the corrections necessary to the raw tithing data, see Poos, 'Population and resources', pp. 64–87; Newton, 'Medieval population statistics', p. 11.

11 Crowley, 'Later history of frankpledge', p. 11.

12 Poos, 'Rural population of Essex', pp. 525–9.

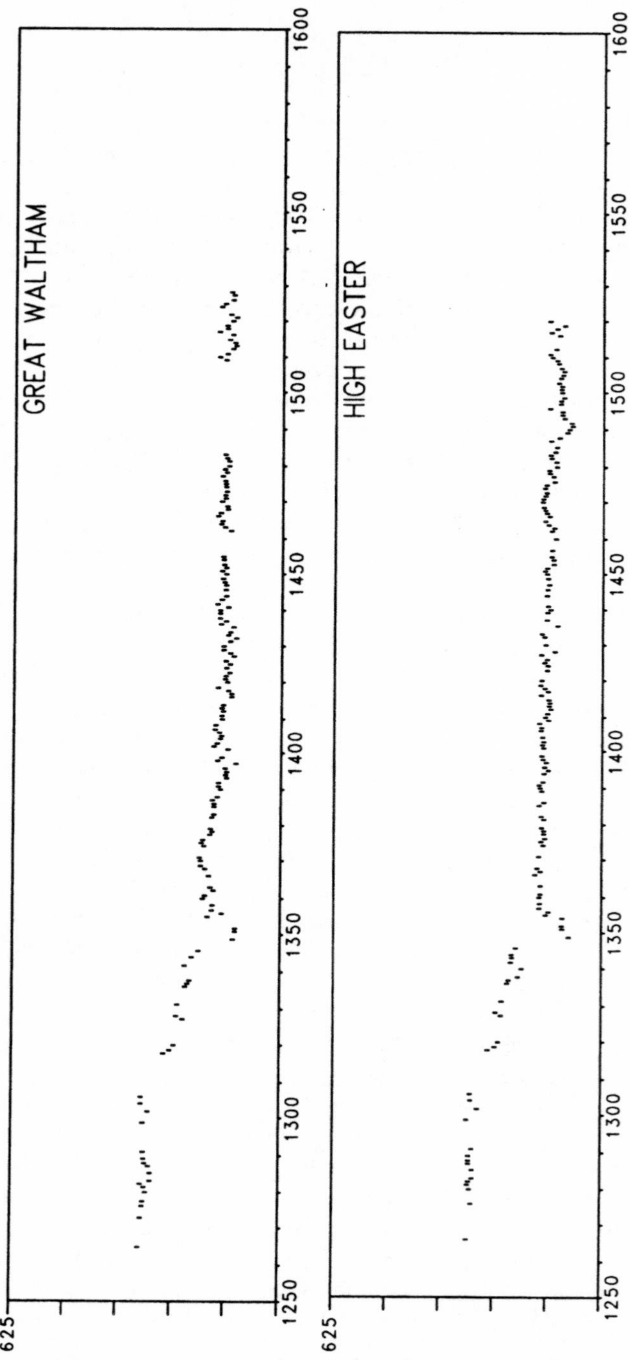

Figure 5.2a. Males aged 12 and older in sixteen Essex communities:
Great Waltham 1265–1528 High Easter 1266–1520

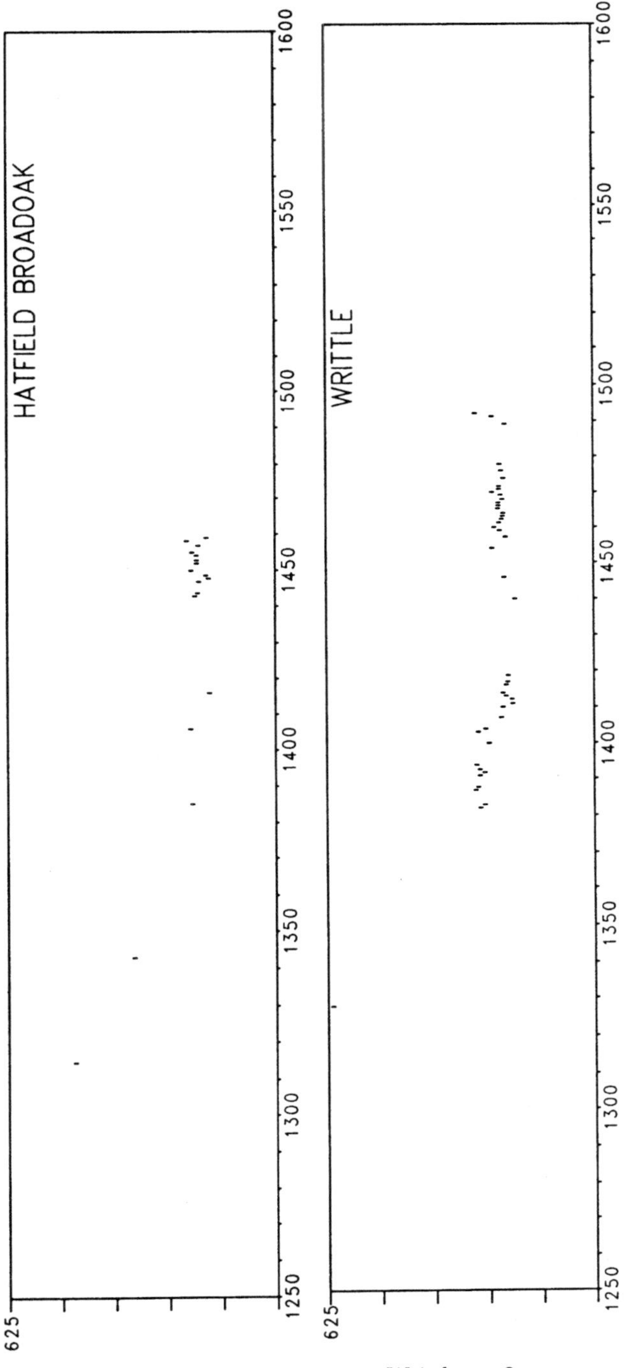

Hatfield Broadoak 1315–1459

Writtle 1328–1492

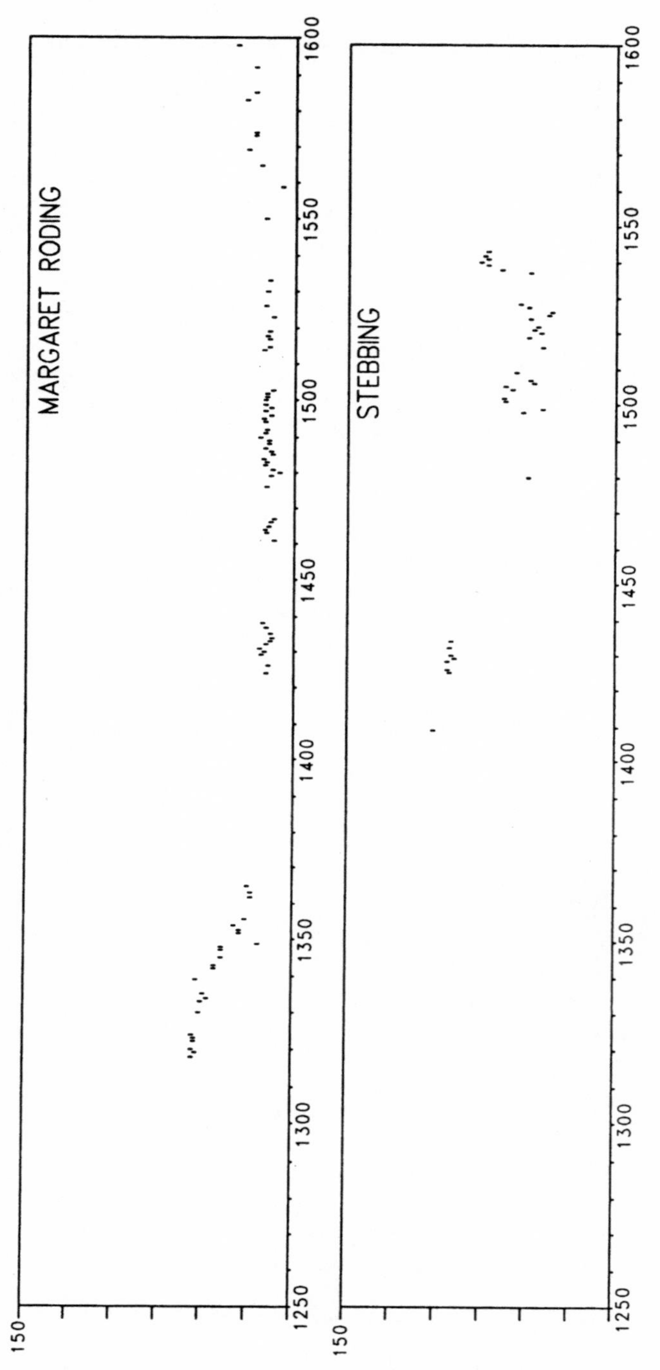

Figure 5.2b. Males aged 12 and older in sixteen Essex communities:
Margaret Roding 1318–1598 Stebbing 1409–1543

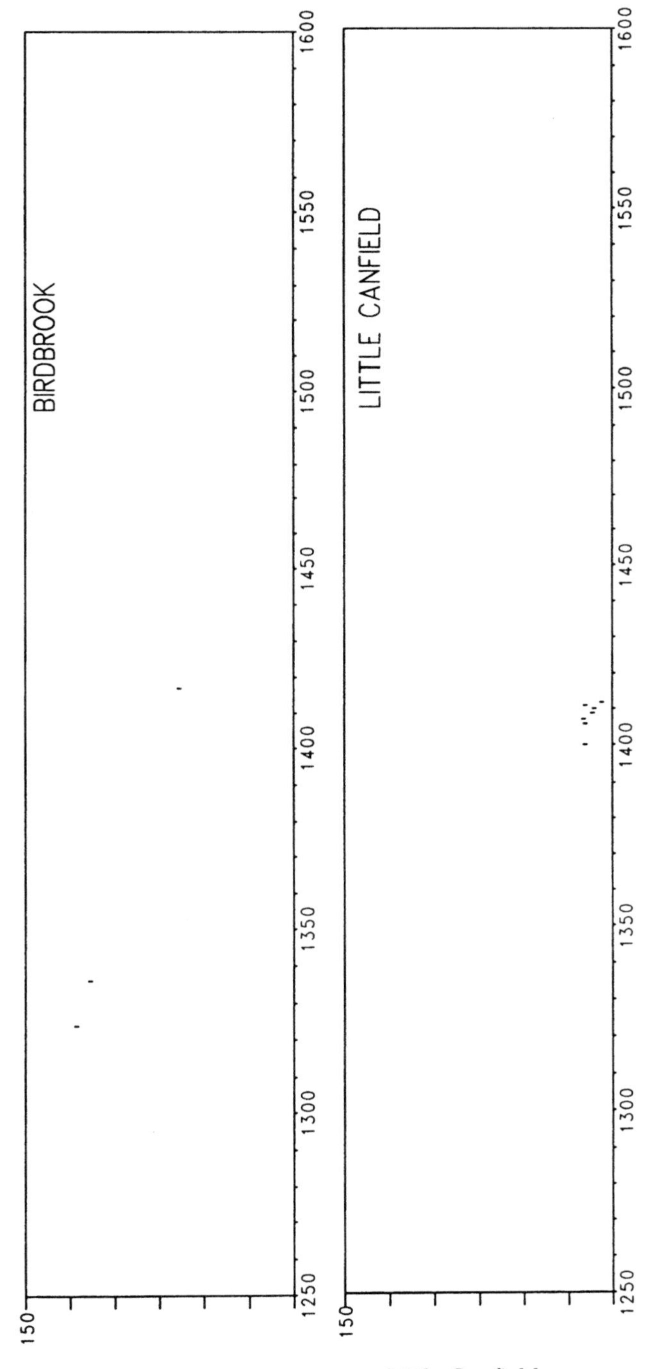

Birdbrook 1325–1420

Little Canfield 1400–12

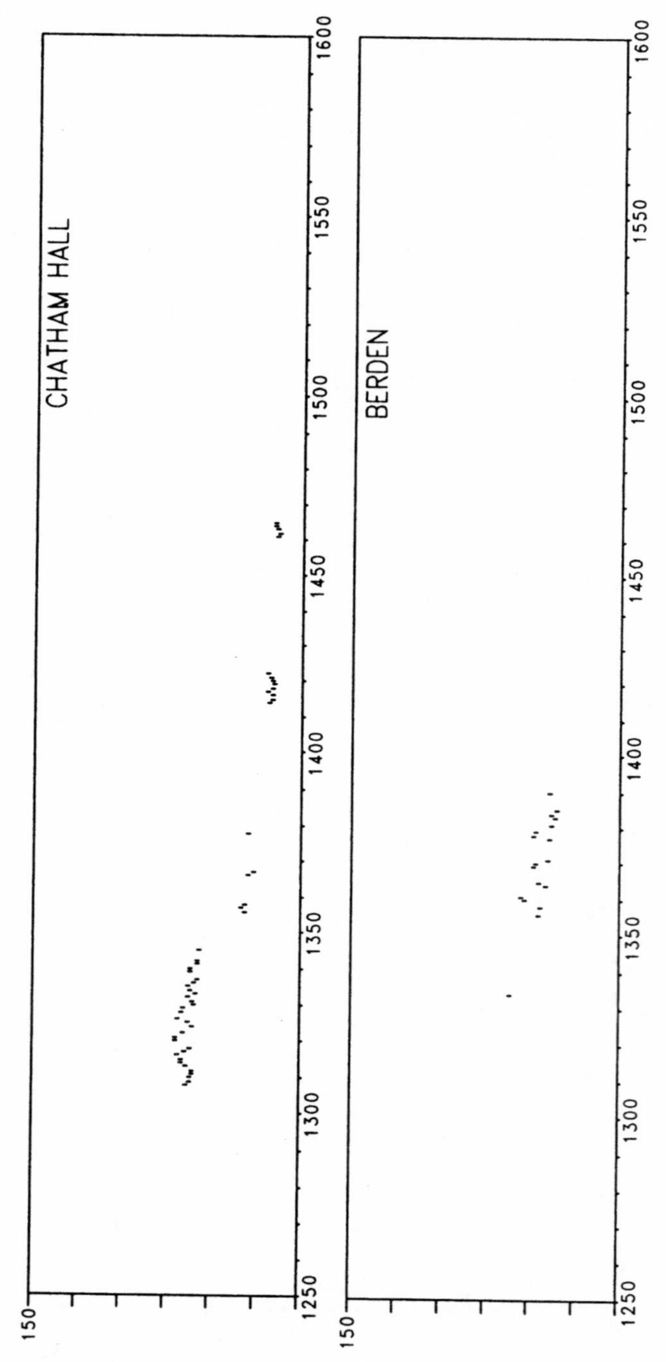

Figure 5.2c. Males aged 12 and older in sixteen Essex communities:
Chatham Hall 1308–1465 Berden 1334–90

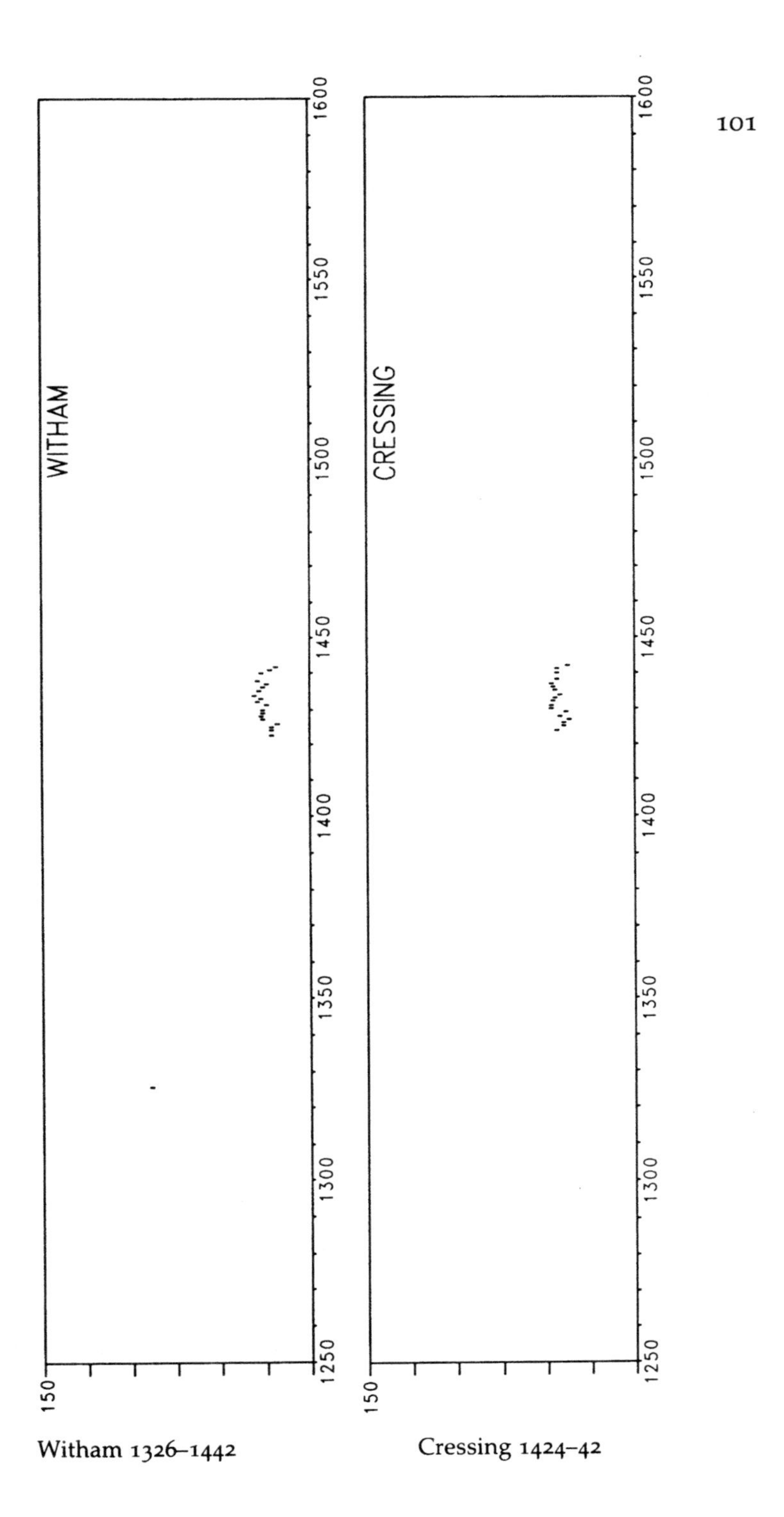

Witham 1326–1442

Cressing 1424–42

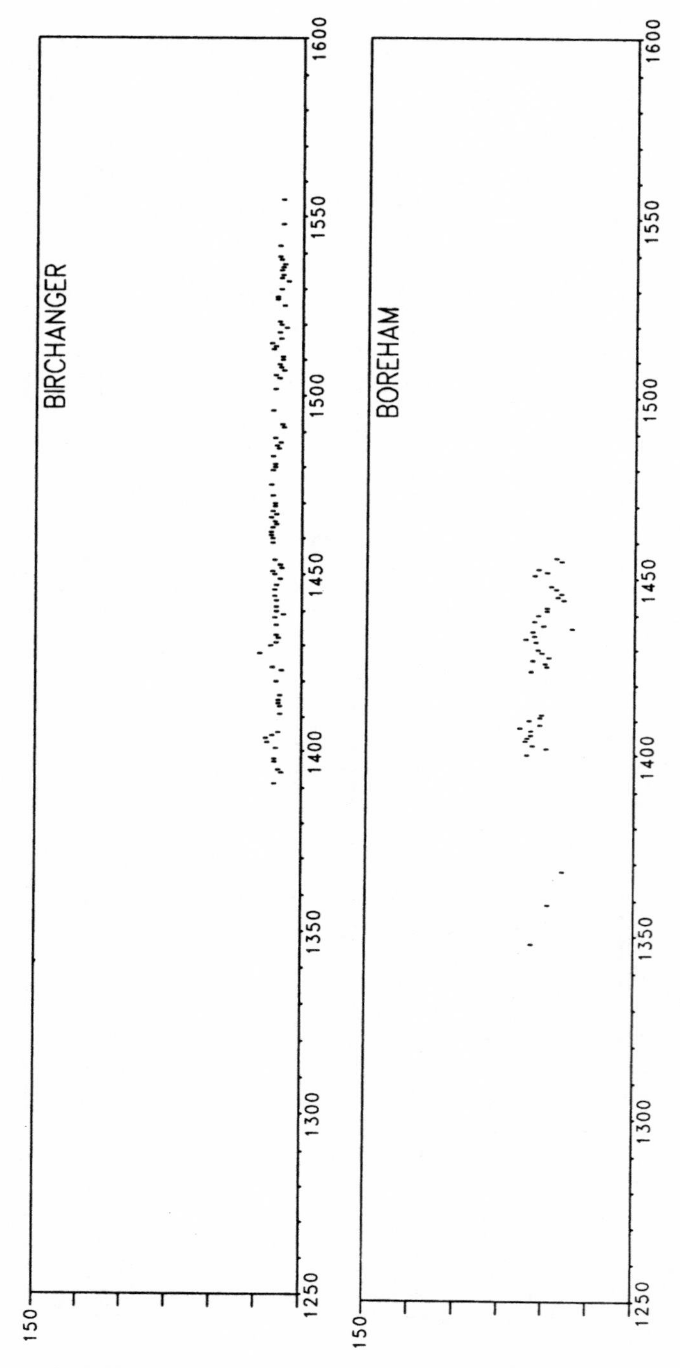

Figure 5.2d. Males aged 12 and older in sixteen Essex communities: Birchanger 1391–1555 Boreham 1348–1456

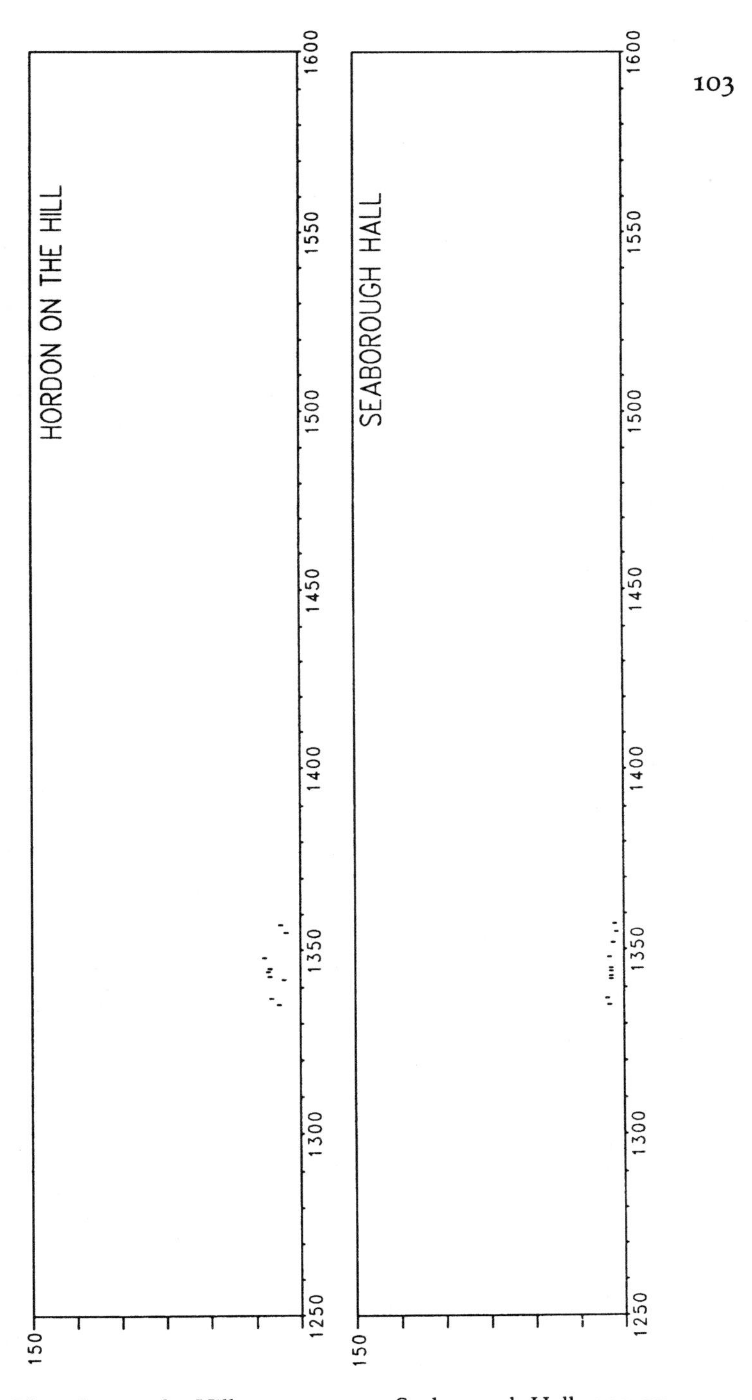

Horndon on the Hill 1335–57

Seaborough Hall 1335–57

given place derived from the tithingpenny data can be checked against a similar estimate from other sources, the agreement between the two is well within acceptable error margins. To make these comparisons is seldom entirely straightforward, for several reasons. The geographical boundaries of frankpledge jurisdictions are seldom exactly coterminous with those of the parish, township, or manor that serves as the basis for alternative estimates. Comparisons like this also make it necessary to make assumptions about the demographic structures of underlying populations before tithing figures or other local data may be expanded to estimates of total local populations.

Nevertheless the results are striking. In the two cases – Margaret Roding[13] and Great Waltham[14] – where tithing series extend far enough into the sixteenth century to be compared with parish-register data, estimated local populations derived from the two sources lie within 5 per cent or so of one another. The 1377 poll-tax returns, though often criticised as reflecting an unknown but possibly large underenumeration,[15] in fact appear to have netted a very high proportion of local people liable for the tax in the five Essex townships where this comparison is available. Table 5.1 summarises comparisons between township totals estimated from tithing data and from 1377 poll-tax returns, where the pertinent data are available.[16] It is noteworthy that in every case where such comparison is possible, township population derived from poll-tax data exceeds that based

13 Margaret Roding parish register, ERO D/P 309/263A. An admittedly crude method of estimating parish population from burial rates is to take observed burials (1.60 per annum during 1551–1600) and inflate by 100/D, where D is the national crude death rate calculated for England during this period (26.10 per thousand per annum, simple arithmetic mean of quinquennial rates: Wrigley and Schofield, *Population history of England*, p. 528). This yields a derived base population of 61.3. The mean number in tithing during 1550–98 (10 data points) was 21.7. This has been inflated by 2.745 (proportion of total population to males aged 12 and older: Princeton Model West life table, population growing by 0.5 per cent per annum, and mortality level 8, which is close to the national e_0 calculated for this period: *ibid.*; see also below, Appendix A). The resulting base population is 59.6.

14 Great Waltham parish register, ERO D/P 121/1/0. From the first 25 years of surviving parish-register data (1567–91), inflated as above from crude death rates for 1566–91 calculated by Wrigley and Schofield, the parish-register-derived base population is 497.4. The latest surviving variable tithingpenny data for Great Waltham come from 1509–28, yielding a mean of 123.1. This must be inflated to take into account the population of Chatham Hall's leet jurisdiction, for which no data survive. Therefore a factor of 0.274 has been added (the ratio of Chatham Hall to Great Waltham tithing memberships during 1308–46), to provide a mean figure for males aged 12 and older during 1509–28 of 156.8, or a total base population of 415.5 (Model West, stationary population, mortality level 8). This in turn must be inflated to take into account demographic growth between the first and fourth quarters of the century. If a very rough approximation may be taken as growth at 0.5 per cent per annum for four decades, this would bring the tithing-derived base population to 507.2.

15 See below, Appendix A.

16 Poos, 'Rural population of Essex', pp. 527–8.

Table 5.1. *Populations derived from poll-tax and tithing data, five Essex townships, 1377*

Township		Poll tax[a]		Tithing[b]	
		Taxpayers	Range of derived base population[c]	Tithing members	Range of derived base population[c]
Berden		86	115–29	39	100–11
High Easter		298	399–447	135	346–85
Margaret Roding		54	72–81	25	64–71
Great Waltham[d]	Great Waltham			162	
	Chatham Hall			29	
	(total)	527	706–90	191	490–545
Writtle		600	804–99	268	688–764

[a] *Sources:* PRO.E179.107.46; E179.107.48; E179.107.55.

[b] Tithing figures tabulated here are those for 1377 if the relevant sources have survived. Otherwise, the surviving figure closest in time to 1377 has been used: for Chatham Hall, 1378; Margaret Roding, 1365; Great Waltham, 1382; Writtle, 1382.

[c] Ranges of derived base populations have been calculated from Princeton Model West life tables, proportions of males aged 12 and older (for tithings) or males and females aged 14 and older (for poll taxes) to total population, assuming population declining at 0.5 per cent per annum and extreme limits of mortality levels 1 and 8 (female $e_0 = 20.0$ and 37.5 years). See also below, Appendix A.

[d] Great Waltham and Chatham Hall frankpledge jurisdictions were both included in Great Waltham township.

upon tithing membership. The most likely reason for this is that males resident in these communities for less than a year – particularly servants – need not have enrolled in local tithings although still liable for poll-tax payment, a situation entirely compatible with the Essex evidence for servanthood and mobility (discussed below, Chapter 9). Other sources, such as the late-medieval or early-Tudor lay subsidy returns and manorial rentals, by contrast are very poor bases for estimating local resident population, and this is likely to be especially true in view of the high proportion of smallholders and landless people in rural Essex.

Taken together, then, these tithingpenny series constitute a set of evidence for late-medieval aggregate population trends from one compact district, unmatched in volume and likely credibility by any records as yet discovered for other parts of England. It would be misleading to imply that the experience of central and northern Essex necessarily mirrored that of England as a whole, or any other region of the country, over the period in question. In some respects, in fact, the Essex data merely appear to confirm general outlines upon which historians have largely agreed. But in other respects they provide strong evidence for the chronology and scale of change over time that have so far been major points of contention.[17]

As has already been shown,[18] central Essex had become remarkably densely populated by about 1300, and the tithing series for these decades are without noticeable trend, indicating that local population then had already reached its apogee of high-medieval expansion. The first major changes arrived with the famine mortality and agrarian crisis that followed upon three consecutive years of disastrous weather in 1315–17, whose effects were felt well beyond Essex and England too. Mortality during this crisis, on the evidence of the tithing data, apparently varied considerably from place to place. The mean aggregate decline in three Essex communities for which comparisons can be drawn was about 15 per cent, towards the higher end of the range of previously attempted estimates from elsewhere in the country.[19] There then followed three decades of sustained demographic

[17] The literature of surveys and speculations concerning these trends and evidence for them is large. Brief overviews of the subject are given in Poos, 'Rural population of Essex', pp. 515–17; Smith, 'Human resources'; Baker, 'Changes in the later middle ages', pp. 187–95; Hatcher, *Plague, population and the English economy*.

[18] Above, Chapter 2.

[19] When the latest available tithing figure before the famine of 1315–17 is set against the earliest available after it for three communities, the decline in numbers of tithing members was: Great Waltham, 20.6 per cent (320–254 for the years 1306 and 1319); High Easter, 13.9 per cent (288–248), for 1306 and 1319); Chatham Hall, 3.2 per cent (63–61, for 1308 and 1318); or a global figure of 16.1 per cent. Most previous estimates

decline. In short, the falling-off from maximum local population levels was rapid and well advanced in Essex even before the Black Death.

Plague arrived in mid-Essex in 1349, and the tithing data from six communities in the district imply an aggregated mean of approximately 45 per cent mortality during this first visitation of the disease, though again with some variation from place to place.[20] This is commensurate with estimates of mortality derived from evidence of manorial tenants' deaths in the same district.[21] And yet the graphed figures for Great Waltham, High Easter and Margaret Roding would appear at first glance to be highly anomalous, since they display upturns in the mid-1350s that resulted in 1363 in these three communities' tithing totals standing at only about 15, 30 and 40 per cent lower, respectively, than their pre-Black Death levels.[22] It is inconceivable that this ostensible upsurge of resident population resulted directly from intrinsic demographic factors, such as an outburst of fertility in the wake of the epidemic. This possibility is unlikely not only because of its sheer scale and abruptness, but also because the upturn in males aged 12 and older came within six years or so of the plague.

It is more likely that a combination of administrative disruption, migration and the method utilised here for deriving estimated resident population is responsible for the tithing data's anomalous and at least partly illusory behaviour after 1349. In 1355, the leet courts of Great Waltham and High Easter recorded redoubled curial efforts to force into tithing resident males who had escaped recruitment during the previous few years; especially vigorous demands were recorded that eligible males be sworn into tithing, and the juries of

for local mortality have been in the range of 10 to 15 per cent, e.g. Titow, 'Thirteenth-century population increase', p. 223 (tithing membership at Taunton, Somerset, declined by 9.3 per cent between 1313 and 1319); Razi, *Life, marriage and death in a medieval parish*, pp. 25, 39–40 (numbers of people appearing in manorial-court proceedings at Halesowen, Worcestershire, declined by approximately 15 per cent during the decade 1310–20); Kershaw, 'The great famine and agrarian crisis', p. 131 (for a 'guess' of about 10 per cent mortality during the famine).

20 When the latest available tithing figure before 1349 is set against the earliest available after 1350 for six communities, the decline in numbers was: Great Waltham, 44.4 per cent (187–104 for the years 1346 and 1351); High Easter, 53.8 per cent (199–92 for 1346 and 1351); Chatham Hall, 44.6 per cent (56–31 for 1345 and 1356); Margaret Roding, 25.6 per cent (39–29 for 1347 and 1352); Horndon on the Hill, 60.0 per cent (20–8 for 1348 and 1355); Seaborough Hall, 25.0 per cent (8–6 for 1348 and 1355); or a global figure of 47.0 per cent.

21 Poos, 'Population and resources', pp. 105–12; Fisher, 'The Black Death in Essex'.

22 Great Waltham, 13.9 per cent (187–161 for the years 1346 and 1363); High Easter, 28.1 per cent (199–143 for 1346 and 1363); Margaret Roding, 41.0 per cent (39–23 for 1347 and 1363).

chief pledges were ordered to compile new lists of tithing members.[23] It is for that same year that the upsurge in tithing data shown in Figure 5.2 was registered, but in that year the basic tithingpenny payments of the two places were essentially unchanged from the previous year (and so, therefore, were basic tithing memberships); the 'upsurge' reflects, rather, curial orders to place into tithing a total of 86 males in the two communities, and these have been added (as noted above) to the numbers already in tithing to produce the totals in Figure 5.2. Only a minority of these 'newcomers' can be identified as having had previous recorded links to the communities, and some doubtless moved on again without ever being enrolled into the local tithings.[24] It seems plausible, then, though it is impossible to prove, that the first few years after the epidemic witnessed especially high migration rates. This migration took several years to register in the tithing data in the form of newly enrolled tithingmen, it resulted also in court orders to enrol many males (thus inflating the data graphed above) who never actually settled in the communities in question, and its varying dimensions from place to place account for the differing degrees of ostensible 'recovery' in the respective datasets in the mid-1350s.

It was only over the following years that actual enrolled tithing memberships climbed to their post-plague peak, observable in several of the series, in the 1360s and 1370s. Thus it seems most plausible to envisage Black Death mortality as indeed at or close to the levels reflected in the tithing data, especially in view of corroborating manorial evidence, although the figures for the early 1350s may be depressed slightly by the inability of manorial administration to enforce recruitment. This would appear to have been especially true for the case of Great Waltham, where tithing membership in the 1360s was closer to pre-1349 levels than in the other communities. This evidence need not preclude a temporary upturn in fertility in the wake of the plague, which would have been registered in tithing membership in the early 1360s, and so have contributed to the peaks in many of the graphed series in that and the next decades.

After this ostensible recovery, however, the nearly unanimous pattern of these communities was continued gentle decline into the

[23] PRO.DL30.64.811 (High Easter leet, 28 May 1355): ' . . . distringantur . . . quorum nomina plene patent in quoddam rotulo de decennarioriis annexato in dorso quod sint ad proximam curiam ad ponendos in decenniam domini Regis . . . et sunt de illis qui fecerunt defaltam videlicet non sunt in decennia Regis xl . . . ' (a similar notice involving 46 'evaders' was recorded at the Great Waltham leet of the same date, *ibid.*); PRO.DL30.64.812 (Great Waltham leet, 16 Jun 1356): 'omnes capitales plegii habent diem ad proximum visum habendo in scripto nomina capitalum plegiorum et decennariorum suorum prout decet sub pena xx s.'.

[24] Poos, 'Population and resources', p. 77.

early decades of the fifteenth century, and no discernible recovery throughout the rest of the 1400s. In fact, several of the series (e.g. High Easter, Stebbing and possibly Birchanger and Boreham) indicate that the last few decades of the fifteenth century saw a new, though milder and briefer, phase of population contraction. Only in the cases of Stebbing and Margaret Roding do the series continue far enough into the sixteenth century to register any unmistakable resurgence of local population. This renewed expansion in tithing members began to make itself felt no earlier than the 1530s (though since these figures register only males aged 12 and older the balance between fertility and mortality may well have altered a decade or so earlier). Even this renewed growth was not necessarily universal within the district before the mid-1500s, however, for if the data are believable (and in this instance it is not possible to cross-check them with parish-register data) the resident population of Birchanger was apparently still declining down to about 1540.

Several broader observations are possible from this evidence. Wrigley and Schofield's exhaustive reconstruction of the early-modern English population, from several hundred series of parish-register data, estimated that compound annual growth rates for the English population at large generally hovered between 0.8 and 1.0 per cent per annum in the 1540s, 1550s and 1560s.[25] Moreover, on the basis of early Tudor tax returns and other authors' estimates from the medieval poll-taxes, they suggested that available empirical data are most consistent with stationary population into the 1510s, followed by growth at approximately 0.8 per cent per annum during the two decades or so before the inception of parish-register keeping by the new Church of England.[26] Such a scenario is in fact perfectly consistent with the Essex tithing data. The rising trends in, for example, the Stebbing tithing series accord well with the growth rates implied by the earliest parish-register data.

Considering the Essex tithing data against the broader perspective of England's post-medieval demographic experience suggests another observation: that the late-medieval Essex demographic depression was the midpoint between two successive maxima of aggregate population growth that were symmetrical in the relative heights of their peaks and troughs though not in the shape of their chronologies. At Great Waltham and High Easter, resident adolescent and adult

[25] Wrigley and Schofield, *Population history of England*, p. 528. The exception to this was the later 1550s, when severe epidemic mortality on a nearly nationwide scale resulted in a negative compound annual growth rate for this quinquennium.

[26] *Ibid.*, pp. 566–9.

males in the third quarter of the fifteenth century totalled slightly fewer than one-half their averages in the same communities in the last quarter-century of the 1200s.[27] By contrast, Wrigley and Schofield's estimates for England's national population fell only slightly short of doubling from 1541 to the 1650s, when the country's next demographic expansion crested (though, once again, growth was most rapid in the earliest decades of this expansion).[28]

Once again, it must not be presumed that Essex necessarily mirrored England throughout this long duration. Different regions doubtless differed in the scale and timing of the course of their population change. Nevertheless, these comparisons suggest that for more than a century the population of this district achieved a remarkably stable equilibrium within its environment and local economy at broadly one-half the level it had previously reached, and one-half the level it would reach again in the mid-1600s. Understanding something of the mechanisms by which that equilibrium was achieved is the object of the following chapters.

[27] For High Easter, the mean total for 1276–99 (11 data points) was 305.6, for 1451–75 (21 data points) 128.5. For Great Waltham, the mean total for 1276–99 (12 data points) was 309.3, for 1451–75 (19 data points) 133.4.

[28] Wrigley and Schofield, *Population history of England*, p. 528.

6

Components of demographic equilibrium

The rural population of Essex achieved a remarkable period of equilibrium at low absolute levels for most of the time from the end of the fourteenth to the early sixteenth century. Emphasis here is upon 'equilibrium', because population adapted itself to its biological, economic and social-structural environment in such a way that mortality and fertility balanced each other out over an extended period of time.[1] Such is clear from the Essex tithing data. But to move beyond mere aggregates in order to consider the components of demographic equilibrium makes much more serious demands upon available empirical evidence. At present it seems unlikely that there will ever be anything like precise measures of broadly based mortality or fertility levels from medieval English sources, or indeed absolute consensus regarding relationships between the two variables. And yet, as the case of Essex demonstrates, that does not necessarily mean that tentative inferences are wholly impossible.

The relative importance of mortality and fertility in defining the course of later-medieval population raises issues that extend far beyond the period's demography narrowly defined. To decipher this equilibrium makes it necessary to understand the social-structural and economic underpinnings of household formation as a process over time. Ultimately, these questions raise the more basic issue of how far later-medieval England's demographic system differed from or resembled the country's population regime in the post-medieval centuries.

A traditional, and still probably the majority, view of the late-

[1] This statement presumes, of course, that net migration into or out of the district was negligible. Though incapable of proof, the observations of Chapter 2 (above) would tend to minimise the possible effects of migration to London or Colchester, when viewed as a proportion of the district's population.

medieval English population would place mortality at centre-stage.[2] In this view, an already unfavourable economic climate resulting from population growth extending into the early 1300s was transformed by the arrival of plague in the country during the Black Death of 1348–9. Quite apart from the swingeing death rates of this first visitation, plague's importance lay in its becoming established as a major factor of mortality for centuries to come. First in the form of a few national or at least supraregional outbreaks (as in 1361, 1369 and 1375) and then of a more steady human wastage manifesting itself in a few (chiefly urban) pools of permanent infection but mostly in highly localised strikes randomly scattered across time and space, there is little doubt that bubonic plague was indeed a new and potent force in England's demographic experience. In this view a high frequency of 'crisis' mortality was also the chief bellwether of high mortality (or low life expectancy) generally.[3] What is most at issue here is not whether the disease became 'endemic'[4] in the country, but rather whether it became – alone or in tandem with other infectious diseases – the harbinger of a distinctly more deleterious phase of mortality.

For underlying these questions is the more fundamental one of how preindustrial demographic systems work. The view sketched out above defines disease-driven mortality as the motive force of demographic change, as an exogenous factor extrinsic to the period's economy and social structure. The corollary of this view is that fertility change was incapable of contributing much to the later-medieval population depression.[5] Though seldom explicitly voiced by medieval historians, this premise derives in turn from several other assumptions. Economic circumstances after 1350 – especially a lower people-to-land ratio and higher real wages – are presumed if anything to have conspired to make marriage easier and earlier, and so to have contributed to boosting fertility; that population did not rise shows that this

[2] It is impossible and unnecessary to recount here the multitude of arguments and empirical supporting evidence that have contributed to this view. For representative summaries see Hatcher, *Plague, population and the English economy*, esp. pp. 55–62; Bolton, *The medieval English economy*, esp. pp. 56–66. The view is critically discussed in Poos, 'Plague mortality and demographic depression'.

[3] Such is the emphasis, for example, in Hatcher, *Plague, population and the English economy*, esp. pp. 57–61, and Gottfried, *Epidemic disease*, pp. 225–30.

[4] Epidemiologically it is impossible for bubonic plague to become 'endemic', despite much use of the term by medieval historians. It could (and it is hard to believe it did not) become 'enzootic', or established in permanent cycles of infection among rodents with further vector spread to humans, in England between 1349 and 1666: cf. Biraben, 'Medical views on plague', and Bradley, 'Medical aspects of plague'.

[5] Again, this perhaps stereotypical caricature is an amalgam of medievalists' opinions: cf. Hatcher, *Plague, population and the English economy*, pp. 56–7; Razi, *Life, marriage and death in a medieval parish*, pp. 135–44; Smith, 'Human resources', p. 210.

response, if it occurred, did not manage to surmount heightened mortality. Or else, nuptiality and fertility were already very high before 1350 and could not respond to a significant degree to such economic stimulus. Or else, in a 'traditional' society like this, nuptiality's timing and incidence were culturally determined and so unlikely to respond to such stimulus in the first place. It is immediately evident, even from such a terse summary of the voluminous debates that medieval English historians have committed to print in recent years, how far beyond demography proper these questions range.

But from the vantage of this study's present goals a view of England's late-medieval demography as essentially mortality-driven is at odds with what is now known of the country's population history from the mid-1500s onward. Medievalists' views of the primacy of exogenous mortality in population change echo what until recently was a principle more widely applied to preindustrial populations generally, often via (partially misunderstood) reference to Malthus as supporting theory.[6] In contrast, sophisticated analysis of parish-register data during the past two decades has shown beyond reasonable doubt that variability in fertility was the chief determinant of aggregate population change in England (though not necessarily elsewhere in Europe) during the early-modern period, and that fertility in turn was chiefly conditioned by changes in nuptiality that themselves were responses to economic environment.[7] Moreover, between the sixteenth and eighteenth centuries the frequency of mortality crises (localised, short-term upswings in death rates usually caused by epidemics) did not necessarily move in concert with general mortality levels.[8] To accept that mortality was chiefly responsible for the late-medieval demographic slump makes it necessary to envisage that England's demographic regime altered fundamentally within a very short space of time around 1500.

Medieval historians have shown great resourcefulness and tapped a wide variety of sources in attempts to investigate mortality and fertility, but the empirical basis for establishing any particularly precise view of the period's population dynamics has remained

[6] A classic statement of the 'exogenous' theory is given in Chambers, *Population, economy and society*, pp. 77–106; this has been recently echoed by Lee, 'Population homeostasis'. Bolton, *The medieval English economy*, p. 56, claimed 'Malthus believed that fertility was constant'. Of course, Malthus believed no such thing: Smith, 'Human resources', pp. 188–9.

[7] This is the chief implication of Wrigley and Schofield, *Population history of England*, and is discussed in more detail in Chapter 7, below.

[8] Wrigley and Schofield, *Population history of England*, esp. pp. 332–42, 645–93: a decline in crisis mortality incidence coincided with a worsening mortality schedule in England in the later seventeenth century.

recalcitrant. Some writers have utilised royal tenurial inquests, manorial-court records, and wills in attempts to calculate 'replacement rates' – numbers of offspring surviving to parents' deaths, in reality a composite measure of fertility, mortality and age of childbearing – but both methodology and the measure itself remain problematic.[9]

More recently the obituary lists of the Benedictine priory of Christ Church, Canterbury, have yielded estimates of mortality and of epidemic frequency among the priory's monks that are quite high during the last decades of the fifteenth century, though more moderate in earlier decades.[10] Temporarily heightened mortality consonant with the Canterbury data may in fact have been responsible for the mild contraction in several Essex tithing series at the end of the fifteenth century (above, Chapter 5). Among the Canterbury monks mortality was so severe at the end of the 1400s that, if they were representative of the late-medieval English population at large, fertility rates would have to have been half again higher than in later Stuart England for the nation's people to have achieved zero population growth. A definitively 'high-pressure' fertility regime would have been needed, in other words, merely to maintain its numbers in the face of an extremely short life expectancy, in sharp contrast to England's post-medieval demographic system.[11] It remains to be seen how this essentially urban group would compare with a broadly based rural population.

Clearly it is highly unlikely that any source or method will emerge that would allow very precise measurement of mortality and fertility in later-medieval Essex to be calculated. Nevertheless, there do survive some data of a more oblique nature, that can yield rough measures of these variables from the district. So long as one is concerned merely with rough approximations rather than aspiring to unattainable precision, it is in fact possible to provide some better-than-order-of-

[9] Russell, *British medieval population*, pp. 92–117; Thrupp, 'The problem of replacement-rates'; Razi, *Life, marriage and death in a medieval parish*, pp. 32–4; Gottfried, *Epidemic disease*, pp. 187–203. A critical examination of these exercises appears in Poos and Smith, 'Legal windows onto historical populations?', pp. 137–9.

[10] Hatcher, 'Mortality in the fifteenth century'.

[11] Hatcher, *ibid.*, pp. 31–2, observes that the Canterbury monks' mortality schedule most closely approximates mortality level 3 in the Princeton Model West life tables, or a life expectancy at birth for males of 22.85 years. (The nature of the Princeton model populations is discussed later in this chapter, and in Appendix A.) At zero population growth in this model population, Gross Reproduction Rate (GRR, the mean number of daughters born to women who passed through their childbearing years experiencing the average age-specific fertility pattern) would need to be 2.682: Coale and Demeny, *Regional model life tables*, p. 107. In later-seventeenth-century England, GRR averaged 1.990 (simple arithmetic mean of quinquennial rates, 1651–96): Wrigley and Schofield, *Population history of England*, p. 528.

magnitude estimates of the components of demographic stasis. And while the approximate nature of the resulting estimates demands repeated emphasis, they not only bear some comparison with England's post-medieval population history but also raise some suggestive partial answers for resolving the puzzle of demographic equilibrium in the later middle ages.

Most attempts to estimate life expectancy among broadly based rural populations below gentry status in medieval England run up against nearly insuperable empirical obstacles. Medieval England has in fact bequeathed to historians innumerable records of deaths, most typically in connection with land tenure and its transfer to heirs. But those who appeared in tenurial death records were almost exclusively adults (those persons fortunate enough to have attained at least minimum legal age for propertyholding in their own right in the first place), whereas in preindustrial populations mortality is invariably most severe in lower age-ranges, for which medieval evidence can normally provide no data. Even within this limitation, such records hardly ever include the ages of the deceased. And so to estimate life expectancy from most medieval death records would require that the decedents in question be identified earlier in their lives, in dated documentary contexts that permit ages to be estimated within reasonably close limits: whether in the case of monks (estimating a standard age at profession of vows),[12] or of manorial tenants (estimating age at which persons typically entered into landholding, or estimating age from the life-cyclical record of tenants' parents).[13] In the case of manorial records in particular, attaching ages to persons in this way is quite problematic, because there is no means of independent verification; any age one chooses in such contexts is likely to be highly arbitrary.[14]

The tithing system that operated throughout the later-medieval period in most Essex communities offers one alternative possibility. The preceding chapter has already outlined this system's essential features. Males who either were already resident within the community, as sons of local people, and who reached the age of compulsory tithing membership (12 years), and males of older ages who settled within the community for at least a year, appeared by name in the records of local leet courts when they were sworn into tithing or when

[12] Hatcher, 'Mortality in the fifteenth century', pp. 26–7.

[13] Razi, *Life, marriage and death in a medieval parish*, esp. pp. 43–5, 128–31; Postan and Titow, 'Heriots and prices'; Hallam, 'Age at first marriage and age at death', esp. pp. 63–8.

[14] These points are discussed in Poos and Smith, 'Legal windows onto historical populations?', pp. 139–41.

the court ordered officials to produce them at the next curial session for swearing-in. In the former case, an age of 12 years can be assigned to someone appearing in such contexts within plausibly narrow limits. And if enough persons thus identified subsequently appeared in court records of tenant deaths, deriving a mean interval in years between tithing entry and death is tantamount to calculating a surrogate life expectancy at age 12 (e_{12}).

The surrogate nature of this measure needs emphasising, for there are many qualifications and difficulties inherent in its derivation. Nominal linkage – that is, determining whether seemingly identical names appearing in different records do in fact refer to the same person – is always difficult with manorial material. In this case it is necessary to include in the group under observation only those males who belonged to families already appearing in local records before tithing entry, in order to ensure that older immigrants into the community are not included (and thus that an erroneously low 'e_{12}' is not subsumed in the dataset). This stricture, combined with the very high migration rates that were prevalent in the district, means that extremely few tithing entrants can be reliably traced through to their subsequent death notices. Similarly strict criteria are necessary to prevent other types of spurious inclusions.[15]

Moreover, even with these qualifications, the group for whom

[15] These rules may be summarised as follows. 'Linkages' between the appearances of ostensibly identically named males in tithing entry and tenant death records were rejected if: the elapsed interval between the two events was shorter than 10 years or longer than 65 years; more then one male with identical name (especially with inconsistently given further descriptors such as occupation, 'junior' or 'senior', or geographical descriptor) can be observed in the same community in the same half-century; the tithing entrant was described as a servant; or no explicit genealogical links can be found between tithing entrant and a family previously visible in the local records. Elapsed time between tithing entry and death notice for each male was reckoned as an integral number of years. With both types of records, it was not uncommon for a given male to appear in the same capacity in several successive years (for example, a male might be ordered sworn into tithing in one or two years and recorded as taking his oath only in the third year); in such cases it was the first recorded mention from which the relevant year of tithing entry or death was entered into the dataset. Death records in these manors usually were careful to specify that the person in question died 'since the previous court', so uncertainty of time lapse between death and death record is unlikely to be a serious methodological problem. Whether such promptness was also observed when a local lad reached the age of 12 cannot be determined; the more lengthy this time lapse typically was, the more calculated 'e_{12}' would be an underestimate. The dates within which tithing and death entries were taken from these manors' records depended mainly upon documentary survival, and were as follows: High Easter 1462–1509; Great Tey, 1400–1546; Great Waltham, 1351–1483. The 110 'linkages' tabulated here resulted from a total of 2,860 individual records of tithing entry or tenant deaths.

Table 6.1. *Mean interval between tithing entry and death, three Essex communities, 1351–1546*

'Birth cohort'[a]	Mean interval ($\bar{X}$)	Standard deviation (σ)	Standard error of mean ($S_{\bar{X}}$)	Number of deaths observed (N)
1351–1400	41.6	14.0	2.1	44
1401–50	39.9	12.6	2.0	39
1451–1500	36.2	12.7	2.4	27
Entire period	39.7	13.4	1.3	110

Note: [a] 'Birth cohort' 1351–1400 means cohort recorded as entering tithing 1363–1412, etc.
Sources: See Bibliography for High Easter, Great Tey and Great Waltham.

surrogate e_{12} is obtainable is far from constituting a complete demographic cohort. The group in question is exclusively male. But more fundamentally, the males in question had to have leapt several demographic hurdles in order to have been included in the group under observation in the first place. First, they had to survive to age 12. But they also had to survive to such a further age (in practice, at least their early twenties) that they were able to assume property in their own right and thus be recorded as tenants when they died. Even for those registered as tithing entrants, then, no calculation is possible if they died in their teens, or died at any age without property, or left their communities after early adolescence. And so this surrogate 'e_{12}' is more like an 'e_{21} plus nine years' or 'e_{22} plus ten years' (or whichever other combination one regards as most plausible).

Table 6.1 presents data for surrogate life expectancy calculated in this way from three communities in central Essex: High Easter, Great Waltham and Great Tey. The dataset is divided into half-century birth cohorts. As the table shows, high mobility and strict criteria for inclusion have resulted in fairly small half-century samples. Nevertheless, the relatively small standard error of mean for each sample means that sample size is not a serious drawback of the data. It does mean, though, that within commonly accepted error margins there is no statistically significant difference in the mean interval between tithing entry and death calculated for the respective samples. In other words, one cannot say that there is any meaningful conclusion to be drawn from the (perhaps superficially counterintuitive) result that calculated

Table 6.2. *Male life expectancies at various ages, Princeton Model West life tables*

	Mortality level 5	Mortality level 6	Mortality level 7	Mortality level 8
e_0	27.67	30.07	32.48	34.89
e_{12}	37.57	38.93	40.28	41.61
e_{21}	31.32	32.54	33.75	34.95

Source: Coale and Demeny, *Regional model life tables*, pp. 44–5.

'e_{12}' for 1351–1400 here is higher than for 1451–1500.[16]

In broad terms, then, the data indicate that for those males who went on to become propertyholders in these communities, e_{12} lay in the range of roughly 38 to 40 years in the post-Black Death period in central Essex. Measures of e_{12} are, however, without much comparative value without reference to life expectancy at birth (e_0), but in this case direct evidence for infant and child mortality in the district is simply not available. The only means of relating these calculated surrogate measures of e_{12} plausibly to an overall mortality schedule is to refer to standardised life tables of preindustrial European populations, and the most appropriate for present purposes are the Princeton Model West life tables.[17] Comparisons of e_0, e_{12} and e_{21} for several respective mortality levels of the Princeton model populations appear in Table 6.2.

If it were possible to take the data for life expectancy derived from later-medieval Essex tithing and death records straightforwardly as a true measure of e_{12}, Table 6.2 implies that this would be compatible with Princeton Model West mortality level 6 or 7, corresponding with a male life expectancy at birth of 30 to 32 years. It is likely, though, that this is an underestimate of true e_0 by a year or two, because reconstitution data indicate that the Princeton Model West tables embody

16 Standard error of mean (sample standard deviation divided by square root of number of cases in sample) is a measure of the likelihood that the actual mean of the population being sampled lies close to the sample's mean. In the case of calculated e_{12} for 1351–1500 at large, the probability is 95 per cent that actual e_{12} (with the strictures noted in the text above) lay within $\pm 1.96 \times$ standard error of mean, or in other words between 37.2 and 42.2. This inference, formally speaking, presumes that the 'samples' tabulated in Table 6.1 are random samples in the statistical sense, which is not strictly true but unlikely to be grossly incorrect.

17 The Princeton life tables are model populations based upon largely nineteenth-century empirical data, adjusted for different presumptions concerning underlying demographic structures. For the appropriateness of Model West for later-medieval England, see Appendix A.

infant and child mortality levels somewhat higher than those empirically derived from the earliest English parish-register data of the sixteenth century.[18] Partly offsetting this underestimation factor, on the other hand, is the fact that the group under observation here omits males who attained the age of 12 but died before reaching adulthood. In practice, however, this latter deviation from a demographically exact e_{12} is unlikely to result in a very large error, simply because in most preindustrial populations age-specific mortality is at its lowest in the teenage years, much lower compared with age-ranges beyond the later twenties.[19] One final consideration is necessary in relating these figures to an underlying level of life expectancy: the data from Essex manorial sources pertain exclusively to males, whereas over the range of e_0 typical of preindustrial England life expectancy for both sexes averaged together was fairly consistently about 1.5 years higher than that for males alone.[20]

In sum, the closest one is likely to get to realistic estimates of life expectancy in late-medieval Essex is an e_{12} for both sexes together of around 40 years and perhaps an e_0 of around 32–4 years. These are estimates, it should be noted, whose continuous and broadly based nature subsumes both periods of large-scale epidemics and 'background' mortality alike. Doubtless they have error margins that are not trivial, but for present purposes they are suggestive enough. Placing them into the longer-term perspective of English population history suggests one partial answer to the conundrum of late-medieval demographic equilibrium. Between 1541 and 1601, e_0 for England at large generally ranged between the middle and upper 30s, though in the conspicuously unhealthy years of the later 1550s and early 1560s life expectancy at birth dipped temporarily below 30 years.[21] England's long-term mortality experience entered a rather more

[18] Schofield and Wrigley, 'Infant and child mortality in Tudor–Stuart England'. The authors note (p. 95n) that the English mortality experience in eight parishes during the later sixteenth century may be best approximated by Princeton Model North mortality level 12 ($e_0 = 44.24$ for males at $r = 0.0$) up to age 10, and Model West mortality level 7 thereafter. At this time e_0 in England generally ranged between 35 and 38 years (Wrigley and Schofield, *Population history of England*, p. 528). The implication is that adolescent and adult mortality at that time was essentially indistinguishable from that calculated here for later-medieval Essex.

[19] For example, in Princeton Model West model populations, at mortality level 7 age-specific mortality for males is 7.89 per 1,000 per annum for ages 15–20, 14.57 for ages 30–35, and 39.81 for ages 55–60: Coale and Demeny, *Regional model life tables*, p. 45.

[20] Wrigley and Schofield, *Population history of England*, pp. 241–2, noting that this convention is an approximation, though a reasonably accurate one.

[21] This and the following observations upon England's early-modern mortality come from *ibid.*, p. 528.

unfavourable period in the latter half of the seventeenth century, when e_0 typically ranged between 31 and 34 years. Viewed from this perspective, the post-Black Death period can usefully be seen as another cyclical phase of relatively severe mortality, followed by the somewhat healthier phase of the later Tudor and early Stuart era and then by another downturn of life expectancy in the later 1600s.

Plague's precise importance within the overall mortality schedule of later-medieval Essex remains virtually impossible to gauge with evidence currently at hand. But it would *a priori* seem difficult to ascribe the fourteenth-century population collapse in the district to plague alone, since the local tithing data show that a substantial part of this decline came before 1349. Over the long run, though, it seems reasonable to conclude that unfavourable mortality was one reason why the Essex population stagnated between 1350 and 1500. But this unfavourable mortality was not of a wholly different order from what early-modern England experienced at times, and it is unlikely to have constituted the entire reason for the prolonged late-medieval depression. The fertility side of the demographic equation demands attention also.

In contrast with the sparse evidence for mortality, direct measures of fertility appear to be virtually nonexistent in England before the early-sixteenth-century institution of parochial registration of baptisms. It is true that in medieval Essex births or baptisms, and burials also, were occasionally recorded in missals, psalters, calendars, or other liturgical books belonging to parish churches, religious houses, or lay families.[22] At least one such book from an Essex family is known to have survived.[23] Inclusion in such entries was, however, usually the province of persons of at least minor gentry status, and so these records are obviously incapable of providing broadly based aggregate fertility measures.

[22] This was often mentioned in proof-of-age inquests, when a witness claimed to have remembered the date of birth of a feudal heir because the birth had been recorded in a book. Essex examples include PRO.C136.101.11 (inquest, 7 Nov 1397): '[two witnesses] dicunt quod hoc bene recolunt per inspectionem cuiusdam libri manualis in eadem ecclesia existentis in quo continetur eiusdem Roberti nativitas videlicet in kalendario eiusdem libri super festum Sancte Agathe virginis anno xlix supradicto in hec verba Robertus atte Chirche filius Johannis atte Chirche natus fuit anno regni domini Regis Edwardi tercij a conquesto xlix . . .'; C135.249.19 (inquest, 5 Sep 1375), for a death record 'in a certain book in the aforesaid church [in quodam libro in ecclesia predicta]'; C135.155.9 (inquest, 8 Mar 1360), for a birth recorded in a missal ['missali ecclesie predicte'].

[23] Ker, 'More manuscripts from Essex monastic libraries', pp. 308–9, describes a fourteenth-century psalter, originally belonging to the parish church of High Ongar.

It is therefore extremely fortunate that one relatively direct fertility measure is available for later-medieval Essex, and in fact this is perhaps unique for pre-1500 England as a whole. The source in question is a series of records, included in the fifteenth-century accounts of the churchwardens of Walden parish, of women purified or 'churched' after childbirth.[24] These records span a period of nearly half a century, from 1439 to 1488, though data for only relatively few years during this period actually survive.

The rationale for churching was rooted in the conviction, stemming ultimately from Mosaic law (Leviticus 12: 1–8) and apparently widespread in medieval popular attitudes, that after childbirth a mother remained in a state of spiritual impurity, which should bar her from entering church and to die in which might even imperil her soul. And so after a suitable interval, conventionally reckoned at one month after childbirth, the ceremony of purification not only cleansed away this impurity but also symbolically welcomed the mother back into the regular human community, thus rendering it an act of great social as well as religious significance.

The medieval church's attitude towards churching was ambivalent. On the one hand its official attitude was to discourage any imputing of spiritual impurity to the act of childbirth and at various times, from Gregory I to a papal decretal at the end of the twelfth century, the right of the mother to enter church immediately after giving birth was reaffirmed. On the other hand, though churching never attained the status of a sacrament, synodal statutes from several English dioceses from the thirteenth century onward reveal it to have been a regular part of parochial life. And as a sanctioned ceremonial custom it was deeply enough ingrained within popular English religious culture to survive the Reformation.[25]

In view of the deep strain of religious nonconformity in this district of northern Essex in the late middle ages (discussed below, Chapter 12), it must also be noted that, just as churching was harshly condemned by the more zealous Protestant reformers of the sixteenth and seventeenth centuries, so too was it one of the many ceremonies of the

Births and deaths of several families were entered into this book during much of the fifteenth century, by which time the book belonged to one of the families involved.

24 ERO D/DBy Q12. The author is grateful to Dr Jeremy Boulton for bringing these records to his attention, and for discussing their data with him.

25 Thomas, *Religion and the decline of magic*, pp. 42–3, 68–9; Gasquet, *Parish life*, p. 193; Heath, *English clergy*, p. 8; von Arx, 'The churching of women'; Payer, *Sex and the penitentials*, pp. 26, 35–6; decretal X 3.47.1, printed in Friedberg, ed., *Corpus Juris Canonici* vol. ii, c. 652; Powicke and Cheney, eds., *Councils and synods* vol. ii, pp. 80, 154, 272, 336, 512, 1116. The author is grateful to Fr Michael Sheehan for the last two references.

Church to fall under the scorn of fifteenth-century Lollards. Though less common than dissenting positions concerning the sacraments proper, objections specifically to churching – directed against paying fees to clergy for performing the rite, apparently, rather than against its underlying rationale as such – are occasionally found in surviving Lollard literature. One example is contained among the heretical opinions imputed in 1389 to William Ramsbury, a Lollard 'priest' active in the diocese of Salisbury: 'Item that no one should pay in church for ... purification of women ... and those who do this are excommunicated from God'.[26] Though no statement of this kind has been located for fifteenth-century Essex, the possibility that such objections may have resulted in some births at Walden not being followed by an entry in the churching records makes it all the more imperative to try to assess whether Walden's churching data appear to constitute a credible reflection of fertility.

Scattered anecdotal references to this ceremony's observance in later-medieval Essex can be found in testimony rendered at proof-of-age inquests, a source whose interpretation is discussed below (Chapter 9). Several witnesses in fourteenth- or fifteenth-century inquests claimed to have remembered events years earlier because they coincided with the churching of their wives or other female relatives. John de Heiham, for example, recalled that one day in 1309 at Great Sampford 'his wife and his wife's daughter were purified of two sons'.[27] And in four instances from the early fifteenth century, Essex witnesses provided the dates of both birth and subsequent churching, separated by intervals of 24, 28, 32 and 39 days, fairly close to the notional optimum of one month.[28]

[26] Printed in Hudson, 'A Lollard mass', p. 121, from Salisbury reg. Waltham fo. 222: 'Item quod nullus debet offerre in ecclesia in exequijs mortuorum, purificacionibus mulierum, solempnitatibus nubencium; et si qui hoc fecerint, sunt excommunicati a Deo'. A statement to the same effect is found in a recantation from 1428 in Salisbury reg. Neville ii (WRO D1/2/9) fo. 32: 'I John Upton ... knowlyche here before yow alle y[t] I ... have made an ordinaunce ... to wythdraw ayenst ye determinacion of holy cherche ... as in wythdrawynge of offerynge in puryficacion of women ... and in sponsall of men and women ...' The author is extremely grateful to Dr Anne Hudson for these references, and for discussing the subject with him.

[27] PRO.C135.33.13 (inquest, 6 Apr 1332): '... dicit quod uxor eius & filia uxoris eius purificate fuerunt de duobus filiis in crastino Purificationis beate Marie ...'.

[28] E.g. PRO.C139.13.52 (inquest, 10 Jun 1424): '[Thomas Holmwode] ... dicit quod ipse Thomas & Johanna uxor sua fuerunt apud Thorp' predictam [i.e. Thorpe-le-Soken] tempore quo prefata Johanna mater predicti Walteri filij se levavit a puerperio ipsius Walteri filij & fecit purificationem suam pretextu nativitatis eiusdem Walteri filij videlicet in festo nativitatis Sancti Johannis Baptiste dicto anno tercio Regis Henrici quarti ...'. [i.e. 24 Jun 1402, or 39 days after the date, given earlier in the inquest, of the heir Walter's birth]; C139.7.54 (inquest, 31 May 1423), for a timelapse of 28 days; C139.13.51 (inquest, 22 Feb 1424), 24 days; C139.31.72 (inquest, 13 Mar 1427), 32 days.

The only modern study to date of churching in England in its cultural, religious and demographic contexts is Boulton's work on the parish of St Saviour's, Southwark, in the early seventeenth century.[29] In this instance nominative records of churchings could be compared with 732 baptisms entered into the parish register. Boulton was able to show that for most women in this parish, churching succeeded childbirth by roughly a month, as in the few cases from medieval Essex where the interval can be recovered. More importantly, in Southwark in the early 1600s, adherence to the rite was remarkably strong. Between 1619 and 1625, 92.6 per cent of women whose children's baptisms were entered in the parish register subsequently were recorded as having been churched, and 'observance was widespread right across the social structure'.[30]

The Walden churchwarden's accounts took as their accounting year the interval between one Easter Monday and the next, and so the 'year' of account varied in actual length as measured in days from year to year, though the variation is relatively slight.[31] Records of churching took two forms. For each of 17 years between 1439/40 and 1487/8, a straightforward sum of money was recorded, representing the fees received by the parish church for performing the ceremonies over the course of the year.[32] For six of these same years, the account book also includes a list of the names of women churched, in two cases on a week-by-week basis over the course of the liturgical calendar.[33]

It is not strictly possible to convert the simple aggregate sums of money into numbers of women churched. This is because although, as the nominative lists make clear, more than three-quarters of the 238 women recorded in these six years paid 1d. for the ceremony, some paid ½d. or 2d., and two paid nothing, in one instance explicitly

29 Boulton, *Neighbourhood and society*, pp. 276–9. Cf. Schofield, 'Did the mothers really die?', pp. 240–1: in the Swedish Lutheran church from the later seventeenth century churching was actually required, aiding the study of mothers of stillborn children.

30 Boulton, *Neighbourhood and society*, p. 278. This percentage excludes women known to have died in childbirth; when these are included the figure is 91.7 per cent.

31 For the years in question, the 'accounting year' varied (depending upon the date on which Easter fell in any particular year) between 347 and 385 days, respectively 5.0 per cent shorter and 5.4 per cent longer than a modern 'average' year of 365.25 days.

32 E.g. ERO D/DBy Q12 fo. 15 (1441/2): 'Item est collez de femys que vyent alglyz pour puryfyr' – xvd. ob.'; fo. 27v (1444/5): 'Item recepta ex mulieribus in tempore purificationis earundem – xvjd.'; fo. 142v (1487/8): 'Item reseyvyd of ye wyvys for yer chyrche goyngg – ijs. iiijd.'. Other annual sums are given on fos. 42v, 47, 90v, 92v, 108v, 111v, 116v, 123v, 126v, 129v, 131v, 135v, 140.

33 *Ibid.*, fos. 3 (1439/40), 92v–94v (1474/5), 102–3 (1475/6), 132v (column 1 = 1484/5, columns 2 + 3 = 1485/6, dated by cross-referencing with yearly sums on fos. 131v and 135v), 136 (1486/7).

Table 6.3. *Churchings of women at Walden, 1439–88*

Year	Churching fees (total)	Women churched
1439/40	38½d.	[41][a]
1441/2	15½d.	
1444/5	16d.	
1452/3	15½d.	
1455/6	42d.	
1473/4	64d.	
1474/5	45½d.	51
1475/6	45d.	49
1476/7	37d.	
1477/8	31d.	
1481/2	33d.	
1482/3	38d.	
1483/4	37d.	
1484/5	28d.	36
1485/6	45d.	49
1486/7	32d.	38
1487/8	28d.	

Note: [a] For this accounting year, first a list of 15 women's names and their fees is given, then a further sum of 22½d. for other churchings is entered. A total of 41 is estimated on the premise that the women whose fees totalled 22½d. paid in the rough proportion of three-quarters (19) at 1d. and one-quarter (7) at ½d. (the proportion observed from all the lists with individual payments).
Source: ERO D/DBy Q12 (for folio references, see notes to text).

because she (or her husband) was 'poor'.[34] The money sums recorded thus cannot be multiplied straightforwardly by any simple per-churching fee to yield numbers of women, but since the fee varied within fairly narrow limits the total annual sums collected doubtless reflect numbers churched to a certain extent. Table 6.3 presents both sums of churching fees and numbers of women churched for the years where these data are available.

There were fairly wide year-to-year fluctuations in numbers churched, as would be expected in any relatively small population due to stochastic variations, and at any rate the small number of lists makes any conclusions drawn tentative. Frequency of churching constitutes

[34] Of the 238 women in these lists, 2 (0.8 per cent) paid nothing, 50 (21.0 per cent) paid ½d., 184 (77.3 per cent) paid 1d. and 2 (0.8 per cent) paid 2d. ERO D/DBy Q12 fo. 102 (1475/6): '... Et de purificatione uxoris Thome Colle eodem die nichil quia pauper'. Boulton, *Neighbourhood and society*, p. 277, notes that in early-seventeenth-century St Saviour's, also, fees varied.

a slight undercounting of birth frequency due to maternal mortality, though the margin of error due to this factor is likely to be quite small.[35] But if it can be presumed that these churchings reflect all or virtually all births in the parish of Walden, albeit at a lapse of one month or so, then in a strictly statistical sense it would be difficult to regard the series of annual totals from the nominative lists as anything but essentially horizontal over this interval of nearly half a century.[36] When fee totals are considered as a time series, a slight rise over the period is observable, but as already noted these totals constitute a less precise measure of actual churchings.[37]

If, then, as these data imply, annual birth totals at Walden were to all intents flat over the mid- and later fifteenth century, then this in turn raises several further possible interpretations. Either the population of the parish itself was essentially unchanged over the interval, and the crude birth rate (births per thousand of parochial population per annum) within the parish was also unchanged; or the parish population rose substantially but its crude birth rate declined; or the parish population fell substantially but its crude birth rate rose.

Unfortunately there is no direct means of estimating Walden's parochial population during the later middle ages, particularly since no 1377 poll-tax return survives for the place. The parish of Walden embraced not only the small market centre at its core but also a large surrounding area of dependent hamlets and open-field and enclosed agricultural land.[38] Its population was thus a composite of rural hinterland and commercialised core. But if Walden's demographic growth rates resembled to any extent the remarkably near-unanimous patterns of other nearby Essex communities, large and small, rural and

35 That is, mothers who died during or soon after childbirth obviously would not have appeared in subsequent records of churching. On the other hand, although no explicit evidence on this point appears in the Walden record, there seems no reason to believe that mothers whose children were stillborn or died shortly after birth would not have been churched, since the rationale for the rite was inherent in the act of childbirth itself. In Southwark between 1619 and 1625, of 732 baptisms, 7 women died in childbirth: Boulton, *Neighbourhood and society*, p. 277. In general, early-modern Swedish evidence is better than English records for maternal mortality. In five Swedish parishes in the later eighteenth and early nineteenth centuries, maternal mortality rates amounted to 7.8 per 1,000 births; for thirteen English parishes during 1550–99, approximate 'best estimate' is 9.3 per 1000: Schofield, 'Did the mothers really die?', pp. 240, 248. There is of course no reason to presume Walden was identical, but if maternal mortality there were as high as 20 per 1,000, churchings' underrepresentation of births due to this factor would amount to 2 per cent.

36 When linear regression is performed with year $= x$ (taking '1439/40' as 1439) and women churched $= y$, slope $= 0.008$, $r = 0.023$.

37 When linear regression is performed with year $= x$ and fees total $= y$, slope $= 0.282$ and $r = 0.383$.

38 Cromarty, *Fields of Saffron Walden*.

small-urban, for which tithing data survive, then its resident population was likely to have been essentially stationary over the course of the 1400s. It follows that Walden's crude fertility rate was also essentially unchanged over the same decades.

In the absence of direct population estimates it is, however, possible to construct a more indirect measure, even if with a probably fairly wide error margin, from Walden's sixteenth-century parish-register data and cross-reference to Wrigley and Schofield's national estimates for early-modern fertility. Surviving records of baptisms in Walden begin in 1559, and during the next 40 years (1559–98 inclusive) a mean of 87.7 baptisms was registered annually.[39] During this period – one of high rates of demographic growth – England's national crude birth rate was about 34 per 1,000 per annum.[40] So, if Walden mirrored this to any great extent, its Elizabethan parochial population totalled roughly 2,600.[41] And if, once more, the course of Walden's absolute population change over the preceding century resembled those of other Essex communities' tithing series, this would suggest that resident totals did not fall far short of doubling over that century, or that Walden possessed approximately 1,400–1,500 souls during the third quarter of the fifteenth century.[42] That would place the parish's crude birth rate – if its 44.0 churchings per annum represented virtually all local births – at around 30 per 1,000 per annum: in other words, quite close to the rate Wrigley and Schofield have calculated for England as a whole during the later seventeenth and early eighteenth centuries, the country's next prolonged demographic stagnation.[43] Such a roundabout means of estimating local population and fertility should not, of course, be taken literally, to imply a spurious precision. But it is worth noting that even if this projection of Walden's fifteenth-century crude birth rate falls short of the parish's actual experience by as much as 20 per cent, that still represents a fertility rate no higher than England's national average in the middle decades of the Tudor era.[44] In short, it is extremely difficult to regard Walden's fertility rates

39 ERO D/P 192/1/1; standard deviation = 11.98 (calendar years taken as in new style).

40 Wrigley and Schofield, *Population history of England*, p. 528: simple mean of quinquennial rates during 1561–96 = 33.68 per 1,000 per annum.

41 The formula is 1,000 × (observed births per year/crude birth rate); here, 1,000 × (87.7/33.68) = 2,604.

42 If the most continuous series over the relevant period, that of Margaret Roding, is taken as an example, mean numbers in tithing in 1438–88 (18 data points) = 13.8, in 1565–98 (8 data points) = 24.0, or an increase of 74 per cent.

43 Wrigley and Schofield, *Population history of England*, pp. 528–9: simple mean of quinquennial rates 1661–1721 (when compound growth rate, by the same mean, was 0.09 per cent per annum) = 30.82 per 1,000 per annum.

44 *Ibid.*, p. 528: simple mean of quinquennial rates in 1541–66 = 36.62.

during the later 1400s as a component of a different demographic system from that of England at large in the early-modern era.

It would clearly be mistaken to imply that Walden's fertility experience, or that mortality in High Easter, Great Tey and Great Waltham, was paradigmatic of all communities thoughout the region. Nevertheless, their data provide a rare and critically important empirical basis for understanding the puzzle of local demography during the period. Once more and from two rather different varieties of evidence, the picture that the tithing data paint of essential stasis is substantiated. On the basis of these data stationary population, until well beyond the turn of the fifteenth and sixteenth centuries, was the product of both mortality and fertility that themselves did not change appreciably for most of the 1400s.

The preceding analysis constitutes something more akin to the social scientist's 'thought experiment' – a researchable, postulated outcome to a series of general-order estimates – than to a precise recovery of empirical reality.[45] And the ultimate test of such an analysis (in this case, of the plausibility of these derived estimates of demographic variables) lies in the estimates' mutual compatibility with observed outcome. In fact, once more on the basis of Princeton Model West model populations, the combination of a life expectancy at birth of slightly more than 32 years, plus a fertility level no higher than that which England possessed in the later seventeenth century, is virtually precisely calibrated to produce zero population growth.[46] In other words, the estimates of mortality and fertility produced above from very different bodies of evidence add up in comparative demographic terms to a plausible scenario with a result identical to the late-medieval Essex population equilibrium.

Another way to visualise this thought experiment is to place it into the context of England's post-medieval demographic history. Figure 6.1 depicts the combined effects of English fertility and mortality changes between 1551 and 1861, and attempts to place estimates

45 McCloskey, *Econometric history*, esp. pp. 16–18, 61–76, contains a witty, elegant and brief discourse on the nature of 'thought experiments' in economic history.

46 Under Princeton Model West assumptions at mortality level 6, intrinsic demographic growth rate will be zero if male $e_0 = 30.07$ years and Gross Reproduction Rate (GRR) = 2.077. The corresponding values for mortality level 7 are male $e_0 = 32.48$ years and GRR = 1.939: Coale and Demeny, *Regional model life tables*, pp. 110–11. (This growth rate assumes that mean age at maternity = 29 years.) In England at large during 1651–96, $e_0 = 33.82$ years and GRR = 1.990: Wrigley and Schofield, *Population history of England*, p. 528 (simple arithmetic mean of quinquennial rates during period in question).

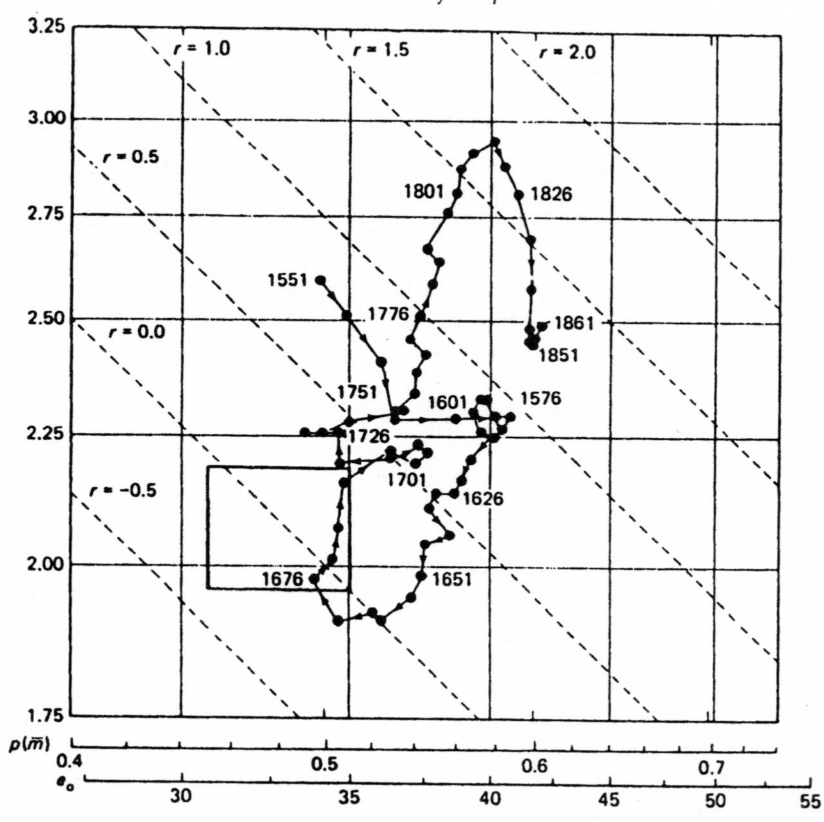

Figure 6.1. The demographic terrains of early-modern England and later-medieval Essex

Note: Y-axis scaling is Gross Reproduction Rate. X-axis scaling is e_o (life expectancy at birth) or alternatively $p(\bar{m})$ (where $\bar{m}$ is mean age at maternity and p is the probability of survival to that age). Diagonal lines represent r (intrinsic growth rate, per cent per annum). The joined dots illustrate combined effects of female English fertility and mortality upon intrinsic growth rates (five-point moving averages of quinquennial data) for England 1551–1861. The box at lower left represents the demographic terrain implied by fifteenth-century Essex data.

Source: Adapted from Wrigley and Schofield, *Population history of England*, p. 243. For further details see text and notes.

derived from later-medieval Essex within this perspective. With some minor simplifications, the figure's axes are scaled so as to be isometric with respect to intrinsic population growth (r): that is, a given horizontal distance across the graph from left to right (increasing e_o) has the same effect in raising intrinsic growth rate as the same distance from bottom to top (increasing GRR, or gross reproduction rate).[47] The figure displays combinations of mortality and fertility that England's early-modern population exhibited in the form of joined data points. The smaller box depicts, with quite generous error margins, the demographic terrain implied by the late-medieval Essex data.[48] The results are suggestive, for they imply that the Essex demographic equilibrium represents a modest deviation from England's post-medieval population regime. They would also imply that the district's population broke free of that equilibrium much more by way of increasing fertility than via a major improvement in life expectancy in the early 1500s.

Beyond this, statistical simulation can hardly be pressed further with evidence presently available. But thus stated, the Essex data suggest that the 150 years after the Black Death represent a further cyclical phase of somewhat higher mortality and lower fertility than the century and a half that followed. It is, in short, difficult to regard the district's demographic equilibrium as a product of a definitively high-pressure fertility regime constantly striving, but failing, to overcome the positive check of disease-driven high mortality. Instead, the district's demography resembles a variation – differing only in relative degree and not in fundamental typology – upon England's early-modern demographic system. Moreover, the Essex evidence strongly suggests that constraints upon fertility were a result of social-structural restrictions upon nuptiality in the later-medieval Essex countryside.

[47] This figure is adapted from Wrigley and Schofield, *Population history of England*, p. 243; its derivation is discussed in more detail *ibid.*, pp. 238–45. In particular, it should be noted that e_0 graphed here represents female life expectancy, approximated by adding 1.5 years to the authors' estimates of e_0 for both sexes taken together.

[48] The box is bounded by $e_0 = 31$ and 35 years, and by values for GRR such that the line representing $r = 0.0$ bisects the box (to denote stationary population). If anything, the box's position errs conservatively, in the direction of lower e_0 and higher GRR than was probably the case in Essex. This is because, in order to be strictly comparable to the early-modern data graphed here (which pertain to female life expectancy), the male Essex data should be increased by up to three years: Wrigley and Schofield, *Population history of England*, pp. 241–2. In Princeton Model West stable populations, mortality level 7, $r = 0.0$, a crude birth rate of 30.79 per 1,000 per annum (consonant with the Walden churching data) corresponds with GRR = 1.939: Coale and Demeny, *Regional model life tables*, p. 111.

PART IV

'While it is so forward between us'

Johanna Corney to her intended husband, Rayleigh, 1488[1]

Migration, settlement, marriage and household formation were processes central to the social structure of the district's population during the later middle ages. Propensity to move or marry, and the ages at which people did so, were personal demographic experiences that differed among different social or occupational groups in the Essex countryside. And the objective measures of these demographic experiences that are available from the district constitute the least ambiguous indices by which late-medieval Essex countryfolk mirrored the lives of their early-modern counterparts.

Marriage was a process with many legal and qualitative or experiential implications. Most importantly from the demographic perspective, it represented the inception of a new household, and thus the accumulation of the material means that made neolocal marriage possible. But in a rural society marked by persistent disparity between richer and poorer at village level, nuptiality varied between occupational subgroups. And so for agriculturalists, marriage was an experience likely to occur earlier in life, or more likely to occur at all, than was the case for craftsmen and retailers, and the differences between agriculturalists and labourers in these respects were even more marked. In short, for all people in the district nuptiality was linked with living standards, while still generally falling, as closely as the available evidence allows one to observe, within the realm of what historical demographers term the 'Northwestern European marriage pattern'.

Only a minority of people in the Essex countryside at the end of the middle ages spent their entire lives residing in a single parish. In fact,

[1] GL MS 9065 fo. 52v; see also below, Chapter 7.

population turnover rates here were already, on the eve of the Black Death, so high as to be virtually indistinguishable from analogous measures calculated for early-modern England. But like marriage, mobility varied greatly by occupation or status, and also by age. For all, the late teens and twenties were the most mobile phases of the life cycle. Agriculturalists were most likely to remain in their parish of birth, labourers least likely. Of those who moved, on the other hand, agriculturalists were likely to settle in a new parish at the highest age, craftsmen at the lowest, reflecting the contrasting circumstances necessary for the respective groups to find niches within the local economy.

Marriage and migration were aspects of demographic behaviour, then, that complemented one another. Both, that is to say, were dimensions of each new generation's fitting itself into the interstices of the district's society and geography.

7

Marriage and household formation

Marriage in rural Essex at the end of the middle ages was a multi-faceted experience. For one thing, rather than a discrete action at a given point in time it was a process with successive stages, that might (or might not, depending upon the participants' predilections and circumstances) draw in friends, neighbours, relatives and ecclesiastical authorities.[1] It was a process with wide legal ramifications ranging from defining the validity of the union itself to affecting the transmission of property. It was moreover a critical lynchpin in demographic processes, signalling the inception of a new family unit and of legitimised procreative careers.

Late-medieval canon law had evolved a conception of marriage based upon the free consent of partners who had attained legal minimum age and who were without inhibiting ties of consanguinity or previous contracts to others.[2] A regular union was to proceed through espousal or 'trothplight', publication of banns in the parish church to help ensure the detection of impediments if such existed, and finally nuptial solemnisation with exchange of vows, again at the church and in the presence of clergy. Nevertheless, unions formed either by the couple's free consent, regardless of parental or seigneurial wishes, and expressed by exchange of vows in the present tense, or alternatively by mutual promise of future marriage followed by sexual intercourse, were also regarded at canon law as legally binding though 'clandestine' and irregular. This potentially uneasy dichotomy between the private or individual and the public – the latter often

1 This point is especially emphasised by Smith, 'Marriage processes'. Accounts, albeit somewhat impressionistic, of this process are given in Homans, *English villagers*, pp. 160–76; Hanawalt, *The ties that bound*, pp. 188–204; Bennett, *Women in the medieval countryside*, pp. 91–9.

2 Helmolz, *Marriage litigation*; Sheehan, 'Choice of marriage partner'; Sheehan, 'Formation and stability of marriage'; Donahue, 'Canon law on the formation of marriage'.

sealed by an exchange of gifts in the presence of witnesses and a feast or other collective social occasion – has led to considerable debate among historians as to whether ecclesiastical imposition of discipline or conformity upon common people's marriage practices was successful in lessening clandestine marriage on the eve of the Reformation.[3]

Various difficulties of evidence stand in the way of any clear understanding of this issue. One of the most tangible records of marriage among medieval English villagers is the entries into manorial court rolls of merchet, the payment for seigneurial sanction for the marriage of servile women.[4] These records have enabled historians to reconstruct the constellation of kinship ties and property settlements that might accompany villagers' marriages, and also to demonstrate the often considerable degree of geographical exogamy among these same marriages.[5] This evidence does, however, relate disproportionately to the upper levels of village society, whose marriages were especially likely both to attract seigneurial scrutiny and to involve land settlements onto the marrying couple.[6] Merchet records, moreover, fade from the court rolls of most Essex manors in the later fourteenth century, one sign of the waning of personal serfdom.[7]

Depositions rendered during matrimonial litigation in ecclesiastical courts, on the other hand, while often providing vivid insight into the social or experiential background to marriage vows, are often problematic evidence precisely because they deal with marriages whose establishment or legitimacy subsequently came to be questioned. By far the greatest number of surviving Essex marriage cases, and apparently the majority of marriage cases in pre-Reformation English ecclesiastical courts generally, were civil suits brought by one of the parties in what the plaintiff believed had been a binding exchange of clandestine vows (rather than a promise of future mar-

3 This debate is discussed by Smith, 'Marriage processes', pp. 47–52, 69–78, and Smith, 'Origins of the "European marriage pattern"', pp. 88–90.

4 Searle, 'Seigneurial control of women's marriage'. It should be noted here that it was not strictly possible for a lord to prevent a canonically valid marriage from taking place, since at canon law (as already stated) seigneurial or parental permission was not required; merchet is usually regarded, rather, as a combination of a tax upon villein marriages and a tax upon land transfers which potentially followed upon such marriages.

5 E.g. Bennett, 'The tie that binds'; Bennett, 'Medieval peasant marriage'; Poos, 'Population and resources', pp. 159–82.

6 Poos and Smith, 'Legal windows onto historical populations', pp. 144–8. For remarkable evidence from Norfolk (parallels to which have not been found in Essex) of direct seigneurial coercion into choice of villeins' marriage partners, see Clark, 'The decision to marry'.

7 Poos, 'Population and resources', p. 170; cf. Razi, *Life, marriage and death in a medieval parish*, p. 132; Hilton, *Decline of serfdom*, pp. 33, 42; Faith, 'Seigneurial control of women's marriage', p. 147.

riage), which the plaintiff was seeking to enforce.[8] It is difficult to discern any unilineal trend toward more universally 'orthodox' (in canonical terms) entry into marriage during the period, or indeed to insist upon any one particular paradigm of individualistic and private versus collectivist and public marriage in actual practice. Individual experiences differed considerably.

It is also very difficult, from a survey of the available evidence, to regard matrimony in fifteenth-century Essex as an institution entered into lightly or with little regard to the binding implications of consensual union.[9] Even the Lollards of the region, who spread heretical doctrines concerning the institution of marriage during the 1400s, were more concerned with undermining the sacramental authority of clergy over the institution than with debasing the notion of marriage itself.[10] While couples recognised that they were permitted to enter marriage of their own free will and with little ceremony or forethought, this freedom was by no means incompatible with a desire to secure the assent of parents or other relatives or friends, at least in cases where the spouses' parents were still alive and residing in close proximity to the couple.[11] Upon familial approval might also depend any endowment of moveable goods or especially land which the couple might hope to receive, though in Essex during this period (because of the patterns of property distribution already discussed) significant endowments in land could have been anticipated in only a minority of rural marriages. The entire process from inception of courtship, through securing whatever familial or other consent was felt desirable, and espousal or mutual promises, to solemnisation or exchange of binding vows could extend over a considerable time. During fourteenth-century inquests to prove the ages of feudal heirs,

8 Donahue, 'Canon law on the formation of marriage'; Smith, 'Marriage processes', pp. 75–8.

9 For discussion of the opinion held by some historians that such was the case, see Smith, 'Origins of the "European marriage pattern"', p. 88; Smith, 'Marriage processes', pp. 52–69.

10 On this point see below, Chapter 12.

11 It is important to recognise the potential magnitude of both of these qualifications. Migration was most pronounced in late-medieval Essex, as in early-modern England, in the youthful age groups; see below, Chapter 8. In early-modern England it has been estimated that by the time they married, up to one-third of all unmarried girls had lost one of their parents, and up to one-fifth has lost both: Laslett, 'Parental deprivation in the past'. Recently Bennett has examined 426 merchet payments on Ramsey Abbey manors from the late fourteenth to the mid-fifteenth centuries, noting that a large proportion of these fines were paid by the brides themselves (rather than their fathers) and interpreting this as evidence of independent economic establishment by the women in question. While this is undoubtedly correct, parental death before daughters' marriages would have accounted for a proportion of these cases also. Bennett, 'Medieval peasant marriage'.

witnesses, some of whom claimed to recall the heir's birth date because the witness had been married at the same time as the birth, distinguished espousal from final wedding in their reminiscences: in 1329 at Tolleshunt, Ralph atte Stokk 'affianced [*affidavit*] Johanna daughter of Ralph Page to marry her', in 1347 at Little Laver, Richard Hunte 'espoused [*desponsavit*] Margaret his first wife', while in 1339 at Springfield, Edmund Lyon 'married [*duxit in uxorem*] Alice ... John Hunte's servant'.[12]

One remarkable case heard in the London diocese consistory court in 1489 touches upon a number of these points.[13] In December of the previous year, at John Pike's house in the parish of Rayleigh, John Corney asked his daughter Johanna whether she had agreed to marry Robert Philipson. Corney was clearly opposed to the match, and she fearful of his displeasure: she replied 'I[n] feith I have made him a

[12] PRO.C135.111.9 (inquest, 24 Mar 1350): '... affidavit Johannam filiam Radulphi Page ducendum eam in uxorem ...'; PRO.C135.211.2 (inquest, 11 Jun 1369): '... desponsavit Margaretam primam uxorem suam ...'; PRO.C135.155.9 (inquest, 8 Mar 1360): '... duxit in uxorem quandam Aliciam filiam Johannis Pese tunc servientem predicti Johannis Hunte ...'. The reliability of these inquests as evidence for social history is considered below, Chapter 9.

[13] This case is sufficiently important to warrant reproducing the major portions of the testimony here:

GL MS 9065 fo. 52v (deposition of Thomas Ame): 'Ad primum & secundum articulos dicti libelli dicit quod quodam die contingente infra quindenam proximam post festum Epiphanie domini ultimum preteritum prefati Robertus et Johanna stando prope quandam sepem in campo vocato Coxslond in parochia de Raylegh communicaverunt ... iste juratus intendens ire ad molendinum in dicto campo transivit prope eosdem et ... audivit dictam Johannam dicentem eidem Roberto Robert While it is so forward as it is betwene us I pray you let us be weddid for I shal have much anger specielly w[t] my dame qui respondit eidem by my feith Johan I wil wedd you fortnyght afor Witsontyde next or fornyght aftir ...'.

GL MS 9065 fo. 53 (deposition of John Heard): 'Ad iij et iiij articulos dicit quod quodam die Mercurij parvo ante festum Natalis domini ultimum preteritum quem diem aliter specificare nescit presens fuit iste juratus in domo Johannis Pike de Raylegh una cum Johanne Pike Johanne Corney patre dicte Johanne & dicta Johanna ubi & quo dicta Johanna interrogata per prefatum Johannem Corney utrum contraxit matrimonium cum Roberto Philipson dixit eidem quod sic I feith I have made him a promise thou hast made no suche bargyn I trow but I know of hit I owgt to know of hit Et medio tempore supervenit dictus Robertus et in eius presencia dixit dicta Johanna eidem Roberto I made you promise but on my faders good will dicto Roberto contrarium asserente et dicit quod dictus Johannes Corney citra recessum suum ultimum a civitate London' dixit huic jurato I love not the law I wil not let them et postea banna fuerunt edita inter eosdem apud Raylegh uno die presente dicta Johanna et nemine contradicente et secunda vice dicta Johanna reclamavit ut communiter dicitur in dicta parochia mediis & instantiiis dicti patris sui Ad v[tum] articulum dicit quod dicto die mercurij dicta Johanna ostendebat tempore dicte communicationis xxxd. in auro unum parem cerothecarum & anulum argentum que fatetur ibidem se recepasse ab eodem Roberto ... et eadem obtulit dicto Roberto qui ea recipere recusat [sed?] dixit dictus Johannes Roberd and you wil take them ageyn it shal never be the wors for you ...'.

promise, thou hast made no suche bargyn I trow but I know of hit, I owgt to know of hit.' To Robert, who arrived during this exchange, she explained 'I made you [a] promise, but on my faders good will.' The deponent who recalled this conversation in court also remembered hearing Johanna's father say on another occasion, 'I love not the law, I wil not let them'. Robert had also given Johanna gifts – 30d. in cash, a silver ring and other items – which she tried to return to him but which he refused. Yet several weeks later the couple were still intending to proceed. Another witness recalled coming upon them as they stood out in a field, Johanna appealing to her intended, 'Robert While it is so forward as it is betwene us I pray you let us be weddid, for I shal have much anger, specielly w^{t} my dame.' Robert replied, 'by my feith Johan, I will wedd you fortnyght afor Witsontyde next or fornyght aftir'. And at some point in the proceedings (it is not clear exactly when), banns were pronounced upon their intended union in Rayleigh church, but on their second reading 'Johanna renounced [them], as is commonly said in that parish, at the instance of her father'.

Several things remain unclear about this case, including whether Johanna and Robert ever succeeded in marrying. But the couple had gone through a courtship over at least several weeks and probably rather longer, during which tentative promises were given and which eventually became 'so forward'. This process was hardly an entirely private affair: one witness claimed that 'in the said vill of Rayleigh and other places, Robert and Johanna are reputed to be persons mutually affianced'.[14] Both they and (to his displeasure) her father knew they were legally entitled to marry if they wanted to, but she at least was unwilling to flout parental opinion entirely, in the absence of a 'bargyn' (a formal agreement including endowment, or simply consent, or even mere tacit acquiescence?) between her father and her intended. Whether the 'dame' whose anger she dreaded was her mother, or was her mistress and Johanna her servant, is also uncertain.

In the process of negotiating matrimony relatives and friends were sometimes enlisted as go-betweens. In 1492 at Walthamstow, John Fynk appealed to his intended's brother: 'Thow haste a sister tanggild w^{t} a knave, I wuld that thow cuddyd rede her frome hym and I wuld maryer my selff, and yff so that thou canne doo itt thow shall not steke for no good frend of myn.'[15] Two years earlier at Stratford Langthorne,

14 GL MS 9065 fo. 52v: '. . . in dicta villa de Raylegh et aliis locis dicti Robertus et Johanna reputantur persone adinvicem affidate . . .'.

15 GL MS 9065 fo. 149.

John Arnold gave Martin Braknale a rosary and a groat coin, 'which [Martin] was to deliver to Marian [Filders], because John desired Marian to make as good a promise as she could, since his neighbours did not want marriage to be solemnised with her, and she replied that she intended to keep the promise that she had made'. Yet half a year later Martin's mother was urging John 'that he make an end to the marriage contracted between them'.[16]

And during the course of these protracted courtship fugues, unscrupulous (or exasperated) suitors might sometimes stoop to sexual slander. When William Marks was pursuing Alice Brigge at Salcott in 1494, the couple met with two of his friends on his behalf and two other men on Alice's, 'named and chosen to hear and oversee the matrimonial undertaking [*negocium matrimoniale*] that William Marks claimed he had contracted with Alice'. But she was unwilling, and William responded by claiming to have had sex with her: 'Be cause she wold not have me, ther for I seid I lay by her, that she shuld be loth to any othir man.'[17]

The majority of these matrimonial suits in the surviving ecclesiastical-court records involving Essex people revolved around what must be classified as clandestine or irregular marriages, usually with the couple exchanging vows in a private house in the presence of a few friends. But their apparent prominence in these records should not be taken to imply that such unions were necessarily the majority experience, though they may in fact have been. Rather, these marriages were conceivably more likely to result in later disagreement and thus litigation than those marriages that followed the prescribed, more public course. As Smith has shown in the case of a similar series of matrimonial suits from Ely diocese in the later 1300s, clandestine

[16] GL MS 9065 fo. 139: '. . . presens fuit iste juratus in domo patris sui ubi & quo dictus Johannes Arnold dedit isti jurato unum parem preculanum & unum grossum quod deliberaret dicte Marione et quod idem J' desideravit eandem Marionam quod faceret tam bonam promisionem pro ipsa sicut scit quia vicini sui nolunt quod matrimonium non solemnisaret cum ea et ipsa respondivit quod tale promissum quod ipsa promisit cum eo vellet custodire & circiter dimidum annum proximum sequentem iste juratus presens fuit in domo proprio suo & audivit quod mater sua dixit dicto Johanne quod faceret finem pro matrimonio inter eos contracto . . .'.

[17] GL MS 9065 fo. 184: '. . . presens fuit iste juratus in domo Johanne Bisshop vidue infra dictam parochiam de Salcote situata una cum Galfrido Dalling Ricardo Badock Johanne Palmer Johanne Brigge dicta vidua quodam cognominato Stobbard & aliis ubi & quo iste juratus & Johannes Palmer pro parte dicte Alicie & Galfridus Dalling & Ricardus Badock pro parte dicti Willelmi nominati & electi ad audiendum & exercendum negocium matrimoniale quod idem Willelmus Marks asserebat se cum dicta Alicia contraxisse Et tandem post aliquod tractatum dictus Willelmus dixit quod voluit habere dictam Aliciam in uxorem & ipsa noluit ut tunc iste juratus interrogavit eandem querentem erga prius diffamavit dictam Aliciam super fornicationem cum eo ut dicebat commissam . . .'.

marriages contested in ecclesiastical courts could have accounted for only a minuscule fraction of all unions taking place within the diocese over the period in question.[18] And not even those 'private' unions that were subsequently contested in court were wholly private, without the presence of friends or neighbours, nor did they invariably lack an element of collective social occasion.

John Arnold and Marian Filders, whose courtship has already been observed, finally exchanged vows in the house of John Hayward at Stratford Langthorne and in the presence of Hayward and his wife:

> . . . after discussion between John Arnold and Marian about contracting marriage between them, John said to Marian, 'May ye nott fynd in your hert to love me as I may fynd in myn to love yow?'
>
> And she answered . . . 'on a condicon, that ye may do the same to me'.
>
> And immediately after, John put his hand in Marian's, saying, 'I John take ye Marion to my wyff, all other to forsake, and therto I plygte the my trouth.'
>
> And then she said similarly to John, 'I Marion take the John to my husband, and therto I plygte the myn trouth.'[19]

Similar scenarios are repeated in more than half a dozen other Essex cases in the surviving church-court records of the later fifteenth century.[20] In the parlour of a house at Bowers Gifford in 1462, one husband sealed the couple's vows with a gift of a gold ring.[21] At another exchange of vows in a house at East Ham in 1476, a deponent remembered, all the witnesses present 'drank ale and ate bread and cheese, of other victuals he does not recall'.[22] At least at the higher echelons of village society, whether a marriage was solemnised *in facie ecclesie* or not, the scale of these collective celebrations might be impressive: in 1468 in Writtle's manor court, Henry Turnor brought a suit of broken agreement against his father-in-law John Baconn, claiming that when he had married Baconn's daughter Anna, Baconn had promised to pay half the nuptial expenses for clothing and drink, his half amounting (so Turnor asserted) to the substantial sum of 35s. 5½d.[23]

18 Smith, 'Origins of the "European marriage pattern"', p. 88.

19 GL MS 9065 fo. 138.

20 GLRO DL/C/205 fos. 86v–87v, 138, 266v–267v, 269v–270v, 271–272, 272v–274; see also Chapter 4, above. It should be emphasised that these cases are not amenable to any quantitative analysis, for example to convert them to a rough percentage of contested marriages to all marriages that were likely to have taken place within the diocese or county over the period these records cover; not only are the deposition records fragmentary (so yielding only a handful of cases) but the procedural and other records of matrimonial litigation in the diocese in the period are not extant, so it is impossible to recover the total number of such suits in the first place.

21 GLRO DL/C/205 fo. 138.

22 GLRO DL/C/205 fo. 270; cf. *ibid*. fo. 87

23 ERO D/DP M270 m.2 (Writtle court, 7 May 1468): '. . . dicit quod ubi ipse Henricus xx° die Aprilis anno regni regis nunc vij cepit in uxorem Annam filiam eiusdem Johannis

Qualitative evidence of marriage processes in this period and district is admittedly sparse and impressionistic, and heavily weighted toward clandestine unions. The picture that emerges from these scenarios, however, is of a popular culture of marriage that generally recognised the gravity and perdurance of unions formed by mutual vows, even when these were not entered in the canonically optimal manner. Indeed, popular culture coincided with canon law in so far as the latter was willing to recognise the former in its definitions of valid matrimony despite its opposition to clandestineness. Though it would be unrealistic to presume that adultery or spouse-abandonment never occurred, there is little evidence that either was sufficiently widespread to undermine the institution seriously.[24] Moreover, even at fairly humble levels of society and even in the case of clandestine marriages that subsequently found their way into litigation, matrimony was customarily undertaken via a series of stages, in many cases entailing successive degrees of mutual commitment and the knowledge and approval of relatives and acquaintances.[25] This relatively

conventum inter predictum Henricum & prefatum Johannem quod ipse Johannes inveniret eisdem Henrico & Anne ad nuptias suas medietatem omnium expensorum ad dictas nupcias factorum & habitorum ut in apparatu vestimentis & aliis necessariis eiusdem Anne & medietatem conbinij ad nupcias predictas que quidam medietas omnium dictorum expensorum extendent ad summam xxxvs. vd. obulum et incontinenti post maritagium predicte Anne ipse Henricus venit ad predictum Johannem & ipsum requisivit se acquietare de predictis xxxvs. vd. obulo . . . tamen eum acquietare noluit . . .'. Little is known about the nature of these marriage celebrations in medieval rural England generally: cf. Smith, 'Marriage processes', pp. 67–9; Homans, *English villagers*, pp. 172–3; Bennett, *Women in the medieval countryside*, pp. 93–4.

[24] In the absence of surviving records from rural deanery or other varieties of ecclesiastical courts exercising jurisdiction over morals in this region during the later middle ages this impression must remain tentative. Evidence from other sources is very sparse. In a somewhat earlier period, and perhaps significantly from a manor with an ecclesiastical lordship, comes what appears to be the closest thing to an extant trace from a medieval Essex manorial court of direct seigneurial intervention in tenants' matrimonial affairs (apart, of course, from merchet fines), and even here the issue appears to centre more upon securing the continuing viability of a customary tenement: Bodl. Essex Rolls 8 (Little Leighs court, 12 Jun 1314): 'Willelmus Carectarius qui desponsavit Agnetem relictam Willelmi Bryan' custumari prioris calumpnatus est ad istam curiam de hoc quod non residet cum uxore sua predicta super terram custumariam qui ponit se in gratiam Prioris Et concessa est eidem licencia de gratia Prioris & Conventus quod non calumpniabitur commorare super eandem terram custumariam usque ad legitimam etatem heredum'. Other evidence, such as the abjuration of adultery by a Great Waltham man in 1372 (Fowler, ed., *Registrum Simonis de Sudbiria* i, p. 223), is equally rare. For a slightly more pessimistic view of rural marriage's perdurability, albeit in a somewhat earlier period, cf. Bennett, *Women in the medieval countryside*, pp. 100–2.

[25] There has, however, been debate about exactly which stage was believed in popular culture and customary law to constitute the binding or irrevocable step in this process: cf. Smith, 'Marriage processes', pp. 57–69; Homans, *English villagers*, pp. 168–70. This uncertainty need not in itself, however, undermine the impression that that same popular culture did regard the outcome of this process as binding.

deliberate quality of the popular marriage process is all the more striking in view of the fact that only a minority of rural marriages in Essex during this period could have entailed significant settlements of landed property, which (so medieval social historians have customarily been predisposed to believe) were the major incentive for strategic familial intervention into individuals' matrimonial experiences. This last point is of crucial importance in understanding how marriage in the aggregate was related to the local economy, household formation and general demographic circumstances during the later middle ages in Essex.

In much of preindustrial northwestern Europe, at least since the early-modern era, marriage coincided with household formation: that is, the founding of a new unit of co-residence, reproduction, consumption, and often to one degree or another of production, whether in the guise of an agriculturalist's landholding, a craftsman's workshop, or a labourer's establishment sustained with wages earned from others plus whatever alternative forms of income were obtained from petty artisanal by-employment or small-scale agrarian production.[26] This conjunction between marriage and household formation was the result of a deeply embedded cultural principle of neolocality, dictating that newly married couples set up their own households, and presupposing that the means to do so had been obtained before marriage could take place. A neolocal household-formation system also presupposes some degree of consciousness concerning material foundations for intended unions, with which the gradual, deliberate nature of late-medieval Essex marriage would seem congruent, although it can scarcely be put more strongly than that on the basis of evidence discussed so far.

If a neolocal principle obtained in any given historical society, one may envisage two alternative hypothetical systems which mediated between economic environment and household formation.[27] In one, which may be termed a 'peasant' or 'niche' model, the means to marry and form a new household were secured by acquiring a 'niche' in the local economy: a viable landholding with residence and requisite tools

[26] The classic statements of the role of this principle in Northwestern European household formation are Hajnal, 'European marriage patterns in perspective', esp. pp. 130–5; Hajnal, 'Two kinds of pre-industrial household', esp. pp. 68–71. Cf. Smith, 'Fertility, economy, and household formation', esp. pp. 599–602. Laslett has applied the term 'noumenal normative rules' to principles such as this one: Laslet, 'Demographic and microstructural history', pp. 354–5.

[27] The arguments of this and the next paragraph closely follow, in substance and largely in terminology, Schofield, 'The relationship between demographic structure and environment'.

and stock, or a craftsman's workshop similarly equipped and able to command sufficient clientele for operation. In situations where the number of these niches was confined below a fairly inelastic ceiling, access to the means to marry could usually be obtained only through the vacating of a niche by the death of its previous incumbent. Such a system is often described as homeostatic, in that upsurges in mortality are likely to spur upsurges in nuptiality (especially in the short term) in a rather direct manner. Autonomous mortality patterns would thus generally be the prime mover of such a system and would, depending upon the *absolute* values of key demographic variables, influence household formation in economically difficult times by suppressing nuptiality, raising ages at marriage, or forcing more people to spend their entire lifetimes unmarried.

Alternatively, a hypothetical opposite extreme, a 'proletarian' or 'real wages' system, may be envisaged in societies where economic differentiation was great and a well-developed market in wage labour with widespread geographical mobility was present. If strict neolocality were still the operating principle of household formation, persons without realistic expectation of 'niches' through inheritance, marriage, or purchase would need to accumulate the means to marry largely through employment. Nuptiality would therefore be highly sensitive to long-term economic changes, in particular the level of real wages, or more generally (and more difficult to define, let alone measure empirically) standards of living, and would be further mediated by a fairly diffuse mechanism of perceiving prospects for the immediate future.

There is no reason why both these systems could not coexist in any particular historical setting, with different elements of the population responding to different aspects of economic change in different ways and with different demographic consequences. The critical question is whether either model was dominant within a particular society.[28] It is generally agreed that preindustrial England since (at latest) the middle

[28] Recently Wrigley has usefully distinguished what he calls the 'tactics' of decisions affecting when or whether to marry – the immediate, short-term circumstances pertaining to an individual's or group's particular position – with the larger-scale 'strategy' that is apparent in broader measures of long-term aggregate behaviour. He observed that a single, persistent value for mean age at first marriage, for instance – a 'strategy' – can conceal considerable variations in short- or medium-term 'tactics' (and, one might add, between different status or occupation groups). Wrigley, 'The means to marry', p. 276. Levine's account of household formation in early-modern England essentially consists of a long-drawn-out process whereby the 'peasant' model gradually became less and less the modal experience at the same time as a 'proletarian' model (though Levine's understanding of this is rather different from the scheme sketched out here) gained importance: Levine, 'Production, reproduction and the proletarian family', p. 111.

of the sixteenth century is best described by the 'real wages' model. As Wrigley and Schofield have conclusively shown, nuptiality moved in broad, long-term cycles, mirroring the cycles of surrogate living-standards indices with a few decades' lagged response. And in early-modern England as a whole, nuptiality proved to be the most important determinant of fertility, exerting at least as much influence as mortality (and more influence as the early-modern period progressed) in setting the course of England's aggregate population change.[29] Nuptiality changes were effected by changes both in age at marriage and in proportions never marrying; in an important addition to Wrigley and Schofield's reconstruction, Weir was able to show that before 1700 changes in proportions never marrying exerted much greater impact upon overall fertility than changes in age at marriage.[30] And it should be emphasised here that it was women's marriage ages, much more than men's, that mattered in setting the perimeters of reproduction and thus the course of fertility patterns over time.

There has, however, been much debate about whether or how the nature of this 'preventive check' via nuptiality (to use Malthusian terminology) was changed by proletarianisation, the latter defined here simply as an increasing proportion of people becoming dependent upon wages earned through labour on other persons' land or for industrial entrepreneurs. Some have argued that by altering the logic of family or household economic strategies, especially through altering considerations surrounding the value of children's work, changes in the forms and institutions of wage labour also undermined the principle of accumulating resources before labouring couples' marriages could take place.[31] Freeing wage-earners from constraints upon nuptiality would tend to lower marriage ages, lower proportions never marrying, and generally raise the intrinsic demographic growth rate of wage-dependent people relative to other population subgroups. This is an argument usually made most forcefully in connection with protoindustrial workers,[32] but Tilly and

[29] Wrigley and Schofield, *Population history of England*, pp. 402–84; Lindert, 'English population, wages, and prices'; Lee, 'Population homeostasis and English demographic history'; Wrigley, 'The means to marry'.

[30] Weir, 'Rather never than late'; Schofield, 'English marriage patterns revisited'.

[31] These arguments and their ideological underpinnings are critically discussed in Smith, 'Fertility, economy, and household formation', pp. 611–15.

[32] Medick, 'The proto-industrial family economy'; Kriedte, Medick and Schlumbohm, *Industrialization before industrialization*, esp. pp. 38–93. These predictive theories of the demographic consequences of protoindustrialisation are critically reviewed in Houston and Snell, 'Proto-industrialization?', pp. 479–84.

Levine in particular have been willing to extend the argument to agricultural labourers, especially from the seventeenth century onward.[33]

It is empirically quite difficult to obtain occupation-specific nuptiality data from much of preindustrial Europe, largely due to problems of sources. What evidence is available does suggest that different occupational subgroups – especially labourers as compared with substantial farmers – did often differ in mean ages at first marriage, or perhaps even more importantly responded differently in this measure to economic changes over time. In fourteen German villages during the eighteenth and nineteenth centuries, both men and women among labourers and cottagers were virtually always older than their farmer counterparts at first marriage.[34] In the French province of Thimerais males and females among the labourers (*journaliers*) married somewhat earlier than larger farmers (*laboureurs*) in the early eighteenth century, but later in the 1700s, when marriage ages rose for both groups, labourers' ages at first marriage rose a great deal more, to stand slightly higher than those of farmers by 1789.[35]

Comparable data from early-modern England are less readily available, but a similar conclusion can be tentatively drawn. Parish-register data from Halifax (Yorks.) in the mid-seventeenth century and Shifnal (Shropshire) in the early eighteenth century show mean ages at marriage for both brides and bridegrooms rather higher – in the case of labourers by as much as five years – than in yeomen's or farmers' marriages.[36] In two larger samples drawn from marriage licences (a possibly less representative but more easily accessible source than parish registers) from several Midlands and southern counties the situation is less clear-cut for bridegrooms, but brides of labourers were still likely in several samples to be older when they married than brides of husbandmen or farmers.[37]

Nevertheless, for earlier centuries it would be hazardous to predict *a priori* any particular mathematical relationship between the marriage behaviours of different occupational or status groups without specific reference to a given society's labour institutions, family culture and local economy. And in all the early-modern settings discussed here,

[33] Tilly, 'Demographic origins of the European proletariat', esp. pp. 38–44; Levine, 'Production, reproduction and the proletarian family', esp. pp. 93–5, 104–15; Levine, *Reproducing families*, esp. pp. 38–93.

[34] Knodel, 'Demographic transitions in German villages', pp. 351–5.

[35] Derouet, 'Une démographie sociale différentielle', pp. 6–11, 41.

[36] Drake, *Historical demography*, pp. 71–6; Watts, 'Demographic facts in eighteenth-century Shifnal', p. 38.

[37] Outhwaite, 'Age at marriage in England', pp. 61–3.

differential marriage ages still remained within the limits set by the 'Northwestern European marriage pattern', first elaborated and recently restated by Hajnal. This marriage pattern consisted of neolocality, life-cycle servanthood, high proportions never marrying, and high ages at first marriage for both sexes – typically mid- to high twenties for men, early to mid-twenties for women – relative to other preindustrial settings.[38]

This much is reasonably clear for England from the beginning of parochial registration of vital events in the middle of the sixteenth century. Whether the England of a century or two earlier possessed an identical marriage and household-formation regime, or a wholly different one, or one intermediate between two forms, remains a critical problem. Much has been written in recent years about whether medieval rural England conformed to the 'Northwestern European marriage pattern', the recent statements by Razi and Hanawalt in particular being notably strongly sceptical that such was the case.[39] Other writers, however, albeit often on highly impressionistic grounds, have been more willing to consider later marriage and many lifetime-unmarrieds as features of the medieval landscape, Hallam claiming to observe 'prudential marriage' in the high middle ages and Russell speaking more generally of the various means by which 'the determination of a people to control the population' was effected.[40] But statements such as these have tended to concentrate rather singlemindedly upon age at marriage as being, in and of itself, the hallmark of such a marriage regime. At the same time, no source or methodology has yet been discovered that can conclusively yield reliable data for marriage ages in rural England before 1500.[41] But it is possible to approach the question in a somewhat more roundabout manner, by considering marriage in the broader context of household-formation systems.

On the topic of neolocality there has been quite broad agreement that marriage in medieval rural England did entail the establishment of a new unit, whose independent creation depended upon securing assets. This has, consciously or not, usually been envisaged by

38 Hajnal, 'European marriage patterns in perspective'; Hajnal, 'Two kinds of pre-industrial household'.

39 Razi, *Life, marriage and death in a medieval parish*, esp. pp. 50–64; Hanawalt, *The ties that bound*, pp. 90–104.

40 Hallam, *Rural England*, pp. 254–64; Russell, *The control of late ancient and medieval population*, pp. 219–20, 234.

41 Attempts to derive this measure from manorial material are epitomised by Razi, *Life, marriage and death in a medieval parish*, pp. 50–64, and Hallam, 'Age at marriage in the Lincolnshire Fenland'. These methods have been criticised by Poos and Smith, 'Legal windows onto historical populations', pp. 144–8.

medieval social historians as essentially the 'peasant' system outlined above, with acquisition of land as the key. This was a central aspect of the first attempted comprehensive sociological analysis of medieval village society, that by Homans almost a half-century ago. Homans drew strong connections between the non-inheriting and the lifetime-unmarried, though it has since been shown that Homans was mistaken concerning the demographic consequences of this principle.[42] Titow has more recently written about the plight of landless men in the village marriage competition during the decades around 1300, while Razi emphasised differential marital prospects between 'richer' and 'poorer' villagers, though he continued to believe that all married relatively young.[43] And studies of rural Essex in the later middle ages have similarly uncovered close connections between marriages and endowment with land for couples from the higher echelons of the tenentry.[44] In another context, arrangements in late-medieval Essex for retirement of elderly property holders that appear to incorporate stipulation of separate or at least quasi-independent household units (if not always 'housefuls') for elderly retirees and new tenants would also appear compatible with a neolocality principle.[45]

It is understandable that the 'peasant' model of neolocal household formation has informed so many of these discussions of medieval marriage to date, since manorial-court records, the primary source of greatest importance for reconstituting village society for the period, demonstrably tend to overemphasise the land and marital transactions of middling and upper ranks in village society, and are much less illustrative of landless labourers' activities.[46] This is not to deny that the 'peasant' variant of household formation may well be an accurate depiction of marriage behaviour among those with substantial land endowments, but merely to point out that in regions of

[42] Homans, *English villagers*, pp. 121–59; Smith, 'Some issues concerning families and their property', pp. 39–49; Poos and Smith, 'Legal windows onto historical populations', pp. 143–4.

[43] Titow, 'Some differences between manors'; Razi, *Life, marriage and death in a medieval parish*, pp. 58–60. Other recent discussions which embrace variants upon the neolocality principle, largely (though not exclusively) echoing the 'peasant' model, include Bennett, *Women in the medieval countryside*, esp. pp. 57–8, and Ravensdale, 'The transfer of customary land'.

[44] E.g. McIntosh, *Autonomy and community*, pp. 170–1; Poos, 'Population and resources', pp. 165–70.

[45] See above, Chapter 4.

[46] This problem is a truism among students of manorial records: e.g. Britton, *The community of the vill*, pp. 10–15. The problem was perhaps the major point of contention in the debate contained in Poos and Smith, 'Legal windows onto historical populations'; Razi, 'The use of manorial court rolls'; Poos and Smith, 'Shades still on the window'; Razi, 'The demographic transparency of manorial court rolls'.

medieval England with marked economic differentiation it was not necessarily the whole, or even the majority, experience.

Adopting a view of medieval English rural marriage as essentially the 'peasant' system sketched out here does appear to pose a further conundrum of great importance for the period of this study. A sudden injection of exogenous mortality of such cataclysmic dimensions as the Black Death would, under the logic of this model, be expected to provoke an immediate upsurge of nuptiality, and over the following decades the much freer aggregate availability of land would wholly alter the balance of homeostatic constraints upon household formation. As Hatcher put it, 'If population had expanded apace in the fifteenth century historians would certainly have had few difficulties in explaining why!'[47] Yet population remained depressed. If this prolonged depression is not entirely to be explained by continuing high levels of mortality, an alternative or at least another contributing factor must be shown to have existed. This conundrum may be more apparent than real, however, if a wider perspective is taken upon household-formation processes, in conjunction with the particular features of land distribution and labour forms present at the local level. Discussion will return to this critically important point below.

The second component of Hajnal's 'Northwestern European marriage pattern' is servanthood, as an institutional alternative to marriage or at least a transitional stage between leaving home and marrying. Again, servants have been widely recognised as a feature of late-medieval English rural life, though their quantitative dimensions and functional relationships with other demographic features are not yet so clear.[48] There is substantial evidence from Essex at the end of the middle ages, though, to suggest that in this region at least servanthood corresponded fairly closely to Hajnal's formulation; this evidence is discussed below (Chapter 9).

If two of the quintessential ingredients of a 'Northwestern European' household-formation pattern were present in late-medieval Essex, it then becomes all the more important to gain some understanding of the parameters of nuptiality. There are several reasons for this. First, in most pre-modern European societies nuptiality (especially female nuptiality) is the strongest influence upon fertility. The former defined the lawful and licit boundaries within which the

[47] Hatcher, *Plague, population and the English economy*, p. 55.

[48] Razi, *Life, marriage and death in a medieval parish*, pp. 76, 146; Hanawalt, *The ties that bound*, pp. 156–68; Bennett, *Women in the medieval countryside*, pp. 55–6, 82–4; Smith, 'Some issues concerning families and their property', pp. 32–9.

latter took place.[49] For this to be true, of course, there must be negligible illegitimacy and negligible fertility limitation by human intervention within marriage. Both of these conditions were true for England for the early-modern era, and what evidence exists would be hard pressed to support any argument that the later fourteenth and fifteenth centuries differed markedly in these respects.[50]

Secondly, to demonstrate empirically differences in marriage patterns between occupational or status groups in Essex, in a manner explicable within a local economic context, would provide a powerful argument for the coexistence of 'peasant' and 'proletarian' household-formation paradigms in the district. And finally, any empirical measure of nuptiality directly comparable to other historical populations would aid in understanding late-medieval Essex in time and space. Though direct measures of marriage ages and proportions never marrying are not feasible, another approach may be taken.

The nominative listings resulting from the later-fourteenth-century poll-tax returns provide the potentially most systematic evidence for nuptiality patterns in late-medieval England. And since a large number of these returns survive from the 1381 collection in Essex, they constitute the single most important set of data for marriage patterns for the purposes of this study.[51] This evidence necessarily relates to

[49] Bongaarts, 'Why high birth rates are so low'; Lesthaeghe, 'On the social control of human reproduction'.

[50] In eight English parishes between 1538 and 1700, for virtually no decade did illegitimate births (as opposed to bridal pregnancies) exceed 5 per cent of registered baptisms, and they were usually well below this figure: Oosterveen, Smith and Stewart, 'Family reconstitution and the study of bastardy', pp. 96–7. Although some writers (e.g. Hilton, 'Freedom and villeinage in England', p. 191; Razi, *Life, marriage and death in a medieval parish*, pp. 64–71) have used records of leyrwite (fornication fines: cf. North, 'Legerwite in the thirteenth and fourteenth centuries') in manorial court rolls to indicate high levels of illegitimacy in medieval villages, this seems doubtful: Poos and Smith, 'Legal windows onto historical populations', pp. 148–51. On the evidence of family limitation, two of the most striking features of early-modern English parish-register reconstitutions are the remarkable stability of marital fertility and the absence of evidence for such limitation before 1750: Wrigley and Schofield, 'English population history from family reconstruction', pp. 168–75. As for the middle ages, Biller, 'Birth-control in the West', has recently argued persuasively that knowledge of contraceptive practices (especially *coitus interruptus*) was more widespread in Western Europe by the early 1300s than historians have appreciated. But Biller's further argument, that contraceptive practices may even this early have been employed on a demographically significant scale, seems less convincing. Especially for England, to accept this view would make it necessary to believe that widespread family limitation before 1500 actually gave way to virtually none at all during 1550–1750.

[51] The Essex returns for 1377 are: PRO.E179.107.46; E179.107.47; E179.107.48; E179.107.50; E179.107.51; E179.107.52; E179.107.53; E179.107.55; E179.107.56; E179.107.57; E179.107.58. The 1381 Essex returns furnishing nominative listings are:

one particular point in time, when the epidemics of the preceding generation may possibly have caused distortions in the age or sex composition of the populations that were purportedly being recorded. But more critical difficulties inherent in the poll-tax returns stand in the way of inferences about marriage behaviour from these data. Particular problems include the terms of reference for each successive taxation (that is, criteria concerning who were liable or exempt), the nature of the collection process, and the resulting systematic shortcomings in the data from the returns as they stand.

These features of the poll-tax evidence are discussed more fully elsewhere (below, Appendix A), but they bear reviewing in the light of their importance. The 1377 returns provide figures for the lay population aged 14 and older resident in each township. Though these figures may be deficient by a non-negligible but probably small factor, they can at least be taken as relatively reliable baseline indicators of township populations when taken in the aggregate. The tax collection resulting in the 1381 listings, which provide nominative data including marital status for lay residents aged 15 and older, netted many fewer taxpayers than in 1377. The nominative and occupational data of the 1381 listings also make it clear that exclusion from the listings was strongly influenced by sex (with single females disproportionately few), occupation or status (with servants, labourers and the poor generally more likely to have been excluded), and probably marital status (since the excluded poor were likely to have included proportionately more single people, if a neolocal household-formation system were indeed present).

All this obviously bears critical implications for how one is to read the poll-tax data for nuptiality patterns. The most widely cited attempt to date to read these data in such a way was made by Hajnal in his seminal article on 'European marriage patterns in perspective'.[52] Hajnal noted that two major nuptiality variables characterised the 'Northwestern European marriage pattern': high mean age at first marriage for both women and men, and large proportions of both sexes who never married, relative to other preindustrial societies. Both variables are reflected in relatively low proportions of both females and males recorded as married in census-like documents. Hajnal's

PRO.E179.107.49; E179.107.59; E179.107.60; E179.107.63; E179.107.64; E179.107.65; E179.107.67; E179.107.68; E179.107.69; E179.107.75; E179.123.44; E179.240.308. The returns for all collections for the entire country are, at the time of writing this, being assembled into a database by Dr C. C. Fenwick under the direction of Dr R. M. Smith; the author is grateful to Dr Smith for furnishing a preliminary copy of this database for the Essex returns, for checking author's previous manual analysis.

52 Hajnal, 'European marriage patterns in perspective', pp. 117–20.

Table 7.1. *Proportions currently married and aged 15 years and older, selected historical European populations*

	Mortality level 3 ($e_0 = 25$ years)				Mortality level 5 ($e_0 = 30$ years)			
	Rate of population growth (% per annum)							
	0.0	−1.0	0.0	−1.0	0.0	−1.0	0.0	−1.0
	men		women		men		women	
Nine English parishes (17th–18th centuries)	54.4	55.9	50.2	52.8	57.6	60.2	51.7	53.5
Sweden (1750)	59.6	60.8	51.4	53.2	61.5	65.4	52.2	53.5
Tuscany (1427)	56.1	60.8	71.2	70.4	56.3	60.4	70.4	69.2
Mishino, Russia (1849)	64.7	69.7	65.4	64.8	71.1	71.6	64.6	61.8
Serbia (1733–4)	65.7	66.0	67.5	62.6	63.7	65.4	65.6	60.8

Source: Smith, 'Hypothèses sur la nuptialité en Angleterre', pp. 115–16.

'very cautious criterion' was that a minimum of 30 per cent of women aged 15 and older being recorded as unmarried would be consistent with a 'Northwestern European' marriage pattern of mean age at first marriage in the mid-twenties.

More recently, Smith has taken data from census-like enumerations of several historical European populations, under a variety of assumptions about underlying demographic structures, in order to provide a series of benchmark figures for proportions aged 15 and older currently married in several 'Northwestern European' and non-'Northwestern European' marriage regimes.[53] For purposes of comparability with the later-medieval English poll-tax data, in which notations of widowhood are too inconsistent to be reliable, 'currently married' in this discussion excludes widows and widowers and thus differs from demographers' more familiar category of 'ever-married'. These figures are reproduced in Table 7.1.

Table 7.1 implies that in a declining population with a mortality level somewhat more severe than that generally prevalent in early-modern England – both factors likely to have been true for the later fourteenth century – approximately 40 per cent of men and 45 per cent of women aged 15 and older would be unmarried in a definitively 'Northwestern European' marriage system. Other nuptiality regimes show considerable differences in this measure: early-fifteenth-century Tuscany, for

[53] Smith, 'Hypothèses sur la nuptialité en Angleterre', p. 116.

Table 7.2. *Comparisons of numbers taxed, Essex poll-tax returns, 1377 and 1381*

Hundred	Number taxed in 1377	Number taxed in 1381	Number of vills
Chelmsford	2,355	1,839	16
Dunmow	2,701	1,537	22
Hinckford	3,476	2,368	29
Ongar	2,098	1,595	25
Total	10,630	7,339	92

A vill's data have been tabulated here only if legible total numbers taxed are recoverable from that vill's returns for *both* 1377 and 1381. Only returns from 1381 which furnish *summe personarum* at the end of the vill's list, or which (failing that) are completely legible and without obviously missing names, are included here. The figure tabulated here is the former where given, or the total number of names listed if no *summa* is available.
Sources: See notes to text.

example, where women married markedly younger, and more recent Russian and Serbian populations where marriage was relatively earlier in life for both sexes.[54]

The task, then, is to overcome the systematic shortcomings inherent in the 1381 Essex data for sex and marital status in order to translate these data into a form directly comparable to that of Table 7.1. It is first necessary to inflate the number of taxpayers recorded in the 1381 returns into a 'global' figure (that is, representing all those of the relevant age-group likely actually to have been resident in the communities in question), since numbers taxed in 1381 are demonstrably far short of all lay residents aged at least 15 at the time. Since the 1377 collection was clearly more inclusive of local residents (though itself possibly deficient in this regard), its data provide the best basis for doing this. Table 7.2 shows that in 92 Essex vills for which both complete 1377 and 1381 returns survive, total numbers taxed dropped by 31.0 per cent from the earlier collection to the later.

When a further factor is added for the difference of one year in minimum age liable to be taxed in the later collection,[55] a final factor of

[54] Cf. Herlihy and Klapisch-Zuber, *Tuscans and their families*, esp. pp. 203–21; Czap, 'Marriage and the peasant joint family', pp. 103–23.

[55] This further factor (0.97023, the ratio of those aged 15+ to those aged 14+) has been derived by calculating ratios of persons aged 14+ and 15+ to total population, from Princeton Model West stable populations with population declining at a rate of 0.5 per cent per annum, mortality levels 1 (female $e_0 = 23.25$) and 8 (female $e_0 = 42.05$), taking the mean of the two ratios (in practice quite close: 0.97092 and 0.98754

Table 7.3. *Recorded sex and marital-status data, all surviving Essex poll-tax returns, 1381*

	Married	Unmarried	Total
Male	3,651	1,771	5,422
Female	3,651	777	4,428
Total	7,302	2,548	9,850

Number of vills = 135
Recorded sex ratio = 122.4
Recorded percentage married (males) = 67.3
(females) = 82.5

Sources: See notes to text.

1.418 is obtained, by which numbers taxed in 1381 should be multiplied to produce a minimum 'global' population of males and females aged 15 years and older and resident in the communities in question in 1381.

Next to be considered are the actual figures for sex and marital status as recorded in the surviving returns for 1381. Table 7.3 presents these.

This table, representing the data for 135 vills scattered throughout Essex but concentrated mostly in the central and northern districts of the county, confirms that there was widespread exclusion of single females from the taxation proceedings, and as a direct corollary of this, quite a high figure for percentage of women currently married in this age group. But multiplying total persons taxed in these returns by the correction factor already derived implies that a plausible minimum figure for persons aged 15+ in the vills in question is 13,971, with a sex ratio in this age group (as calculated from Princeton Model West stable populations) of about 94.3.[56] Some of these 'missing' or 'excluded' persons can be recovered by adding single females to bring the sex

respectively): Coale and Demeny, *Regional model life tables*, pp. 42, 45, 55, 62, 105, 112. Model West is used here because it appears to fit most closely the characteristics of infant and child mortality (the most critical factor in deriving proportions of those 14+ and 15+ to total population) observable in the earliest English parish registers: Schofield and Wrigley, 'Infant and child mortality in Tudor–Stuart England'. The nature of derivations like this from the Princeton tables is discussed further below, Appendix A. No major epidemic is known to have occurred between 1377 and 1381, so it seems reasonable to treat underlying or 'global' population as essentially unchanged between the two dates.

56 This theoretical approximation is in fact likely to be reasonably close to empirical reality. In 100 English community listings between 1574 and 1821, the aggregate sex ratio for the entire sample population (including under-15s) was 91.0: Laslett, ed., *Household and family in past time*, p. 74.

Table 7.4. *Sex and marital-status data, all surviving Essex poll-tax returns, 1381, corrected for sex ratio only*

	Married	Unmarried	Total
Male	3,651	1,771	5,422
Female	3,651	2,101	5,752
Total	7,302	3,872	11,174

Number of vills = 135
Sex ratio = 94.3
Percentage married (males) = 67.3
(females) = 63.5

Sources: See notes to text.

ratio up to this figure, on the presumption that in a population and geographical area as large as this, localised sex-specific migration patterns resulting from employment practices are likely to have been cancelled out. Table 7.4 presents the result of recovering these single females.

This exercise of 'reinserting' some of the excluded females into the dataset has the effect of dropping the proportion of females currently married down to slightly less than 65 per cent: in other words, just within Hajnal's 'very cautious criterion' for a 'Northwestern European' marriage pattern, though still rather higher than the empirical data for early-modern England. But this exercise in itself accounts for only *some* of the exclusions from the raw data, and so a more accurate impression of marital status among the 'global' population at large must turn upon the likely composition of the remaining 'exclusions'. Three limiting scenarios can be constructed, each of which 'reinserts' the remaining 'exclusions' and maintains a sex ratio of 94.3, but rests upon extreme alternative assumptions concerning the marital status of the 'excluded' members of the region's population. These scenarios are shown in Table 7.5.

In order to choose between the respective likelihoods of each of these scenarios' reflecting the actual marital status of Essex inhabitants in 1381, it is necessary to revert to the broader issue raised earlier, that of whether different subgroups within the region's population can be shown to have had markedly different nuptiality experiences. This question is best considered by looking at the raw data – that is, as recorded in the returns and with no 'corrections' – for marital status among those Essex taxpayers listed in 1381 with occupational or status designations. These are given in Table 7.6.

Table 7.5. *Sex and marital-status data, all surviving Essex poll-tax returns, 1381, corrected for all 'exclusions'*

Scenario A: All 'exclusions' unmarried

	Married	Unmarried	Total
Male	3,651	3,128	6,779
Female	3,651	3,541	7,192
Total	7,302	6,669	13,971

Number of vills = 135
Sex ratio = 94.3
Percentage married (males) = 53.9
(females) = 50.8

Scenario B: Half of (male) 'exclusions' married

	Married	Unmarried	Total
Male	4,329	2,450	6,779
Female	4,329	2,863	7,192
Total	8,658	5,313	13,971

Number of vills = 135
Sex ratio = 94.3
Percentage married (males) = 63.9
(females) = 60.2

Scenario C: All (male) 'exclusions' married

	Married	Unmarried	Total
Male	5,008	1,771	6,779
Female	5,008	2,184	7,192
Total	10,016	3,955	13,971

Number of vills = 135
Sex ratio = 94.3
Percentage married (males) = 73.9
(females) = 69.6

Sources: See notes to text.

Several comments are necessary concerning the nature of these samples. First, isolated for tabulation here are only those persons given such designations and their spouses (in practice, where married couples are recorded it was without exception the husband who was given an occupation); servants, children and other dependents of these persons are excluded, so the samples undoubtedly comprise married household heads plus wives, and unmarried or widowed

Table 7.6. *Sex and marital-status data, all surviving Essex poll-tax returns, 1381, by occupation*

Agriculturalists	Married	Unmarried	Total
Male	334	49	383
Female	334	25	359
Total	668	74	742
		Recorded percentage married (males) = 87.2	
Craftsmen and retailers	Married	Unmarried	Total
Male	264	113	377
Female	264	6	270
Total	528	119	647
		Recorded percentage married (males) = 70.0	
Labourers	Married	Unmarried	Total
Male	536	250	786
Female	536	94	630
Total	1072	344	1416
		Recorded percentage married (males) = 68.2	

Sources: See notes to text.

persons (again, mostly men, since unmarried women were given such designations only relatively infrequently). Thus sex ratios and percentages of women currently married in these samples are irrelevant, since the sample does not approximate a total population in any meaningful sense. What is of more concern here are the differences among males currently married in the respective subgroups. For it is clear that agriculturalists were rather more likely to have been married than either craftsmen/retailers or labourers, the figures for the latter in particular, however, probably being more maximal owing to the nature of systematic exclusions in collection.[57] These differences in the

[57] When the database currently being assembled under the direction of R. M. Smith for the entire country's surviving returns is available it will be possible to speak authoritatively about whether this is a pattern observable more broadly throughout England. Preliminary analysis by hand by the present author with the returns from Yorkshire and Leicestershire indicates, however, that Essex was by no means unique in this respect.

data as recorded are statistically significant at the 0.001 level.[58]

Several tentative conclusions, then, can be drawn from this exercise with the poll-tax data. First, in very broad terms it seems most likely that the nuptiality experience of this region's overall population fell somewhere between Scenarios 'A' and 'B' in Table 7.5. Among the 'exclusions' whom one must take into account in any analysis of returns of this taxation process, unmarried servants, labourers (who from the Essex evidence were the subgroup least likely to be married), and more generally the poorest (again, as argued elsewhere, less likely to have been married than those who actually paid the tax)[59] were undoubtedly predominant, so Scenario 'B' is most likely the limiting (i.e. maximal) case of currently-married incidence.

This in turn implies that when Essex society after the Black Death is put into a broader comparative perspective among the historical European populations represented in Table 7.1, it would be difficult on this evidence alone to conclude (as did Hajnal, forced as he was to rely upon Russell's treatment of the few 1377 Northumberland listings) that this region's nuptiality regime was markedly dissimilar from that which England experienced in the early-modern era. This, then, reinforces Smith's remarks concerning the 1377 Rutland material, about which he came to similar conclusions.[60] And finally, it should be reiterated that this exercise with the 1381 Essex material, based as it is on the 1377 returns as the benchmark for local population (a benchmark itself deficient, due to similar patterns of selective underenumeration), is likely to overstate the currently-marrieds by a further factor stemming from that same selective underenumeration. Since the above exercise inflates 1381 taxpayer numbers in line with the 1377 returns, that is, if the latter are lower than the actual resident population in question, a higher reconstructed 'global' population would lead to a lower estimate of currently-marrieds.

If this is indeed true, then the low proportions of both sexes currently married in later-fourteenth-century Essex are all the more striking in view of the conundrum mentioned earlier: that the generation after the midcentury plague was precisely the period when one might expect high nuptiality under a 'peasant' or 'niche'-based system of household formation. And if these proportions were so low, and

[58] The result of a chi-square test, with males married and unmarried in each of the three occupational categories forming six cells, is 77.73 (2 degrees of freedom).

[59] See below, Appendix A.

[60] Smith, 'Hypothèses sur la nuptialité en Angleterre', pp. 109–15. Hanawalt, *The ties that bound*, pp. 95–6, makes a contrary argument based upon the 1381 Suffolk returns, but her conclusions may be questioned on a number of interpretational grounds; see below, Chapter 9.

persisted into the fifteenth century, they would help to account for the modest fertility implied by both the Walden churching evidence and, more generally, by the prolonged late-medieval population slump.

Obviously, reaching these tentative conclusions has made necessary some extensive manipulation of the raw poll-tax data, and this is especially true for the experiences of women, whose marriage patterns were in fact more pivotal both in influencing fertility and in defining the particularity of Northwestern European marriage. By themselves the data for the population at large may well not bear the weight of such an interpretation. But when placed beside other evidence, some already presented and more still to be considered, that point in the same direction, the poll-tax data are more telling.

Even more significant, with regard to household formation, are the differentials of marriage behaviour as recorded (and the actual differentials were likely to have been quite a bit wider) between occupational groups. If agriculturalists married either younger or more invariably (or both) than the other groups, this does correspond well to a 'niche' variant of a household-formation system in which niches were indeed more freely available to that segment of the Essex population. For craftsmen and retailers, entry into marriage was either slightly later in life or slightly less likely to occur at all, though the contrast with agriculturalists is modest. Once more, then, in terms of demography as well as structures of production, this district fits poorly into any predictive model of protoindustrialisation.[61] For many more labourers, marriage and household formation was quite a bit later, or quite a bit more difficult ever to achieve. Occupation-specific differences in nuptiality implied by the Essex data, in turn, heighten the importance of employment forms for both sexes, to which discussion will return below (Chapters 9–10).

In 1504 at Littlebury a last will and testament was rendered by Elizabeth Thomys, 'sengylwoman', and six years later the term was echoed in the will of Richard Smyth the younger of Fingringhoe, 'syngilman'. In these wills the testators left money and sundry household goods to siblings, other relatives and friends, the relicts of the unmarried.[62] Thus was contemporary Essex terminology of social typology extended to embrace those who passed their lives unmarried. But when viewed as an aggregate demographic process, marriage and household formation in the district erected social-structural barriers to the married state for labourers in particular. These barriers to marriage must relate to one or the other (or more likely a combination) of two factors. Either the late-medieval Essex economy was

[61] See above, Chapter 3. [62] ERO D/ACR 1/86; D/ACR 1/176.

inimical to rapid accumulation of the means for labourers to marry, despite what appear to have been propitiously high real wages; or the structural components of that economy made it tactically more difficult for labourers to settle and found new households. Wage levels and forms of employment will be taken up later. Differential migration and settlement patterns among these same groups must first be considered.

8

Migration and settlement

Only a minority of rural people in late-medieval Essex spent their entire lives in the same community. In one respect, migration was the means by which people found places in the local economy to fit into. Despite the variegated economic complexion of the Essex countryside, persons who were of a certain age and possessed certain skills could not necessarily always find positions that would yield them a livelihood within their own communities; few rural places in the district would have afforded viable livelihoods to an unlimited number of carpenters or tailors, for example.

In addition to being an economic phenomenon, migration was also a demographic experience that, like marriage, differed among different social groups. And besides occupation, age was an extremely important influence upon geographical mobility. Movement from parish to parish was in part a function of the life cycle, since Essex country people were most likely to migrate in their teens and early twenties and to settle down in their late twenties. This last point is of considerable importance for understanding household formation also, because if a person typically achieved a place in the local economy and so tended to attain stable geographical settlement only towards the end of his third decade in life, this was also the time when the means to marry most likely either had been secured or were expected in the near future.

The notion that medieval villagers all spent their entire lives rooted to one plot of soil has of course long been discarded.[1] But historians have also been long predisposed to view the decades following the Black Death as a time of especially heightened geographical mobility in rural England, stemming both from the loosening of traditional bonds through the waning of serfdom and through new opportunities

[1] Cf. Poos, 'Population turnover in medieval Essex', pp. 3–5, and sources cited there.

unleashed in a more fluid economic environment.[2] It is, however, easy to mistake contemporary concern about mobility for mobility itself. Officialdom at most levels of English society during these same decades made such concerns manifest. The Statute of Labourers, a product of the labour turbulence that came in the wake of the midcentury epidemic, sought to stem workers' movements by legal coercion, probably to little effect.[3] Manorial lords, under the customary law of most Essex manors, in theory possessed compulsive powers of restraining their villeins' movements away from their estates. Many lords redoubled their efforts to do just that in the second half of the fourteenth century, with apparently rather limited results, often after having shown little zeal in this respect earlier.[4] A profusion of documentary illustrations of mobility must not be confused with its underlying persistence.

For extensive geographical mobility had already become an integral experience of country life in Essex well before the Black Death. Attempts by authorities to stem the tide were not a reaction to a new phenomenon, though contemporaries may well have thought of it as such, but a wholly unrealistic attempt to curtail what was an essential component of local social structure. There are no direct means of comparing geographical mobility mathematically before and after 1350. By the 1320s and 1330s, though, rural Essex communities experienced rates of resident population turnover roughly equal in magnitude to those of English communities three hundred years later.

The evidence for this comes from four communities: Birdbrook, Chatham Hall in Great Waltham, Margaret Roding and Messing, all in central and northern Essex.[5] From these communities survive lists of names of all males enrolled in local tithings, largely corresponding to all males aged 12 and older and resident within their communities for at least a year. Where two or more successive tithing lists are available for the same community within a space of a decade or two – as is the case with these four communities – comparison of names between lists yields annual rates of population turnover. 'Turnover' here is defined as the annual rate at which persons present in the community at the time an earlier list was drawn up had 'exited' the community by the later compilation, either by death or by emigration, and the rate of

[2] Dyer, *Lords and peasants in a changing society*, pp. 274, 366–8; Raftis, *Tenure and mobility*, pp. 153–66; Hilton, *Decline of serfdom*, pp. 33–5; Bolton, *The medieval English economy*, pp. 236–7.

[3] Traditional accounts, in particular Ritchie, 'Labour conditions in Essex', have emphasised Statute of Labourers proceedings as evidence of vastly heightened mobility after 1350; cf. below, Chapter 9, for a somewhat revisionist view.

[4] See below, Chapter 11.

[5] Poos, 'Population turnover in medieval Essex'.

Table 8.1. *Annual population turnover rates: four early-fourteenth-century Essex communities compared with other preindustrial communities*

Place and dates	Group under observation	Exits	Entries
Weighted mean of four Essex communities, 1293–1339	Males aged 12+	4.1	5.2
Clayworth (Notts.) 1676–88	Entire population	5.1	5.3
Cogenhoe (Northants.) 1618–28	Entire population	5.2	5.3
Hallines (France) 1761–73	Entire population	3.8	4.3
Longueness (France) 1778–90	Entire population	3.8	3.0
Dedham (Massachusetts) 1640/48–1700	Males aged 21+	2.7	3.8
Krasnoe Sabakino (Russia) 1814–34	Servile males, all ages	1.9	–

Note: 'Exits' and 'entries' refer to mean number of persons disappearing from and appearing in recorded group under observation per 100 persons under observation per annum.
Source: Poos, 'Population turnover in medieval Essex', p. 21.

'entries' represented by new immigrants' arrivals or the coming of age and enrolment of local adolescents. The technical details of these sources and of calculation of turnover from them, and likely margins of error, have been discussed elsewhere.[6] Weighted aggregate turnover rates (exits and entries expressed as percentages of recorded population under observation per annum) from these four communities are presented in Table 8.1, along with comparative figures from a variety of other preindustrial settings.

Comparison is less than straightforward because, as the table indicates, the age and sex composition of groups with which the Essex data are to be compared varies from case to case. Projections based upon model populations imply that, if the group under observation in the Essex data were males of all ages, turnover rates expressed as percentages of total population would in fact be somewhat higher than those tabulated here.[7] Nevertheless, the results indicate that, as in the

[6] *Ibid.*, pp. 13–17. [7] These factors are discussed further *ibid.*, pp. 17–20.

English Midlands parishes of Clayworth and Cogenhoe in the seventeenth century, in these Essex communities during the early 1300s roughly half the residents of a given year were likely to have disappeared a decade later. Reference to model life tables under a wide range of assumptions about underlying demographic structures also indicates that no more than about one-half of the 'entries' and 'exits' in the fourteenth-century Essex communities can be accounted for by intrinsic demographic factors (i.e. deaths and comings of age); the remainder resulted from migration.[8] In broader comparative perspective, while early-fourteenth-century Essex appears virtually indistinguishable from the seventeenth-century Midlands, it appears to have possessed a wholly different social order from that of the early-nineteenth-century Russian servile population tabulated here. And so if one envisions geographical mobility as indeed increasing after 1350 it was against the background of these already high levels; it seems more plausible to argue that widespread mobility was already an integral feature of Essex rural society, and the post-Black Death attempts to stem its tide were futile outcries against an entrenched reality.

Migration, then, was commonplace, but it took place within a localised field. Essex people moved, not aimlessly or randomly over long distances, but to and from communities within, typically, a radius of ten or fifteen miles, longer-range resettling being relatively much rarer. They moved in order to settle with new spouses, take up tenements through purchase or kinship connections, assume employment, or transact other licit or illicit business in communities that were usually near enough to home to imply previous acquaintance or contacts in their new places of residence. As an example, a composite plot of several indices of geographical interactions is given in Figure 8.1.

This map plots evidence from the manorial-court records and criminal cases from royal circuit-court justice pertaining to the communities of Great Waltham and High Easter between 1327 and 1389. It includes destinations of local serfs who either paid fines to emigrate legally, or else were cited in the courts for illegal absences, from their home manors; origins of persons appearing in the communities' local courts who were explicitly denoted as being from elsewhere (in the form 'A.B. of C.'), whether to pursue litigation, take up tenements, or marry local villein women and assume their property; and the sites of felonies committed by indicted Waltham and Easter people and origins of persons indicted for felonies committed at Waltham and

[8] *Ibid.*, pp. 17–20.

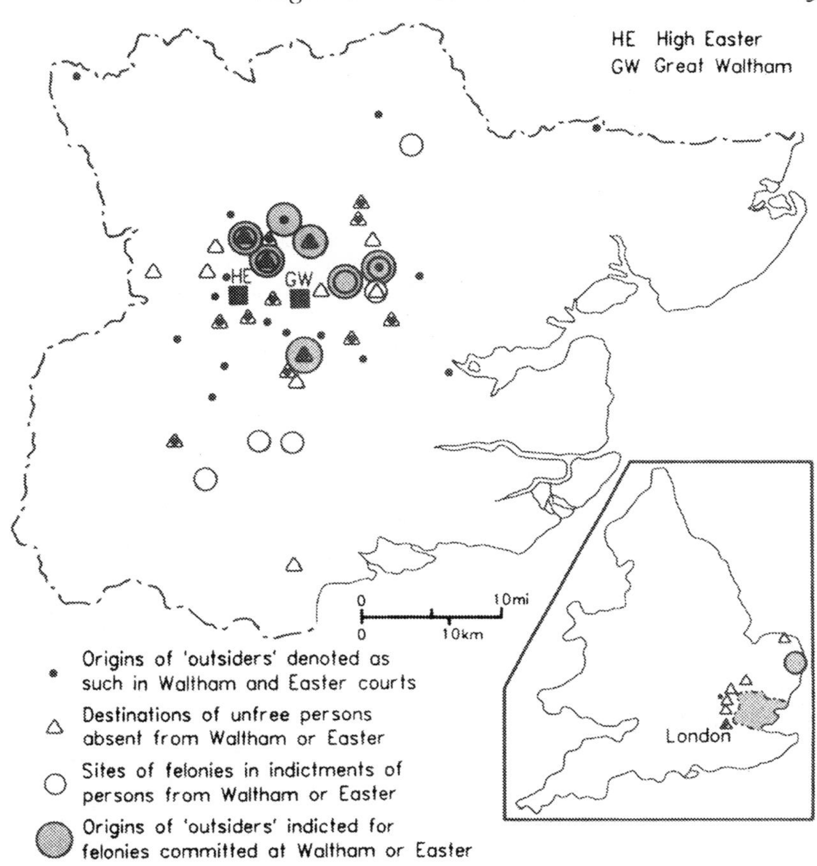

Figure 8.1. Extra-local contacts, High Easter and Great Waltham, 1327–89

Easter.[9] Each of these indices of movement is sporadic and uncovers only the tip of a doubtless much larger iceberg of migration activity, and the resulting figure is a composite of the two communities' migration fields.[10] But taken together they yield a credible impression of the depth of local migration fields: dense within a dozen miles or so, much less so further out, and strikingly similar to a comparable plot of

[9] This evidence is discussed further, and documentary references are given, in Poos, 'Population and resources', pp. 48–50, 180–2.

[10] This composite nature of the plot is unavoidable, because in several of these categories of migration evidence is sparse for either community taken on its own, and the two communities held a single manorial court between them before the 1350s, making it difficult to disentangle the contributions of the respective manors to the scatter of absentee serfs.

the 'social area' (as the authors put it) of the central-Essex parish of Terling in the sixteenth and seventeenth centuries.[11]

High levels of geographical mobility are merely another corollary of a densely settled, highly stratified local population containing a large proportion of landless, wage-dependent people, such as later-medieval Essex had. Migration in the specific contexts of servanthood and wage labour is best considered in the light of these institutions (below, Chapters 9–10). But much more revealing information is available on the age- and occupation-specific qualities of migration in Essex during the later fifteenth century.

One of the most important sources utilised by historical demographers in recent studies of migration and settlement patterns in early-modern England is the mass of autobiographical details given by deponents testifying before ecclesiastical courts. During instance causes – that is, suits of litigation which were brought by plaintiffs and which in the majority of cases dealt with matrimonial, testamentary, tithe, or defamation disputes – in both the later middle ages and the sixteenth and seventeenth centuries, the plaintiff's initial statement of charges and the defendant's countering interrogatories were followed by the examination of deponents, individually and without the parties to the cause being present.[12] Consistent with the civil law's stress upon weighing the quality of evidence, importance was placed upon evaluating the deponent's status, character and familiarity with the persons and events in the cause.[13] Therefore a preamble, entered in the record before the text of the witness's deposition, often stated the deponent's age, status or occupation, parish of current residence and length of residence there (or, alternatively, a statement that the person had lived there since birth), and often also contained notes of previous moves and places of residence. The preamble also usually recorded how many years the deponent claimed to have known the principals in the cause, and often whether the deponent was literate or not.[14] Since these depositions survive in large numbers after 1500 and the witnesses were drawn from a fairly broad spectrum of early-modern English society, their data have proved invaluable in the explication of migration experiences for different age, sex, occupational groups and geographical contexts.[15]

[11] Wrightson and Levine, *Poverty and piety*, pp. 74–82.

[12] Helmholz, *Marriage litigation*, pp. 11–22; Houlbrooke, *Church courts and the people*, pp. 38–54.

[13] Donahue, 'Proof by witnesses in the church courts', pp. 127–58.

[14] These literacy data are discussed below, Chapter 13.

[15] E.g. Clark, 'Migration in England'; Souden, 'Pre-industrial migration fields', pp. 25–149. The author is grateful to Dr David Souden for permission to cite his

Historians interested in the phenomenon of migration in England during the later middle ages have barely begun to tap these sources, although the substance of the depositions has attracted the attention of historians investigating medieval marriage.[16] In part, no doubt, this lack of detailed research may be due to the fact that in relatively few surviving collections of medieval cause materials was the full complement of autobiographical detail recorded as a matter of procedural or scribal convention. In one otherwise detailed volume of depositions from the early-fifteenth-century Canterbury diocese, for example, length of residence is recorded only very sporadically and occupation is likewise usually absent.[17] At times it is, however, possible to infer such information from the deposition itself.[18]

Fortunately, three full volumes of deposition material from the latter half of the fifteenth century survive from the consistory court of the diocese of London (within which Essex was located), and in many cases the pertinent data are included for a preliminary exploration of migration and settlement in the county near the close of the medieval period.[19] This material represents depositions taken between 1467 and 1497. No act books or similar records of other procedural stages of the causes in question, apart from the depositions themselves, appear to have survived from the London consistory court before 1500.[20] It is therefore impossible to learn the outcome of each cause from the surviving evidence, and the nature of the suit (matrimonial, testamentary, and so forth) must be inferred from the substance of the recorded testimony. These limitations of the available evidence are none the less unlikely to affect the quality of migration and settlement data contained in the deposition preambles.

More serious for present purposes is the domination in the consistory court business of causes relating to persons within the city of London itself. Of the total of 822 deponents included in the three surviving volumes of testimony, 517 (62.9 per cent) were city residents at the time of their depositions, 81 (9.9 per cent) were resident within

unpublished data, and for discussing the early-modern deposition evidence with him.

16 E.g. Sheehan, 'Formation and stability of marriage'; Donahue, 'Canon law on the formation of marriage'; Goldberg, 'Marriage, migration, servanthood and the life-cycle'.

17 CALC X.10.1: see fos. 8v, 30–32 for occasional mentions of length-of-settlement data.

18 Cf. Goldberg, 'Marriage, migration, servanthood and life-cycle'. The York cause papers of the fourteenth and fifteenth centuries, the most voluminous source of depositions from the later middle ages, do not usually include migration data in deposition preambles.

19 GLRO DL/C/205; GL MS 9065; GL MS 9065B. In the latter volume, much smaller than the other two, only deponents resident in the City of London appear.

20 Wunderli, *London church courts and society*, p. 7.

the diocese of London, outside the city but in Middlesex or Hertfordshire, 34 (4.1 per cent) resided entirely outside the diocese, and the parish of residence of a further 5 (0.6 per cent) was illegible or otherwise unidentifiable. This means that only 185 Essex residents remain for analysis, a figure small enough to invite a degree of caution in drawing firm inferences.

The composition of the Essex deponent sample imposes certain further limitations. Most obviously, investigation is virtually entirely restricted to males, since only 7 (3.8 per cent) of the 185 Essex deponents were females. There was no formal prohibition of women's testimony before medieval ecclesiastical tribunals,[21] but the bias against female deponents in the London consistory court during the later fifteenth century was remarkably strong, much stronger than was shown in the early-modern courts.[22] Secondly, although deponents in the Essex sample ranged in age from the late teens to over 60 years, the majority were in mid-adulthood when they rendered their testimony: their mean age as recorded in the deposition preambles was about 40, though, as will be shown, this must be viewed as only approximate due to the obviously only approximate accuracy of the ages as recorded.[23] Moreover, the Essex deponents were drawn predominantly from rural and small market communities (only 15, or 8.1 per cent, of the 185 witnesses were residents of Colchester, Chelmsford and Maldon, the most important urban centres in the county). The communities represented are scattered throughout Essex, although there was some tendency for deponents to be drawn from places in the southwestern quadrant of the county. This is understandable, since propinquity to the city doubtless facilitated recourse to the consistory court itself. A similar pattern has been observed among seventeenth-century deponents.[24] Thus for all intents this is essentially a male, rural, mostly mid-adult sample.

Finally, even within these constraints the Essex deponent sample represents a cross-section of only the middling levels of rural society in the county, as the designations of status or occupation within the

[21] Donahue, 'Proof by witnesses in the church courts', pp. 130–1.

[22] Cf. Souden, 'Pre-industrial migration fields', p. 85. In Souden's seventeenth-century sample of deponents, rural males outnumbered rural females by the ratio 4410:957, or a sex ratio of 460.8, compared to a ratio of males to females in rural medieval Essex of 178:7, or 2542.9.

[23] For all 184 deponents (not counting one whose stated age is illegible), mean age was 39.6 years (standard deviation = 11.7). A slightly different mean age at deposition is given below, where the dataset in question comprises deponents for whom length-of-residence data are also recorded.

[24] Souden, 'Pre-industrial migration fields', p. 65.

Table 8.2. *Composition of Essex deponent sample by occupation, 1467–97*

Agriculturalists[a]	23 (31.5%)
Craftsmen/retailers[b]	31 (42.5)
Clergy	8 (11.0)
Labourers	10 (13.7)
Servants	1 (1.4)
Total	73

All occupational designations tabulated here are taken from deposition preambles; none has been inferred from the substance of depositions.
[a] Comprises 16 *agricultores*, 3 *husbandmen*, 2 *coloni* and 2 *yomen*.
[b] Comprises 10 *fysshers/piscatores*, 4 *taylors*, 3 *carnifices*, 2 *textores/wevers*, 2 *fabri* and 1 each *allutarius*, *baker*, *carpentarius*, *clothmaker*, *hospes*, *pelliparius*, *pogger*, *pulter*, *tinator* and *waterman*.
Sources: GLRO DL/C/205; GL MS 9065.

deposition preambles make clear. Table 8.2 summarises these designations.

Only 73 (39.5 per cent) of the 185 Essex deponents were actually given such designations (and all of these were males). Obviously, even in comparison with the cognate distribution recorded in the 1381 poll-tax returns (which, it was argued above, themselves doubtless understated servants, labourers and other lower-status groups), these same groups were grossly underrepresented among deponents. It seems clear that parties in the causes, and perhaps the court itself, tended to value especially the testimony of more substantial and longer- or better-established members of their communities, and a similar impression emerges from seventeenth-century depositions.[25] Conversely, no persons identifiable as members of the gentry or peerage appear in the deponent sample, and clergy make up a relatively modest proportion of witnesses. Therefore, although paucity of data renders it difficult to recover much of the experience of humbler members of Essex rural society at the end of the middle ages, it seems fair to characterise this deponent group as broadly representative of the middling range of adult male country-dwellers in this region.

[25] Donahue, 'Proof by witnesses in the church courts', pp. 144–6, cites a York cause of 1367 in which the plaintiff attempted (unsuccessfully) to exclude two of the defendant's witnesses because, among other things, they were serfs, and 'ignoble, vile, and abject persons [ignobiles, viles, et abiecte persone]'. Cf. Souden, 'Pre-industrial migration fields', p. 81: among rural males in Souden's seventeenth-century sample, yeomen and husbandmen comprised 1,173 (68.1 per cent) of the total of 1,722 deponents.

A few examples of details contained in the depositions' preambles will help to illustrate the strengths and limitations of this material:

[1474] John Fuller, of the parish of Saint Peter, Coggeshall, common labourer, where he has lived for six years, and before that time in the vill of Combs Ford in the county of Suffolk for 14 years, illiterate, of free condition, 36 years of age as he says, witness etc. He says that he has well known James Whytyngdon for six years, and Agnes Rogers since the feast of All Saints last past, as he says . . .[26]

[1472] John Corant of [Great] Holland, *agricultor*, where he was born and has dwelt from the time of his birth, illiterate, of free condition, 48 years of age and more as he says . . .[27]

[1473] Thomas Cheseman, of the parish of Horndon on the Hill, London diocese, tailor, where he has dwelt for four years, and before that time in the city of Worcester in the parish of Saint Michael for six years, and before that time wandering through England and beyond the sea, illiterate, of free condition, 34 years of age as he says . . .[28]

These examples demonstrate the range of information which *may* be available in individual preambles. But unfortunately it is relatively rare for the entire range of information to be offered for any one deponent. One preamble may contain the deponent's occupation but no information on length of residence, and the next preamble vice versa. Subdividing the dataset into occupational categories thus yields quite small groups for whom migration and settlement profiles can be derived. Furthermore, it is only relatively rarely that the preambles allow one to observe more than one movement backward in time: that is, when migration information is given it usually simply states length of residence in present parish, and in fact seldom names previous place of abode (as do the examples of John Fuller and Thomas Cheseman, above). So for the bulk of the Essex deponent sample one may only view movements backwards from the 'present', in terms of how recently they arrived where they were living in mid-adulthood, rather than reconstructing movements from birth onward.

[26] GLRO DL/C/205 fo. 225: 'Johannes Fuller de parochia Sancti Petri de Cogsale communis laborarius ubi moram traxit per vj annos Et ante illud tempus in villa de Combesforth in Comitate Suffolch' per xiiij annos illiteratus libere condicionis xxxvj annorum etatis ut dicit testis &c Dicit quod Jacobum Whytyngdon per vj annos & Agnetem Rogers a festo omnium sanctorum ultimo preterito bene novit ut dicit'.

[27] *Ibid.* fo. 89: 'Johannes Corant de Holond agricultor ubi fuit oriundus & moram suam traxit a tempore nativitatis sue illiteratus libere condicionis xlviij annorum etatis & amplius ut dicit . . . '.

[28] *Ibid.* fo. 138: 'Thomas Cheseman de parochia de Horndon on the Hill London' diocesis Taylor ubi moram traxit per iiij annos Et ante illud tempus in Civitate Wigorn' in parochia Sancti Michaelis per vj annos Et ante illud tempus vagando per partes Anglie & ultra marem illiteratus libere condicionis xxxiiij annorum etatis ut dicit . . . '.

One may begin with a relatively straightforward question: what proportion of the Essex deponents were 'lifetime stayers', still living at the time of their testimony in the parish where they were born? Even such a rudimentary measure as this can yield an impression of the typicality of migration in this society, and moreover similar measures are available for comparison from early-modern deposition evidence. To derive this measure simply requires that all deposition preambles furnishing residence data (regardless of presence or absence of occupational information) be isolated, and the proportion taken of deponents who claimed to have been born where they were then living. Yet there is reason to believe that this proportion of 'lifetime stayers' will be only a *maximal* estimate. The deposition preambles are reticent as to short-term or short-range migrations, and this is occasionally implied in such preambles as the following:

[1490] Richard Twety of Buttsbury, where he was born and has dwelt for the most part from the time of his birth, of free condition, 26 years of age as he says . . .[29]

[1472] Thomas Bogays of Kirby[-le-Soken], *agricultor*, where he was born, and he has dwelt in the said vill of Kirby and in Frinton[-on-Sea, a coastal village approximately two miles from Kirby] from the time of his birth, of free condition, 38 years of age and more as he says . . .[30]

In both cases, these deponents had apparently moved out of and back into the parishes of their birth, but for present purposes they have been tabulated as 'lifetime stayers' because of the ambiguity of this information. Once more, this problem occurs also in seventeenth-century depositions.[31] Table 8.3 compares proportions of 'lifetime stayers' among the Essex deponents with the same measures derived from early-modern deposition material.

Considerable variation is apparent in the various figures for the seventeenth and early eighteenth centuries calculated by Clark. The more detailed work of Souden, however, demonstrated the broad and consistent regional variations over southern England: East Anglia during the seventeenth century witnessed rather more migration (at least by this measure) than the southern Midlands and southwest, with proportions of 'lifetime stayers' rising from east to west.[32] No

[29] GL MS 9065 fo. 70v: 'Ricardus Twety de Buttsbury predicta ubi fuit oriundus et pro maiori parte moram traxit a tempore nativitatis sue illiteratus libere condicionis xxvj annorum etatis ut dicit . . . '.

[30] GLRO DL/C/205 fo. 88: 'Thomas Bogays de Kyrkeby predicta agricultor ubi fuit oriundus & moram suam traxit in dicta villa de Kyrkeby & Frynton a tempore nativitatis sue illiteratus libere condicionis xxxviij annorum etatis & amplius ut dicit . . . '.

[31] Cf. Souden, 'Pre-industrial migration fields', pp. 41–2, 73–4.

[32] *Ibid.*, pp. 73–4.

Table 8.3. *Percentages of 'lifetime stayers' among English ecclesiastical-court deponents*

Essex 1467–97[a] (N = 137)	24.1
Eleven counties in southern/ midland England 1660–1730 (rural males)[b] (N = 3,337)	31.3
Norfolk 1660–1730 (rural males)[b] (N = 1,356)	21.5
Suffolk 1660–1730 (rural males)[b] (N = 308)	16.6
Six dioceses in southern/midland England 1601–1710 (rural males)[c] (N = 5,538)	34.0

[a] Sources: GLRO DL/C/205; GL MS 9065. Among Essex deponents for whom migration data are available, only 7 (5.1%) were women and only 13 (9.5%) were residents of the three major towns in the county (Colchester, Chelmsford, or Maldon). Thus it appears reasonable to compare this group with rural male samples from the early-modern data.
[b] Source: Clark, 'Migration in England', pp. 64–5. The eleven counties are Derbyshire, Dorset, Gloucestershire, Kent, Norfolk, Oxfordshire, Staffordshire, Suffolk, Warwickshire, Wiltshire and Worcestershire.
[c] Source: Souden, 'Pre-industrial migration fields', p. 73. The six dioceses are Bath and Wells, Exeter, Lincoln (Leicester archdeaconry only), Norwich, Oxford and Salisbury.

such calculations have been made from the early-modern London diocese records, so it is undoubtedly more pertinent to compare the Essex data with the figures from Norfolk and Suffolk than with the broader samples of early-modern national data. In this perspective it is striking (particularly in view of the maximal nature of the Essex figure) how closely later-fifteenth-century Essex resembled East Anglia of two centuries later. It should be noted here that mean age of deponent at the time of testimony in the early-modern records was roughly identical to that of Essex deponents, so comparisons among these datasets appear fully warranted.[33]

Such a crude measure of course obscures a potentially great diversity of experiences. The most obvious variables likely to be associated

[33] Neither Souden nor Clark appears to give mean age of deponents in their respective samples, but a rough-and-ready reconstitution from Souden's data (*ibid.*, p. 91) indicates that his rural male deponents were on average aged just over 44 years.

Table 8.4. *Percentages of 'lifetime stayers' among English ecclesiastical-court deponents, by occupation*

	Agriculturalists		Craftsmen/retailers		Labourers	
	%	N	%	N	%	N
Essex 1467–97[a]	28.6	14[b]	30.8	13[c]	0.0	4
Six dioceses in southern/midland England 1601–60 (rural males)[d]	39.8	543	37.5	100	–	–
Norfolk and Suffolk 1601–60 (rural males)[e]	31.3 (yeomen) 27.6 (husbandmen)		48.8 (weavers) 26.7 (smiths) 18.5 (tailors) 15.4 (food trade)		–	–

[a] Sources: GLRO DL/C/205; GL MS 9065.
[b] Comprises 9 *agricultores*, 2 *husbandmen*, 2 *coloni* and 1 *yeoman*.
[c] Comprises 3 *fysshers*, 2 *tailors*, 2 *wevers/textores*, and 1 each *carnifex*, *carpentarius*, *clothmaker*, *faber*, *pogger*, and *tinator*.
[d] Source: Souden, 'Pre-industrial migration fields', p. 81. 'Agriculturalists' comprises 176 yeomen and 367 husbandmen. 'Craftsmen/retailers' comprises 50 weavers, 20 tailors, 19 smiths, and 11 food traders. No data are available in this dataset for labourers.
[e] Source: *ibid*. The format of this tabulated source does not permit citation of Ns for individual dioceses.

with migration, and open to scrutiny from the deposition evidence, are those of occupation and age. To observe this is merely to state the obvious, but to move beyond simple aggregates requires more caution. As already noted, calculating proportions of 'lifetime stayers' on an occupation-specific basis yields quite small samples. Table 8.4 displays these.

Clearly with such scanty data only tentative inferences can be drawn. Yet it is again striking how closely the proportions of 'lifetime stayers' among late-medieval Essex agriculturalists, which is probably the 'hardest' of the pre-1500 figures, resemble their early-modern East Anglian counterparts: slightly more stable geographically by this measure than the entire deponent sample, in which it has already been argued they were overrepresented in proportion to their numbers in the local population, but somewhat less so than seventeenth-century farmers further west.

Although data are available for nearly as many Essex craftsmen and retailers as for agriculturalists, this figure is problematic in that in this category especially any mean will probably conceal greatly divergent patterns resulting from different occupation-specific opportunities or structures of trade organisation. This was certainly the case in the seventeenth century, when the differences between, say, weavers and tailors were marked. There would appear to be no reason to suppose *a priori* that the situation was different in the later 1400s. Nevertheless, late-medieval Essex does not seem to have been radically dissimilar in this regard from the early-modern Norwich diocese.

Finally, though it would obviously be unwarranted to claim the only four labourers in the sample as paradigmatic of all their contemporary brethren, to find them with much greater geographical mobility than the other groups – indeed, in this minuscule sample, with universal mobility – is hardly startling, since this is consonant with much recent writing on the position of the landless or otherwise marginal members of medieval rural society,[34] and this theme will be taken up again below (Chapters 9–10). But underrepresented as they are here, it is worth reiterating that on the evidence of the poll-tax returns labourers formed roughly one-half of the 'households' in the county less than a century earlier, and it is their experience which was modal in late-medieval Essex.

Migration was, then, affected in part by status, occupation, or economic circumstances. But the Essex deposition evidence demon-

[34] See for example the remarks, drawn from a variety of contexts, of Hilton, *Decline of serfdom*, pp. 33–4; Dyer, *Lords and peasants in a changing society*, p. 359; Raftis, *Tenure and mobility*, pp. 173–4; Britton, *The community of the vill*, pp. 146–7.

strates that age was also an important variable in migration and settlement behaviour. In fact, the age-specific nature of movement was at least as marked in the later fifteenth century as it was in the early-modern era, where this subject has been extensively studied.[35] But there are certain further difficulties in specifying this relationship from the medieval evidence.

For those deponents who were not 'lifetime stayers' it is fairly straightforward to calculate a mean 'age at arrival in current parish of residence', simply by subtracting number of years resident there from age at deposition. For the 104 Essex deponents for whom these data are available, this 'mean age at arrival' is 28.3 years.[36] Hence for the majority of deponents who did move at least once during their lifetimes, settlement in 'home' parish occurred well into young adulthood. But there is a positive statistical relationship between age at deposition and 'age at arrival': the older the deponent at the time of rendering testimony, the older he or she was likely to have been at settlement.[37] The reason for this is simple: a 50-year-old deponent could obviously testify to having settled in his current parish of residence at any age up to 50, whereas a 25-year-old deponent could only testify to movements up to age 25. Put another way, this means that 'mean age at arrival' by this simple calculation is partly conditioned by the age structure of the deponent sample itself, and so it is necessary to try to control for this.

Another feature of the evidence further complicates matters. This is the nature of the ages which the deponents reported for themselves in the deposition preambles. The preambles themselves sometimes imply that reported ages were only approximate. This imprecision is discernible in phrases such as '48 years of age and more [*et amplius*]' in the preamble of John Corant (above), '50 years or thereabouts [*vel circiter*]',[38] 'nearly [*fere*] 21',[39] and so forth. Thus the deponents themselves gave somewhat hazy estimates of their ages,[40] and this is compounded by a tendency for reported ages to bunch at integral multiples of ten years. There are certain standard tests for this 'age heaping', to use census-takers' terminology, none of which is exactly applicable to the present situation since such tests were developed for census collections and so are predicated upon the assumption of a

35 E.g. Schofield, 'Age-specific mobility'; Wall, 'Age at leaving home'.
36 Standard deviation = 12.4.
37 When linear regression is calculated with x = age at deposition and y = age at arrival in parish, $r = 0.590$.
38 E.g. GL MS 9065 fo. 3v.
39 E.g. GLRO DL/C/205 fo. 265v.
40 For observations on this subject in early-modern England, see Thomas, 'Age and authority'.

Table 8.5. *'Age at arrival' by ten-year increments, English ecclesiastical-court deponents* (percentages in all cases)

	Proportion of deponent sample 'arriving' within age group		
'Age at arrival'	Essex 1467–97[a]	Six dioceses in southern/midland England 1601–60 (rural males)[b]	Norfolk and Suffolk 1601–60 (rural males)[b]
0–10	8.7	8.1	5.9
11–20	25.0	18.5	20.5
21–30	25.0	36.7	32.6
31–40	26.9	21.6	20.3
41–50	6.7	9.0	11.2
51–60	6.7	4.5	7.4
61+	1.0	1.6	2.2
N=	104	1,272	–

[a] Sources: GLRO DL/C/205; GL MS 9065.
[b] Source: Souden, 'Pre-industrial migration fields', p. 99. (No totals are available for individual dioceses.)

regular life-table-like age structure in the underlying population, whereas the deponent sample obviously does not conform to such an assumption. But by any measure age heaping is fairly severe in this dataset, and thus mean 'age at arrival' can be only approximate.[41]

Table 8.5 presents 'age at arrival' for the Essex deponents and compares this with seventeenth-century data. Of the entire group of deponents, regardless of occupation, for whom settlement data are available and who were not 'lifetime stayers', the proportion who arrived in parish of current residence in each ten-year age range is tabulated.

[41] On tests for accuracy of reported age in census collections, see Shryock, Siegel *et al.*, *The methods and materials of demography*, pp. 114–29. One of the simplest of these tests is Whipple's Index, which assumes rectangularity within a ten-year age range; this is not, of course, wholly realistic for the deponent sample, but as the sample rises to a peak in the thirties and declines again it may be useful to cite the resulting index. This is:

$$\frac{\sum (P_{20} + P_{30} + P_{40} + P_{50} + P_{60}) \times 100}{(1/10) \sum (P_{18} + P_{19} + P_{20} \ldots + P_{65} + P_{66} + P_{67})}$$

or 513.7.

Although it is necessary to be cognisant of the great variety of experiences which comprised the overall sample, a relatively clear picture of age-specific migration patterns in early-modern England is now available, from a number of other sources in addition to deposition evidence. Studies of this problem have generally emphasised the later teens and twenties as the characteristically most mobile stage of the life cycle, representing movements of young persons from parental household to positions as servants or apprentices or periodic movements between masters in such positions, or to other employment opportunities in towns, or (especially for women) movements coincident upon marriage.[42] This is reflected in the seventeenth-century deposition data, with settlement especially common between the ages of 15 and 30.

The medieval Essex data appear broadly similar, except that instead of showing clear peaks in the twenties the range of ages most commonly observed as coinciding with settlement is spread more widely between teens, twenties and thirties. This may conceivably be an artefact of the greater tendency among Essex deponents to report both age and length of settlement in multiples of ten years, a large number of deponents thereby being classed as having settled at ages 20, 30 and 40. Still, within the limits imposed by the nature of the evidence it seems likely that this same interval of late adolescence and early adulthood was also when late-medieval Essex rural dwellers were most typically on the move.

Table 8.6 rearranges the Essex data into subdivisions, based upon the age at which the deponent rendered testimony before the consistory court, and then presents mean 'age at arrival' for each subdivision. The advantage of this arrangement is that it allows some assessment of the influence of age at deposition upon calculated age at arrival. For deponents aged 30 or younger, settlement had occurred fairly early, on average at about the age of 20. But for deponents aged 31–50, mean 'age at arrival' was only about seven years higher. This implies that the distribution of the previous table was not strictly an accident of the deponent age structure itself, but rather that the twenties really were typically the most mobile phase of life in this region and era. It also, incidentally, confirms the greater variability of age at settlement reported by the oldest deponents. Put another way, the range of ages at settlement tabulated in Table 8.5 does not merely reflect the last movement prior to deposition of persons equally likely to move at any point throughout their adult lives. Nevertheless, a significant minority

[42] Schofield, 'Age-specific mobility'; Laslett, 'Clayworth and Cogenhoe', pp. 70–5.

Table 8.6. *Mean 'age at arrival' by age at deposition among Essex ecclesiastical-court deponents, 1467–97*

Age at deposition	Mean 'age at arrival'	Standard deviation	N
0–30	20.1	7.0	24
31–50	27.4	9.7	62
51+	42.6	14.4	18

Sources: GLRO DL/C/205; GL MS 9065.

of deponents migrated rather later in life, and this is a warning against over-simplistic generalisations upon youthful tendencies to migrate.[43]

Finally, this exercise may be taken one step further by looking at mean 'age at arrival' for the different occupational groups already isolated. Table 8.7 presents these.

Once more, small samples dictate caution, and are doubtless the reason why the respective occupational groups' ages at settlement are not, strictly speaking, statistically significant.[44] Yet again, in the absence of larger datasets which could conceivably be derived eventually from more widely drawn pre-1500 English deposition evidence, it is difficult to discern major differences in the experiences of agriculturalists between the fifteenth and seventeenth centuries. The case of craftsmen and retailers is rather less clear-cut, again no doubt due in part to the more heterogenous group from which these data are drawn.

But comparisons between the three groups represented in this table are complicated by the very different age structures of the deponent samples. At the time of rendering testimony, agriculturalists were on average aged 46.9 years,[45] craftsmen and retailers 38.7 years,[46] and labourers 36.5 years.[47] These differences are themselves suggestive. Might 'occupation' itself have had a life-cyclical dimension, with accumulation in earlier life from either inheritance or craft or agricultural labour helping to promote these persons substantially in later life, thus allowing them to cross boundaries of occupational desig-

[43] See the cautionary remarks concerning diversity of ages at migration in different contexts by Wall, 'Age at leaving home'.

[44] The arrays of 'ages at arrival' for the three respective occupational groups were compared, two at a time, by the Mann-Whitney nonparametric test. The results fall well short of the 0.05 significance level: between labourers and craftsmen/retailers, significant only at 0.537; between craftsmen/retailers and agriculturalists, significant only at 0.191; between labourers and agriculturalists, significant only at 0.396.

[45] Standard deviation = 13.1 (N = 10).

[46] Standard deviation = 8.7 (N = 9).

[47] Standard deviation = 5.9 (N = 4).

Table 8.7. *Mean 'age at arrival' among English ecclesiastical-court deponents, by occupation*

	Agriculturalists			Craftsmen/ retailers			Labourers		
	age	standard deviation	N	age	standard deviation	N	age	standard deviation	N
Essex 1467–97[a]	30.7	10.2	10	21.2	15.1	9	26.3	12.6	4
Six dioceses in southern/midland England 1601–60 (rural males)[b]	31.4	13.9 (yeomen)	270	26.3	12.8 (weavers)	66	–	–	–
	28.2	13.2 (husbandmen)	553	27.0	11.4 (tailors)	54			
				28.8	8.0 (smiths)	28			
Norfolk and Suffolk 1601–60 (rural males)[b]	33.0	14.9 (yeomen)	–	28.3	16.1 (weavers)	–	–	–	–
	29.8	14.7 (husbandmen)	–	25.5	10.7 (tailors)	–			
				31.4	8.4 (smiths)	–			

[a] Sources: GLRO DL/C/205; GL MS 9065. 'Agriculturalists' include 6 *agricultores*, 2 *husbandmen*, and 1 each *colonus* and *yeoman*. 'Craftsmen/retailers' include 2 *tailors* and 1 each *carpentarius*, *clothmaker*, *faber*, *fyssher*, *pogger*, *tinator*, and *wever*.

[b] Source: Souden, 'Pre-industrial migration fields', pp. 107–8. No totals are available for individual dioceses, and no data are available for labourers in this dataset.

nation which were fluid to a certain extent anyway? Anecdotal examples of such a process can certainly be produced,[48] though it would seem impossible to demonstrate conclusively (one way or the other) whether social promotion of this sort was widespread enough to undermine the inter-group comparisons drawn here. But for present purposes these differences bear directly upon how differential settlement experiences are to be interpreted from the deposition material.

By the measure of proportion of 'lifetime stayers', Essex agriculturalists appeared to have been slightly more stable than the deponent sample as a whole. But they also had the highest 'mean age at arrival', implying that for those who did move, establishment in a viable economic niche within the regional economy – in this case, acquisition of property – took longer to accomplish. And yet the agriculturalists as deponents were rather older than the other two groups. By contrast the labourers in this sample, though highly mobile in terms of 'lifetime staying', would appear under this analysis to have accomplished 'settlement' earlier in life. But this is misleading, because of the youthfulness of the labourer deponents. In other words, labourers were more likely to have continued to move about longer over the course of the life cycle (as implied by the smaller gap between ages at deposition and arrival), whereas agriculturalists who did move – those who did not achieve their niche by inheritance, endowment at marriage, or other means early in life – would have accomplished this later on but, once having done so, would more likely have stayed put. This was a function of the availability of land, to acquire which, even at a time of relative land abundance in comparison with population levels, required capital and the vacation of a tenement by the previous tenants, as well as, perhaps, an interval of youth spent acquiring practical experience in service to others.

The record of the third group, craftsmen and retailers, is as ever an amalgam of diversity. But from the evidence presented here, 'establishment' in these occupations was both easier (more 'lifetime stayers') and earlier. This is plausible, since establishment in these occupations probably required less initial capital than acquiring land did and, except for the more skilled crafts, perhaps less experience also, as well

[48] See for example Poos, 'Population and resources', pp. 271–2, 275, for the examples of two brothers from High Easter, indicted as common labourer and ploughman respectively under the Statute of Labourers in 1389 (and aged about 19 and 26 respectively on the basis of admission into tithing), who later in the same year received a half-virgate of land from their father, then retiring. Other examples from later-fourteenth-century Essex are given in Dyer, 'Social and economic background', esp. pp. 21–2.

as being probably less directly dependent upon the vacating of a 'niche' by another person. Thus, in the developed rural economy of late-medieval Essex, one was less likely to have to go further afield to achieve establishment. As already shown, the economic geography of the district, and particularly the structure of the rural cloth industry sketched out earlier (above, Chapter 3), were amenable to this. Beyond this point the deposition evidence can be stretched no further, and other varieties of evidence must be invoked.[49]

In sum, though the available sources are insensitive to change over time, the overall incidence of migration implied by the medieval Essex deposition material buttresses the fourteenth-century turnover data cited earlier. Both in gross measures of migration levels and in the age-specific nature of movements, this demographic region appears to have been virtually indistinguishable from early-modern East Anglia. Moreover the occupational subdivision of these data suggests, as did the poll-tax evidence, rather different patterns of personal demographic experiences between different occupational or status groups.

The migration patterns and the characteristics of late-medieval rural nuptiality discussed earlier were interlocking pieces of a single puzzle of demographic experience in the district. Not only do the overall demographic differences of migration and marriage between this society as a whole and early-modern rural England appear to be too small to discern within the broad error margins imposed by the quality of the early evidence, but these two aspects of the life cycles of individuals also reinforce each other. It was inherent in the logic of this district's social structure that, whereas the geographically more stable agriculturalists and craftsmen achieved their niches at somewhat younger ages, the much more numerous labouring people remained unsettled until later in their lives. And so this is consistent with differential nuptiality patterns, particularly labourers' being likely to marry later in life or more likely not to marry at all, relative to the other groups. The nature of wage labour institutions in the district is therefore critical to understanding how this disparity could have existed.

[49] For a similar line of inference from seventeenth-century deposition data, see Souden, 'Pre-industrial migration fields', pp. 98–120.

PART V

'She came that day seeking service'

Eleanor Robard, explaining her journey from Hornchurch to Corringham, 1488[1]

Since such a high proportion of the district's residents worked for wages, the local labour market's structures were significant features of the rural economy, but they also bore major implications for demography and social structure. It was a labour market that had not developed into full proletarianisation: money wages were merely one component of most workers' overall standard of living. Available sources for reconstructing structures of hiring are mostly oblique and partial. For example, the Statute of Labourers (1351) and its subsequent reenactments and enlargements, notably the Statute of Cambridge (1388), attempted to restrain wage-rate increases and regulate terms of employment, but recorded indictments under its terms present only one particular, problematic perspective upon hiring.

The district's labour force comprised both servants and labourers. Servants were largely young, unmarried, and resident in employers' households, and they received a major portion of their remuneration in the form of bed and board. They were highly mobile, often changing employers annually. For many in the district, servanthood was what came after early adolescence and before marriage.

Labourers, on the other hand, largely occupied their own households, though less likely to be married than contemporary agriculturalists. They too were mobile, likely to change residence further through the course of their lives than other occupational groups, and especially moving about on a short-term basis during harvest season. Their pay was much more exclusively in money, but their work patterns were highly seasonal and discontinuous. Despite the higher

[1] GL MS 9065 fo. 67; see also below, Chapter 9.

per diem wage rates of the period than before or after, then, their actual earnings as a whole were not enhanced proportionately. Relative labour shortage during the period had most impact on the sectors of the labour market – particularly the seasonal sectors – of highest marginal labour demand.

Though it is impossible to prove empirically, the circumstances of the local economy probably enhanced the numerical importance of servants *vis-à-vis* labourers after the Black Death, and also provided incentives for employers to substitute cheaper female for more expensive male workers where this was feasible. Both the muted nature of earnings enhancement for labourers, and the quantitative shifts in servanthood and female workers, had potentially wide-ranging effects upon local nuptiality and fertility and, ultimately, the prolonged nature of the late-medieval population depression. In fact, these structures of local labour markets help to resolve the conundrum of modest fertility and prolonged demographic contraction in an era of high wage rates.

9

Servants

In any highly differentiated rural society, with many individuals and families partly or heavily dependent upon wages earned through working for others, forms and institutions of hiring are obviously of critical importance to the local economy. In late-medieval Essex agriculturalists, craftsmen and even a few labourers took on non-familial workers to augment their own or their families' capacities. Labour forms and institutions had to be flexible enough to adapt to many different circumstances, arising from agrarian regimes and industrial occupations that varied over time and space, from changes in wage and price levels, and from the many other factors that affected the supply and demand of workers.

But labour forms and institutions in this society did not reside solely in the realm of abstract economic forces. On the contrary, they were at the same time products of, and influences upon, social structure and demographic change. They were the means by which employers evened out the cyclical disparities between their own intrinsic labour reserves – those of their own biological families, if such they had residing with them – and the less readily changeable configurations of land resources or workshops' capacities that they possessed. And from the employees' perspectives, accumulating the practical experience and the material wherewithal to establish themselves in life was likely to be much affected by the ways they were deployed within the matrix of familial and non-familial labour.

In the early-modern English rural economy the most fundamental distinction between labour forms was that between labourers and servants. Put most simply, labourers were generally adults, living within their own households, and hired by others on a short-term basis, often by the day.[1] Their employment was heavily seasonal, and

[1] Everitt, 'Farm labourers'.

in periods of slack demand for their work they typically resorted to by-employments or quite small-scale farming. Labourers in this sense comprised an occupation, whereas servanthood is more usefully understood as a phase of life.

Servants in husbandry in early-modern England were youthful, usually leaving their parental homes in their early or middle teens and spending up to a decade or more as servants for a succession of masters.[2] Servants lived in their employers' households and so received a large portion of their remuneration in kind – food and lodging – and only part in money. They were almost always unmarried: servanthood, for many boys and girls in sixteenth-century England, was what came after puberty but before marriage and establishment as husbandmen, labourers, or the like. Servants were employed on a long-term basis, usually for a year at a time with one employer before moving on to another household and often another parish. They were thus highly (though, as Kussmaul put it, 'ambiguously') mobile as well.[3] Finally, by mediating between leaving home and establishing neolocal households, servanthood was an integral component of Hajnal's 'Northwestern European' marriage system.[4]

These are the senses in which the terms 'labourer' and 'servant' are understood by historians of post-medieval England. Broadly speaking, these two variants of labour forms were the chief constituents of wage workers in late-medieval Essex also, and the same terminology will be applied here. But several serious problems need to be addressed before assuming that the two historical settings were very similar in this regard. The first problem is, once again, the basic one of terminology.

Late-medieval England did not possess a completely unambiguous terminology to denote what historians understand by 'servant' and 'labourer'. To be sure, the later-fifteenth-century sumptuary statutes, which proscribed excessively costly apparel for different degrees and statuses of English people, placed at the very bottom of their social hierarchy the 'servant in husbandry, common labourer, and servant to any artificer' (*Servaunt al husbandrie . . . comyne laborer . . . Servaunt al ascune Artificer*), as if these were taken for granted as established components of English social structure.[5] And in fact the Latin terms employed most frequently in contemporary documents to describe these workers were *serviens* and *laborator* or *laborarius* respectively. But

[2] Kussmaul, *Servants in husbandry*.

[3] Kussmaul, 'The ambiguous mobility of farm servants'.

[4] Hajnal, 'Two kinds of pre-industrial household formation', esp. pp. 92–9.

[5] 3 Edw. IV c.5; 22 Edw. IV c.1; *Statutes of the realm* vol. ii, pp. 399–402, 468–70.

it would be mistaken to translate, automatically, every occurrence of these terms into the English words that they so closely resemble.[6]

Etymologically *serviens* connotes someone 'serving' (in the sense of 'subservient to') another. The word theoretically could, and occasionally actually did, denote sons or daughters residing in their parents' homes. The one example of this in the surviving 1381 Essex poll-tax returns was 'John the son [and] *serviens*' of Edmund Tanner, listed as such at Great Baddow.[7] In this sense the term closely resembled 'mainpast' (*manupastus*), or anyone residing in the household of, and legally and morally the responsibility of, the household's head.[8] Some examples survive (though none has been found in Essex) of *servientes per dietam*, apparently workers not residing with their employers but possibly still contracted to them on a long-term basis.[9] And notably absent from the Essex poll-tax listings and most other contemporary documents were craftsmen's apprentices, some of whom doubtless are lurking among the *servientes* of the listings. To confuse matters further, *serviens* is familiar to students of manorial account rolls as the Latin equivalent of 'sergeant', an administrative official.[10] But in the great majority of late-medieval Essex sources persons described by the term were attached explicitly to a master or mistress, in the form 'A the *serviens* of B'. Less ambiguous, but also less commonly encountered in the documents, are *ancilla* ('maidservant') and *garco* ('boy' or 'servant-boy'). There is ample evidence to indicate (as this chapter is intended to show) that such words employed in this fashion do mean 'servant' in the sense elaborated above. It is necessary to emphasise this, since Hanawalt recently claimed that 'The evidence for live-in servants is hardly overwhelming.'[11]

On the other hand *laboratores*, as Hilton noted, are hardly ever described as attached to other people's households, and so seem

[6] Putnam, *Enforcement of the statutes of labourers*, pp. 79–80, noted in surveying occupations of those indicted under the Statute of Labourers, 'It must be remembered that the ambiguous term *serviens* is very frequent, with no clue as to the nature of the occupation'.

[7] PRO.E179.107.63 m.1: 'Edmundus Tanner & uxor Johannes filius serviens eiusdem'. Cf. Hilton, *The English peasantry in the later middle ages*, pp. 30–1.

[8] Examples of this use of the term are given later in this chapter.

[9] Hilton, 'Some social and economic evidence', p. 121.

[10] E.g. PRO. SC6.838.21 (account roll, Claret Hall in Ashen, 1346/7); cf. Harvey, *Manorial records*, p. 6.

[11] Hanawalt, *The ties that bound*, p. 165. She also admits (pp. 163–4) that servants as proportions of the recorded poll-tax populations were as high as in early-modern England (for this see below). The circumstantial details of servants' lives discussed later in this chapter, however, derive from unpublished sources largely unconsidered by Hanawalt.

mostly to have been the labourers of this study's terminology.[12] But here too caution is necessary. *Laboratores* as a group shade off at their upper ranks into the lesser husbandmen, since cross-reference between poll-tax listings and manorial rentals reveals that some labourers held land and a few possessed more than five acres.[13] On the other hand, *laborator* could simply be used to describe anyone employed, whether occasionally or otherwise, by another. It would seem to have been in this sense that one suit in an Essex manorial court in 1383 spoke of a boy hired *in officio laborarij* and two sentences later referred to the time he was a *serviens*, both phrases pertaining to the same annual employment contract.[14]

Perhaps most ambiguous of all were the *famuli*. *Famulus* – etymologically, one of the household or *familia* – before 1300 most commonly referred to the permanent staff of workers employed on the manorial demesne, as opposed to the extra workers hired for a few days or weeks at harvest or haymaking.[15] But by the later fourteenth century, the word could be used as a synonym for *laborarius*: the 1381 listings for several townships in Hinckford Hundred lumped together *famuli et laborarij* under one heading, in nearly all cases not being explicitly attached to masters and apparently living in their own households.[16] And yet occasionally in the poll-tax returns, and often in other documents including many that provide corroborating circumstantial detail, people described as 'A the *famulus* of B' clearly were servants as the term is being used here.[17]

This protracted discussion of the terminology of labour forms in late-medieval Essex does not spring from mere etymological quibbling. Any discussion of the quantitative weight and qualitative significance of servanthood in the period must display great sensitivity to the ambiguities of these words, for tax listings and other contemporary sources demonstrably varied a great deal from place to place and context to context in how they used the terms. This chapter is concerned with servanthood in its economic and social-structural

[12] Hilton, *The English peasantry in the later middle ages*, p. 34.

[13] See above, Chapter 1.

[14] ERO D/DP M190 (Writtle court, 7 Feb 1383): '. . . Johannes Melford . . . servivit dicto Johanni Hurtlynd in officio laborarij per unum annum . . . in defectu ipsius Johannis tempore quo fuit serviens eius perite fuerunt duo bidentes . . .'. Other examples of similar terminology in manorial-court litigation appear in ERO D/DP M214 (Writtle court, 11 Oct 1410) and ERO D/DGe M251 (Hatfield Broadoak court, 19 Nov 1418).

[15] Postan, *The famulus*.

[16] PRO.E179.107.68, township listings for Belchamp Walter, Gestingthorpe, Halstead, Pebmarsh, Great Yeldham and others.

[17] Examples of this use of the term are given later in this chapter; cf. Hilton, *The English peasantry in the later middle ages*, p. 30.

aspects in the district at the end of the middle ages; Chapter 10 will deal with labourers and with the considerations surrounding how these two labour forms were balanced in the Essex workforce. The next problem to address here is how, quantitatively, servanthood in this district compared with the England of two centuries or so later. The only source likely to yield much of a systematic sense of the prevalence of servanthood is the 1381 poll-tax listings, and from the foregoing discussion it is clear that strict criteria must be followed to identify who might reasonably safely be considered servants. Only those described as 'A the *serviens/famulus/ancilla/garco* of B' can meet this demand.

By this criterion the Essex returns are of relatively little value, even when compared with the listings of other counties. Only 269 servants (under such a strict definition) appear in the surviving listings – 183 males, 82 females and 4 people whose sex is unspecified or illegible in the documents – representing 2.7 per cent of all persons listed (i.e. of the age group 15 years and older). This is a remarkably low percentage, in comparison with estimates from the tax returns of other counties and from other types of sources. In the 1381 Leicestershire returns servants constituted 24.8 per cent of all taxpayers; Hilton's studies of the returns from several western counties imply proportions not much lower.[18] By contrast, in the early-modern English parochial listings amenable to analysis, servants comprised typically 10 per cent or so of a parish's entire population, although the mean figure for 29 communities between 1650 and 1749, a period in which servanthood was especially extensive, was 18.4 per cent.[19] But early-modern servants did constitute a much higher proportion of older adolescents and young adults: in Ealing (Middlesex) in 1599, for example, servants comprised four-fifths of all males aged 15 to 24 years.[20] Perhaps

18 The Leicestershire (Gartree Hundred) returns' data include servants who were listed in a second tax collection after escaping payment in the first: author's calculation from PRO.E179.133.35; cf. Poos, 'Population and resources', p. 150n. Hilton 'Some social and economic evidence', pp. 122–4; Hilton, *The English peasantry in the later middle ages*, pp. 31–5. Another aspect of the prevalence of servanthood recoverable from the poll-tax returns and possibly other sources from other counties is proportions of households containing servants, which could range from estimates of 20 per cent in Rutland in 1377 to 40 per cent (based, less reliably, on manorial-court-roll data) in early-fourteenth-century Halesowen (Worcs.), if anything rather higher than cognate figures from early-modern England: Smith, 'The people of Tuscany and their families', p. 123.

19 Kussmaul, *Servants in husbandry*, pp. 12–13; Wall, 'Regional and temporal variations in English household structure', p. 94. It should be noted that, since servants were concentrated in the ages 15–24 in early-modern England, they comprised a much higher fraction of this particular age group: Kussmaul, *Servants in husbandry*, p. 3.

20 Kussmaul, *Servants in husbandry*, p. 71.

slightly more credible in the Essex poll-tax evidence are the patterns of servants' dispositions among employer-'households'. In the great majority of cases 'servant-keeping households' had only one servant each; agriculturalists and craftsmen were apparently equally likely in proportional terms to have employed servants, though a very few labourers had them also; and married couples and single 'household' heads were also seemingly equally likely, proportional to their recorded appearance in the tax lists, to have had servants.[21]

Many more Essex servants may be hiding behind the appellation *famulus*, otherwise unspecified. But since servants, especially female servants, were notoriously among the most likely to be excluded from this tax collection, and since the 1381 collection in Essex was in turn notoriously deficient in comparison with earlier collections,[22] poll-tax-derived data from this district are unfortunately of little value in assessing the proportions of servants within the general population. In order to understand the circumstances of late-medieval Essex servants, and in particular their marital status, ages, mobility and hiring terms, it is necessary to turn to an array of other evidence.

The bulk of the medieval Essex evidence indeed supports the impression that fourteenth- and fifteenth-century servants were almost exclusively unmarried, and hints also survive that contemporaries, especially their employers, regarded this as an integral aspect of servanthood. Only three servants – at Great Yeldham, Fyfield and Shelley – were listed as married in the surviving poll-tax returns for the county.[23] A less systematic survey of the returns from other counties yields the same impression.[24]

[21] Among the 207 'servant-keeping households' in the surviving 1381 Essex returns, 170 had one servant, 28 had two, 5 had three, and 4 more 'households' had four, five, nine and ten servants each. Of those 82 'servant-keeping households' whose heads were listed with occupations, 25 were agriculturalists, 22 craftsmen or retailers, 10 were labourers, and 5 were gentry; 20 more were represented by clergy, who of course did not appear themselves in the returns of this laity-based tax but whose servants often did. Of the 207 total 'servant-keeping households', 143 were headed by married couples, 22 by single males and 22 by single females, again with 20 more headed by clergy.

[22] That is, when enrolled-account totals for taxpayers in each county in 1377 and 1381 are compared, only nine counties – all in the sparsely populated far north and west of the country – experienced greater proportional drops than Essex in taxpayer totals. Thus the especially large numbers of 'excluded' potential taxpayers in Essex perhaps allows greater concealment of servants. Figures calculated from Oman, *The great revolt of 1381*, pp. 163–5.

[23] PRO.E179.107.68 (Great Yeldham): 'Johannes famulus Johannis Charyr Margeria uxor eius'; E179.107.60 m.3 (Fyfield): 'Simon Clerk Johanna uxor eius Willelmus serviens eius Alicia uxor eius'; *ibid.* m.20 (Shelley): 'Johanne Hierde serviente Johannis Bataylle Margeria uxore eiusdem Johannis Hierde'.

[24] It was Hanawalt's inattention to the shadings of social terminology that led her to conclude that a significant fraction of 'servants' in the 1381 Suffolk listings were

Married servants do occasionally appear in other contexts: for example, the wife of a butcher's servant was churched after childbirth at Walden in 1474.[25] And scattered among suits for broken agreement or debt concerning wages in Essex manorial courts in the later fourteenth and fifteenth centuries are a few instances in which husband and wife appeared together as plaintiffs, seeking unpaid wages for the wife's prior employment as a servant from her former master. In a typical case, from Writtle in 1419, William Fynch and Alice his wife sued John Whelere for Alice's wages for four years' employment with Whelere more than five years earlier.[26] It is conceivable that Alice was married during her time as a servant, but although not explicit, in this or similar cases, it is likely that Alice's leaving her position with Whelere preceded her marriage to Fynch.[27] A coincidence between exit from service and marriage is hinted at by evidence from other regions of England at the time, such as a number of licences to migrate granted at East Midlands manors of Ramsey Abbey in which women were given permission to enter service until they married their employers.[28]

That marriage and servanthood were ordinarily regarded as incompatible in the later middle ages is also implied by occasional vignettes issuing from testimony rendered at hearings establishing proof of ages of feudal heirs. These inquests were required when heirs or heiresses to property held in chief from the Crown prepared to assume tenure

married. Hanawalt, *The ties that bound*, pp. 95–6, calculating from the 1381 Suffolk returns published in Powell, *The rising in East Anglia*, observed that percentages listed as married in these records were quite high for all social groups, including 'servants'. But Hanawalt has taken *laborarii* and *servientes* in this county's returns as unproblematically equivalent to 'labourers' and 'servants' in the early-modern sense. This is unlikely, since many of these vills were composed wholly or nearly wholly of persons of these statuses (and so *laborarii* and *servientes* most likely include smallholders and labourers respectively), and since relatively few of these 'servants' are explicitly attached to employers' households in these returns.

25 ERO D/DBy Q12 fo. 93v: '. . . Item de purificatione uxoris servientis Johannis Danbery jd. . . .'.

26 ERO D/DP M223 (Writtle court, 7 Jan 1419): 'Willelmus Fynch & Alicia uxor eius optulerunt se versus Johannem Whelere . . . de placito debiti . . . quia predicta Alicia deservivit eidem Johanni a festo Sancti Michaelis anno regni regis Henrici quarti . . . xj° per iiij^or annos integros . . .'.

27 Clark, 'Medieval labor law', p. 338 n. 28 discusses cases such as these and argues that wives in such disputes married after leaving service. It was the convention (or perhaps in some manors the requirement) that married women bring litigation in manorial courts jointly with their husbands, even in matters pertaining only to the woman, which resulted in husbands' appearances in such contexts. This point is discussed, though not directly with reference to ex-servants' disputes, by Bennett, *Women in the medieval countryside*, pp. 108–10.

28 E.g. Dewindt, ed., *Liber Gersumarum*, pp. 172 (nos. 2024–5, 2027), 194 (no. 2293).

upon reaching the age of majority (21 for males, 14 for females).[29] Witnesses were required to swear to their memory of the heir's birth, and testimony focused, typically, upon events with mnemonic value, such as having been present at the heir's baptism, having acquired property or suffered misfortune on the day of the heir's birth, and the like. Many of these narratives were somewhat stereotypical, being repeated at different hearings by different witnesses with only minor variations of detail. Some historians have therefore chosen to question their strict factual accuracy, and undoubtedly it would be foolhardy to lend blind credence to the exact dates or circumstantial minutiae of every individual testimony.[30] Nevertheless, so long as one is concerned merely with the general plausibility of situations detailed in their testimonies, particularly where these are less stereotypical, there is no reason to reject unreservedly the notion that the vignettes represent experiences actually drawn from everyday life.

An example will illustrate how cautiously one must tread with this material. In one inquest, Robert Danyell testified that in 1401 at Little Laver, when he was 27 years old, he 'married a certain Rosa, recently his wife, until then the servant of Elizabeth the mother of the said Thomas [the heir] . . . '.[31] This would seem *prima facie* to support, albeit anecdotally, the impression that for at least some female servants exit from service coincided with marriage. But confidence in the strict veracity of Danyell's vignette is rather undermined by the fact that a nearly identical story – that is, in nearly identical language and in two instances with 'Rosa' given as the servant's name, though with different employers' names – was told by three other people at three other Essex proof-of-age inquests within a few months.[32] It would obviously strain one's credulity to believe that all four men had had such identical experiences, on the exact dates and with the particular people given in their testimonies. On the other hand it is less credible to regard such a story as an absolute fabrication, wholly unlikely ever to have happened in real life, than as either the actual experience of one witness which was then echoed as a likely-sounding account by later jurors, or else as a scenario which represents a familiar or at the least a plausible experience within late-medieval Essex society. And

29 Walker, 'Proof of age of feudal heirs'.

30 E.g. Hunnisett, 'The reliability of inquisitions', p. 206, speaks of the 'artificial nature of many "proofs of age" . . .'

31 PRO.C139.13.51 (inquest, 22 Feb 1424): ' . . . dicit quod ipse Robertus . . . duxit in uxorem quandam Rosam nuper uxorem suam adtunc servientem Elizabethe matris predicti Thome filij . . . '.

32 PRO. C139.7.54 (inquest, 31 May 1423); C139.13.52 (inquest, 10 Jun 1424); C139.13.55 (inquest, 21 Jul 1424).

slightly less scepticism is called for when the testimony is especially laden with circumstantial detail, or is not paralleled by other near-identical testimonies. It is with this degree of caution that proof-of-age inquests have been used in this and other chapters.

Since the point was to attest to the heir's birth date, many witnesses testified to having been servants in the household in question and thus in a good position to have been privy to family events. Typical of the more commonplace narratives rendered in this context is that of John Ledet, who in 1369 recalled that 21 years earlier at Little Laver 'he was then a servant of the father of the said John [i.e. the heir in question] . . . and he rode a horse to fetch John's godfather and fell into a pit and broke his arm, and so he well remembers the said John's age'.[33] Ten years later in another typically stereotypical account, John Palmer claimed to have been a servant of the heir's grandfather in 1358 at Totham, and to have been present in church at the heir's baptism.[34]

But on rare occasions the narratives of these former servants are rather more revealing of domestic aspects of their positions. In 1372 at Kirton in eastern Suffolk (a few miles north of the Essex border), William de Strate recalled that 21 years earlier he had been a servant, had espoused a female servant in the same household without the permission of the maidservant's mistress, and as a result had been struck and wounded by the master of the house: a violation of the sexual etiquette, or merely the domestic discipline, of servants within their households?[35] Further afield from Essex and somewhat earlier, a more explicit sign of contemporary incompatibility between servanthood and marriage was expressed in the testimony of Henry del Hill, who remembered that he had been a servant at Spaldington (Yorks.) and 'because he had married he was removed from his position'.[36]

One final qualitative insight into the domestic life of servants from this testimony can be drawn from the narrative of Thomas de Hodyng,

[33] PRO.C135.211.2 (inquest, 11 Jun 1369): '. . . tunc tempore ipse fuit serviens patris predicti Johannis filij Willelmi & sicut equitavit pro compatre ipsius Johannis filij Willelmi cecidit in foveam & fregit brachium suum . . .'.

[34] PRO.C136.11.7 (inquest, 26 Jul 1379): '. . . ipse fuit serviens Johannis de Cogeshale militis avi predicti Willelmi Cogeshale chivalri tempore nativitatis ipsius Willelmi Cogeshale chivalri & fuit cum Willelmo de Wauton milite ad ecclesiam ville de Todham ad baptizationem . . .'.

[35] PRO.C135.231.17 (inquest, 19 Jul 1372): '. . . tunc tempore ipse fuit serviens predicti Johannis de Londham & Johanne uxoris & quia desponsavit Margeriam ancillam prefate Johanne sine licencia sua idem Johannes de Londham ipsum Willelmum vulneravit & percussit digitum suum . . .'.

[36] PRO.C135.33.17 (inquest, 3 Feb 1332): '. . . idem Henricus fuit tunc serviens ibidem & quia dat se in maritagium amotus fuit ab officio suo . . .'.

who in 1357 testified that he remembered the birth of John de Liston at Braintree because at about that same time he (Thomas) had had a son born to himself and Agnes, a servant of his father's.[37] That young, unmarried female servants were at an especial risk of sexual predation by masters, masters' male relatives, and other men would seem to be borne out by the proceedings of rural deanery or other local ecclesiastical courts that dealt with correction of morals offences. Though disappointingly few such records survive, and none, apparently, from Essex, the point is illustrated by a series of consistory courts held in the diocese of Rochester (just across the Thames, south of Essex) in 1363–4, where of 65 citations for fornication or adultery, 17 cases pertained to women explicitly denoted as servants.[38]

Indeed the theme surfaces also in a late-fourteenth- or early-fifteenth-century poem on the subject of 'the servant-girl's holiday', combining a fairly conventional theme (the pregnancy lament) with especially vivid details of maidservants' domestic duties. In this poem the servant-girl in question was impregnated on her holiday, and ended by lamenting:

> durst y nat my dame telle
> Wat me betydde Þis holyday.[39]

Late-medieval servants, then, with occasional exceptions were unmarried. The texts of the later-fourteenth-century labour legislation hint that to contemporaries it was commonplace for servants in husbandry to commence service at a quite youthful age. The Statute of Cambridge (1388) contained a hopeful clause to this effect: 'It is ordained and assented that he or she who is accustomed to work with plough or cart, or other labour or service in husbandry, till they be aged 12 years, shall henceforth remain at the same work and not be put to any handicraft'.[40] To discern the typical ages of servants in this period in any systematic manner is more difficult, and the Essex evidence is largely restricted to male servants because the few contexts in which this information was proffered – most importantly, depositions before ecclesiastical courts and testimony at proof-of-age inquests – were usually male preserves. In the only other systematic attempt to assess medieval servants' ages from ecclesiastical-court

[37] PRO.C135.138.2 (inquest, 16 Aug 1357): '. . . habuit unum filium nomine Thome procreatum de quadam ancilla patris sui nomine Agnetis . . .'.

[38] SJCC D57.170.

[39] Robbins, ed., *Secular lyrics*, pp. 24–5.

[40] 12 Ric. II c.5, printed in *Statutes of the realm* vol. ii, p. 57: 'Item ordeinez est & assentuz que celuy ou celle que use de laborer a la charue & charette ou autre labour ou service de husbandrie tanquil soit del age de xij. ans, que delors enavant il demoerge a cell' labour sanz estre mys a mistier ou artifice . . .'.

data, Goldberg has recently drawn upon the rather fuller York evidence for the fourteenth and fifteenth centuries to examine female servants. In a sample of thirty female servants, approximate ages clustered closely in the late teens and early twenties.[41] By contrast, only one Essex servant appeared as a deponent in the surviving church-court depositions before 1500: in 1487 Robert Brightmay, a smith's servant in Prittlewell, aged 28 'or thereabouts', testified to having been present in a house where one of the parties in a matrimonial suit had expressed her willingness to contract a marriage.[42]

But, as has already been shown, a small group of Essex men testified at proof-of-age hearings to having been servants at the time of the birth of the heir in question. Where the ex-servant/witness's age at the time of the inquest was recorded, simple subtraction of years elapsed since the heir's birth from deponent's age at rendering testimony yields an estimate of the servant's age at the time of the remembered incident. Such age estimates will inevitably be only approximate. For one thing, the same phenomenon of 'age heaping' is apparent among recorded ages of witnesses at proof-of-age hearings as was discussed above concerning the church-court depositions, with a disproportionate number of witnesses giving their ages as integral multiples of five or ten years.[43] Again, it seems plausible to assume (though there is no proof) that if there is any systematic error in these age estimates, it was probably upward: that is, the testimony of ostensibly older

41 Goldberg, 'Marriage, migration, servanthood and life-cycle', pp. 150–2. This sample includes both servants who rendered testimony and whose ages were given in the records, and women who according to their testimony had earlier been servants and whose ages when in service can be calculated 'retrospectively', by subtracting years elapsed since events described from age at deposition.

42 GL MS 9065 fo. 21v (deposition, 27 Jun 1487): '. . . presens fuit iste juratus in aula dicti Roberti & audivit quod prefata Agneta in parlura ibidem . . . advocere quod ipsa voluit habere prefatum Johannem in maritum suum . . .'.

43 The ages of witnesses at these inquests were almost always recorded, though sometimes betraying their approximate nature, e.g. PRO.C135.239.8 (inquest, 21 Oct 1374): '. . . Thomas Caitere etatis triginta nonem annorum & amplius juratus & diligente examinatus . . .'. When Whipple's index (cf. Shryock, Siegal *et al.*, *The methods and materials of demography*, pp. 114–29) is calculated from the stated ages of all witnesses (i.e. not just those of ex-servants) in inquests used here to derive servants' ages (see below for references), and calculated as:

$$\frac{\sum (P_{40} + P_{50} + P_{60}) \times 100}{(1/10) \sum (P_{38} + P_{39} + P_{40} \ldots + P_{66} + P_{67})}$$

the result is 322.4. The mean age of all witnesses in this sample was 51.1 (standard deviation = 7.5), compared with 49.0 (standard deviation = 7.1) for ex-servant/witnesses.

witnesses was perhaps regarded as more credible, so there is no reason to suppose that the range of servants' ages thus reconstructed is a dispassionate reflection of the actual range of ages of servants in service.

Moreover, many (though by no means all)[44] of these witnesses claimed to have been servants of tenants-in-chief: in other words, persons of at least minor gentry status. They are for this reason also, then, less than perfectly representative of all Essex servants including those in households of less elevated status, because 'servants' of gentry may more likely have included longer-term retainers, again rendering these servants' estimated mean ages maximal. Finally, when this analysis is restricted to only one county, a very small sample of (ex-) servants is available; undoubtedly a country-wide sample would be worth compiling.

For the entire fourteenth and fifteenth centuries, the ages of only 17 Essex servants can be reconstructed in this manner from the surviving proof-of-age inquests.[45] These reconstructed ages range from a low of 15 years to a high of 39, the mean being 28.4 (standard deviation = 7.2). Again, if anything, this mean is likely to be an overestimate. The implication is that, for males at least, servanthood was most typically an experience of one's mid-to-late teens through later twenties or even early thirties, although servants of a fairly wide age range can be found. Thus, while to a substantial degree medieval Essex servanthood was probably life-cyclical, this paradigm must not be pressed too far, since some males remained servants at least well into middle age.

The relative youthfulness of some servants is, however, reflected in the fact that occasionally the father of an ex-servant sued the latter's former employer in manorial court, implying that the ex-servant himself or herself was still too young to pursue such litigation in his or her own right. In one such case from Writtle in 1383, John Melford, a tailor, brought a suit claiming that he had agreed to hire his son to John Hurtlynd for one year, for which he (the father) had yet to receive 15d.

[44] E.g. PRO.C139.13.52 (inquest, 10 Jun 1424), for a servant of the vicar of Thorpe-le-Soken; C139.31.72 (inquest, 13 Mar 1427), for a servant of the bailiffs of Colchester. Omitted from this sample are a few cases where *serviens* appears to mean '(manorial) sergeant', e.g. C135.67.7 (inquest, 2 Sep 1342): '... serviens manerij de Wokyndon ...'.

[45] These cases are taken from PRO.C135.19.2; C135.67.7; C135.147.2; C135.147.11; C135.155.9; C135.180.92; C135.211.2; C135.239.8; C136.11.7; C137.64.83; C139.13.51; C139.13.52; C139.13.55; C139.31.72; C139.113.3 (two ex-servant/witnesses); C139.120.51.

of the agreed 5s. stipend. Hurtlynd replied that the boy had broken a pot and wounded two of his sheep, and that the wages had been withheld as compensation for these damages.[46]

Essex servants in the fourteenth and fifteenth centuries were thus for the most part both unmarried and youthful, and their resemblance to their early-modern counterparts extended to their migration behaviour. For medieval Essex servants regularly moved from village to village or parish to parish when they entered or left employment or exchanged one master for another. The age-specific mobility evidence discussed in the previous chapter accords well with this impression, since the late teens and twenties were shown in that evidence to have been the most mobile stages of the life cycle for all occupational groups.[47] But although unfortunately almost no evidence of servant migration as such is contained in the surviving London diocesan courts of the period, fleeting and indirect glimpses of this mobility can be found in this and other types of evidence. John Whitypoll of Corringham (in southern Essex) deposed that in February 1488 one Eleanor Robard came to his house.

> . . . and he asked why she had come and what she wanted, and she replied that she had come that day from Hornchurch [a distance of about nine miles] to seek service there, because her master at Hornchurch had not given her an adequate stipend, and since she did not have any contract [*convencio*] with him she came seeking better service . . .[48]

Termination of a servant's employment and subsequent migration might come about for a variety of other reasons: Simon Maynard recalled at a proof-of-age hearing that in 1309 he had been in service at Little Sampford, but that his master had died and 'soon thereafter

[46] ERO D/DP M190 (Writtle court, 7 Feb 1383): '. . . dicit quod quidam Johannes Melford filius suus ex convencione per ipsum facta servivit dicto Johanni Hurtlynd in officio laborari per unum annum capiendo salarium per statutum provisum videlicet vs. . . . [John Hurtlynd] dicit quod in defectu ipsius Johannis tempore quo fuit serviens eius perite fuerunt duo bidentes ipsius Johannis Hurtlynd precij xld. & eciam ipse Johannes fregit unam tibiam unius olle enee precij vjd. . . .'. Similar cases are discussed by Clark, 'Medieval labor law', pp. 342–4, and Hilton, *The English peasantry in the later middle ages*, pp. 51–2.

[47] These occupations referred, of course, to the positions deponents had achieved in middle age, and the ecclesiastical-court depositions are mostly silent as to whether earlier movements stemmed directly from servanthood.

[48] GL MS 9065 fo. 67 (deposition, 1 Feb 1488): '. . . interrogavit eam iste juratus quare illa venit et quid vellet que respondit quod eodem die venit a parochia de Hornchurch quesitura ibidem servicium pro eo quod eius Magister apud Hornchurch non dedit ei stipendium competens et quia non stetit cum eo in aliqua convencione venit quesitura melius servicium . . .'.

Simon was dwelling with' the previous tenant-in-chief whose heir's age was at issue, at Great Sampford (about two miles away).[49]

Another oblique glimpse of this sort of mobility may be gleaned from the quite rare surviving pre-1500 wills of persons explicitly described as servants. When William Pole, then the servant of John Eton at South Mimms (Middx.), composed his will in August 1464 he left small cash bequests to parish churches as widely scattered as Southam (Warwicks.), Bloxham (Oxon.), and Monken Hadley (Herts.), and made further disposition of his goods in Warwickshire, Oxfordshire, Middlesex and Essex.[50] Testators of all statuses in this period regularly made bequests to churches in communities where they had previously dwelt or where they had family connections.[51] In the case of a servant like Pole, these places probably included scenes of former employment, and the wide geographical range of communities which Pole chose to remember at the close of his life was usually characteristic only of the wills of testators of much more elevated status.

It was, of course, one of the central features of the Statute of Labourers and its successive reenactments to attempt to restrain the mobility of labour. The Statute of Cambridge (1388) in particular devoted considerable attention to stipulating that servants, even at the end of their terms of employment, not travel outside their hundred or wapentake to seek another position without letters under the king's seal.[52] And apart from straightforward charges of receiving excessive pay, no indictments in surviving sessions material are more frequent than charges that workers left their employers, and often their communities, before the end of their contracted employment term. As already noted, this evidence has long been cited by historians arguing that the post-Black Death decades witnessed a marked increase in rural mobility.[53]

But it would be mistaken to magnify this evidence so far as to imply, as some authors have done, that wholesale, unlawful desertion by

[49] PRO.C135.33.13 (inquest, 6 Apr 1332): '... idem Simon fuit in servicio domini de Parva Sanford qui quidem dominus obiit die nativitatis predicti Willelmi & statim postea dictus Simon commoravit cum predicta Johanna de Kenefyld ...'.

[50] GL MS 9171/5 fo. 365v: '... Ego Willelmus Pole modo trahens moram in servicio cum Johanne Eton ... ecclesie beate Marie virginis de Monkenhadley ... lego vjd ... ecclesie de Bloxham xijd. ... ecclesie de Southam xijd. ... omnia alia bona mea res & catalla cuiuscumque condicionis aut speciei sint & in quorumcumque manibus aut locis fuerint vel inveniri poterint tam in parochia de Bloxham quam in parochia de Southam Item infra comitates Warwic' Oxon' Essex' & Midd' & alibi infra regnum Anglie ...'.

[51] Cf. Fitch, ed., *Index to testamentary records in the Commissary Court* vol. i, pp. v–vi.

[52] 12 Ric. II c.3; *Statutes of the realm* vol. ii, p. 56.

[53] E.g. Ritchie, 'Labour conditions'; Hilton, *Decline of serfdom*, pp. 33–4.

servants of their masters was in any sense a typical experience during these years. An admittedly very rough-and-ready calculation can illustrate this point. During the Essex peace sessions held within the county between January 1377 and September 1379, a period of roughly two and a half years, 15 indictments were made of employees either explicitly leaving service illegally or else simply workers illegally migrating in search of higher pay, these mobility-related cases being far outnumbered by simple instances of receiving excessive wages. These 15 cases may be compared with the likely number of servants actually present in the county at the time of the 1381 poll-tax collection: 269 recorded servants in the surviving returns for six hundreds (or about one-third of the county), itself, as already argued, probably a gross underenumeration of actual servant numbers. At the most extreme, then, it is hardly likely that as many as one-half of one per cent of all Essex servants in any given year became the focus of legal proceedings through deserting their employers, even at the height of Statute of Labourers prosecution activity.[54]

Nevertheless, both the texts of the labour legislation itself and the substance of indictments brought under its terms leave no doubt: contemporaries were well aware that both servants and labourers moved from community to community as a matter of course while changing employers, and also that restraining this movement would be extremely difficult. And sacred as well as secular authorities were forced to recognise the ubiquity of servants' mobility, since parochial clergy would need to confront the spiritual needs of these strangers from elsewhere, only temporarily within the parish boundaries. John Myrc's fifteenth-century 'Instructions for parish priests' directed clergy to hear confessions of servants even if their 'home' parish were elsewhere:

> . . . Or ȝef a mon be servaunt
> In Þy paresch by covenaunt . . .
> And hys howseholde be elles where
> Pareschen he ys Þenne Þere . . .[55]

The manner in which this particular kind of mobility registered most frequently in local authority was the echoes in manorial courts relating to sanctions against 'newcomers' into communities. For when

[54] Furber, ed., *Essex sessions of the peace*, pp. 137–77.

[55] Myrc, *Instructions for parish priests*, p. 27. A statute for the Archdeaconry of London dated between 1241 and 1270 similarly declared that servants remained parishioners of their 'home' parishes even when employed elsewhere, and incidentally lends further weight to the impression of early establishment of servanthood and its attendant mobility in southern England. Powicke and Cheney, eds., *Councils and synods* ii, p. 336: 'Si vir alicuius mulieris domicilium habentis necessitate ductus alicui

migrants took up residence, even temporarily, within the precincts of manorial jurisdiction there was commonly concern on the part of either court or community notables to ensure that these newcomers be made amenable to local jurisdiction. This took several forms. Adolescent and adult males, as already shown (above, Chapter 5), resident for at least a year were supposed to be sworn into tithings, which would then assume some degree of responsibility for offences committed by their members. By their peripatetic nature one might expect servants to be prominent among males sworn into tithings (even if many servants were ordinarily resident within the community for only a year or so before moving on). And in fact this was so, since persons explicitly labelled 'A the servant of B' figured in orders to swear into tithing in the later middle ages in Essex in numbers that appear disproportionately large relative to their likely prominence in the local rural populations. To take merely one example, at 30 leet-court sessions of the manor of Boreham Hall in central Essex, extending from the beginning of the fifteenth century to the mid-1450s, a total of 131 names was entered into the court records of males who ought to have been sworn into tithing but who as yet had not been.[56] Many, perhaps most, of these were the young sons of residents, who had just attained the age of 12, rather than actual immigrants. But 17 (13.0 per cent) of the 131 (and thus a rather higher proportion of actual newcomers) were explicitly denoted as servants of local residents, such as 'John Hikkes servant [*serviens*] of the vicar of Boreham church'.[57] Possibly others in these lists were also servants but were not denoted as such. And at any rate, servants resident in one place for no more than a year before moving on – as will be argued, probably the majority – had no reason under the terms of the frankpledge system ever to become members of tithings.

The mobility of workers in general, both servants and labourers, intersected with employers' responsibility also at certain points, when communal sanctions extended to local residents who 'received' or 'harboured' [*recepit, hospitavit*] outsiders. This of course was not limited strictly to those who found places in local households for employment, whether for shorter or longer periods, and the purposes for such 'receptions' are seldom made explicit in the court records, but

servierit, tantum parochianus illius ecclesie erit in cuius parochia uxor eiusdem moram facit, quia in hoc casu vir uxorem sequi tenetur . . .'.

56 PRO.SC2.171.25; SC2.171.30; SC2.171.32; SC2.171.33.

57 PRO.SC2.171.33 (Boreham court, 30 Jun 1447): 'Johannes Hikkes serviens vicarij ecclesie de Boreham [and eight others] sunt etatis xij annorum & amplius & residentes infra precinctos istius visus per unum annum & ultra & extra decenniam domini Regis . . .'.

undoubtedly labour hire was involved in many such situations. In the case of newcomers who escaped enrolment into tithing, leet courts also sometimes amerced those who had 'received' them, as in the case of Thomas le Bakere at South Hanningfield in 1350, when John Bolour, who 'received him' and whose mainpast he was, was also amerced 3d.[58]

At times communities had bans or by-laws against potentially trouble-making outsiders. Ault and Raftis, in their studies of village by-laws, noted examples of these sanctions and the early fourteenth century in particular seems to have witnessed a heightened concern over this.[59] This is perhaps to be expected, since at the height of demographic expansion around 1300 there were likely to have been many rather desperate people on the road, and in this sense concerns about vagabondage prefigured similar fears three centuries later, at the next peak of population growth in the late sixteenth and early seventeenth centuries. At Birdbrook in 1294 a manorial ordinance forbade free and customary tenants to receive or harbour any 'outsider' (*extraneus*) during the coming autumn, and went on to make it clear that harvest workers were the object of concern.[60] At Little Leighs about ten years later, Milicent Tyler harboured [*hospitavit*] John Pistor 'against the assise'.[61]

Yet such regulations were by no means limited to this particular period, and references are scattered throughout the later middle ages, such as the presentment (also at Birdbrook) of Elizabeth de Bridbrok, who in 1390 harboured Henry Tyel 'against the statute'.[62] Ault pointed out that well before the Statute of Labourers itself, some English communities had ordinances forbidding local labourers to move outside the village during harvest, when their labour was needed locally,[63] and a similar action may have lain behind the refusal of locals in Rettendon in 1351 to allow labourers from elsewhere to find work

58 ERO D/DP M874 (South Hanningfield court, 24 Feb 1350): '. . . Thomas le Bakere moratur in feodo domini per unum annum & unum diem & non est in decena . . . & Johannes Bolour quia ipsum recepit & manupastus fuit in misericordia . . .'.

59 Raftis, *Tenure and mobility*, pp. 130–8, 268–70; Ault, 'Open-field husbandry', pp. 59, 84.

60 WAM 25568 (Birdbrook court, 31 Jul 1294): 'Preceptum est omnibus tenentibus domini tam liberis quam customariis ne alicuius hospicem nec receptes aliquem extraneum seu notum in autumpno proximo venturo penes quos fuerit suspectum de dampnis in bladis faciendis . . .'.

61 Bodl. Essex Rolls 8 (Little Leighs leet, 19 May 1304): '. . . Milicencia tegulatrix hospitavit Johannem Pistorem contra assisam ultra unum annum et unum diem qui est extra decenam . . .'.

62 ERO D/DU 267/30 (Birdbrook leet, 20 Jul 1390): 'Elizabetha de Bridbrok hospitavit Henricum Tyel contra statutum . . .'.

63 Ault, 'Open-field husbandry', pp. 13–16.

there.[64] It remains an open question, especially in view of the patterns of ordinary migration already seen in the Essex evidence, how far these sanctions may have had any perceptible effect in practice.

Finally, and more immediately, servants were under the direct legal responsibility of their employers while in their households. It was this position of dependence (along with their non-tenure of land) which largely rendered them invisible to most of the proceedings of manorial jurisdictions, for (apart from matters relating to tithing membership and occasional litigation arising from employment disputes) servants were most likely to appear in manor-court proceedings when they had committed petty crimes punishable in leet courts, such as assault or bloodshed, or infractions against manorial custom. It is this relative invisibility which has led historians such as Britton and McIntosh to conclude that little can be learned about servants from manorial records alone.[65] Under many circumstances it was the servants' employers or masters who were held responsible for offences they committed. Any Essex court-roll series from the later middle ages recorded a random, fairly uninformative scattering of such infractions. In 1357 at Great Waltham, John Sponere was amerced because his '*famulus* and mainpast' stole fruit from another person's garden;[66] in the same year at High Easter, Geoffrey Poleyn was held responsible for trespasses committed by his *ancilla*.[67] Ultimately a leet court might attempt to exercise the extreme sanction of banishment from the community, against wholly unacceptable servants, as at Great Tey in 1545 when Robert Dawe was ordered to remove from his household one Thomas Bratherton, a 'common scandal-monger and ... irritant'.[68]

[64] Furber, ed., *Essex peace sessions*, pp. 105–6: '... nolentes permittere dictum Walterum ... securitatem invenire ad commorandum in dicta villa officium suum exercendo ...'.

[65] Britton, *Community of the vill*, pp. 92, 135–7; McIntosh, *Autonomy and community*, p. 162.

[66] PRO.DL30.64.813 (Great Waltham court, 1 Feb 1357): '... quidem famulus et manupastus ... intravit clausum et gardinium ... asportavit fructos ... pira et poma ...'.

[67] *Ibid.* (High Easter court, 30 Jun 1357): '... pro herbagio messo et asportato per ancillam suam ...'.

[68] JRL Tey Magna rolls (Great Tey leet, 1 Jun 1545): '... Et quod Robertus Dawe forisfecit domino penam suam xls. quia ipse ... custodivit & manutentus fuit commorare infra domum suam quendam famulum suum nominatum Thomam Bratherton qui fuit communis barectator scandalorum & opprobriosus verborum suorum ac legeorum domini Regis generalis perturbator & inquietator ad eorum grave nocumentum ... contra speciale preceptum quod dictus Robertus habuit in hac parte ad ultimum visum ... Et preceptum est eodem Roberto ... quod ipse non amplius dictum Thomam recipiat seu manuteneat commorare in aliqua domo ipsius Roberti infra hanc villatam ...'.

This responsibility stemmed simply from any household head's obligation, at common as well as customary law, to account for the actions of his household's members; in the mid-thirteenth century Bracton had written that if a criminal fled, either his tithing or, failing that, anyone whose mainpast he had been was to answer for his offence, and that anyone might claim damages for injuries done to those 'in his household, such as his servants or bondmen'.[69] The relevance of this principle to servants hired by villagers is neatly illustrated by a case in a thirteenth-century precedent book for manorial courts, in which a man whose servants allegedly mowed his lord's meadow was acquitted after claiming that the 'servants' were not his mainpasts but had been hired 'from day to day'.[70]

In this legal sense a household head's responsibility for his servants was essentially identical to that for his own spouse or children. At Birdbrook in 1378, in two consecutive presentments in court for illicitly taking sheaves of grain from the lord's field, first one man was summoned for his wife's offence, and then 'Alice the daughter and servant of Richard Prentys' was presented for doing the same.[71] Like their early-modern counterparts, Essex servants in the fourteenth and fifteenth centuries were, socially and legally, both largely invisible to secular authority and subsumed within their employers' households and responsibility.[72]

The Statute of Labourers explicitly recognised that annual hiring of servants was, already by 1351, a well-established convention: 'carters, ploughmen and ploughholders, shepherds, swineherds and dairy-maids and all other servants' were to be hired 'by the whole year or other usual terms'.[73] This usually meant hire from Michaelmas (29 September) to Michaelmas, and as was the case with early-modern servants this coincided with the cycles of the arable agricultural year and also the traditional accounting year. In the 1389 Essex indictment roll containing several hundred Statute of Labourers infractions, Michaelmas-to-Michaelmas hiring was the term universally mentioned when details are recorded.[74] In a proof-of-age inquest in 1359,

[69] Bracton, *On the laws and customs* vol. ii, pp. 350, 438: '. . . in familia sua sicut servientes suos et servos . . .'; *cf.* Pollock and Maitland, *History of English law* vol. i, pp. 419, 568.

[70] Maitland, ed., *The court baron*, pp. 55–6.

[71] ERO D/DU 267/30 (Birdbrook court, 25 Sep 1378): '. . . Alicia uxor Henrici Jekel cepit & asportavit extra campum domini ij fassiculos avene sine licencia Ideo preceptum est distringere dictum Henricum . . . Agneta filia & serviens Ricardi Prentys cepit & asportavit . . . [etc.]'.

[72] Kussmaul, *Servants in husbandry*, pp. 3–10.

[73] 25 Edw. III c.2; *Statutes of the realm* vol. i, p. 311: '. . . qils soient allowes de servir per lan entier ou autres termes usuels . . .'.

[74] PRO.KB9.25.

similarly, Roger Sayot recalled that in 1345 at Easton he had been the servant of John de Lovayne, 'and he left the said John's service at the next Michaelmas';[75] at another inquest in the same year Roger Prat testified virtually identically concerning his previous service at Totham.[76]

But Michaelmas-to-Michaelmas hiring was not universal, and it is unlikely (since contrary examples can be drawn from a small district of central Essex) that these variations can be related directly, as Kussmaul did in the case of early-modern servants, to the different rhythms of the agricultural year in different ecological zones of England.[77] A series of fourteen suits concerning breaches of hiring agreements heard in Writtle's manorial court between 1381 and 1419, and one plea each in the courts of Great Dunmow and Hatfield Broadoak, demonstrates this variety.[78] Some servants were hired from Michaelmas to Michaelmas: such was the case with John Osteler during 1397–8 and John Illeghe during 1399–1400, both at Writtle.[79] But John Bakere had been hired in 1409 to work for John Fynchyngfeld from that All Saints' Day (1 November) to the next.[80]

And although most hiring agreements appear to have been made for one year it is possible to find examples of shorter, or indeed longer, terms. In 1418 at Hatfield Broadoak, John Bukke agreed to became William atte Watere's servant from Michaelmas to Easter;[81] in 1403 at Writtle, Nichola Aylett was William Johann senior's servant from the

[75] PRO.C135.147.11 (inquest, 18 Jul 1359): '... fuit in servicio predicti Johannis ... & recessit a servicio eiusdem Johannis in festo Sancti Michaelis tunc proxime sequente ...'.

[76] PRO.C135.147.2 (inquest, 28 Feb 1359): '... fuit commorans cum predicto Johanne ... & in festo Sancti Michaelis tunc proxime sequente recessit a servicio eiusdem ...'.

[77] Kussmaul, *Servants in husbandry*, pp. 49–69.

[78] ERO D/DP M189 (Writtle court, 14 Dec 1381); D/DP M190 (Writtle court, 7 Feb 1383); D/DP M197 (Writtle court, 29 Jul 1391); D/DP M199 (Writtle courts, 18 Oct 1393, 1 Dec 1397, 14 Jun 1404); D/DP M204 (Writtle court, 18 Jun 1401); D/DP M209 (Writtle court, 25 Jul 1405); D/DP M213 (Writtle court, 1 Feb 1410); D/DP M214 (Writtle court, 11 Oct 1410); D/DP M219 (Writtle court, 25 Jan 1416); D/DP M223 (Writtle courts, 7 Jan 1419, 11 Mar 1419); D/DP M227 (Writtle court, 23 Jan 1423); ERO D/DMg M39 (Great Dunmow court, 9 Dec 1389); ERO D/DGe M251 (Hatfield Broadoak court, 19 Nov 1418).

[79] ERO D/DP M199 (Writtle court, 1 Dec 1397): '... Johannes Miles convenit cum predicto Johanne Osteler ut predictus Johannes Osteler deserviret eidem Johanni Miles a festo Sancti Michaelis anno regni regis nunc xx usque <idem> festum tunc proxime sequens ...'; D/DP M204 (Writtle court, 18 Jun 1401).

[80] ERO D/DP M214 (Writtle court, 11 Oct 1410): '... Johannes Bakere retentus fuit cum predicto Johanne Fynchyngfeld in servicio ipsius Johannis Fynchyngfeld a festo Omnium Sanctorum anno regni regis nunc x^{mo} usque idem festum Omnium Sanctorum proxime sequens ...'.

[81] ERO D/DGe M251 (Hatfield Broadoak court, 19 Nov 1418): '... predictus Johannes retentus fuit in servicio predicti Willelmi a festo Sancti Michaelis anno regni regis nunc quinto usque festum Pasche tunc proxime sequens ...'.

feast of St Peter *ad vincula* (1 August, the traditional beginning of 'autumn' and of the harvest season) to Michaelmas;[82] in 1418, also at Writtle, Thomas Heel hired his son to William Page from St Peter *ad vincula* to Michaelmas and then from that Michaelmas to the next.[83] As already shown in the case of Simon Maynard (above), the death of one's employer could terminate a servant's position at any time. And in the case of Eleanor Robard, the lack of a definite contract or agreement apparently justified, to her at least, withdrawal from an unsatisfactory position.

And at any rate not all hiring contracts were for fixed-length terms. One such agreement, at Writtle in 1393, included the stipulation that the employee give a quarter-year's notice before withdrawing.[84] Clearly, then, servanthood was a flexible institution, and the 'or other usual terms' mentioned in the Statute of Labourers is a reminder that other terms than annual hirings were permissible. Hiring could be for longer or shorter duration, to suit the needs of employers and the desires of servants.

From the available evidence it appears likely that most servants moved on when their annual hiring term expired. The Essex Statute of Labourers cases involving servants include no case in which the same servant explicitly stayed longer than one year with a master. This, though, is of course hardly conclusive in itself, since the primary objective of such indictments was more likely to emphasise those hirings which were terminated prematurely than those which were long-lasting. Most of the litigation in manor courts concerning disputes over hiring points to the same norm, though with the same reservation.

But none the less some servants did stay longer with one employer. Walter Porter recalled at a proof-of-age inquest that in 1339, when he was 24, at Springfield 'at the next Michaelmas after the birth of the said Abel [the heir in question], he came to the house of John Hunte, Abel's

82 ERO D/DP M199 (Writtle court, 14 Jun 1404): '. . . pro stipendio predicte Nicholae servientis predicti Willelmi a festo Sancti Petri quod dicitur ad vincula usque festum Sancti Michaelis proxime sequens . . .'.

83 ERO D/DP M223 (Writtle court, 11 Mar 1419): '. . . Thomas deliberavit predicto Willelmo unum puerum ipsius Thome deservientem predicto Willelmo a predicto festo Sancti Petri usque festum Sancti Michaelis tunc proxime sequens . . . Et eciam . . . a predicto festo Sancti Michaelis usque festum Sancti Michaelis tunc proxime sequens . . .'.

84 ERO D/DP M199 (Writtle court, 18 Oct 1393): '. . . Johannes Breton convenit cum predicto Johanne Miles quod quo tempore quod predictus Johannes Breton recedere vellet a societate predicti Johannis Miles . . . ipsum Johannem Miles premuniet per unum quarterium anni ante recessionem suam . . .'. It is perhaps debatable whether this agreement, between a sawyer and his employee, should strictly be classed as a 'servant' agreement.

father, to serve him, and so he remained in John's service for the next ten years, that is, until the death of the same John Hunte'.[85] Agnes Burton was the servant of William Herolf at Writtle for four and one-quarter years in the early fifteenth century.[86] And also at Writtle a few years earlier, John Ayllet claimed that William Johann senior promised to enfeoff him of a cottage 'for the long service given by John to the said William'.[87]

There is little evidence to show the exact nature of tasks which most Essex servants in the later middle ages performed, another way in which the medieval evidence of servanthood is reticent. What little indication survives implies that the particular kinds of work done, and the degree of specialisation achieved, by servants varied greatly as a function of the sex, age and experience of the servant in question. At one extreme, some servants were described in such a way as to imply that they were responsible for one primary, fairly highly skilled job. This is familiar from the context of manorial hiring, in the examples of shepherds, pigmen and the (almost invariably female) dairy-servants. Less frequently this was the case with villagers' servants also: in the 1381 poll-tax returns for Springfield, for instance, one married couple who were taxed on tenure (and thus presumed 'agriculturalist') had two servants, one of whom was a male 'servant [and] *herde*', and the rector of Springfield had among his four servants one cook.[88] Several dozen men who were indicted in 1389 for Statute of Labourers violations in Essex had been employed by the year for wages and meals, and thus were probably 'servants' in the sense used in this discussion, but were described as ploughmen or carters.[89] And, as already noted, some servants were also called *laborarij*: such was the case with John Bakere at Writtle, hired in 1409 for one year 'in the position of *laborarius*, that is, threshing, digging ditches, and doing other manual work'.[90] Some suits for broken agreements imply that servants might occasionally be paid extra on a *per diem* or piecework basis for tasks additional to their usual work; one female Writtle

[85] PRO.C135.155.9 (inquest, 8 Mar 1360): '. . . in proximo festo Sancti Michaelis . . . venit ad domum predicti Johannis Hunte patris ipsius Abeli ad serviendum ei & sic stetit in servicio ipsius Johannis per x annos sequentes usque ad mortem eiusdem Johannis Hunte . . .'.

[86] ERO D/DP M213 (Writtle court, 1 Feb 1410): '. . . predicta Agnes deservivit predicto Willelmo Herolf per iiij annos & unum quarterium unius anni . . .'.

[87] ERO D/DP M199 (Writtle court, 14 Jun 1404): '. . . predictus Willelmus convenit cum predicto Johanne quod ipsum Johannem feoffaret in uno cotagio . . . pro prolixo servicio predicti Johannis predicto Willelmo impenso . . .'.

[88] PRO.E179.107.63 m.16. [89] PRO.KB9.25.

[90] ERO D/DP M214 (Writtle court, 11 Oct 1410): '. . . deserviens eidem Johanni Fynchyngfeld in officio laborarij videlicet trituratoris fodens fossatum & alia opera manualia . . .'.

servant claimed to be owed a stipend for her term in service, plus extra money for spinning and reaping.[91]

Yet since, to judge from the poll-tax evidence, the great majority of servant-employing households had only one lone servant each, undoubtedly many agricultural or artisanal servants found themselves performing miscellaneous domestic duties. This was true in the case of Walter Stonere at Great Dunmow, when he claimed he had agreed with William Michel in 1379 'that he would serve him [William] as carter, and do other necessary things in his house'.[92] Similarly, when John Osteler was hired at Writtle in 1397 by John Miles, he was employed 'in the service of sawing, and when the said John Miles was not occupied with sawing the said John Osteler would work at John Miles' house in various other work'.[93]

Just as tasks performed depended upon servants' experience and capabilities, so too did the monetary wages they earned. This was taken for granted by the framers of the Statute of Labourers and its revisions. The Statute of Cambridge, for example, set out a tariff of maximum wages for a variety of servant types: shepherds and carters 10s. per annum, ploughmen 7s., swineherds, dairymaids and 'women labourers' (*femme laborer*) 6s., 'and every other labourer and servant according to his degree'.[94] Carters and ploughmen indicted in Essex in 1389 often had received as much as 30s., 40s., or even more for a year's employment, whereas those described simply as 'servants' seldom had taken more than 20s.[95] As already shown, on the other hand, John Melford's young son contracted for a year's work at only 5s., and 5s. was also the usual rate for manorial maidservants.[96] And yet another Writtle hiring indicates that the wages a servant received from a given master might increase as his or her age and experience increased: Alice Fynch was John Whelere's servant for four years

91 ERO D/DP M209 (Writtle court, 25 Jul 1405): the plea charged that the defendant 'detinet vs. pro stipendio ipsius Agnetis deservientis eidem Emme per unum annum & unam quartam partem anni . . . lxd. pro filacione lx librarum lane . . . [and several other spinning tasks] . . . vjd. pro messione bladi in autumpno per vj dies . . . [etc.]'.

92 ERO D/DMg M39 (Great Dunmow court, 9 Dec 1389): '. . . convenit cum predicto Waltero ut ei deserviret in officio carectarij & faciendo alia necessaria domus sue . . .'.

93 ERO D/DP M199 (Writtle court, 1 Dec 1397): '. . . predictus Johannes Osteler deserviret eidem Johanni Miles . . . in servicio sarrandi . . . & per quod tempus predictus Johannes Miles non esset occupatus in servicio sarriandi predictus Johannes Osteler laboraret ad domum predicti Johannis Miles in aliis diversis laboribus capiendo per diem stipendium suum ad modum laboris . . .'.

94 12 Ric. II c.3; *Statutes of the realm* vol. ii, p. 57.

95 PRO.KB9.25.

96 ERO D/DP M190 (Writtle court, 7 Feb 1383). Manorial maidservants' stipends in several Essex manors remained 5s. per annum for most of the later fourteenth and early fifteenth centuries: e.g. WAM 25474–25500 (Birdbrook), ERO D/DM M81–3 (Moulsham).

beginning in 1410, and took for those years respectively 12d., 4s., 5s. and 6s. 8d.[97]

In Essex at the end of the middle ages, then, servanthood was a flexible institution. It permitted many different kinds of work, lengths of service, and degrees of expertise on the part of both male and female servants. Moreover, it was not merely a form of employment but also a facet of social structure. Like their early-modern counterparts, servants in this late-medieval district were unmarried, young, mobile, and so comprised a distinctive demographic component of this rural population that reinforces the tentative impressions drawn earlier concerning nuptiality and migration. Servanthood, in fact, provides one key to understanding the process of household formation. Although in Essex itself the quantitative dimensions of servanthood cannot be strictly assessed, the mixture of servants and labourers within the local workforce bore critically important implications for the district's economy and demography.

[97] ERO D/DP M223 (Writtle court, 7 Jan 1419): '... predicta Alicia deservivit eidem Johanni ... per iiij[or] annos integros ... capiendo pro primo anno ... xijd. pro secundo anno iiijs. pro tercio anno vs. et pro quarto anno vjs. viijd.'.

10

Wages and labourers

Both labourers and servants played important roles in the rural workforce of later-medieval Essex. But in comparison with servants, unfortunately, local sources during the period are much more reticent about the qualitative or experiential details of labourers' lives. Litigation in local courts concerning simple daily hiring was rare, doubtless less worthwhile pursuing because of the smaller sums involved than was the case with servants' annual stipends. Debt and contract suits in which short-term employees did appear as plaintiffs in these courts dealt most often with situations where employers hired workers along with their equipment or animals, or where employer and employee were entangled in other financial transactions as well.[1] At Hatfield Broadoak in 1413, for example, William Lancastre sued Johanna atte Watere for 2s. 4d. for two days' ploughing he had done for her (using his implement) plus 4d. for pasturing her animals on his land.[2] The evidential filter of the legal tribunal necessarily emphasises these more complex cases at the expense of ordinary day-labourers' hire.

Nevertheless, previous chapters have outlined a quantitative profile of the district's labourers. Comprising about one-half of local 'households', labourers were more mobile, settled later in life, and were less likely to be married than their contemporaries. They were a great deal more likely to dwell in households of their own, in contrast to servants, but this was not universal: John Fuller, a 'common labourer', deposed in 1474 that he had lived in Coggeshall with William Oldale

1 Clark, 'Debt litigation', pp. 254, 261–2. The author is grateful to Professor Clark for sharing her insights regarding the composition of wage-related litigation.

2 ERO D/DGe M251 (Hatfield Broadoak court, 21 Jan 1413): '... predictus Willelmus queritur quod predicta Johanna ei iniuste detinet ijs. viijd ... quia predictus Willelmus certis die & anno aravit terram ipsius Johanne cum caruca ipsius Willelmi per ij dies capiendo pro dictis duobus diebus ijs. iiijd. ... & eciam ... iiijd. pro bestiis ipsius Johanne in pastura ipsius Willelmi agistatis ...'.

and William's father for the past six years, but before that he was in Combs Ford (Suffolk) and 'lived by himself' [*tenuit familiam per se*].[3] Many, probably the great majority, of Essex labourers occupied rungs near the bottom of the persistently stratified landholding ladder. Some found by-employment in industrial or artisanal work.

The few surviving wills of Essex labourers before 1525, scattered throughout the county, support this impression of modest means and multiple pursuits. The 1485 will of John Leveson of Barking left to his eldest son 'my hows y^{t} I dwelle yn', a cart and two horses plus a few household goods, to his other son a cow, four sheep and a pot, and a bullock and a girdle to each of his daughters.[4] In 1521, Lawrence Wyberd of Chigwell bequeathed a bullock to each of his three children and a hopeful admonition to his executors to try to recover a debt of 16s. owed him.[5] At West Mersea in 1504 John Sewall left his widow one 'tenement' and directed that another be sold to pay his debts;[6] at Walthamstow two years earlier, Richard Gamone left only a cow to pay for lights in the parish church.[7] And it is on the whole likely that only the better-off labourers actually left wills.

From the labourer's perspective, then – the supply side of this labour market – wages were one component of their standard of living, elusive as that concept is of empirical recovery. To the employers of workers – the demand side, by the early fifteenth century the multitude of middling and larger agriculturalists rather than manorial lords – wages were a much more direct input factor of their operations. Medieval England generally has left historians much information about wage rates, but little about typical earnings that workers accrued over the course of the year. But the structure of labour demand, especially the seasonal or task-specific fluctuations of demand and the balance of servants and labourers, was the chief determinant of these earnings. The later fourteenth and fifteenth centuries were a period of relative labour scarcity, but scarcity made itself felt first and foremost in seasons of high marginal demand. Imperfect as the evidence is, all these matters bore directly and in complex ways upon social structure and household formation, ultimately with important implications for the district's local demography. And so it is necessary to consider how

[3] GLRO DL/C/205 fo.225: 'Johannes Fuller de parochia Sancti Petri de Cogsale communis laborarius ubi moram traxit per vj annos Et ante illud tempus in villa de Combesforth in Comitate Suffolch' per xiij annos ... Et dicit quod moram traxit cum Willelmo Oldale & Willelmo patre suo per vj annos Et ante illud iste juratus tenuit familiam per se'.

[4] ERO D/AEW 1/209.

[5] ERO D/AER 3/82: 'Item I will if Margery my wyff and John my son cane gett of William Parrar xvjs. of trew dett that my ij doughters have vjs. be twixt theym ...'.

[6] ERO D/ACR 1/84. [7] ERO D/AER 2/6.

the structure of labour supply and demand, especially the balance of servants and labourers in the local workforce, may have shifted from before to after 1350, and to place these patterns also into the context of England's post-medieval rural labour market.

The general trends of wages in later-medieval England at large have long been known. A number of historians have calculated *per diem* wage rates for different categories of worker from manorial and building accounts, and series of real wages (adjusted for the costs of 'baskets of consumables', primarily consisting of foodstuffs) are also available.[8] In the first three decades after the Black Death money wages rose typically by one-third or more, and their upward drift continued at less rapid rates of increase into the middle decades of the fifteenth century. Rises in real wages were more muted in the decades immediately after 1350 because of the persistence of high grain prices into the 1370s, but the declining costs of agricultural produce thereafter boosted real wages proportionately higher, to reach a plateau in the middle and latter parts of the 1400s. It is thus necessary in economic terms to keep the distinction between current and real wages clear, though the distinction finds little echo in the hostile reaction of those who drafted the labour legislation after the arrival of plague, for whom the pennies they paid for a day's work were the salient reality. 'Servants and labourers will not serve and labour, and have not for a long time, without outrageous and excessive pay, much more than has been given to such servants and labourers in any past time', began the Statute of Cambridge in 1388.[9]

None of the wages series available for the fourteenth and fifteenth centuries is entirely satisfactory.[10] Hiring of daily workers done by stewards for manorial demesne work (and thus recorded in the surviving manorial account-roll series most commonly studied) necessarily pertains disproportionately to large-scale agricultural concerns that made major inroads into the local labour market at key seasons like harvesting and haymaking. This evidence, then, is not a perfect mirror of the entire, year-round aggregate hiring of the many lesser agriculturalists who also employed labourers. Moreover, the usefulness of manorial accounts for the purpose of recording agricultural

[8] Phelps Brown and Hopkins, *Perspective of wages and prices*, esp. pp. 1–59; Beveridge, 'Westminster wages'; Thorold Rogers, *History of agriculture and prices*; Farmer, 'Crop yields, prices and wages'; Hatcher, *Plague, population and the English economy*, pp. 47–54.

[9] *Statutes of the realm* vol.ii, p. 57.

[10] The following points are discussed more fully by Dyer, *Standards of living*, pp. 217–22; Hatcher, *Plague, population and the English economy*, pp. 47–50; cf. Loschky, 'Seven centuries of income reconsidered'.

hiring becomes limited after 1400, since few demesnes were operated directly by their landlords' administrators thereafter and so this kind of hiring drops from the records. Builders' wages, on the other hand, involved a small and distinctive sector of the labour market, though one having at least the advantage of more surviving empirical data throughout the fifteenth century. And especially in urban contexts, as Rappaport has recently pointed out in connection with sixteenth-century London prices,[11] but doubtless to a certain extent in the countryside also, small-scale consumers forced to purchase food would often have bought finished or 'retail' items (bread, ale, butchered meat) whose purchase price contained an element of labour or dealer's profit. Thus to base the price of a 'basket of consumables' on raw grain or animal prices – the 'wholesale' price, that is, the price contained in manorial accounts – is to understate the real cost of the 'basket' in periods like the fifteenth century when labour was relatively expensive, and in areas like central and northern Essex that supported a considerable provisioning trade. Under these circumstances 'retail' and 'wholesale' prices would not necessarily have moved in exactly proportional concert with one another; the former declined less than the latter during the later medieval period, and rose less quickly than the latter during the Tudor century.

Nevertheless, the upward trend in *per diem* wage rates is unmistakable over this period, lending much weight to the traditional aphorism that this was a 'golden age' for the English worker.[12] This impression is complemented by wage data drawn from Essex sources. Figures 10.1 and 10.2 present wage data from the manorial accounts of eleven estates in the district from the early fourteenth to the early sixteenth century, respectively for wages paid to carpenters and labourers. Sources and derivation of these data are set out in Appendix B.

These figures represent current wages in pence per day, with no attempt made to adjust for costs of consumables. Over the period, the dataset contains 1,479 days worked by carpenters and 2,016 by labourers. Strict criteria were adopted to limit inclusion of recorded employment to instances likely to be meaningfully comparable to one another: carpenters' wages plotted here were typically paid for repairs to the buildings, mills or equipment of manors,[13] while the labourers

[11] Rappaport, *Worlds within worlds*, pp. 127–8. The author is grateful to Professor Rappaport for providing a copy of his study's data and text before it was published.

[12] The phrase seems to have originated with Thorold Rogers: Dyer, *Standards of living*, p. 216.

[13] Conventions for drawing these statistics from the accounts are set out in Appendix B. Typical of entries concerning carpenters are ERO D/DM M69 (Moulsham account, 1338–9): '... j carpentario conducto per j diem & dimidium pro parietem cuiusdam

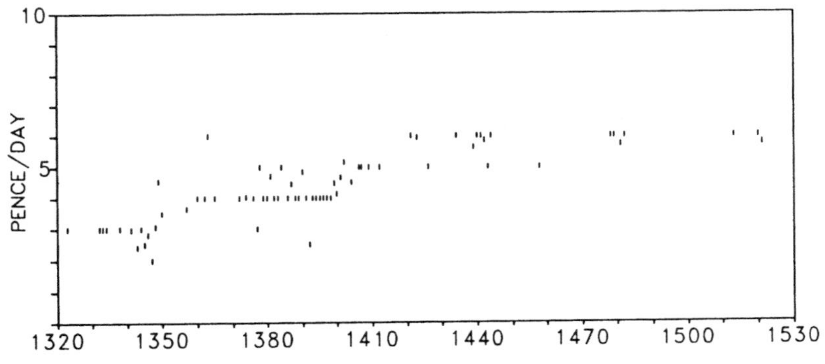

Figure 10.1. Daily wages of carpenters in Essex 1323–1521

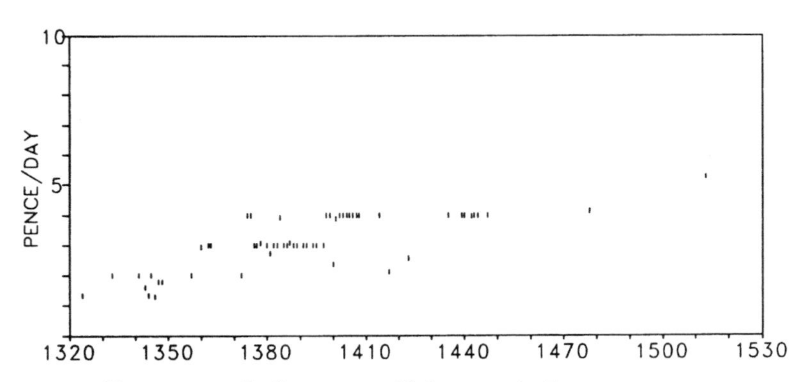

Figure 10.2. Daily wages of labourers in Essex 1324–1513

represented in the graph were hired for digging, carrying or other fairly unskilled work.[14] And so while these data are still far from being perfectly representative of the totality of the district's labour market, they obviate at least a few of the drawbacks of other published series. The data also confirm, incidentally, how little a factor wage labour

camere apud le Bromhous faciendo & emendendo videlicet in carpentria plastrando pariettem predicte camere & emendatione muris ijd. q. capiendo per diem jd. ob.'; PRO.SC6.839.9 (Claret Hall in Ashen account, 1374–5): 'In stipendio Johannis Nichel carpentari per iij septimanias emendendi tibias dagshoos & le Fullyngstoks molendini fullonici ibidem vijs. vd. per diem vd.'.

[14] Again, conventions for inclusion are discussed in Appendix B. Examples: CALC Beadles' Rolls, Bocking (Bocking account, 1387–8): '... in iij hominibus conductis ad auxiliandum cariagium per j diem xijd.'; PRO.DL29.43.826 (High Easter account, 1439–40): 'Et Johanni Bataille laborario & Johanni Eve laborario pro j die & dimidio tam ad stokkandum argillam pro tecto dicte grangie cum eadem argilla crescendo utroque eorum per diem iiijd. – xijd.'.

hired by manorial officials became within the local labour market during the period: at the small manor of Birdbrook, mean carpenter-days hired per annum declined by one-half from the last quarter of the fourteenth century to the second quarter of the fifteenth, while labourer-days fell over the same interval by 90 per cent.[15]

In general the Essex evidence confirms the traditional picture. For both kinds of workers the later fourteenth century witnessed a sharp wage hike, while in the early decades of the next century a new, higher plateau was reached that persisted for most of the period to just beyond 1500. The new regime of higher wages also produced a slight narrowing of the gap between more skilled (carpenters') and less skilled (labourers') wages, as one would expect in a period of relative labour shortage: whereas carpenters before the Black Death typically earned 3d. per day and labourers 1½–2d., by the mid 1400s the most commonly paid rates were 5–6d. and 4d. respectively.

But daily wage rates by themselves reveal little about workers' living standards in this period without reference to structures of employment, because where labourers were concerned the late-medieval Essex labour market was highly episodic and discontinuous. For agricultural workers hired by the day, both employment and wages were very irregular over different portions of the year, and so annual wage earnings garnered by workers bore no simple linear relationship to *per diem* wages.[16] Unfortunately almost all evidence for wages from the period is generated from the hirer's perspective, making it quite difficult to reconstruct a 'typical' labourer's earnings from all his or her different employments. In fact, no one source is completely informative on this score, and one must fall back upon a variety of partial, oblique perspectives on workers' earnings.

One of the most remarkable pieces of evidence for the structure of agricultural hiring in late-medieval Essex is a unique farmer's account from Porter's Hall in Stebbing for the agricultural year 1483–4.[17] The

[15] For sources, see Bibliography. Hirings tabulated here pertain only to employment strictly defined by the criteria set out in Appendix B. The variability in volume of hiring from year to year is also noteworthy.

Period	Years (accounts) in sample	Carpenter-days		Labourer-days	
		mean	st. dev.	mean	st. dev.
1376–1400	25	21.1	21.4	39.8	88.0
1401–25	10	23.6	18.9	16.1	17.2
1426–50	8	10.5	12.4	3.8	5.3

[16] Cf. the comments by Dyer, *Standards of living*, pp. 222–9.
[17] BL Add. Roll 66051.

owner of this estate was William Capell, second son of a minor gentleman from Stoke by Nayland (Suffolk).[18] William went on to prosper as a London draper, eventually being knighted and serving as MP, sheriff and Lord Mayor of the city. His business affairs included widespread moneylending and the acquisition of a number of rural properties. One of these was Porter's Hall, which Capell bought in 1481. Two years later William's older brother John was managing the Stebbing property, and it was John who compiled the 1483–4 account. This document combines some of the standard features of earlier manorial accounts (recording arable land and livestock operations and their associated cash receipts and expenditures) with household and travel expenses and payments ranging from customary duties to the parish church to repairing buildings and shoeing horses.

Porter's Hall was being run at that time as a demesne farm, with slightly more than 300 acres under crops and several dozen cattle and other livestock bought and sold within that year, most likely for fattening and sending to local markets. Its mixture of arable and pastoral production was thus in line with the district as a whole during the period, but the scale of its operations obviously was much larger than all but the most affluent agriculturalists in the area. Capell was, in fact, almost certainly the largest employer in the parish by a wide margin. The account's details of hiring include names of employees, tasks performed, wages paid and (usually) number of days worked, as well as some broad indication of periods over the course of the year in which the work was done. For all these reasons it is a quite different document from a typical manorial account of the high-medieval period, and the agricultural concern to which it pertains was more akin to an early-modern, market-oriented farm than a traditional manorial demesne. This information is summarised in Table 10.1.

The structure of hiring at Porter's Hall in 1483–4 embraced the gamut from a few persons employed for the whole year or at least periods of a month or more, to a rather larger number of employees working for Capell for just a few days each. Capell had eleven year-round servants – ten male, one female – and although the account makes no explicit mention of the nature of their work (merely recording 'payd to John Royston on hys yer wages xiijs. & viijd.' and

[18] The following description of Capell's career and his acquisition of Porter's Hall is taken from BL Add. Ch. 65,357 (charter of acquisition); *CCR 1476–85*, p. 295; *CCR 1485–1500*, pp. 144–5; SRO (Bury) R2/9/78 (will of John father of William Capell, 1449); PRO. PROB11.18.13 (will of William Capell, 1515); *Essex feet of fines* vol. iv. pp. 80, 81, 86; Morant, *History of Essex* vol. ii, pp. 401–2; Copinger, *Manors of Suffolk* vol. i, p. 227; Minet, 'The Capells at Rayne'; Bindoff, ed., *House of Commons* vol. i, pp. 569–70.

Table 10.1. *Labour hired at Porter's Hall, Stebbing, 1483–4*

Type of work	Person-days worked			Persons hired			wage rate	Total wages paid
	men	women	total	men	women	total		
I Daily hiring								
Harvesting	161	73	234	27	16	43	4d./day (men) 3d./day (women)	£3 9s. 6d.
Sowing	0	50	50	0	5	5	1d./day (women)	4s. 2d.
Threshing	51	0	51	4	0	4	1½–2d./day (men)	6s. 7½d.
Harrowing	10	0	10	2	0	2	1–2d./day (men)	1s. 4d.
'Work'	20	13	33	5	1	6	1–2d./day (men)	3s. 5d.
Total	242	136	378	31[a]	21[a]	52[a]		£4 4s. 0½d.
II Long-term hiring								
Servants			(4,026)[b]	10	1	11	3s. 3d.–22s. 5d./yr	£6 7s. 6d. + ?[c]
Plough-drivers			(111)[b]	2	0	2		6s. 9d.
Total				12	1	13		£6 14s. 3d. + ?[c]

Source: BL Add. Roll 66051.

Notes: [a] Total persons hired is number of different people hired in all capacities, not sum of above columns.

[b] Notional total 'person-days worked' here is: for servants, number of servants multiplied by 366; for plough-drivers, one man hired for 5 weeks, another hired 'from Candelmas to Easter' (11 weeks) plus 15 days more, taking a work week notionally as 6 days.

[c] One male servant is listed in account without a wage being noted.

so on)[19] they must have consisted mainly of domestic, transport, herding and other continual or intermittent tasks, plus occasional work such as hay-mowing for which no other hiring arrangements are mentioned. The servants' annual cash wages varied widely, from 3s. 3d. to 22s. 5d., and while again the account provides no direct indication it is likely that these widely ranging sums were related to the varying ages, experience and skills of the servants in question.[20] These annual cash wages were, of course, only part of the servants' total remuneration, since the value of their bed and board would have been substantial also, though buried in the account among the various cattle and grain recorded as 'spent in ye hushold'. Capell also employed two men for several weeks each as plough-drivers.

By contrast, Capell hired 52 other people for agricultural or other work on a daily basis over the course of that year; these day-labourers worked at Porter's Hall as few as one day or as many as 30 days during 1483–4.[21] The episodic nature of day-labourers' seasonal employment patterns at this estate (though not necessarily its mixture of servants and labourers) bears a striking similarity to comparable establishments more than a century later and in a quite different economic environment.[22] Stebbing tithing data indicate there were probably not many more than 100 adolescent and adult males and females living in this community at the time, so at first glance it would appear that half or more of the potential workforce of the community was drawn into employment at Porter's Hall at least occasionally.[23] This, however, is likely to be an overstatement, since, at seasons of peak demand especially, workers were apt to find employment with a number of employers over a wider geographical area, and so, while some of Capell's reapers doubtless also found work for other employers during harvest, his own employees were not exclusively drawn from Stebbing alone. In fact, the list of harvest workers in Capell's account

19 The quotations cited in this and the following five paragraphs are all taken from BL Add. Roll 66051.

20 See above, Chapter 9.

21 These figures do not include a very few other casual hirings noted in the account, whose length in days cannot be ascertained or whose nature does not fit into the task-categories tabulated above.

22 Hassell Smith, 'Labourers in late sixteenth-century England'. At the estate of Stiffkey (Norfolk), with more than 600 acres and substantial building going on, in 1593–4 there was a stark contrast between a few specialist day-labourers who enjoyed steady employment and the majority who found very little work over a typical year with this employer. Of 25 male day-labourers employed that year, 14 worked no more than 52 days each, and the majority of these worked fewer than 20 days, mostly in harvest and haymaking.

23 This statement is based upon the 49 males in tithing (i.e. aged 12 and older) resident in 1480: BL Add. Roll 65929; cf. Chapter 5 and Appendix A.

includes men from Bocking, Braintree and Nayland (respectively 5, 5, and 20 miles away).

Hiring at Porter's Hall neatly illustrates, albeit on a much larger scale, the tactical decisions that many Essex agriculturalists confronted in balancing continual and sporadic labour needs over the various agricultural seasons. Almost two-thirds of the person-days worked by employees hired on a daily basis were expended during the harvest, or in other words within a few weeks at the end of the summer. Other agricultural work that fell into particular seasons, such as sowing and harrowing, consumed comparatively much less labour, while threshing and otherwise unspecified 'work' done by day-labour, as well as servants' work, were spread much more evenly throughout the calendar.

It was this widely varying intensity of demand for labour that accounted for the fluctuation in *per diem* wage rates for daily workers. During harvest, when many other employers would have been seeking labourers at the same time and when constraints of weather made it imperative to marshal the maximum effort from reapers within a short period, cash wages doubled or tripled from their more modest levels of the remainder of the calendar. And even this understates the value of harvest employment to workers, because Capell provided meals to harvest workers whereas there is no clear evidence of this in connection with daily workers at other times: Capell wrote that 'in harveste I spent' 3 steers, 7 sheep, 40 cheeses, 25 bushels of wheat and 42 bushels of malt.

This differential in wage rates between 'autumn' (medieval terminology for the harvest season) and other times of the year, and also the intensity of demand for labour that led workers to find employment over a wider geographical area to the dismay of potential employers, are familiar from indictments under the Statute of Labourers. Presentments made in Essex peace sessions in 1379 that John Essex of Dunmow 'is a common labourer and takes in winter and summer 2d. per day and food, and in autumn 4d. per day and food',[24] and in 1378 that John Mory of Castle Hedingham 'moves from place to place in autumn for excess [pay]',[25] and the presentment in Birdbrook's leet court in July 1366 that three men 'do not wish to work within the vill'[26] are not only

[24] Furber, ed., *Essex peace sessions*, p. 174: '. . . est communis laborator et capit per diem tam in yeme quam in estate ijd. et cibum contra statutum, etc., et in autumpno iiijd. et cibum contra statutum'.

[25] *Ibid.*, p. 160: 'devillat in autumpno pro excessu'.

[26] ERO D/DU 267/29 (Birdbrook leet, 20 Jul 1366): 'Item presentant quod Robertus Wolfrich nativus domini non vult operare infra villatam Ideo preceptum est seisire corpus eius & c [two other men similarly charged]'.

typical of Statute cases but also entirely compatible with the scenario encapsulated in Capell's account a century later.

The other noteworthy wage differential at Porter's Hall was that between men and women. Females accounted for a strikingly large proportion of the daily-employed in 1483–4, amounting to roughly one-third of all the person-days worked, and approximately the same proportion of harvest work. The gender-specific nature of other tasks was more marked: sowing at Porter's Hall was exclusively women's work, threshing and harrowing, men's. Nor were these female employees exclusively spinsters, widows, or others unencumbered with the domestic demands of married life or in economically precarious solitary households. On the contrary, of the 16 female harvest workers 6 are explicitly called wives of named husbands, and in 5 of these instances the husband also was hired to harvest, as was the case for example with 'Richard Boknam ys wyfe' who reaped for one day while Richard himself was hired to do so for ten and a half days. Similarly, among the five female sowers two were explicitly called wives. But despite recent suggestions by historians that in some instances there was little or no real wage differential in medieval England between men and women for identical agricultural tasks during harvest,[27] a woman's day's work at Porter's Hall was clearly less expensive than a man's. The difference was less marked at harvest – as one would expect, given the heightened intensity of demand for labour that would have tended to iron out disparities – than at other times, when the difference in wages was more typically two-to-one.

Unfortunately very little can be known about the personal circumstances or background of the great majority of Porter's Hall employees in this single agricultural year. They are just names in a list. For a few, though, some clues to their likely economic position within the community can be gained through cross-reference to a rental of local tenants that was drawn up a few years later, in October 1487.[28] Several of the Porter's Hall workers fit well into the paradigmatic profile of the late-medieval Essex labourer sketched out earlier in this study. Richard Hall possessed only a messuage and garden, and his wife did twelve days' milking for Capell for the sum of 4d. John Pyknote, listed in the rental as holding only a 'piece' of land and a pasture, harvested for Capell for five days and also sold him some chaff for 6d.

[27] Penn, 'Female wage-earners', pp. 7–11; Middleton, 'Sexual division of labour', esp. p. 161. It is, in fact, strictly speaking not possible to say that men and women hired for harvesting at Porter's Hall did exactly the same work, since Penn points out that men may have been more likely to wield the sickle, women to gather or bind sheaves.

[28] BL Add. Roll 66054. All the tenurial information given in this paragraph is taken from this 1487 rental.

But members of the middling to upper ranks of the community were not all so exclusively preoccupied with their own affairs as to preclude a few days' paid work also, even in autumn. Stephen Lytyl, holder of a messuage and more than 14 acres of land, did five and a half days' harvesting for Capell; William Caffyl, tenant of a holding of roughly equivalent size, also did six days' harvesting, two more days of unspecified work plus 'j day ye cart', and he also was hired 'for beryng of mett & drynke to feld for iij days' in harvest. Local craftsmen were also drawn onto Capell's payroll for agricultural work. John Mechyll did seven days' harvesting, his wife one day, and 'John Mechyll & ys man' one further day each. Mechyll, tenant of a messuage and garden in 1487, doubtless gained much of his livelihood as a carpenter, because he was also paid 20d. later in the year 'for makyng of the berne dor', 'ys man' receiving 4d. for two days' work at the same time, and Mechyll at another time earned 12d. 'for iij day work in the garden & att melle'. Clearly, then, more than just the landless or near-landless labourers of the community were drawn into harvest work in particular, but also a variety of other tasks and transactions with the community's dominant employer.

Porter's Hall, then, was by no means a 'typical' employer in late-medieval Essex, either in scale or, necessarily, in the composition of its labour demands. But the unique insight into wage employment that its account lends does point to some features of the district's wage-labour market that are likely to have wider significance, beyond this one farm and through the later middle ages generally. It is useful, again, to distinguish between the demand and supply sides of this market.

Balancing the demands for long-term and short-term hiring, or between servants and labourers, bore important implications for the cost of labour from the employer's perspective. A very rough-and-ready impression of the costs of a day's labour to its employer can be glimpsed from Table 10.1. Harvest claimed more than three-quarters of the cash cost of daily labour, both due to the large number of person-days worked and to their higher *per diem* cost (and their true cost is underrepresented in the table because there the cost of harvest meals is not included). At the same time, the actual cost of the eleven servants and two ploughmen was much greater than, perhaps even double or more than, what the table implies, due to the unknown cost to Capell of the servants' bed and board. It is difficult also to estimate the number of 'person-days' of work the servants actually would have rendered over a year; the table presents a notional figure of potential work assuming that servants could be called upon every day of the calendar, but that is doubtless quite unrealistic and the actual figure would in reality be smaller by some fraction, perhaps by as much as one-quarter. But all the same and with all these qualifications, the cost of a servant's day's work to his or her employer was clearly very much smaller than that of a day-labourer's.

From the worker's perspective, then, employment by the day was much more remunerative, and there was thus a sound economic basis for the charge made in many Statute of Labourers indictments that a labourer 'does not want to serve anyone by the usual and accustomed terms, except only by the day'.[29] Indeed, as writers from Ritchie to Dyer have noted, it would seemingly not have taken too many weeks' work at the rates prevailing in the later fourteenth and fifteenth centuries to accumulate as much in cash terms as many servants did over an entire year.[30] But the critical question is whether the demand for labour, and the objective differences in circumstances between servants and labourers, were such as to make this trade-off a realistic prospect for many workers.

The Porter's Hall evidence, even though pertaining to only one employer in this community, albeit the largest, tends to undermine the expectation of such an unlimited demand throughout the calendar that day-labourers could easily and regularly have found enough employment over enough days to match servants' annual earning in cash and kind. Among all those who worked on a daily basis over this year, the mean employment was for 7.3 days, earning 19.6d. (for men, 7.8 days and 24.0d.; for women, 6.5 days and 13.1d.). The majority of this work, again, came in harvest season: when only harvest workers and their earnings are considered the means are 5.4 days for 19.4d. (for men, 5.8 days and 22.7d.; for women, 4.6 days and 13.8d.). Many, perhaps, the great majority, of these people found work for other employers at Stebbing and elsewhere, so the typical earnings of ordinary agricultural labourers would be some unknown multiple of these figures. Still, when these earnings are compared with servants' (typically 10–20s. plus bed and board), the employment Capell alone provided would need to have represented one-tenth or less of all the hirings that his day-labourers managed to find over the year for them to have accrued what his servants earned. This seems unlikely, and it is clear that labour demand levels generally, the seasonal constraints of the harvest weeks and the lower wage rates of the remainder of the calendar imposed stricter limits

[29] PRO.KB9.25 m.11: John Pipe of Arkesden 'est communis laborarius ad laborandum & non vult servire alicui per terminos usuales & consuetos nisi per diem ...'.

[30] Ritchie, 'Labour conditions in Essex', p. 93; Dyer, *Standards of living*, pp. 222–5.

upon the earning potential of the daily labour supply than is apparent at first glance.

Indictments under the terms of the Statute of Labourers provide another perspective upon earnings. This evidence is traditionally cited to point out the high levels of daily wage rates that labourers attained after the Black Death, with the usually only tacit implication that earnings were correspondingly high.[31] However, in many cases the charges brought against Statute offenders included an assessment of the total sum that a worker earned at 'excessive' rates from different employers over the course of a regnal year. For example, among a long series of indictments brought against Essex labourers in 1389 it was charged that 24 men in Dunmow Hundred 'are common labourers and refuse to serve by the usual terms but only by the day, taking per day in the twelfth year of the present king [i.e. Richard II, or 1388–9] in winter 2d. and meal and in autumn 4d. and meal ... And so each of them took by extortion 2s.'.[32] Doubtless these earnings assessments should not be taken too literally, but in view of the aims of Statute enforcement they are unlikely to err on the side of minimising the scope of illegal earnings.

When viewed in this way, Statute indictments data underscore the intermittent nature of wage employment in late-medieval Essex, and cast some doubt upon the notion that the period's illicitly high wages necessarily translated into a workers' bonanza. In indictments brought in 1389 against 130 daily-employed labourers (all male) in Chelmsford, Dunmow, Freshwell and Uttlesford Hundreds, workers were charged with earning at illegal daily rates as little as 12d. to as much as 10s. per year. The mean was 56.9d., probably representing at most a few weeks' work.[33] Similarly in 1352, when fines collected under the Statute were applied to offset the county's liability for a lay

[31] E.g. Ritchie, 'Labour conditions in Essex'.

[32] PRO.KB9.25 m.8: '...sunt communes laboratores & nolunt servire per terminos usuales nisi solummodo per diem capiendo per diem in anno xij domini Regis nunc tempore yemali ijd. & prandium & tempore autumpno iiijd. & prandium videlicet de Willelmo Mannyng & de aliis hominibus hundredi predicti apud Altam Rothyng & alibi in hundredo predicto Et sic ceperunt quilibet eorum per extorcionem usque ad summam ijs.'.

[33] PRO.KB9.25 mm. 4, 6–9, 10–11. One can construe the language of these cases in two different ways. One is to read it to mean that the 59.6d. was the total earned at the 'excessive' rates, or about 15 (at 4d. per day in harvest) to 30 (at 2d. in other seasons) days' work. Alternatively, 59.6d. may have been meant to represent the difference between what *was* earned and what *should* have been earned at legal rates (set in 1351 as what had been customary in the decade before the Black Death, in Essex 2–3d. in harvest and 1½–2d. otherwise). This would reflect up to two months' employment. One should not, of course, take these estimates as anything other than order-of-magnitude; the point here is simply to show that indictments like these indicate a modest hiring season during which such inflated wates were earned.

subsidy assessment, an estreat roll was drawn up that lists, community by community, the name of each Statute offender and the 'excess' of illegal over legal earnings received by each.[34] Among 7,556 offenders, roughly 80 per cent of them men and 20 per cent women, the mean 'excess' was 22.9d. Once again, this evidence is partial, limited as it is to earnings at 'excessive' daily rates, though in these Statute cases the earnings in question were apparently meant to represent what was taken from all the workers' employers who paid those rates. Nevertheless, as with the Porter's Hall evidence of a century later, the impression remains that high *per diem* wage rates did not inevitably translate into proportionately high earnings.

One final glimpse, though perhaps the most problematic of all, of workers' earnings comes from the very end of the period of this study, in the form of assessment of wages in the early Tudor subsidies. The subsidy collections of 1524 and 1525 assessed liability upon wages earned on a daily, weekly, or yearly basis, and so at least in theory netted both servants and labourers who earned at least 20s. per annum.[35] Among those taxed upon earnings in Witham Hundred in 1524 (probably the most consistently recorded return from Essex), 218 (80.1 per cent) of 272 wages-based assessments fell at the minimum taxable level of 20s., and a further 38 (14.0 per cent) were assessed at up to 30s.[36] The difficulty here is to know how literally one may take this as a realistic assessment of annual earnings of the labourers (and, probably, some servants) constituting this group. It is unlikely to be more than an order-of-magnitude indicator.[37] In short, each of these oblique glimpses of workers' earnings is imperfect, but derived as they are from several very different contexts of evidence, taken as a whole they are consistent with one another. Labour shortage during the later middle ages meant, not that enhanced wage-earning opportunities at

[34] PRO.E137.11.2; cf. Poos, 'Social context of Statute enforcement'.

[35] See Chapter 1 for discussion of these subsidies' tax bases.

[36] PRO.E179.108.154 (returns for 15 townships). Earning assessments among 272 taxpayers were distributed as follows:

20s.	20s.1d. – 30s.	30s. 1d. – 40s.	40s. 1d. +
218 (80.1%)	38 (14.0%)	14 (5.1%)	2 (0.7%)

[37] Cornwall, *Wealth and society*, pp. 14–28, 205–10, does not discuss this problem in any detail but appears to treat relative assessments in the Tudor muster rolls and subsidy returns as realistic in comparative terms. Phythian Adams, *Desolation of a city*, pp. 132–3, on the other hand, suspects 'extreme artificiality' and questions whether, in an urban context, the returns for Coventry (where most wage-earners were assessed at 40s.) could realistically reflect total earnings.

high daily rates of pay were the norm throughout the calendar, but rather that marginal supply and demand, and thus realistic prospects for high earnings, became more intensified along seasonal or task-specific lines for labourers hired by the day. In the light of this it is all the more important to consider how the conditions of the district's late-medieval economy may have influenced the mixture of servants and labourers within the local workforce, and specifically how this mixture may have shifted from before to after the Black Death and from the recessionary fifteenth to inflationary sixteenth century.

Kussmaul has persuasively demonstrated that the importance of servants in husbandry within the agricultural workforce of early-modern England was by no means constant.[38] They were demonstrably less prevalent in the later sixteenth and early seventeenth centuries than during the next hundred years or so, and their numbers declined again thereafter. Several economic factors influenced servanthood's cyclical incidence, or more specifically the demand for this form of labour, especially agricultural change over time, levels of wages and prices, and (intimately tied up with both) aggregate population. Economic and demographic influences upon early-modern servanthood in turn pose some suggestive parallels for understanding labour demand in late-medieval Essex as well.

In pre-modern England generally, upward population pressure, as in the late thirteenth or late sixteenth century, tended to force up agricultural productivity per unit of land by shifting production towards grain and away from animals. Demographic decline or stagnation exerted the opposite effect. Arable agriculture's labour demands – as the Porter's Hall evidence incisively shows – is intensive in certain periods of the year but slack for the remaining months. Animal-raising, on the other hand, requires work more evenly distributed over the calendar. Of course, even strictly grain-producing farms of any size had animals, so this dichotomy is not absolute. Wage labourers hired on a daily or short-term basis were ideally suited, from the employer's perspective, for grain-growing, servants for stock-rearing. And so long-term swings in the balance of arable and pastoral between 1500 and 1850 were accompanied by shifts in the composition of labour demand.

Since a large part of a servant's remuneration was in food, higher food prices tended to make servants less attractive to employers. Or to put this another way, lower real wages relative to food prices made wage labourers more attractive. Such was characteristic of the later

[38] Kussmaul, *Servants in husbandry*, pp. 22–7, 97–119, from which this and the following three paragraphs are derived.

1500s and early 1600s. By contrast, higher real wages made servants more desirable and labourers less so later on in the early-modern period.

Long-term swings in England's national population influenced both agriculture and real wages, but demography influenced servanthood in other ways also. In England's early-modern, fertility-driven demographic regime, contracting or stagnant population resulted in there being fewer adolescents, the age-group from which most servants were drawn, as a proportion of total population than in times when population was growing. Thus, even if the number of servants remains unchanged relative to total population, those servants represent a higher proportion of adolescents during times of demographic decline. And early-modern servanthood and marriage stood in an inverse relationship of sorts to one another. At the aggregate level, more prevalent servanthood in the later 1600s and early 1700s coincided with higher mean ages at marriage and with proportionally more people never marrying. From the individual's perspective the trade-off was that between prolonging one's status as a servant an extra year or two before marrying or indeed passing one's lifetime unmarried, as opposed to leaving service sooner and being more likely to take a spouse.

The sources simply do not exist to demonstrate empirically whether the same forces acted with equal effect in England before 1500. But under the logic of the mechanisms sketched out here, both Kussmaul and Smith have argued that backward extrapolation of the early-modern cyclical patterns is plausible, and that the weight of agricultural labour was probably tilted more towards servants and away from labourers during the century and a half after 1350 than the preceding and succeeding periods.[39] The earlier chapters of this study have shown that in central and northern Essex during the later middle ages, the requisite components of economic environment certainly obtained. Population remained in decline or stagnation until the early sixteenth century; agriculture in the district did shift towards pastoral production in the 1400s; wages were relatively high and grain prices low; and employers clearly made tactical hiring decisions balancing servants and labourers.

Nevertheless, several medieval economic historians have questioned whether the importance of servants in the later-medieval workforce could have been greater than before 1350. On the basis of references to servants in manorial-court proceedings, Razi argued that

[39] *Ibid.*, pp. 97, 168–9; Smith, 'Some issues concerning families and their property', pp. 35–8.

the proportion of households having servants in one West Midlands manor declined by one-half during the 1300s; the difficulties inherent in this source's selective inclusion of lower-status individuals in the written record have, however, already been noted.[40] Other writers, most recently Dyer, cite the many cases of Statute of Labourers indictments charging that employees had abandoned their positions or refused to serve 'by the usual terms but only by the day', as *prima facie* persuasive evidence of workers' widespread aversion to long hiring contracts.[41] But the previous chapter showed that in Essex, at any rate, when put into quantitative perspective it is more difficult to regard such cases as an expression of massive resistance to the institution.[42] Moreover these cases, and contemporary moralists' castigation of servants' laziness and untrustworthiness,[43] cut both ways. One can read them equally as an expression of preference on the part of employers, who in many cases were the immediate Statute-enforcers, to preserve a norm of servanthood which was already established but whose economic logic was all the more compelling to all employers, even those of quite humble status.[44]

Ultimately one's choice of interpretation here turns partly upon one's perception of relative bargaining and coercive power in a labour 'market' rather less fluid or capitalised than a modern one. Indictments for violating the labour laws of the period thrust into prominence the recalcitrant. But Clark, in an important recent study, has illuminated another, previously neglected aspect of how the Statute of Labourers affected hiring.[45] In local courts throughout England – including Essex manorial courts – employers invoked the Statute to quash workers' claims in litigation for arrears of wages. At Writtle in 1410, for example, John Bakere sued John Fynchyngfeld for 20s., the stipend they had agreed upon for one year's service; Fynchyngfeld, while not denying the agreement, replied that since the labour statute of 1388 set 13s. 4d. as a servant's maximum pay, he was not obliged to reply to Bakere's suit.[46] Clark concluded that the

[40] Razi, 'Family, land and the village community', pp. 31–2; see above, Chapter 9.

[41] Dyer, *Standards of living*, pp. 213, 224–5.

[42] See above, Chapter 9.

[43] Cf. Hilton, *The English peasantry in the later middle ages*, p. 24; Coleman, *English literature in history*, pp. 148–9.

[44] Poos, 'Social context of Statute enforcement'.

[45] Clark, 'Medieval labor law and English local courts'.

[46] ERO D/DP M214 (Writtle court, 11 Oct 1410): '. . . Johannes Bakere retentus fuit cum predicto Johanne Fynchyngfeld . . . per unum annum integrum deserviens . . . pro quo servicio predictus Johannes Fynchyngfeld solvisset per convencionem . . . xxs. & xld. pro vestura sua . . . predictus Johannes Fynchyngfeld defendit vim & iniuriam . . . dicit quod ordinatum est & provisum per quoddam statutum factum in tempore Ricardi nuper Regis Anglie quod nullus serviens laborarius per annum deserviens capere debeat pro salario suo per annum ultra xiijs. iiijd. unde petit iudicium si contra

legislation thus provided masters with a means of recourse (or barred workers from a means of recourse) in a way that 'readily worked to most masters' benefit'.[47] In short, surviving Statute of Labourers material does not necessarily speak unanimously to a labour market in which it was workers who had the upper hand in setting terms.

Undoubtedly the legislation failed to have much impact in limiting wage rises, but in one important respect it would be misguided to view cases of refusal to serve 'by the usual terms' as meaning that employees could switch back and forth, from being servants to being labourers and the reverse, at will. Servanthood was, once again, a phase and condition of life, not just an alternative occupation. From the supply side of the labour market only certain servants, of more advanced age and with a minimal wherewithal (skills, and a cash reserve and prospects for imminent settlement, for example), were likely to be able to make the transition to being labourers capable of sustaining their own independent households. Here too, these particular workers are thrust into ostensible predominance by the evidential filter of legal tribunals (in this case, indictments under the labour statutes). It was primarily from the demand side, or the employers' perspective, that the two alternative labour forms could be juggled.

In quantitative terms, the weight of each within the rural economy of late-medieval Essex cannot be empirically demonstrated. But these forms and structures of employment do have some critically important implications for social structure, household formation, and the conundrum of late-medieval demographic depression.

The weight of evidence demonstrates the prominence of servants in the district's economy and social structure. Economic logic, albeit not empirical demonstration, suggests that they played a role at least as important in the district's workforce as before 1350 or after 1520, and quite likely rather more. But even if servants' numbers (relative to total population) were unchanged from before the Black Death, they almost certainly accounted for a higher percentage of the adolescent age-group.[48] That, in itself, would have delayed marriage and depressed fertility in the district.

formam statuti predicti predictus Johannes Bakere istam actionem versus eum manutenere debeat ...'. Bakere subsequently was amerced for not pursuing his suit: *ibid.* (Writtle court, 18 Apr 1411).

47 Clark, 'Medieval labor law and English local courts', p. 344.

48 Coale and Demeny, *Regional model life tables*, pp. 55, 62, 105, 112, provides a rough impression of how large this factor potentially could be, depending upon mortality levels and intrinsic growth rate (r). In Model West stable populations (see below, Appendix A), under mortality scenarios ranging from extremely severe to roughly equivalent to England's sixteenth-century experiences (Coale and Demeny's level 1, where female e_0 at $r = 0$ is 20.0 years, to level 8, or $e_0 = 37.5$ years), the percentage of all

The condition of wage labourers during the period is more paradoxical. *Per diem* wage rates rose, but the structure of local agricultural hiring means that any rise in yearly earnings they enjoyed was more muted. At the same time, labourers in central and northern Essex were not the beneficiaries of a wholesale redistribution of land after the Black Death. On the contrary, landholding profiles remained highly stratified, so that that potential component of enhanced living standards was denied them. Some, though probably not a high proportion, found by-employment in local industries like clothmaking. And migration data imply that if enhanced opportunities were to be had in the late-medieval Essex countryside, they came at the cost of more frequent, more inevitable mobility and later settlement than for other occupational groups. All this, then, makes more comprehensible labourers' nuptiality patterns – less likely to marry, or likely to marry later in life than others – and their differential fertility, indeed the fertility of the district's population as a whole due to the numerical preponderance of labourers, was restricted accordingly. And so (to follow on from Chapter 7's observations upon the marriage process) there is no need to view demographic stagnation in a time of high *per diem* wage rates as a conundrum, nor to doubt the efficacy of the 'real wages'-sensitive nuptiality model for wage-earners.

It was, once again, women's nuptiality experiences that were the more pivotal for influencing overall demographic growth, and here too wage-labour opportunities were of great importance. Women were extensively involved in many aspects of agricultural and industrial work, as shown by the female workers at Porter's Hall in 1483–4 or the 1,559 women (only 235 of them explicitly married, appearing in the record as 'A the wife of B') fined for Statute violations in Essex in 1352.[49] Indeed, their appearances in other Essex Statute material (few in number, doubtless due in part to the selective vagaries of the

males and females represented by the age-group 15–24 years varied as follows:

Mortality level	*r*	Males	Females
8	−0.5% p.a.	16.46	15.73
	0.0	17.38	16.71
	+0.5	18.17	17.57
1	−0.5	19.15	18.32
	0.0	19.68	18.93
	+0.5	20.06	19.39

And so, for instance, the share of total females represented by 15-to-24-year-olds drops by 10.5 per cent when *r* falls from 0.5 to −0.5 per cent per annum (mortality level 8).

[49] PRO.E137.11.2; Poos, 'Social context of Statute enforcement'.

indictment process)[50] imply many similarities with their male counterparts. In 1378 'Isabella, daughter of Gilbert Rouge of Sturmer, takes 4d. per day and food in autumn'; each of three women in Ashen takes 'excess pay in autumn, that is, 4d., and also moves from place to place [*devillat*]'[51]; such entries suggest a mobile female harvest workforce. Medieval employers had long been quite well aware that women were cheaper to hire. A late-thirteenth-century manual of husbandry recommended that for stock-keeping 'it is always advisable to have a woman there for much less money than a man would take'.[52] And so it is likely that some substitution of cheaper female for dearer male workers took place in the countryside when wage rates rose after 1350, as was the case also in certain late-medieval English towns.[53] Moreover, although it has been shown that by no means all female wage-earners in the district were single, independent agents, expansion of employment opportunities would in balance have had the same effect as for males of delaying marriage for women who followed this life-course as servants or labourers.[54]

In formal econometric terms it will never be possible to specify the parameters of agricultural labour as an input factor, or labour supply and demand, during the period, or to balance the implications of labour supply from a local population reduced by one-half against the district's contracting arable production and expanding textile output. The wide variety of evidence addressed here, however, suggests that historians need to direct more attention to the structure of labour than to simple person/land balances. And in many respects employment, particularly in the case of servants, in this society was a matter of social structure as much as a strictly economic phenomenon. It is precisely for that reason that the significance of servanthood and

50 Penn, 'Female wage-earners', p. 5, notes that in Somerset in 1358, females indicted for Statute offences comprised more than one-third of all offenders, but notes the variability of women's share in these indictments from county to county and session to session. In Essex peace sessions during 1377–9, only six women appeared among 170 Statute indictments: Furber, ed., *Essex peace sessions*, pp. 158, 159–60, 163, 166.

51 Furber, ed., *Essex peace sessions*, pp. 158, 159–60.

52 Oschinsky, ed., *Walter of Henley*, pp. 426–7: 'si est tut iurs bon de aver une femme leynz a plus leger souz qe lem puyt . . .'.

53 Goldberg, 'Marriage, migration, servanthood and life-cycle'.

54 Cf. Bennett, 'Medieval peasant marriage', esp. pp. 207–8, 212–14. Citing the fact that one-third of the merchets recorded in the Ramsey Abbey estates' *Liber Gersumarum* in the early fifteenth century (a body of data having no parallel in Essex during the period) were paid by the women involved themselves and not their parents, Bennett argues that this was the result of these women's economic independence and more advanced age, both probably the result of employment in many cases.

wage labour is so wide-ranging, and also that the cultural and even political experiences of the various occupational and status groups comprising the late-medieval Essex countryside's population demand equal attention.

PART VI

'Beware of such holy men'

William Kirkham, rector of Beauchamp Roding, to his parishioners, 1494[1]

The district was the centre of a deeply rooted strain of anti-authoritarianism during the later fourteenth and fifteenth centuries, which manifested itself both in rural revolts and uprisings and in a persistent subculture of religious nonconformity. In both these respects, once again, late-medieval Essex foreshadowed the county's predispositions towards dissent from that time on to the Civil War. Civil unrest and religious unorthodoxy were inextricably linked with each other, and with the social structure in which they flourished.

The great revolt of 1381, which convulsed much of southeastern England, began in Essex, and the district's countryfolk participated in other large-scale revolts in 1413–14, 1450 and 1471. But quite apart from these relatively well-known events there were many more, smaller-scale episodes against local and national authority. It would be misguided to claim one distinct pattern of motivation, target, or participants for all uprisings in the district during this period: political, economic, religious and seigneurial factors, and pre-existing personal or local enmities, contributed to revolts in different permutations. Each rising was multi-layered, with different patterns of motive, clientele and target at local, regional and extra-regional levels.

Nevertheless, two patterns of continuity formed a constant refrain through the unrest of the period. Large-scale revolts grew to significant proportions when they were able to co-opt participants with diverse immediate aims and allow them to coalesce under a unifying rubric. And each uprising drew upon a local culture of anti-authoritarianism, for which religious nonconformity was a contribu-

[1] GL MS 9065 fo. 217v; see also below, Chapter 12.

tory ingredient. Towards the end of the middle ages purely anti-seigneurial strikes, although important in the later 1300s when manorial economies and personal serfdom were in states of flux, became progressively more submerged among factors that were more overtly political, or that fitted in other ways into the ever-important issue of local authority.

Lollardy was firmly established in Essex during the early fifteenth century, but beyond formal heretical belief lay a less articulated culture of popular religion that made the district amenable to nonconformity of various degrees and shadings. This culture was anti-sacramentarian and anti-clerical, but primarily in the sense of favouring an evangelical stance over hierarchical authority. Religious attitudes complemented (though they did not deterministically 'cause') civil unrest. At the same time, lay people at the parochial level claimed a more activist role in community affairs that was in certain respects encouraged by nonconformist tendencies.

The participants in both rural revolts and formal religious heresy sprang from the broad middling band of village society: modest agriculturalists, artisans, and smaller numbers of labourers and clergy. It is ironic, then, that labourers, craftsmen and retailers lagged well behind agriculturalists at the end of the medieval era in acquiring basic literacy, a skill widely presumed to have been central to the transmission of religious and political subversion. It was, instead, the industrialised, commercialised nature of the local economy and the persistent disparity of richer and poorer at village level that were the critical factors predisposing the district to unrest.

11

Authority and rebellion

Rural society in Essex at the end of the middle ages stood near the epicentre of many of the period's most spectacular social and agrarian revolts and uprisings. Moreover, in addition to the better-known, larger-scale episodes the period was also punctuated by many more localised and modest eruptions of discontent with authority. In this respect the later fourteenth and fifteenth centuries provide the backdrop to a heritage of radicalism in the county stretching forward in time to at least the Civil War, when Essex would be the most Puritan and the most Parliamentarian of constituencies.[1] Civil turbulence was the crossroads where a volatile, stratified social structure and local economy merged with an entrenched anti-authoritarian mental culture.

The most serious of these uprisings – especially the great revolt of 1381, which was sparked off in Essex, but also including Oldcastle's revolt (1413–14) and Cade's rebellion (1450), and even Essex participation in Thomas Fauconberg's attempted *coup* in London (1471) – derived their immediate impetus from a variety of factors, political, fiscal, seigneurial, social and economic, and religious. In this era, common people only extremely rarely left explicit statements in the written record, relayed by relatively unbiased authors, of their personal motivations and aims. And so historians can deduce motives only very cautiously, and only by reconstructing as much as possible of the circumstances, background and individuals in each episode. Even then, only inferences are possible. And even in the larger-scale uprisings of the middle ages that did bequeath to modern eyes articulated programmes or demands, these programmes may have

[1] Hunt, *The Puritan moment*. Hill, 'From Lollards to Levellers', pp. 89–91, attempts to trace a continuity of religious radicalism and social unrest in Essex from the later middle ages to the Civil War.

been rallying-calls which managed to impel to action groups holding rather more diverse underlying grievances than the manifestos may imply on the surface.

It would in fact be misleading at the outset to imply that all of Essex people's experiences of these revolts can be entirely assimilated into a common scheme. Each evolved from its own distinctive roots, and within its own temporal circumstances. And yet the common threads that run through all these episodes are precisely the facts that, in each, more than one distinct if overlapping factor or motive impelled different sectors of rural society to coalesce temporarily into common action, and that each episode managed, even if only inadvertently, to tap into an underlying stream of more diffused anti-authoritarian unrest among ordinary rural people.

Nowhere is this more true than in the 1381 revolt, one of the most-debated events of English social history, and the one which will provide the present chapter's point of departure. The topic of 1381 is too vast, and the evidence and its interpretation too varied, for this discussion to attempt wholesale revisionism. The religious component of local dissent throughout the period will be taken up in Chapter 12. What follows here is an attempt to reconstruct some local contextual framework for the background and participation in that revolt, to trace some lines of parallel and contrast with other rebellions and disorders within the county, and ultimately to describe what there was about the district's social structure and economy that helps to lend meaning and continuity to the Essex anti-authoritarian tradition. It will be helpful first to review the basic narrative of events in the great revolt in general, then to inspect more closely what can be reconstructed of the pattern of local events within the county, and next to examine some salient points of the background and precursors to the revolt in Essex, before going on to other selected episodes of local unrest over the following century.[2]

Most deeply rooted among the background factors contributing to friction on the eve of the great revolt were the rapid economic restructurings of rural society in the post-Black Death era. Manorial economies were being transformed in some places, while in others lords attempted to reinforce their traditional claims for bond labour obligations and incidents of personal serfdom. To this discontent was

[2] The summary of the following two paragraphs has been taken largely from Oman, *The great revolt of 1381*; Hilton, *Bond men made free*, esp. pp. 137–43; Dobson, ed., *The peasants' revolt of 1381*, esp. pp. 36–44; Brooks, 'The organization of the peasants in 1381'.

added the friction caused by attempts (in Essex, at least, largely futile ones) to stem geographical mobility and wage increases under the auspices of the Statute of Labourers. Political uncertainties and fiscal demands compounded tensions: when Richard II assumed the throne as a minor in 1377 the English war effort in France had been turning sour, a collective regency council held the central government, and demands for revenue were pressing. It was the third poll tax within four years, voted by the Commons in late 1380, that ignited the spark within this volatile atmosphere. It soon became apparent that the proceeds coming in from this levy were seriously below expectations, and during the spring of 1381 commissions were appointed to investigate and remedy the collection's shortfall.

On 30 May at Brentwood (in southern Essex) men from at least fifteen nearby communities attacked a party of officials, including John de Bampton and John Gildesburgh, both prominent Essex-based gentry, who had been sent to enforce poll-tax collection. Events moved swiftly from there. During the first few days of June rebel groups in Essex and Kent, clearly operating in some degree of communication with each other, were stirring revolt in their respective districts. Insurgents attacked the property of manorial lords and of figures, like Bampton and Gildesburgh, who were associated in the popular eye with the loathed poll-tax and local law enforcement. Manorial court rolls, rentals and other documents, the tangible tokens and practical tools of manorial lordship and customary law, were seized and burnt. On 12 June Kentish rebels assembled at Blackheath (south of the Thames and about five miles from London), while on the same day Essex insurgents arrived at Mile End, east of the city, the contingents from each county probably numbering into the thousands. The city was entered with the aid of Londoners on 13 June. During the next three days the rebels executed Simon of Sudbury (Archbishop of Canterbury and Richard's Chancellor), Robert Hales (prior of the order of Hospitallers and Treasurer of England), and many others. The London palace of the much-despised John of Gaunt, Duke of Lancaster and Richard's uncle, and the property of other notables were looted and burnt. Meanwhile news of the events in London radiated north, generating secondary uprisings in East Anglia, the northern Home Counties, and further afield. After two colloquies between Richard and the rebels, the Essex and Kentish insurgents began drifting home in the middle days of June, and with little capacity for sustained resistance the last group of Essex diehards was routed at Billericay on the 28th.

The dramatic quality of the London events has tended, until fairly recently, to overshadow close analysis of the sequence of incidents in the rural, opening stages of the revolt. The nature of the evidence is partly responsible for this: chroniclers tended to be best informed about the capital and to treat the invading rebels as a faceless mob, while the criminal records available have their own serious *lacunae*. Only with the recovery of a great volume of civil litigation for damages brought by victims in the wake of the revolt, largely through research by Andrew Prescott, has it been possible to piece together the succession of events within Essex at ground level.[3] As a product of this research the names of nearly 1,000 Essex rebels are known now, though the painstaking work of tracing their local background has barely begun.

What has become increasingly clear is to what a great extent the revolt in rural Essex was a multi-layered as well as a multi-faceted phenomenon. That is to say: at one level there were the myriad attacks upon seigneurial authority, mounted largely by a given manor's tenantry and inhabitants against its own lordship. At another level were strikes at figures notorious for their involvement at county-level government, at the hands of assailants of geographically more widely dispersed origins. At yet another level were the bands, drawn from different corners of Essex, who made the exodus to London and often helped to incite those more localised disturbances along the way, and who participated in the assaults upon property or persons of national notoriety. In addition, at each of these levels the outbreak of revolt triggered attacks upon individuals as a result of pre-existing conflict or enmity between victim and assailant.[4] The lid lifting off the pressure-cooker provided opportunity and pretext for scores to be settled. This multi-layered nature of the revolt in the countryside has obscured clear comprehension and frustrated historians in search of synthetic interpretation of the revolt's meaning. And yet it was precisely the fact that the revolt garnished participants with such widely ranging grievances that permitted it to assume the remarkable dimensions it attained.

The evidence now available makes it clear how widely the attacks against manorial lordship were spread and how many there were. The most tangible evidence for this comes from manorial documentation

[3] Prescott, 'Judicial records of the rising'; Prescott, 'London in the peasants' revolt'; Prescott, 'Essex rebel bands in London'. The author acknowledges with deep gratitude Dr Prescott's extraordinary generosity in sharing and discussing evidence of the events in Essex in 1381 which is drawn upon below.

[4] Prescott has shown that that was often the case during violence among Londoners themselves during the uprising: Prescott, 'London in the peasants' revolt', pp. 131–7.

itself. From surveys of manorial court-roll series whose records either explicitly mention the burning of previous courts' entries or whose surviving series commence (or recommence after a gap) in 1381 or soon after, and from other reports in civil- or criminal-court processes, it turns out that documents were destroyed at more than eighty Essex manors in the revolt. When only evidence from the manorial records alone is considered, this means that just over two-thirds of manors with available surviving material suffered that fate.[5] The manors in question were spread absolutely throughout the county, from Little Chesterford in the northwest to Moze in the northeast to Little Wakering in the southeast to Barking in the southwest. Moreover, in the heat of the moment many villagers seized the opportunity provided by the breakdown of manorial authority to encroach upon landed property or other resources, for example seizing upon and enclosing pieces of land or violating parks or common grazing ground.[6] The groundswell of popular revolt, and almost certainly (though it is impossible to prove exactly) the largest numbers of participants in the events of 1381 in Essex, comprised those who struck out at their immediate lordships and went little further.[7]

In contrast, attacks against prominent figures within Essex were mounted by bands drawn from many different places. The chronology of these assaults, the widespread geographical origins of those charged with participating in each of them, and the very language of legal proceedings relating to them, all make it clear that the logistical enterprise of spreading news, recruiting and co-ordinating attacks was astonishingly swift and efficient.[8]

One indictment recorded that at Bocking on 2 June – in other words, three days after and two dozen miles away from the initial eruption at Brentwood – a meeting was held that drew attenders from nine surrounding communities within a radius of more than ten miles. According to the relevant indictment, at this meeting those present 'swore to be of one mind, to destroy various of the king's lieges and his common laws and also all lordships . . . [and] to have

[5] Wood, 'Essex manorial records and the revolt', p. 67, and accompanying gazetteer, pp. 85–98. A map of places in Essex where records were destroyed in 1381 is given in Liddell and Wood, *Essex and the peasants' revolt*.

[6] E.g. Wood, 'Essex manorial records and the revolt', pp. 74–6, and accompanying gazetteer, pp. 88, 92; Poos, 'Population and resources', pp. 54–5.

[7] Prescott, 'Essex rebel bands in London', p. 65, notes that in northwestern Essex 'the rising assumed the form of old fashioned village riots directed against the local lord' whereas in the southeast of the county 'there was a more cogent and sophisticated protest'.

[8] Brooks, 'The organization of the peasants in 1381', esp. pp. 269–70.

no other law in England but those that they themselves made to be ordained'.[9]

During the next few days messengers were circulating to proclaim revolt and recruit followers in at least fifteen Essex communities.[10] 'Thomas Bakere of Fobbing and William Goldebourn feloniously sent Robert Berdon of Orsett as their messenger to the vill of Rayleigh on 7 June ... to raise the men of the said vill against the king's peace'.[11] 'John Geffrey, bailiff of East Hanningfield, made all the men of the vills of East Hanningfield, West Hanningfield, and South Hanningfield go against their wills' to make attacks elsewhere in the county on 10 and 17 June, 'and he was their leader [*ductor*] ... and he went voluntarily with an evil band'.[12] As the Essex rebels prepared to make their last stand, on 26–27 June Geffrey also sent his servant to warn people in surrounding villages 'that unless they were [assembled] at Great Baddow church the next day to go with his evil band ... they would be killed and their houses burnt ... and he made them swear that they would rise up against the lord king whenever they were ordered'. Geffrey was subsequently hanged for his agitation.[13] John Glasene and John Webbe of Manningtree confessed that on 13 June Henry Baker, bailiff of Tendring Hundred, coerced them and many others to join the men of Colchester on the journey to Mile End.[14]

[9] PRO.KB145.3.6.1 (quoted in Brooks, 'The organization of the peasants in 1381', p. 252n.): ' ... et ibidem iuraverunt essendum de uno assensu ad destruendum diversos ligeos domini regis et communes leges suas et etiam omnia dominia diversis dominis spectantia ... dicendum et iurandum quod noluerunt aliquam legem in Anglia habere nisi tantummodo certas leges per ipsos motas ordinandum ... '.

[10] Brooks, 'The organization of the peasants in 1381', pp. 255, 257.

[11] PRO.KB145.3.6.1 (quoted in Brooks, 'The organization of the peasants in 1381', p. 255n.): 'Thomas Bakere de Fobbyng et Willelmus Goldebourn felonice miserunt Robertum Berdon de Orsete ut nuntium eorum ad villam de Reyle ... ad levandum homines ville predicte contra pacem regis'.

[12] PRO.KB9.166.2 m.4 (incompletely translated in Sparvel-Bayly, 'Essex in insurrection', p. 218): ' ... fecit omnes homines villarum de Esthanyngfeld Westhanyngfeld & Southanyngfeld ire contra voluntates eorum ad templum Prioris Sancti Johannis ... ad Kirsyng & erat ductor eorum & surrexit & ivit cum comitiva iniqua voluntarie ... '.

[13] *Ibid.*: [on 26 June] ' ... misit Johannem Devenys servientem suum ad domos Johannis Baron junioris ... & aliorum & dixit eis quod nisi essent ad ecclesiam de Magna Badewe ... ad eundem cum comitiva iniqua adversus comitem Bukyngham & alios ligeos domini Regis essent interfecti & domos eorum combussi essent ... [on 27 June] ... congregavit omnes homines villarum de Esthanyngfeld & Southanyngfeld Wodeham Ferers & Retyngdon apud Retyngdonwode & fecit eos iurare quod surgerent adversus dominum Regem quotienscumque per ipsum periniuncti fuerint ... '; cf. Wood, 'Essex manorial records and the revolt', pp. 76–7.

[14] PRO.KB27.485 Rex m.5: ' ... Henricus Baker de Manytre ballivus hundredi de Tendryng ... percepit eidem Johanni sub pena forisfacturi que erga ipsum Regem forisfacere possit & ... quampluris aliis ville de Manytre ut se levarent pararent & insurgent & apud Colchestre se accederent facturi prout alij eiusdem de Colchestre

On 10 June a large mob, drawn from more than forty communities throughout the county and including Geffrey's recruits from the Hanningfields, attacked and destroyed the Hospitallers' priory at Cressing Temple. Later that same day they moved on three miles to Coggeshall, where they assaulted Sir John Sewale, the sheriff of Essex, and pillaged his house. At the same time they killed John Ewell, the county's escheator. The next day this group had moved on to Chelmsford, where Sewale and Ewell's official documents were ceremoniously burnt.[15]

It is scarcely difficult to account for the motives of these attacks. Hales, the head of the Hospitallers and soon to lose his own head at the Tower on the 14th, was publicly vilified in his role as Treasurer and chief administrator for the poll tax. Sewale and Ewell, in addition to their county offices and visible roles as local agents of the Crown's criminal law and property rights enforcement, had also been commissioned earlier that spring to take responsibility for the follow-up enforcement of the tax's collection in Essex.[16] A similar identification in the popular mind branded John de Bampton, who had also been estate steward for Barking Abbey and whose property at Canewdon was attacked on 11 June.[17]

The same was again true of John Gildesburgh. Apart from his presence with Bampton on the panel attacked at Brentwood, he had been Speaker of the Commons when the last poll-tax was voted. On 11 June Gildesburgh's houses at High Easter and Wennington were broken into, his charters and muniments destroyed, and his servants driven off.[18] The origins of the assailants in these incidents, shown in Figure 11.1, echo the spatial distributions in the attacks upon Cressing, Sewale and Ewell.[19] Passions inflamed to hatred over the poll-tax and co-ordinated by able organisers drew rebels from long distances in a way that it is unlikely simple intramanorial enmity often did.

Finally, Prescott has shown that the roughly 170 Essex rebels who

facerent quiquidem Johannes & alij . . . eadem die accederunt exinde . . . cum eisdem hominibus de Colchestr' apud Milende . . . '.

15 Brooks, 'The organization of the peasants in 1381', pp. 255, 259–62.

16 *Ibid.*, p. 62.

17 Dyer, 'Social and economic background', p. 39; *CPR 1381–5*, pp. 24, 76.

18 PRO.KB145.3.6.1; PRO.CP40.489 m.491v; CP40.490 mm. 263v, 278. The author gratefully acknowledges these references from Andrew Prescott. The places of assailants' origins mapped in Figure 11.1 are taken from these references. It should be pointed out that these sources do not allow one to distinguish whether (or which of) these assailants were present at one, the other, or both attacks. A house of Gildesburgh's at Fambridge was also attacked on 11 June: Wood, 'Essex manorial records and the revolt', accompanying gazetteer, p. 90.

19 Compare with Brooks, 'The organization of the peasants in 1381', maps on pp. 257, 261.

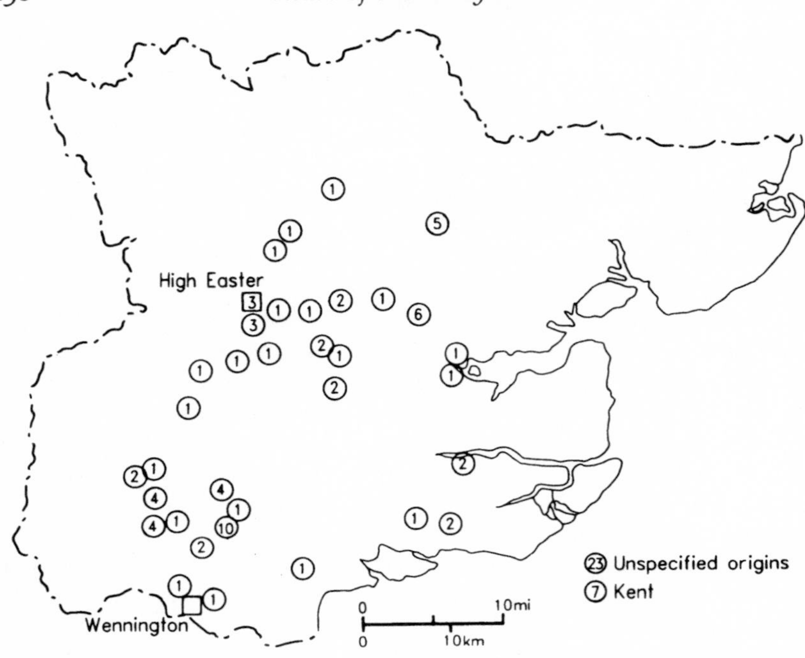

Figure 11.1. Origins of attackers at Sir John Gildesburgh's houses at High Easter and Wennington, 11 June 1381

are known by name to have reached London and joined in the attacks on Gaunt's Savoy palace and John Butterwick's houses at Westminster, Ebury and Knightsbridge, were by no means drawn into a general, random or indiscriminate drift.[20] Rather, three nuclei formed separate contingents that recruited and incited others as they moved and eventually joined in the London fray. One group, from Manningtree and surrounding villages in the northeastern corner of the county, joined up with the main band of insurgents in Chelmsford. After returning from Mile End, on 17 June they destroyed the house of Thomas Hardyng at Manningtree, in what must have been a definite score-settling since Hardyng had been a notorious manipulator of food prices and a litigious harasser of his neighbours in previous years.[21] Another group, drawn primarily from Thaxted and Ware (Herts.), attacked Gaunt's house at Hertford and incited village revolts on its way to London. A third Essex group in London had been drawn

[20] Prescott, 'London in the peasants' revolt', pp. 127–9; Prescott, 'Essex rebel bands in London'.

[21] Prescott, 'Essex rebel bands in London', pp. 58–60; PRO.KB27.485 Rex m.5.

from North Weald Bassett and thereabouts in the southwestern quarter of the county. In the attacks in London, Londoners predominated. Nevertheless, these patterns suggest, once again, that rebels who joined in events at the capital did so through co-ordinated networks of contacts and served as linchpins between village-level violence and assaults upon nationally notorious public figures.

This brief survey, it should be emphasised, barely scratches the surface of events in Essex during June of 1381, and a full retelling of the local rural revolt must await another venue.[22] But the multilayered nature of the revolt, and its selection of targets and details of organisation and dissemination, are keys to comprehending unrest in the district not only during 1381 but also through the variety of less spectacular uprisings that followed in the succeeding century. Some historians have concluded that 1381 witnessed a general eruption against lordship and authority that was unable or disinclined to distinguish between agents of royal government and of manorial lordship, or (for instance) between Hales' position as Treasurer and his position as lord of villeins. Hilton claimed that 'it is doubtful whether the peasant of medieval Europe was able to see much distinction between the agents of the State and those of the landed aristocracy'.[23] There is certainly ample evidence for a deep anti-authoritarian strain in this district. But the evidence for rebel organisation in Essex is unmistakable, even if contemporary charges may have exaggerated its conspiratorial nature. And the evidence clearly shows that rebels chose specific targets beyond their own personal lords with full knowledge of the identity and connections with local government or national politics of their targets, and of the locations of their victims' properties.

What little is now known of the rebels themselves bears this out. Dyer recently reconstructed the backgrounds of 48 Essex rebels from manorial evidence. This group represented a broad spectrum of rural society, with a slight bias towards the better-off at the village level and encompassing both agriculturalists and artisans. The most striking feature of this group was the high proportion who had had previous experience as officials of township or manorial administration, as jurors, reeves, constables and the like.[24] A similar pattern emerges from a group of six men from Great Waltham and High Easter who appeared in civil and criminal proceedings relating to attacks outside

22 Prescott, 'Judicial records of the rising', p. 260, notes that 33 civil pleas have been found that relate to Essex persons or events.

23 Hilton, 'Peasant society, peasant movements and "feudalism"', p. 82.

24 Dyer, 'Social and economic background', pp. 15–22.

their home manors, in the aftermath of the revolt. Of these, three had held manorial offices of one kind or another; three or perhaps four had paid the poll tax that year; at least five held customary land or were of unfree personal status, two or three as substantial tenants but one as a smallholder; one was primarily employed as a butcher.[25] People who had experience of local organisation and of the higher reaches of county legal authority were natural and informed leaders at the local level.

Much has been made of the demands that the rebels presented to Richard at Mile End and Smithfield.[26] They apparently included an end to serfdom, a dismantling of much of the endowment and institutional structure of the church, and a general dismembering of 'lordship'.[27] If these aims have not been too much garbled or sensationalised by hostile chroniclers then they constitute, not a programme as such, but a collection of aspirations appealing to a diversity of anti-authoritarian urges and a corresponding diversity of audiences and clientele. In this respect, though the aims or motivations varied, it was a phenomenon that would be repeated on later occasions when coinciding, multiple urges coalesced to spark common action in the district.

There is ample evidence that in Essex during the three decades or so before 1381, traditional and novel forms of authority were stiffening in ways that, with hindsight, can be seen to have amounted to little more than a rearguard action to slow the pace of change, but that in fact provoked a great deal more tension. These have, indeed, long been recognised as important background factors to the revolt: the poll tax itself, the recent attempts to enforce the Statute of Labourers, and more broadly the complex pattern of postures that different manorial lords and their administrators adopted regarding the operation of their manors and their demands both for labour services from customary tenants and for other obligations stemming from the personal liabilities of serfdom. Yet the evidence now available lends some tangible dimensions to this picture. The result was a rising crescendo of resistance to these irritants, in part in the form of individual acts of defiance but also, it would appear, increasingly in the form of group actions that prefigured the main events of the great revolt.

Some simple figures underscore the scope of this defiance. The

[25] Poos, 'Population and resources', pp. 59–63, reconstructs these persons and gives full documentary references.
[26] E.g. Hilton, *Bond men made free*, pp. 219–30.
[27] Dobson, ed., *The peasants' revolt of 1381*, pp. 164–5, 177, 183, 186, 257, 324.

decline in numbers paying the poll tax in the county at large from its first collection (1377) to its third and last (1381), with only relatively trivial differences in the population groups in theory liable to pay, was from 50,917 to 32,357, a fall of 36.5 per cent.[28] The 1377 collection itself is unlikely to have been absolutely successful in netting everyone who was liable to pay, so resistance to the tax four years later was doubtless even higher than that dropoff percentage would indicate. In 1352 alone, 7,556 persons (about 20 per cent of them women) were fined for Statute of Labourers violations in Essex, and the estreat roll recording these fines does not cover seven of the county's eighteen hundreds.[29]

Thus it is likely that, at a crude estimate, roughly one in seven Essex people older than their mid-teens, or nearly one in four Essex males in the same age-range, were fined for violating the labour legislation in a single year. The proportion of all male *labourers* would thus have been even higher.[30] Due to the chance nature of document survival it is simply impossible to gauge the weight of Statute enforcement in comparative terms over the years down to 1381, though one series of indictments in Essex from 1389 contains 791 Statute cases.[31] The sheer numerical weight of Statute enforcement in the county, if these data are at all indicative of the period, makes much more vividly comprehensible the ferocity directed towards county-level agents of law enforcement (like Bampton, Gildesburgh and Sewale) by a rural society so heavily infused with wage labour and rural industry.

But in addition, Statute enforcement was extremely divisive at the village level. Officials within the community – constables, chief pledges and jurors drawn from the higher ranks of village society – bore the immediate brunt of enforcing the labour laws and faced the animosity of offenders who, even if largely labourers beneath them in the community hierarchy, were after all their neighbours.[32] The confrontation could turn violent: in 1353 'Richard Warde, constable of Cavendish [Suffolk, just over the River Stour from Essex], chased Richard Bridder, labourer, to the church of Pentlow [Essex] in order to take him before the justices of labourers, and assaulted him and drew

28 Russell, *British medieval population*, p. 132; Oman, *The great revolt of 1381*, p. 163. The age-group differences between the two collections and the most plausible interpretations of the dropoff in numbers paying are discussed in Chapter 7 and Appendix A.

29 Poos, 'Social context of Statute enforcement'.

30 This projection is based upon dividing persons fined in 1352 by the 1377 enrolled taxpayer total. The latter is certainly an underestimate of the actual 1352 population, both because the 1377 total taxed would understate the actual age-group in 1377 and because the tithing series discussed in Chapter 5 show decline between 1352 and 1377. But as the estreat roll does not cover 7/18 of the county's hundreds it too is an underestimate, if anything by an even greater factor.

31 PRO.KB9.25.

32 Poos, 'Social context of Statute enforcement'.

blood from him'.[33] Some Essex manorial or leet courts themselves occasionally fined Statute offenders during the 1350s and 1360s, which entailed a similar dynamic of enforcement by village notables but turned animosity towards manorial jurisdiction.[34] Village officials did not necessarily welcome this role. In 1378 all the constables of the Hundred of Dunmow in central Essex were cited for not compelling labourers to swear oaths to obey the Statute of Labourers.[35] It was, in fact, an act of noncompliance that was to be echoed on the eve of the revolt by villagers holding manorial offices also.

As elsewhere in England, during the rapidly changing economic circumstances of the later fourteenth century Essex manorial regimes fell into the familiar pattern of dwindling production – especially arable production – on the lord's demesne lands as hired labour became more expensive and, after the mid-1370s, grain prices began falling. The lords' dilemma was compounded by the growing difficulty of relying upon customary labour services owed by unfree tenants as a significant portion of their labour input. Resistance to this obligation grew, and on a piecemeal basis lords increasingly commuted these obligations to cash for sitting tenants or were forced to re-let vacant tenements at strictly monetary leases for terms of years. By 1400 few manors in central and northern Essex were still practising the traditional demesne cultivation nearly ubiquitous a century earlier. Either the demesne land had been rented out straightforwardly on cash leases, or else – as a kind of intermediate option adopted in some places during the later fourteenth and early fifteenth centuries – a farmer might enter into an arrangement with the lord for a certain number of years to assume the demesne land and buildings, claim whatever bond labour was still owed by the manor's tenants in villeinage, pay a fixed sum annually to the lord, and hope to profit by farming the land himself. The exact strategy and chronology of these changes varied widely from manor to manor, even within individual Essex lordships, with correspondingly wide variations in how long and how forcefully servile labour obligations were demanded.

[33] Bodl. MS Ch. Essex 1187 (Pentlow leet, 5 Jan 1354): '[jurors] presentant quod Ricardus Warde constabularius de Cavendish prosecutus fuit Ricardum Bridder laborarium iusque ad ecclesiam de Pentelawe ad ducendum eum coram justiciariis laborariorum & eum verberavit & sanguinem de eo traxit per quod dictus Ricardus levavit hutesium super dictum Ricardum juste . . . '.

[34] E.g. ERO D/DP M874 (South Hanningfield leet, 24 Feb 1354); PRO.DL30.64.811 (Great Waltham courts, 13 Nov 1354, 9 Feb 1355); ERO D/DU 267/29 (Birdbrook leet, 20 Jul 1366).

[35] Furber, ed., *Essex sessions of the peace*, p. 169: ' . . . nullus constabularius hundredi de Dunmowe fecit officium suum faciendi laboratores iurare ad deserviendum et capiendum salarium secundum statutum'.

Most of the evidence available from central and northern Essex comes from manors belonging to great religious houses and to the higher nobility. In general, these estates had enforced quite heavy labour services to the eve of the Black Death. Among the estates of Canterbury Cathedral Priory, labour services were still being claimed in the later 1380s at Lawling but at Bocking had basically been entirely commuted by 1369.[36] At Thaxted, whose lords were the Earls of March, regular bond labour had ceased on the demesne by 1362 but servile tenants were occasionally called upon to give unpaid rough labour in emergencies, like repairing buildings damaged by storms, to the later 1370s.[37] At the small manor of Claret Hall in Ashen, under the same lordship, virtually all customary 'works' were still being claimed in the 1350s, but from 1364/5 onward the whole demesne was leased out, almost all the 'works' were compounded in cash, and demesne grain production ceased.[38] By contrast, at the Westminster Abbey manor of Birdbrook, though some pieces of the demesne had been sloughed off in leases by the 1380s, it was not until 1405/6 that the entirety of the remaining demesne was let out at farm and grain sales stopped.[39]

The history of the large Bohun estates was more complex. At Great Waltham and High Easter only about one-third of the customary 'works' were being remitted by 1400, as the result of leasing out what had previously been customary tenements. Farmers had taken over the demesne and claimed labour from bond tenants for a few years in the 1370s and again in the 1410s, on the latter occasion sparking off conflict when tenants claimed that the farmers were demanding more work than was owed. Well into the 1430s customary services were being commuted or tacitly allowed to lapse on these manors.[40] At Writtle, under the same lordship, similar arrangements were followed and harvest work was still being demanded in the 1440s, though this ended a decade or so later.[41] Some lords eventually came to collective agreements with tenants to commute labour obligations on a *pro rata* basis, like that agreed upon at Priors Hall in Widdington in 1432 that allowed every virgator to pay the manor's farmer 5s. 4d. each year in lieu of harvest work.[42]

36 Mate, 'Labour and labour services', pp. 62–3.

37 Newton, *Thaxted*, pp. 25–6.

38 PRO.SC6.838.24–30; SC6.839.1–12.

39 WAM 25447–25509.

40 Poos, 'Population and resources', pp. 28–34; PRO.DL29.42.815; DL29.42.817; *VCH Essex* vol. ii, p. 318.

41 Newton, *Writtle*, pp. 68–85.

42 NCO 3621 m.9 (Priors Hall in Widdington court, 16 Jun 1432): 'Concordatum est ex assensu & consensu domini & tenentum huius manerij quod quilibet tenens j virgati terre solvet in festo sancti Petris quod dicitur ad vincula firmario huius manerij pro operibus autumpnalibus vs. iiijd. & quilibet tenens minorum quantitatum terre debet

If the chronology of seigneurial demands for labour services, one of the benchmark indices of villein discontent, was thus highly variable before 1381, the case is different with other aspects of the lord–serf relationship in later-fourteenth-century Essex. The primary instrument at lords' disposal for enforcing seigneurial rights was the manorial court. It was in the manorial court that lords enforced tenant obligations, fining those who failed to perform labour services, for instance, and also collecting entry fines when property was transferred from tenant to tenant and penalties for infractions of manorial custom. On many manors there was some flexibility as to how high these fines and amercements could be set in a given situation. The zeal with which lords, or their stewards, who ordinarily presided at manorial courts, chose to pursue infractions of customary laws obviously influenced how many fines or amercements were imposed. For these reasons the lord's income from manor-court business is a rough reflection of the weight of lordly control.[43] 'Court perquisites', as this income was called, were seldom more than a small fraction of total seigneurial revenues, as compared with rent, but they were an especially flexible source of income at a time when rent and other revenues were falling. Table 11.1 presents mean annual court perquisites by decade for three Essex manors before the great revolt.[44]

At Moulsham perquisites between 1350 and 1380 had risen markedly over their levels in the 1340s. At Claret Hall and Birdbrook perquisites were not so visibly higher, if at all, than their pre-plague levels. But these perquisites were being levied from manorial populations that had declined by a good deal, probably by at least a third if not more, since the 1330s, so the practical weight of seigneurial fines and amercements in manorial courts on a *per capita* basis must have been a great deal heavier than the table implies. Dyer has demonstrated that court perquisites rose at four manors in areas touched by revolt in Kent, Hertfordshire and Suffolk over the same period, and draws similar conclusions.[45] In Essex, as elsewhere, increased curial revenues were achieved by increased levels and frequencies of entry fines for land transactions, the frequency of which, at any rate, was

solvere secundum quantitatem & si contingat quod firmarius non poterit cum dicta summa subportare onera autumpnalia tunc quilibet tenens virgati terre solvet in proxima curia tenta post festum sancti Michaelis extunc proximum sequentem dicto firmario jd.'.

43 Dyer, 'Social and economic background', pp. 28–9.

44 In the cases of Moulsham and Claret Hall these data represent all the legible evidence in the surviving account-roll series. For Birdbrook, a random sampling had been taken for other purposes from the (virtually continuous) series of account rolls surviving for the manor.

45 Dyer, 'Social and economic background', pp. 28–9.

Table 11.1. *Perquisites from manorial courts, selected Essex manors, 1320–79*

	Birdbrook		Claret Hall in Ashen		Moulsham	
	annual mean	N	annual mean	N	annual mean	N
1320–9			£1. 8s.6d.	4		
1330–9	£2. 2s. 5d.	2	£1.16s.7d.	3		
1340–9	£1.18s. 6d.	3	£1.12s.3d.	7	£1.12s. 9d.	3
1350–9	£3. 9s. 9d.	3	£1.14s.6d.	4	£2. 7s. 5d.	4
1360–9	£2. 4s. 3d.	6	£2.19s.7d.	3	£2.12s. 3d.	3
1370–9	£2. 9s.10d.	6	£1. 4s.8d.	5	£3.13s.10d.	3

Note: Accounting year 1329/30 is tabulated here as 1330 etc.
Means have been rounded to nearest penny.
'N' refers to number of years included in decadal sample.
Sources: Birdbrook: WAM 25434, 25436–7, 25441, 25443, 25447, 25449, 25454–6, 25458–9, 25461, 25463, 25465, 25469, 25471–4.
Claret Hall: PRO.SC6.838.10–30; SC6.839.1–12.
Moulsham: ERO D/DM M70–83.

more a function of demographic turnover and land market activity than seigneurial policy as such. But perquisites also grew because of increased fines for brewing ale against the assize, for trespasses and public nuisances, and for failure to repair dilapidated buildings on tenements.[46]

It was, however, the personal incidents of serfdom that represented the crux of seigneurial demands *vis-à-vis* their villeins during these years. The evidence is clear-cut only in the relatively few cases where manorial court-roll series are voluminous and continuous enough to permit comparisons before and after 1350. At Great Waltham and High Easter merchets (fines for the lord's permission for unfree women to marry) clearly were subject to greatly increased seigneurial scrutiny. At these two manors during 1327–49, 51 servile marriages were registered in the surviving court rolls, of which only 7 were fines for marriages that had occurred without the lord's permission. During 1350–89, the surviving records contain notices of 46 more servile marriages, but in 20 of these cases the lord's steward was demanding punitive fines because the marriages had already taken place without merchet having been paid.[47] By the end of the 1380s this lordship had

[46] *Ibid.*, p. 29, gives some Essex examples of this.
[47] Poos, 'Population and resources', pp. 170–8.

tacitly admitted defeat, since virtually no merchets were levied thereafter. At Birdbrook, merchets were being levied even more frequently in the 1370s than in preceding decades.[48] Clearly then these lords, while not imposing new obligations as such upon their unfree subjects, were certainly seeking to exploit as fully as possible the traditional seigneurial incidents at their disposal.

Much the same was true of chevage, the fine due to the lord for permission for a serf to leave the manor, temporarily or permanently. At Great Waltham and High Easter, the surviving court rolls for 1327–49 record only eight notices of villeins absent from the manor (that is, villeins who either paid chevage or who were recorded as having left the manor illegally, without paying), and all of these came in the 1340s. But 62 absences are noted in the same manors during 1350–89, the great majority being orders for illegal emigrants from the manor to return. Orders like these were often repeated in court after court for years in connection with a single absentee, and in these manors the courts were ordering the return of serfs as late as the 1460s.[49] But unless the absentee had left property behind the lord possessed virtually no real sanction to compel a serf's return, and so there is an almost whimsical quality to these repeated orders to return escaped serfs. In 1378 two men obliged themselves by bond to the Abbot of Westminster to seize and return a serf to the Abbey's manor of Birdbrook a few months later, but evidence of such extreme attempts at compulsion are rare in Essex and it is hard to see any evidence that they were ever very successful.[50]

As was observed earlier, this was an extremely mobile society long before the Black Death, and manorial lords simply lacked the practical coercive means to change that.[51] The heightened concern expressed in manorial-court proceedings, then, can hardly be taken, as some historians have done, as clear evidence of increased migration. Rather, as was the case with merchet, incidents of personal unfreedom that before 1350 had been relatively little worth pursuing were now pursued with much more zeal, both as a reassertion of lordship but

48 Dyer, 'Social and economic background', p. 23.

49 Poos, 'Population and resources', pp. 48–9.

50 WAM 28079: 'Noverint universi nos Dominum Ricardum Hardesell de Carlton capellanum & Willelmum Toppysfeld teneri . . . Nicolao Abbati Westm' in viginti marcis . . . Condicio huius obligacionis talis est quod si infrascripti Ricardus & Willelmus habeant Thomam filium Roberti Stobulonn nativum domini apud manerium de Brydbrok ad proximam curiam ibidem tenendam ante festum Michaelis proximum futurum . . . quod extunc hoc scriptum pro nullo habeatur . . . '.

51 See above, Chapter 8.

also as a source of expanded curial revenue, though it could have meant relatively little as a component of total seigneurial income.

In the light of this pattern of seigneurial retrenchment, it is hardly surprising that the years leading up to 1381 witnessed a number of small, localised acts of discontent, aimed for the most part at local lords for a variety of reasons that must have been primarily, though not in all cases exclusively, anti-seigneurial in nature. Actions of this sort did of course have a long history through the middle ages, and recent research into the background to 1381 in several parts of England has uncovered a number of these events. Already before the Black Death Essex had generated one of the more noteworthy documentary artefacts of tenant–lord clashes, the early-fourteenth-century petition by the tenants of the manor of Bocking to the prior of Christ Church, Canterbury. Complaining about the abuses of an over-zealous steward, it was, as Dobson put it, 'the work of a group of peasants fully conscious of their common interests and remarkably skilled in presenting their grievances in an articulate legal form'.[52]

More prosaically, during the decades before the great revolt a number of Essex manors' records reveal acts of tenant defiance aimed at particular features of the manorial regime. Any Essex court-roll series contains a scattering of cases where individuals tried to evade labour services, but in these decades hints emerge of actions of a more collective nature. In 1375 the customary tenants of Fingreth Hall in Blackmore 'utterly refused' to elect a rent collector from among their number and a penalty of 20s., previously threatened, was ordered to be collected from them.[53] At Ingatestone in 1379 the tenants offered their lord 40s. to set fixed monetary sums for rents and services.[54] At Great Leighs in 1378 two servile jurors conspired to testify falsely at the manorial court concerning the servile status of a village woman accused of marrying without paying merchet.[55]

Actions like these tested the limits of seigneurial administration and betray considerable local discontent. It is impossible to show that such

[52] Dobson, ed., *Peasants' revolt of 1381*, p. 75.

[53] ERO D/DHt M92 m.47 (Fingreth Hall in Blackmore leet, 9 Jun 1375): 'Cum ad curiam precedentem preceptum fuit omnibus customariis quod unum collectorem redditus domini eligerent secundum consuetudines manerij prout antea &c sub pena xxs. qui hoc facere omnio recusarunt Ideo consideratum fuit quod predicti xx [sic] de eis levendi sed positum fuit in respectum & adhuc ponitur quousque colloquium cum domino habuerimus'.

[54] ERO D/DP M22 (Ingatestone court, 19 Dec 1379): during a case in which the manor's homage had been asked to apportion services between cotenants, 'Omnes homagiarij proferunt domine de fine xls. ad faciendum certa . . . de redditu & serviciis'; cf. Dyer, 'Social and economic background', p. 33.

[55] Dyer, 'Social and economic background', p. 31.

acts of defiance were definitely more frequent in the period, though their apparent clustering in the 1370s is impressive. But acts of a more overtly violent or insurrectionary nature can be found in the same years, within a small area of central Essex, and in these cases the motivation was not always so obviously anti-seigneurial.

The site of one of these was Pleshey Castle, the chief residence and administrative centre for a huge aristocratic estate consisting of a number of Essex manors. Its previous lord, Humphrey de Bohun, Earl of Hereford and Essex, had died in 1373 and the patrimony would pass three years later to Thomas of Woodstock, Bohun's son-in-law and son of King Edward III, and eventually Duke of Buckingham. The mysterious actor in this drama was one John Irland, who had been ordained priest in 1362 and had been a parochial chaplain at Pleshey and by 1374 chantry priest in the castle chapel. In the intervening years Irland appeared sporadically in the court records of the manors of Great Waltham and High Easter, both belonging to the Bohun lordship, on a variety of charges including trespass and hedge-breaking in the lordship's park. In July 1374, it was later charged, he entered the castle chapel, broke open a chest found there, and carried away charters, court and account rolls, and other muniments in a manner remarkably anticipating the widespread document destruction that was to occur in 1381. Irland then drops from the records and his fate is unknown.[56]

Four years later at Hatfield Broadoak, just seven miles west of Pleshey, a much larger-scale uprising took place that, though its exact nature or motivation is less clear-cut, prefigured 1381 in other respects.[57] The victims were the prior and convent of Hatfield Priory, a small Benedictine house whose cloister adjoined, and whose brothers shared with the parishioners the parish church.[58] No records of the uprising apparently now exist beyond a petition by the prior to the

[56] Fowler, ed., *Registrum Simonis de Subdiria* vol. ii, pp. 2, 59 (for D'Irlond's ordination); PRO.DL30.65.819 (High Easter court, 15 Sep 1362): John Dyrlond 'custos ecclesie de Plesseto'; *ibid.* (Great Waltham court, 31 Jan 1363): John Dyrlond 'custos instauri ecclesie beati Nicolai de Plesseto'; PRO.DL30.65.823 (High Easter courts, 17 Dec 1366 *et seq.*): John Dyrlond *capellanus* for trespass in Old Park (' . . . sepem domini fregit . . . occasione cuius . . . xv bestia . . . destruxerunt germina domini'); *CPR 1374–7*, p. 19 (for D'Irlond's grant of the free chapel of Pleshey Castle); PRO.DL30.66.829 (Great Waltham leet, 14 Jun 1375): on 20 July 1374, 'Johannes Irland capellanus . . . intravit castrum de Plesseto et similiter intravit capellam in dicto castro cituatam et quandam cistam in dicta capella existentem fregit et cartas scripta rotulos curie rotulos compoti et alia munimenta in dicta cista existenta tanquam domino Comite cepit et asportavit et alia bona et catalla . . . '; *CCR 1374–7*, p. 362: order to sheriff of Essex for stay of arrest of D'Irlond.

[57] This incident is discussed in *VCH Essex* vol. 8, p. 182; the author is grateful to Ray Powell, formerly editor of the Essex *VCH*, for his insights into the matter.

[58] *VCH Essex* vol. 2, pp. 107–10; Morant, *History and antiquities of Essex* vol. ii, pp. 501–11; Pevsner, *Essex*, p. 234.

royal council,[59] a consequent special commission of *oyer et terminer* to investigate,[60] and a bond in which the prior and convent sought the aid of three of the neighbourhood gentry as arbitrators in the dispute.[61]

The petition related that on 8 June 1378 sixty men named in the text, the first in the list being the vicar of Hatfield Broadoak, along with 'the greater part of the common people of Hatfield' had armed themselves and forced their way into the priory, torn down some of its cloister, walls and hedges, assaulted the prior and his monks and servants in the church and driven them away.[62] The bond, signed in early August of the same year, put the priory under obligation to its arbitrators over 'certain conflicts between the prior and convent ... and the commoners and parishioners of the same vill, touching the parish church'.[63]

The priory held substantial property in the parish, although the vill's largest manor in fact belonged to the Bohun patrimony; the priory also claimed the parish's tithes.[64] But the point of contention here was apparently the church itself: parish and priory had previously shared one structure, but soon thereafter the building was divided into two separate liturgical spaces. And so the issue was prerogative as much as religious or fiscal conflict. What is noteworthy about the incident is its large number of participants, its overt violence which nevertheless failed to end an apparently longstanding conflict, and its leadership by a parish priest.

In Essex, then, 1381 signalled neither the end of serfdom nor a sudden upheaval of protest of a wholly novel variety. In the immediate background of the revolt lay a scatter of individual and small-group actions varying from passive obstruction, to selective refusals to co-operate, to occasional violence against the instruments of authority or even its personal embodiments. Nor did small-scale actions of this sort disappear, or their anatomy altogether alter, after the great revolt.

In England generally in the three-quarters of a century or so after 1381,

59 PRO.SC8.10737. 60 *CPR 1377–81*, pp. 304–5. 61 BL Add. Ch. 28604.

62 PRO.SC8.10737: ' ... John Cok vicar de Hattefeld susdit & autr's sur cest bill endoses & la greindre partie de tout la comunaltie de la ville de Hattefeld avantdit par graunt malice entre eux purprense viendront en la ville avantdit a la dit priorie ... & graunt partie de lor Cloistr' & des mures per queux le dit Priorie iadis estoit enclose ount abatuz & les huys de la dit Priorie ount deffermes & en la Eglise le dit Priorie entreront & tiele manere de fray dens' lez ditz Prior & ses moignes firont ... '.

63 BL Add. Ch. 28604: ' ... tout la agard & arbitrement queles surraunt faitz dune acord sur certainz debatz esteauntz pur entre les Priour & convent de Hatfeld Roys & les communes & Parochiens de mesme la ville touchant la Esglize parochiel ... '.

64 *VCH Essex* vol. 2, pp. 107–10, and vol. 8, pp. 168–9.

tenants' attempts to roll back the burden of rents and services at the expense of manorial lords persisted. Dyer has shown that on the estates of the Bishopric of Worcester during the middle decades of the fifteenth century there were rent strikes and partial or selective withholding of customary payments, usually by this time more to do with money rent or manorial resources or prerogatives than with vestiges of serfdom.[65] The situation in Essex was similar. In 1386 the Dean and Chapter of St Paul's in London complained that bondmen on three of their manors in northeastern Essex 'have withdrawn their customs and services . . . and have in divers assemblies colleagued to resist them'.[66] A similar complaint was made in 1397 by a lay lord at Great Bromley, also in the northeast of the county and the scene of local insurrection during the great revolt, 'that bondmen and bondage tenants . . . have long withdrawn the customs and services due for their holdings . . . leaguing together by oath to resist him and his ministers'.[67] Nor did resentment of royal taxes, economic legislation, or overbearing, unpopular local government figures subside entirely as issues. In 1382 an Essex man allegedly 'incited the commons of the county to resist the payment' of a subsidy of a fifteenth and tenth on moveable goods,[68] while, as already shown, both attempts to enforce the Statute of Labourers and defiance of it persisted through the later fourteenth century.

And occasionally, as in 1381 but on a much smaller scale, anti-seigneurial action continued to merge with anger directed at these other irritants. Waltham Abbey had been the target of rebels in 1381, when its estate archives were burnt.[69] The abbey's strict, conservative stance towards its villeins is epitomised by a surviving roll of cases from its manorial courts, largely comprising exemplary texts from proofs of servile status and other cases pertaining to legal incidents of the unfree, apparently drawn up shortly before the great revolt.[70] The abbey was the scene of violence also in August 1410 and again some time in 1423 or shortly before, when groups of men drawn from several nearby communities of which the abbot was lord (including Nazeing, Epping, Chingford, Loughton and Waltham itself) congregated at Waltham to assault the sheriff of the county. On Sunday, St

[65] Dyer, *Lords and peasants in a changing society*, pp. 187–90, 275–6, 279–80.
[66] *CPR 1385–9*, p. 256.
[67] *CPR 1396–9*, p. 309; for attacks in 1381 by 'all the tenants of this manor in bondage' at Great Bromley, Dyer, 'Social and economic background', p. 12.
[68] *CPR 1381–5*, p. 250.
[69] Liddell and Wood, eds., *Essex and the great revolt*, p. 97; Dyer, 'Social and economic background', p. 12.
[70] Bodl. MS Top. Essex b.5 (R).

Bartholomew's Day 1410, it was charged, two hundred entered the abbey and assaulted both abbot and sheriff,

> crying with one voice let us kill the sheriff, because the sheriff arrested one Richard Grene and others by virtue of a writ at the suit of William, abbot of Waltham, to appear before the justices of the Bench for certain trespasses . . . and others by virtue of a precept to the justices of the peace to have them before the justices to find security for good behaviour towards the abbot and his servants, on account of which clamour and laying of hands on the sheriff the prisoners escaped from his custody.[71]

A dozen years or so later a seemingly virtually identical attack at Waltham was directed towards Lewis Johan, another sheriff, 'and [the assailants] so threatened him with death and mutilation . . . that for a long time he could not execute a certain writ of the said king directed to him as sheriff'.[72] The 20 men specifically named in connection with this later attack included 10 husbandmen, 3 clothworkers (a weaver, a tailor and a draper), 3 leatherworkers (2 skinners and a tanner), plus a carpenter, a carter, a fletcher, and a schoolmaster. In the same year,

> certain bondmen or bond tenants [*terram native tenentes*] of the abbot of Waltham Holy Cross, lord of the manors of Waltham, Nasyng, Eppyng and Lucton . . . at those manors having rebelliously gathered themselves together at the procurement of certain [of] their councillors, aiders and abettors, refused to perform their services due to the said abbot for their tenures, and bound themselves to each other by oath to resist him and his ministers.[73]

It is just conceivable that the hints of conspiracy contained in these charges relating to the Waltham, Bromley and St Paul's tenants were products of seigneurial paranoiac hyperbole. But from the evidence of 1381 and later rebellions collective action uniting agriculturalists and craftsmen and co-ordinated by local 'aiders and abettors' was by no means beyond the capabilities of rural Essex society in these decades, and may even have been a lasting legacy of the great revolt. The long-simmering Waltham disturbances also show how attacks on lords *qua* lords could be exacerbated when those lords were seen to exercise influence with the agents of county government.

In addition to these collective defiances, individuals also continued acts of defiance at particular servile conditions, such as the continued ignoring of impotent restrictions on movement outside the manor already alluded to, refusal to render labour services, or simple disobedience. The 1380s and 1390s seem to have witnessed quite a number of these petty incidents, implying that hard feelings continued to fester. Richard Gamelyn paid a large fine for having removed himself from his manor at Fyfield to avoid doing harvest work in

[71] *CPR 1408–13*, pp. 285–6. [72] *CPR 1422–9*, pp. 216–17. [73] *Ibid.*, p. 174.

1388.[74] At the manor of Priors Hall in Lindsell, one man was amerced 10s. in December 1381 'because he was insubordinate in court and refused to behave according to law', and also for assaulting two inquisition jurors, and two years later in the same place another man was amerced the even harsher sum of 20s. for insubordination towards the steward.[75]

And so there remained an undercurrent of conflict between seigneurs and villagers, sometimes collective but more often individual, and by that very fact less likely to have left much trace in the records. It was an undercurrent in the process of being very slowly transformed from a more lord–villein to a more landlord–tenant pattern of confrontation. It would appear to be still an open question how far memories of 1381 helped to restrain the responses of authority in dealing with such defiance. At any rate this particular conjunction of grievances was not again capable of causing rural Essex society to flare up into more broadly based rebellion.

Popular uprisings did recur in Essex beyond 1381 and through the 1400s, however, even if none approached the scale of the great revolt, and actions striking directly at immediate seigneurial authority became progressively more submerged within outbreaks of unrest. The larger-scale Essex episodes for which much evidence survives fell increasingly into a pattern that would be familiar in the mid-Tudor era: outbursts of popular enmity against publicly prominent or notorious figures, or adventurist plots by political hopefuls who managed to raise popular support.[76] That popular support, in turn, was susceptible of being mobilised on the basis of a constellation of local concerns – including the political, the economic and the religious, shifting in balance from episode to episode – and was effectively tapped in part precisely because the larger uprising enabled individuals or groups within it to settle scores or pursue individual pre-existing grievances. In this regard at any rate later uprisings, and Essex participation in them, present a picture of continuity from 1381 and its antecedents.

But this becomes apparent only when local rebellions are traced over a considerable length of time. Four uprisings, rather serendipitously

[74] ERO D/DCw M97 (Fyfield courts, 13 Nov 1388, 26 Mar 1389): ' . . . Ricardus Gamelyn qui est tenens domini in nativis se elongavit per totum ultimum autumpnum extra istud dominium & renuit metere & deservire . . . ', fined 6s. 8d.

[75] NCO 3655 m.3 (Priors Hall in Lindsell court, 23 Dec 1381): 'Thomas Templer quia rebellis in curia & se noluit justiciare secundum legem ac eciam pro insulto facto duobus hominibus inquisitionis postquam jurati fuerunt & voluit illos percutere & illos minavit contra pacem Ideo ipse in gravi misericordia'; *ibid.* m.5 (Priors Hall in Lindsell court, 29 Dec 1383): 'Item Johannes Pecche quia fuit rebellis in curia contra senescallem & alios Ideo in gravi misericordia'.

[76] Cf. Fletcher, *Tudor rebellions*.

falling one each into four successive reigns of Lancastrian and early Yorkist kings, demonstrate that continuity, but also the wide range of particular circumstances that propelled Essex people to collective action.

The scene of the first of these incidents was once again Pleshey Castle. In early January 1400 a circle of conspirators, led by the Earl of Huntingdon and comprising a group of former friends of the recently deposed Richard II, seized Windsor Castle in a reckless attempt to capture Henry IV.[77] Easily thwarted, Huntingdon made for the southern Essex coast along the Thames estuary, and was captured there by locals and imprisoned at Pleshey. On 15 January inhabitants from the surrounding villages, called by one chronicler 'common folk and craftsmen', 'peasants from the neighbourhood' by another,[78] gathered at the castle and demanded that Huntingdon be produced and beheaded. Apparently crowding into the castle bailey and intimidating its keeper, they led the Earl out of the keep and executed him on the spot. Their motives, as Goodman has shown, are intriguing in that they were if anything pro-seigneurial, the crowd 'dispersing apparently without making tenurial or economic demands on their own behalf'.[79] Thomas of Woodstock, previous lord of Pleshey and several of the large neighbouring manors from which many of the crowd came, had been abducted from the very spot of Huntingdon's death by King Richard three years earlier, and murdered soon after. In short order Woodstock had become in popular eyes a political martyr, and in that respect the Essex villagers' action was one of revenge for their late lord as well as striking out at a figure associated with a discredited tyranny. This was, to be sure, a minor passage in the annals of Essex unrest, and there appears to be no precise evidence for the incident's participants or organisation. It was, though, of a piece with more serious later insurgences: political conflict or intrigue at high levels was capable of mobilising common people to assemble and act quickly and with surprising forcefulness and knowledge of political events and personages, when their actions could simultaneously serve a more immediate local end.

A rather different variation on the theme of popular revolt in Essex was played out during the winter of 1413–14, in the strange affair of Sir

77 This account is taken from Goodman, 'The countess and the rebels'.

78 Thompson, ed., *Chronicon Adae de Usk*, p. 42: ' . . . per plebeyos et mecanicos decapitatur'; Williams, ed., *Chronique de la traison de Richard*, p. 97: ' . . . les villains du pais qui furent la assemblez bien viii mille ou plus . . . '.

79 Goodman, 'The countess and the rebels', p. 270.

John Oldcastle.[80] Oldcastle, an able military veteran and boon-companion of Henry V before and after the latter's accession to the throne, had come under suspicion of being a Lollard as early as 1410. Refusing to heed warnings given by a king and an archbishop who were seemingly reluctant to bring the full force of law down upon him, Oldcastle obdurately clung to his beliefs, was tried and convicted of heresy, and imprisoned in the Tower in the autumn of 1413 in the hope that he would recant. In mid-October he escaped. Over the next two months Lollard groups around southern and Midlands England prepared to join Oldcastle in a quixotic, desperate bid to capture and destroy the king's household and, so it was later charged, rid the kingdom of its nobles and strip the church of its possessions.[81] In early January 1414 the arriving insurgents were easily scattered and broken by a forewarned and well-prepared king west of London. Oldcastle himself eluded capture until December 1417, when he was hanged and burnt. The actual danger to the kingdom had been slight, but Lollardy and sedition, and the threat to property implied by both, would henceforth be intertwined in official attitudes. The covert vogue that the sect had enjoyed in some high circles was broken.

The events of 1413–14, most historians concur, exposed the numerical paucity of committed Lollard support. Despite the very wide geographical area from which adherents advanced in Oldcastle's support, fewer than 300 individual participants are known to have answered the call to arms from the country at large. Those who did respond, with a few exceptions, were craftsmen, small farmers, and some clergy, ill-equipped to topple a government.[82] Essex was no exception to this pattern. Despite what McFarlane called the 'lively response' from the county,[83] no more than about two dozen Essex men (that is, outside Colchester, a notorious hotbed of the sect) were indicted in the wake of the incident, and it is by no means clear that all those indicted actually joined the march to London, as opposed to merely aiding the *coup*'s adherents or supporting the sect generally.[84] This need not, of course, mean that there really were so few people

[80] The account that follows is mostly taken from McFarlane, *Wycliffe and English non-conformity*, pp. 144–68; Aston, 'Lollardy and sedition'; Powell, 'Restoration of law and order', pp. 61–3.

[81] Aston, 'Lollardy and sedition', pp. 24–7.

[82] Powell, 'Restoration of law and order', pp. 61–2. McFarlane, *Wycliffe and English non-conformity*, pp. xv, xvii, provides a map of communities known to have been involved in the episode. These range from Nottingham and Loughborough to the north, to Sutton near the Welsh border and Bristol to the southwest, to Davington in Kent.

[83] McFarlane, *Wycliffe and English non-conformity*, p. 156.

[84] See below, Chapter 12.

inclined towards heresy in the district – on the contrary, the evidence is that a string of communities stretching from Thaxted to Colchester had been touched by religious nonconformity for decades before 1413. On the other hand, not all who joined in the exodus to the capital were necessarily Lollards by conviction, since local supporters recruited companions to the movement for pay. Two brothers, weavers from Pattiswick, were indicted for recruiting three other weavers at Kelvedon (who were not specifically charged with heresy as such) on 1 January to join them for 6d. per day.[85]

Despite the specifically religious context of the events that sparked off Oldcastle's revolt and inflamed many of its local partisans, then, the episode fits well into the longer-term history of Essex participation in anti-authoritarian unrest. Even if Lollardy was not precisely a creed for social revolt, it meshed easily with a predisposition to join in mass movements under a unifying rallying cry. This point, and Essex experience of Lollardy in general, are taken up in the next chapter. Leadership of a charismatic figure intending (albeit wholly impossibly) a re-ordering of government at the very least, exodus to London as the focal point of authority, and an apparently quite efficient network of communications to local organisers who in turn recruited among locals: in these respects, at least, Oldcastle's revolt resembled earlier and later episodes of Essex insurgency. The pattern would recur a few decades later, at considerably more peril to the kingdom.

Cade's rebellion in the summer of 1450 was the most serious outbreak of popular unrest in fifteenth-century England, made especially dangerous because in it common people were mobilised in a crisis coinciding with extreme division at the upper levels of aristocratic politics.[86] John Cade was a man of uncertain origins who adopted the surname Mortimer as a pretence of kinship with the Duke of York and began raising a mass following in southwestern Kent, where sporadic unrest had been festering for some years, as self-proclaimed 'captain of Kent' in late May. By 11 June the rebel host had encamped at Blackheath. Retreating after an inconclusive parley with a delegation from Henry VI, the rebels defeated a small troop sent out to pursue them and had returned to Blackheath around 29 June. Within the next few days 'cam a greet ffelawship out of Essex ordeined by the seid capitaigne', numbering perhaps as many as several thousand, who assembled at Mile End to assail the

[85] PRO.KB9.204.1 m.9; see also below, Chapter 12.

[86] The account that follows relies largely upon the meticulous, detailed reconstruction of Griffiths, *Reign of Henry VI*, pp. 610–49.

city from the east.[87] On 3 July Cade and his followers entered the city, which had been abandoned by the frightened king a week earlier.

Over the ensuing weekend 'the captain' intimidated justices into holding *oyer et terminer* sessions at the Guildhall that indicted several officials of treason, followed by public beheadings of Lord Saye (the king's treasurer and a notorious member of the hated royal-court clique), the sheriff of Kent, and various other targets of the rebels' rage.[88] Sacking and looting ensued, along with other killings lacking even a veneer of legal formality. Among these events of Cade's brief reign of terror was the sole incident with which the Essex contingent in the city are specifically known to have been associated. On 5 July 'the capitaigne beheded in Suthwark a gentilman which the men of Essex delivered to him called Thomas Mayn of Colchestre'.[89] Another chronicler identified Mayn as the keeper of Colchester Castle, which contained the county gaol, the constable and steward of which were also notorious members of the royal court.[90] As with a number of Cade's victims with identifiable previous connections with Kent, here a general hatred of discredited political figures merged with what was likely to have been pre-existing enmity toward officials at the local level.

But Cade's control of the city was brief. By the evening of the 5th the Londoners had regrouped and repulsed the rebels across London Bridge. Fleeing, Cade was captured in Sussex on the 12th and his head decorated the same bridge soon after, the traitor's fate. 'And so the Kentishmen melted back into Kent, the Essex men into Essex.'[91]

Both the parallels and the contrasts between 1381 and 1450 are striking. Though the heart of this rising was Kentish, Essex was quickly drawn in, probably with similar lines of communication (especially if the Essex 'ffelawship' really had been 'ordeined by the seid capitaigne'). In both revolts, military humiliation at French hands, royal weakness and the perceived greed, corruption and self-enrichment of officials both close to the throne and in the counties were a major impetus to rebellion. But Cade's rebellion, unlike 1381, produced a lengthy, detailed programme or manifesto, melding professions of loyalty to the king with demands for reforming royal

[87] Quoted from Flenley, ed., 'Bale's chronicle', *Six town chronicles*, p. 132; cf. *ibid.*, p. 133, and 'Gough's chronicle', *ibid.*, p. 155, for the Mile End location. The most conservative estimate for the rebels' numbers, though probably still an exaggeration, was 20,000 from Kent and 6,000 from Essex: Harriss and Harriss, eds., 'Benet's chronicle', pp. 199–200; cf. Griffiths, *Reign of Henry VI*, p. 619.

[88] Griffiths, *Reign of Henry VI*, pp. 614–15, 626–7.

[89] Flenley, ed., 'Bale's chronicle', *Six town chronicles*, p. 133.

[90] Harriss and Harriss, eds., 'Benet's chronicle', p. 201 and note.

[91] *Ibid.*, p. 201: 'Et sic abierunt Cancii in Canciam et Essexi in Essexiam'.

government abuse and with complaints specific to Kentish local government.[92] Among the various versions of this programme that have survived, 'political' demands far outweigh 'social' or 'economic' concerns, the latter limited to a brief complaint against the Statute of Labourers, specific mention of a few abusive estate officials in Kent, and possibly some animus against the participation of royal officials in the Kentish land market and against inept handling of trade policy that resulted in disruption of cloth exports. And yet as Griffiths observes, as the episode progressed Cade broadened his ostensible goals beyond parochially Kentish concerns, to appeal to an audience geographically and socially more diverse.[93] And indeed it was necessary to do so, if the stated aims of the rebel leader were to be capable of co-opting a broadly based following from other counties.

One major source of information for the Essex rebels in Cade's rebellion is the series of royal pardons issued in the wake of the episode.[94] These include 168 people from 24 Essex communities, roughly 8 per cent of the entire group pardoned in all counties, though in addition some entire Essex villages and hundreds were exculpated.[95] Griffiths has shown that this evidence does not necessarily constitute an entirely reliable profile of the rebel host, since it is possible to show that some Kentishmen appearing in the lists in fact opposed the uprising; non-rebels, he concludes, sought pardons to forestall possible future recriminations in an uncertain political climate.[96] The pardon lists do, however, appear to provide a general impression of the geographical origins of Cade's support, and (perhaps less firmly) some clues to its social composition.

A substantial portion of Cade's Essex following would thus seem to have been drawn from the southwestern quadrant of the county, those areas closest to London and in easiest reach of communication with Kent. But more scattered support apparently came from the county's central areas and from as far away as Colchester, and nearly half the Essex men pardoned were from two places: the port town of Maldon, on the east coast (28 names), and the central-district village of Great Waltham (60 names).[97] As for social composition, about one-half (72) of the Essex people appearing in the lists were given status or

92 Griffiths, *Reign of Henry VI*, pp. 628–40; Dobson, ed., *Peasants' revolt of 1381*, pp. 336–42.

93 Griffiths, *Reign of Henry VI*, pp. 635–8.

94 *CPR 1446–52*, pp. 338–74.

95 E.g. *ibid.*, pp. 342 ('and all men in Chafford hundred'), 343 ('and all others in Dakynham and Berkyng').

96 Griffiths, *Reign of Henry VI*, pp. 619–23.

97 *CPR 1446–52*, pp. 338, 340, 342–4, 348, 350, 354–5, 361, 363, 365, 369–71, 373–4. The southwestern Essex hundreds provided 66 names (Barstaple 9, Becontree 28, Chafford 7, Ongar 22).

occupational designations; of these, roughly half (35) were agriculturalists (husbandmen or yeomen) and another quarter (19) craftsmen or retailers. A few esquires and gentlemen were also included, but in these cases it is less likely that appearance among the pardoned implies actual support for Cade.[98] In all, then, Essex support for the assault upon London was broadly representative of the middling ranks of local rural society.

But a quite different dimension of the unrest of 1450 is unveiled in the returns made by the judicial commissions sent out from September of that year onward to investigate and suppress disorder.[99] For in the aftershocks of the events at Mile End, a spate of disturbances persisted for two months or longer, widely scattered around Essex, as indeed was the case elsewhere in the southeast of the country for quite a while longer. In many cases the leaders in these Essex incidents explicitly invoked Cade as their inspiration, while in others Lollard motives were imputed by their accusers, perhaps spuriously.[100] Either rebels returning from London carried their fervour back to their home communities, or else news of revolt induced secondary uprisings among others.

The ringleaders of one cycle of unrest, William Betyll and Thomas Drake, respectively a husbandman and a weaver from Great Tey, roughly six miles west of Colchester, led a group of forty at their home village who 'treacherously raised the people ... to destroy the lord king and his laws ... as heretics and Lollards ... saying that all things should be held in common, against the lord king's peace' and compelled others to join them on 24 July.[101] On 28 August, Betyll was

[98] The composition included 12 gentry (5 esquires, 7 gentlemen), 35 agriculturalists (20 yeomen, 15 husbandmen), 19 craftsmen and retailers (4 smiths, 3 tanners, 2 tailors, and one cordwainer, 'coverlydwever', 'colyer', cook, draper, dyer, 'hakeneyman', pulter, tallowchandler and sherman), 4 labourers and 2 clergy (the latter, however, included the Abbess of Barking, whose reason for seeking a pardon was seemingly to protect her 'men, tenants and servants': *CPR 1446–52*, p. 355).

[99] Griffiths, *Reign of Henry VI*, pp. 643, 648; *CPR 1446–52*, p. 431.

[100] This aspect of the events is discussed in the next chapter. Cf. Griffiths, *Reign of Henry VI*, p. 643: 'To label such men as lollards and heretics who were anxious to turn all things to common ownership, was nothing more than a device whereby the common stock of contemporary charges could be assembled to ensure conviction for treason'.

[101] PRO.KB9.268 m.19: William Betyll, along with Lawrence, a chaplain, and Thomas Drake, a weaver, both also from Great Tey, '... aggregati eis quampluribus rebellionibus & inimicis ... & pacis perturbatoribus ad numerum quadraginta personarum ... apud Magnam Teye predictam insurrexerunt & guerram contra dictum dominum Regem & populum suum proditorie levaverunt & proponi fecerunt ad destruendum predictum dominum Regem & leges ipsius Regis ac politicam gubernacionem regni sui ... ut heretici & lollardi dampnabiliter ... dicentes & affirmantes ipsos & simul eis omnia habere & tenere in communi ... &

housebreaking at West Bergholt,[102] and more than two weeks later Betyll and Drake were leading another revolt at Aldham.[103]

Another key figure in leading the events of these weeks was Robert Helder, yeoman *alias* weaver of Bocking in the county's central district, who was charged with publicly proclaiming Lollard views in his home town on 5 September and, four days later, led an uprising eight miles to the north at Sible Hedingham that resulted in the murder of the parish's rector.[104] In the south of the county, at Horndon on 11–12 September, a labourer from Grays Thurrock named William Broun '*alias* Long Wyll' incited an insurrection 'in the name of John Cade ... recently great Captain of Kent ... saying that the aforesaid John Cade was still living ... and that they vowed to live and die with [Cade] and his opinions ... '.[105] Similarly in Colchester, a brickmaker who had 'levied war against the king' on 10 September and had been imprisoned in the county gaol was freed five days later by a group of Colchester men who 'affirmed ... that they would stand with [Cade] and die in his treasons'.[106]

Several patterns emerge from the Essex experiences of the summer of 1450. To judge from the indictments (as with the pardon lists) the core of these disturbances sprang from a combination of middling agriculturalists and craftsmen, with smaller elements of labourers and clergy.[107] Violence was spread over many corners of the shire, imply-

false & proditorie moverunt ut ... ligei domini Regis ibidem cum eisdem ... transirent & in opinionibus & prodicionibus suis predictis starent & viverent ... '.

102 *Ibid.* m.21.

103 *Ibid.* m.18: a husbandman and a tilemaker from Aldham received and aided Betyll, Drake, and Peter Bussh, a labourer from Copford (' ... felonice receptaverunt cibaverunt & confortaverunt ... & alios proditores domini Regis qui dicto xv° die Septembris ... levaverunt guerram contra dictum dominum Regem ad eum destruendum & leges & regnum suum Anglie totaliter subvertendum ... ').

104 *Ibid.* m. 41 (for Helder's supposed Lollard views, see below, Chapter 12), mm. 40a, 41, 43.

105 *Ibid.* mm. 32, 34: Broun, along with Richard Stodley, husbandman of Grays Thurrock, and James Tyler, tiler of Barking, ' ... insurrexerunt sua propria temeritate ac nomine Johannis Cade alias dicti Johannis Mortymer nuper magni Capitanei Kancie proditoris rebellis ... adtunc mortui tamen predicti Willelmus Ricardus & Jacobus asserentes affirmantes & dicentes predictum Johannem Cade fore viventem & in plena vita & cum ipso in opinionibus suis & prodicionibus voluerint vivere & obire ... '.

106 *CPR 1446–52*, pp. 415, 503.

107 PRO.KB9.268 mm. 18–19, 21, 24–9, 32, 34, 40a, 41, 43; *CPR 1446–52*, pp. 415, 503. Care has been taken to try to isolate, from the names appearing in the judicial returns and *capias* writs, only names apparently implicated in the events discussed above, but the connection is not always necessarily clear. Of 41 persons appearing in these returns, 11 were agriculturalists (4 yeomen, 7 husbandmen), 15 craftsmen or retailers (two tilers, two butchers, two weavers, and one baker, brickmaker, carpenter, chapman, fuller, glover, miller, millwright and tailor), 8 labourers, 3 clergy, 2 'soudyours', one groom and one widow.

ing a charged atmosphere saturated with rumours of rebellion that were capable of setting off subsidiary affairs far afield and many weeks after Cade's death. At the same time, local instigators like Helder and Betyll were apparently capable of ranging over a radius of a half-dozen miles or more within a few days, implying that the rumours flew fast but also found receptive ears. And despite the more extravagantly alarmist language in which their charges were couched, the concrete crimes in these affairs were usually housebreakings, burglaries and assaults that betray no obvious rationale as to choice of specific targets or victims and may have resulted from pre-existing enmity, as in Mayn's death in London, or simple opportunism.[108] As in 1381, Essex was quick to join fortunes with Kent against the capital.

In this latter respect, a similar pattern would evolve again 21 years later. In 1471, after Edward IV had reclaimed the crown he had temporarily lost and was engaged elsewhere in defeating partisan forces, a rebellion was fomented in Kent in support (at least initially) of the anti-Yorkist cause.[109] The leader of this uprising was Thomas Fauconberg, a bastard son of William Neville, who led a naval brigade and drew garrisons from Calais and the Cinque Ports. In May 1471 Fauconberg managed to raise in addition a large contingent of Kentishmen, drawn from throughout the county and containing a substantial element of yeomen and some gentry, and led them to the gates of London. Refused entry by the city, the rebels attacked but (unlike 1381 or 1450) were driven off after a few days' fighting, to be run down and dispersed eventually after the king's forces arrived. Fauconberg resembled Cade in his rashness and his charisma, notably his ability to draw with him a Kent following numbering at least in the hundreds. As another echo of Cade's rebellion this rising, once in progress, again drew adherents from Essex, who joined in the rebels' assault upon Aldgate. Little information can now be recovered about the Essex participants in the episode, who subsequently were forced to pay some £250 in penalties for their part and a few of whom paid with their heads.[110] Nevertheless, at least one near-contemporary source imputed an economic motive to the Essex recruits; the *Great Chronicle of London* claimed

> . . . Whereof the ffame beyng blowyn Into Essex, The ffaynt husbandys cast ffrom theym theyr sharp Sythys and armyd theym wyth theyr wyvis smokkis chese clothis and old shetis and wepenyd theym wyth hevy & grete Clubbys and long pycchfforkis and asshyn stavys, and soo In all haast sped theym

[108] PRO.KB9.268 mm. 18, 21, 32, 34, 41, 43 records seven such incidents.
[109] Ross, *Edward IV*, pp. 173–5, 181–3; Richmond, 'Fauconberg's Kentish rising'.
[110] Richmond, 'Fauconberg's Kentish rising', pp. 681–6.

toward london, makyng their avaunt as they went that they wold be Revengid upon the mayer [of London] ffor settyng of soo easy penyworthis of their Buttyr Chese Eggis pyggis & all othir vytayll, and soo Joynyd theym unto the kentysh men.[111]

The symbolic significance of 'wives' smocks, cheesecloths and old sheets' escapes the modern reader. But if this writer is to be believed, and as a prominent Londoner commercial circumstances are unlikely to have been foreign to him,[112] resentment over perceived inequities in urban–rural marketing reinforced whatever more purely political motives may have impelled the Essex contingent.

In the long-term perspective of common action by Essex people over a century or more, the welter of diverse motives, aims and irritants are likely to obscure some basic points of continuity. The core of these episodes, as a variety of evidence of widely differing natures routinely implies, was the middling band of agriculturalists, craftsmen and retailers with a smaller sprinkling of the most well-off villagers and some labourers. Where organisation can be glimpsed it appears to have rested upon that network of village notables and petty officialdom prominent in local organisation from the outset of the period. Certain features intrinsic to local society in rural central Essex helped to shape the configuration of disorder. In addition to its characteristic social structure, the absence of common fields and much in the way of communal grazing resources meant that in this district anti-enclosure violence, the most ubiquitous form of village revolt in much of the rest of England from the end of the middle ages onward, was largely unknown. On the other hand, the close proximity of London, a necessary but not a sufficient precondition of politically motivated action, helped Essex to epitomise the 'comparatively high degree of political awareness' attributable to the larger-scale disturbances in southeastern England during the later fourteenth and fifteenth centuries.[113]

But the strongest continuity between these disparate episodes is the fact that the most large-scale of these uprisings united groups whose discernible or imputable motivations differed but who joined a common cause under a unifying rubric. A shifting calculus of grievances fuelled revolts. As purely anti-seigneurial concerns waned,

111 Thomas and Thornley, eds., *The Great Chronicle of London*, p. 218.

112 The author was Robert Fabian, a draper and later Sheriff of London: Ross, *Edward IV*, p. 431.

113 Manning, *Village revolts*, p. 309.

economic and social factors of different sorts, legal and political volatility (which the proximity of London doubtless helped stoke), and even religious nonconformity conspired to unite, albeit briefly and frangibly, a disparate rural society.

12

Religious nonconformity and parochial activism

Longstanding political volatility in the Essex countryside was matched by a persistent strain of religious nonconformity. The northern portion of the county in particular has long been recognised as a place where Lollardy, the quintessential English heresy of the later middle ages, fell upon especially fertile ground, and no survey of anti-authoritarian activity in the district can ignore it.[1] Indeed, as already emphasised, in episodes like Oldcastle's revolt or Cade's rebellion it can be quite difficult to assign relative importance to political, social and religious factors. All sprang in part from the same roots, deeply embedded in local social structure and mentality. Religious nonconformity was an extremely complex phenomenon. Doctrinally it ranged from (at one extreme) the formal theological heresies of John Wyclif, of academics sympathetic to his views in the years surrounding his death in 1384, and of more isolated clerics and writers at a later date, to (at the other extreme) a relatively looser collection of anti-clerical and anti-sacramentarian attitudes at the humbler social levels of the laity.[2] It is precisely this underground quality, as an often only partly articulated belief system, mostly perpetuated in small cells through written texts and by minor unbeneficed clergy or lay people, that

[1] The account of Lollardy which follows is derived primarily from Hudson, *The premature reformation*; McFarlane, *Wycliffe and English non-conformity*; Thomson, *Later Lollards*; Kightly, 'Early Lollards'; Cross, *Church and people*, pp. 9–52; Davis, *Heresy and reformation*, pp. 1–5; Aston, 'Lollardy and sedition'; Aston, 'William White's followers'; Hudson, 'A Lollard compilation'; Hudson, 'Examination of Lollards'; Tanner, ed., *Norwich heresy trials*, pp. 7–30; Dickens, *English Reformation*, pp. 22–37; Hill, 'From Lollards to Levellers'.

[2] This view, it should be noted, takes a rather different conception of religious nonconformity, and indeed of Lollardy specifically, as a phenomenon from the recent impressive synthesis of Hudson, *The premature reformation*, which emphasises doctrinal content and transmission and so would be reluctant to ascribe a 'looser collection of attitudes' to Lollardy *per se*.

makes it difficult to chart its dimensions and clientele for much of the period.

Post-Black Death Essex was no stranger to dissident clerics with disturbing messages. As early as 1367 the Archbishop of Canterbury was issuing warnings to the deanery of Bocking, which was under his direct or 'peculiar' jurisdiction, against the preaching of the notorious John Ball, 'pretending himself to be a priest', and later famed as a shadowy protagonist in the 1381 revolt.[3] His sermons apparently advocated a radical if crude egalitarianism: according to a celebrated passage by the chronicler Walsingham 'he tried to prove ... that servitude had been introduced by the unjust and evil oppression of men, against the will of God'.[4] He also advocated withholding tithes from sinful priests, a standard Lollard position. Hostile commentators did not hesitate to try to link him with Wyclif, but Wyclif's influence upon Ball, if any, was certainly unintended and secondhand. Historians have generally been reluctant to see links between the two, but Hudson has recently argued that these disclaimers may be overstated.[5] Whether or not Wyclif's ideas concerning the limitations of earthly lordship or property did provide inspiration in any way for the 1381 rising, Ball's views seem to represent a more generalised, widespread and submerged hostility to social hierarchy, perhaps with eschatological overtones.

Against such a background, heretical attitudes meshed easily with anti-authoritarian tendencies. Within the last few years of the fourteenth century one Lollard evangelist in Essex, John Becket of Pattiswick (roughly ten miles west of Colchester), probably a layman, had attracted the attention of the authorities. In 1400 Becket was absolved after abjuring his errors, and the surviving list of his condemned opinions contains much that is familiar from other Lollards' examinations, though it also expresses some less conventional positions. Priests in mortal sin cannot administer valid sacraments; kings and spiritual or temporal lords in mortal sin are undeserving of obedience; reverence is not to be given to the cross or saints' images; priests and persons in religious orders may marry; sexual intercourse outside ecclesiastically sanctioned matrimony is permissible and sinless.[6]

[3] Wood, ed., *Registrum Simonis Langham*, pp. 149–50.

[4] Quoted in Dobson, ed., *Peasants' revolt of 1381*, p. 375.

[5] Aston, 'Lollardy and sedition', pp. 4–6; Hudson, *The premature reformation*, pp. 66–9.

[6] LPL reg. Arundel fo. 408: 'Assertere quod presbiter existens in mortali peccato non conficit consecrari nec baptizari Item assertere quod Regibus & secularibus potestatibus vel quibuscumque cohercionem spiritualem vel temporalem habentibus dum fuerint in mortali peccato subditis & subiectis nullatinus obediendi vel obtemporandi existitunt ... Item assertere quod dominalia sive reverenciam cruci & sanctorum ymaginibus a Christi fidelibus nullatenus exhiberi ... Item assertere quod presbiteri &

Both in Essex and in England generally the early decades of the fifteenth century saw a hardening of attitudes by church and secular authorities alike towards this heresy, initially aimed at its extirpation from university circles and then from the ranks of gentry among whom it enjoyed a brief popularity. The sympathy of the gentry largely collapsed after Sir John Oldcastle's abortive attempt at rebellion against Henry V.[7] But Oldcastle's revolt in the early days of 1414 attracted popular support from a wide geographical area, and, as has already been shown, a number of people from Essex went to London to take part. Judicial commissions hastily sent out in the wake of the collapse of the revolt uncovered several Essex Lollard groups, in and around Thaxted, at Pattiswick (perhaps a legacy of Becket's early activity?), and in Colchester.[8]

A local jury charged that a certain chaplain named William was a 'common Lollard' and had 'used books written in English [*libris anglicis*] to preach to the king's people, heretically and ... against the catholic faith in Maldon and Thaxted and many other places in Essex' since 1402.[9] William's fate is unclear, but Kightly has suggested he was the 'prest of Thaksted' burnt for heresy in 1431 at Smithfield.[10] Preoccupation with possession of English-language texts, as virtually an indication of heresy in itself, stemmed from the Wycliffite conviction of the primacy of Biblical texts in Christian understanding, and the desirability of vernacular Bibles as well as treatises and sermons for lay people's study. The connection drawn between vernacular texts and heretical tendencies would recur in judicial proceedings at times of heightened suspicion for much of the century.[11]

The other major Thaxted leader in 1414 was a cobbler named John Smyth, a 'great Lollard' who had also used English books 'to teach the king's people against the catholic faith' for five years pre-

constituti in sacris iure divino nubere possunt sine periculo & peccato ... Item assertere quod actus carnalis sive choitus extra matrimonium secundum formam & observanciam ecclesie constructum est licitus & permissivus ac iure divino fieri potest sine periculo anime & peccato ...'.

7 See above, Chapter 11.

8 PRO.KB9.204.1 mm.1–13; PRO.KB27.619 Rex m.2v.

9 PRO.KB9.204.1 m.2: '... dominus Willelmus capellanus nuper parochialis sacerdos ville de Thaxstede ... est lollardus & utitur libris anglicis predicando populis domini Regis heretice et sic utebatur predicare contra fidem Catholicam in villis de Maldon & Thaxstede & in multis aliis locis in comitate Essex' ...;' m.4: '... et quod Willelmus nuper capellanus parochialis de Thaxstede est communis Lollardus & tenet opiniones Lollardas ...'.

10 BL MS Cotton Cleopatra C.IV fo. 37: '... ther whas a prest of Thaksted that whas viccory somtyme there whas brent in Smythfeld ...'; cf. Kightly, 'Early Lollards', p. 387.

11 Hudson, *The premature reformation*, pp. 166–8; Hudson, 'Lollard book production', p. 182; Thomson, *Later Lollards*, p. 227.

viously.[12] Fourteen other Thaxted men, including Smyth's servant John Chichely, were cited for possession of *libri anglici* or for going to London to support Oldcastle.[13] And at Pattiswick two brothers, John and Thomas Cok, both listed as weavers, organised and even paid for others there and in surrounding communities to make their way to London.[14] With the possible exception of William the chaplain, none of these participants in the events of 1414 is known to have been executed.[15]

It is characteristic of Lollardy that the spotlights thrown onto its adherents' activities follow a chronology more probably dependent upon the authorities' efforts to extinguish it than upon its own development as a heretical movement. The next period of intensified anti-Lollard action came in the late 1420s. Best known today among these persecutions is that conducted by Bishop Alnwick in Norwich, and the testimonies of suspected heretics during Alnwick's proceedings are among the richest sources for understanding the movement's propagation.[16] Unfortunately no comparable material is available for Essex, but Colchester was touched by one of the East Anglian heretics' activities. In that town John Abraham, probably originally from Woodchurch in Kent, was at the centre of a Lollard conventicle, and he was burnt for heresy in 1428 or 1429.[17] A tailor from Mundham (Norfolk), William Hardy, confessed that 'before this tyme Y have be conversant, familier and hoomly with heretikes . . . in the hous of John Abraham, cordewaner of Colcestre, kepyng and holdyng scoles of heresie, of whom Y have herd, conceyved and reported the errours and heresies whiche be writen and contened in this indentur'.[18]

Lollardy was spread through these 'schools' , or rather meetings in houses and shops where ideas were exchanged and texts disseminated among friends and acquaintances made through personal networks.[19] This may well have been the pattern for the 'teaching' that John Smyth did at Thaxted, and others like him. And though little can now be recovered of heresy proceedings in the diocese of London

[12] PRO.KB9.204.1 m.2: '. . . Johannes Smyth libere condicionis sowter de Thaxstede est Lollardus & utitur libris Anglicis docendo populis domini Regis heretice et sic utebatur docere populis domini Regis contra fidem catholicam in villa de Thaxstede . . .'; m.4: '. . . predictus Johannes Smyth soutere est magnus Lollardus . . .'; PRO.KB27.619 Rex m.2v.

[13] PRO.KB9.204.1 mm.3,4; PRO.KB27.619 Rex m.2v.

[14] PRO.KB9.204.1 mm.4,5,6,9.

[15] Kightly, 'Early Lollards', pp. 385–6.

[16] Tanner, ed., *Norwich heresy trials*; Aston, 'William White's followers'.

[17] Aston, 'William White's followers', p. 81.

[18] Tanner, ed., *Norwich heresy trials*, pp. 152–3.

[19] Hudson, *The premature reformation*, pp. 155–7, 180–200.

during these years, they resulted in a spate of executions in Essex and the metropolis during the next few years. Apart from Abraham and the 'prest of Thaksted' another priest was burnt at Colchester in 1430, as was an unnamed tiler at Maldon in the same year, while in 1431 Thomas Bagley, the elderly vicar of Manuden and a relapsed Lollard, was burnt in London after what Griffiths called 'a show-trial . . . with the maximum publicity' that failed to stem widespread Lollard unrest over much of southern England a few months later.[20]

Thereafter the movement's recoverable history in this district down to the early 1500s is confined to intermittent and shadowy references sufficient only to show some degree of continuing presence. In the first few decades of the sixteenth century the sect apparently took on new life in Essex, with more than a hundred heretics being examined and abjured in the county between 1510 and 1532.[21]

One other noteworthy episode, however, came at the time of Cade's revolt in 1450. Although, as already shown, this revolt is best understood as primarily politically motivated but tapping reserves of rural social turbulence, in the cases of many of the Essex participants scattered throughout the county, suspicions of Lollardy were mingled with charges of rebellion in the ensuing indictments.[22] As was possibly the case to a lesser degree with Oldcastle's rebellion also, official consternation may well have encouraged fanciful charges of heresy where little cause existed. But singled out for especially prolix attention among these rebels was Robert Helder of Bocking, yeoman *alias* weaver, the ringleader of several local incidents in September 1450.[23] His indictment charged that on 5 September 1450

> . . . at Bocking . . . in the presence of trustworthy men, he treacherously and heretically announced and proclaimed that it is not necessary to baptise an infant . . . [and that] it is not necessary for a sinful man to be shriven of his sins before any priest, because . . . the church ordained that priests of the church be held and reputed in honour, and have men in their dominion, and for no other cause was confession established . . . [and that] all goods and chattels of every person should be common to all, and should be divided equally among all

20 Riley, ed., *Annales a Johanne Amundesham* vol. i, pp. 50, 51; Jacob, ed., *Register of Henry Chichele* vol. iii, pp. 221–3, 226; Griffiths, *Reign of Henry VI*, p. 139; cf. Kightly, 'Early Lollards', p. 420.

21 Thomson, *Later Lollards*, pp. 132–8; Cross, *Church and people*, pp. 37–40; Dickens, *English Reformation*, pp. 28–9.

22 PRO.KB9.268 mm. 18–21, 24–9, 32, 34, 40a, 41. Charges of Lollardy were made in language like that of m.19: '. . . guerram contra dictum dominum Regem & populum suum proditorie levaverunt . . . ad destruendum predictum dominum Regem & leges ipsius Regis ac politicam gubernacionem regni sui necnon dominos ipsius Regis spirituales & temporales . . . contra legem catholicam ac leges & consuetudines regni predicti ut heretici & lollardi . . .'.

23 See above, Chapter 11.

people, so that no person should have property separately [and] for himself . . .[24]

The anti-sacramentarian echoes of Lollard persuasion are unmistakable in these charges. The levelling or communitarian demand of the last portion is more remarkable, though it echoes remarks allegedly made occasionally by other Lollards elsewhere, and may derive from a passage in Wyclif's *De Civili Dominio* that was subsequently popularised.[25] Whether or not Helder actually advocated such a view, it is surely telling that he was charged with advocating it.

Somewhat more conventionally Lollard, but still displaying the beliefs that posed such a threat to parochial clergy's authority, were the tenets abjured in 1457 by 'A lewd felaw . . . that was brought out of Essex':

Primus articulus that a childe borne schuld not be crysted tyl xiiij yere of aghe.
Also confessyon' ys not be mad to prestis but oonly to god.
Also that matrimon' shold not be solempnyzed in holy chyrche but that hit ys suffycient to make a contracte by endentre.
Also that a prest hath no power to make the sacrament of the auter.
Also he that ys best man ys best prest.
Also that the pope that lyvyth not os seynt Peter ys not pope.
Also and ymages owyth not in no wyse to be worschype.[26]

Apart from the anti-sacramentarian bent of these beliefs *per se* it is quite striking that one Lollard tenet current in Essex in the fifteenth century, the conceptualisation of marriage as an essentially private contract, supported by canon law even if discouraged by pastoral discipline as 'clandestine', was entirely consonant with popular attitudes towards the marriage process that had been unencumbered with heretical innuendo before the rise of the sect.[27] Some local Lollards went further. Two who abjured heretical opinions in the Norwich proceedings of 1428–31, one a tiler originally from Colchester, the other a Norfolk man who admitted having learnt his

24 PRO.KB9.268 m.41: '. . . apud Bokkyng . . . in presencia fidedignorum hominum proditorie & heretice pronunciavit & publicavit quod non est necesse infanti nati baptizari . . . quod non est necesse homini peccanti alicui sacerdoti de peccatis suis confiteri quia . . . ecclesia hoc ordinavit ut sacerdotes ecclesie in honore haberentur & reputaverentur & homines in domigerio suo haberent & quod pro nulla alia causa quam pro ea intencione huiusmodi confessio fuit ordinata . . . quod quecumque bona & catalla quarumcumque personarum essent omnibus personis communia & inter omnes personas equaliter dividenda quod nulla persona separatim pro se proprietatem huiusmodi bonorum & catallorum haberet . . .'.

25 Hudson, *The premature reformation*, pp. 374–5; Aston, 'Lollardy and sedition', p. 30; Cohn, *Pursuit of the millennium*, pp. 200–1. Hudson believes that 'anticipation of communism in Wycliffite thought has been exaggerated by modern criticism'.

26 Harriss and Harriss, eds., 'Benet's chronicle', pp. 220–1.

27 See above, Chapter 7.

heresy partly in Colchester, believed that 'oonly consent of love betuxe man and woman is sufficiant for the sacrament of perfit matrimon, withoute ony contract of wordes and withoute ony solennizacion in churche'.[28] Here too, the heresy fell upon fertile ground in part because it meshed with and reinforced predispositions in the rural population.

Historians seeking to understand the sect's nature and propagation have often debated whether Lollardy had a distinctive clientele. The problem of evidence in this respect is especially acute, since records of trials or accusations seldom attribute occupation or status to a very high percentage of suspects. It is, perhaps, at best only a suggestive pattern that emerges.[29] In Essex, as in England as a whole, Lollards whose occupations are given in the relevant records were drawn disproportionately from craftsmen and artisans, as well as the lower ranks of secular clergy. Table 12.1 presents occupational information for Essex persons charged with Lollardy at different chronological stages of the movement's development, drawn from the more easily available manuscript and printed sources.

Extended search would doubtless uncover more such information, and individuals tabulated here are only those (again, often the minority) for whom occupations were stated. Still, the pattern seems consistent. Only the indictments resulting from Cade's rebellion, which, as already noted, are less likely to be entirely credible accusations of Lollardy as such than the other contexts from which these data are drawn, present a picture at all different. Predisposition to religious nonconformity, so far as can be determined from available evidence, existed at all levels of rural Essex lay villagers but most strongly within the middling, non-agriculturalist ranks.

The reasons for a socially distinctive appeal of this sort constitute perhaps the most tantalising question concerning the sect. Discussions on this point are usually based upon assumptions that craftsmen were much more geographically mobile and more literate than their contemporaries, and that their detachment from the manorial order and their assimilation into a commercialised, urban-influenced menta-

28 Tanner, ed., *Norwich heresy trials*, pp. 144–7, 181–7.

29 Hudson, *The premature reformation*, pp. 128–33, is especially pessimistic of this evidence's ability to reflect Lollards as a social group at all faithfully. She argues that suspects of higher status may not have been so readily charged, whereas labourers either were genuinely less drawn to the sect, or were thought less worth pursuing by officials, or were less likely to be given occupational or status designations in the records. Cf. Dickens, *English Reformation*, p. 30; Tanner, ed., *Norwich heresy trials*, pp. 25–6.

Table 12.1. *Occupations of Essex Lollards 1414–1530*

	Oldcastle's rebellion (1414)[a]	Miscellaneous (1428–31)[b]	Cade's rebellion (1450)[c]	Miscellaneous (1511–30)[d]	Total
Clergy	3	3	3	3	12
Agriculturalists	0	0	11	0	11
Craftsmen/retailers	16	2	15	3	36
[clothworkers]	[6]	[0]	[3]	[2]	[11]
Labourers	0	0	8	0	8
Total	19	5	37	6	67

Sources: [a] PRO.KB9.204.1 mm.2–7, 9–10.
[b] See notes to text.
[c] PRO.KB9.268 mm.24–9 (includes only those whose indictments impute Lollardy).
[d] Foxe, *Acts and monuments* vol. iv, pp. 180–1, 214–16, 585–6.

lity also facilitated their absorption of religious nonconformity.[30] But it has already been shown that in Essex, artisans were not the most mobile social group, and the notion that they were distinctively more literate than others is cast into doubt by the Essex literacy evidence (see below, Chapter 13). Nor are the often-cited links between heresy and clothworkers outstandingly apparent here. Emphasising the commercialised or precocious nature of the local economy, on the other hand, would seem to explain why the district, rather than its artisans, was especially receptive to Lollardy.

If the ostensible occupational distinctiveness of the sect is not entirely an artefact of the way personal details of the accused were reported or recorded, then the movement's appeal to craftsmen may relate to their equivocal position, midway between the wealthier agriculturalists and the poorer and, in Essex, virtually universally illiterate wage labourers. Thomas argued that Lollards were 'mostly men of humble means and little learning', less dependent than husbandmen upon the vagaries of nature and quasi-magical practices of the traditional piety of humble laity. All these circumstances, it seems plausible to argue, were likely to make artisans better predisposed to a religious mentality that was individualistic, evangelical, disdainful of the wealthy, and sceptical of the totemic quality of images and sacraments.[31] Tying popular religion deterministically into social and economic matrices is always perilous, though, and the more fundamental problem remains of the attitudes and predispositions of local people.

Religious dissent, then, was a variegated experience. To study Lollardy primarily through surviving heretical tracts or curial examination of suspected heretics' opinions tends to focus attention upon a cluster of key doctrinal and pietistic principles: disparagement of sacraments and the material aspects of religious observance, emphasis upon scriptural authority and an internalised, individualistic lay spirituality. But it is likely that many more humble lay people never consciously articulated these ideas, when or if they encountered them, into a coherent belief system. Instead, ordinary lay people were receptive to the general tenor of the sect because it complemented attitudes already present in local society. Among these attitudes simple anti-clericalism was certainly a part, though after all a smattering of that was present in any historical Christian society. What

[30] Davis, 'Lollard survival and the textile industry', pp. 193–4; Aston, 'Lollardy and literacy', p. 202; see also below, Chapter 13.

[31] Thomas, *Religion and the decline of magic*, pp. 85, 794–6. Hudson, *The premature reformation*, on the other hand has re-emphasised the links between educationally oriented Lollard conventicles and the heresy's dissemination.

distinguished this era, it would seem, was disdain of clerical authority at its upper reaches absolutely, and at its lower reaches when it was not accompanied by an evangelical stance.

At the same time, as Aston has argued, especially after 1414 church and state concurred in viewing Lollardy and sedition as inextricably intertwined.[32] The connection was neatly encapsulated in one witness's testimony at an Essex proof-of-age hearing, when John Kemp recalled that at Horndon in October 1413 (doubtless, but not explicitly, referring to some otherwise unknown events related to Oldcastle) 'many Lollards congregated with insurgents against the church's power and privilege and, like disturbers, destroyed the king's peace'.[33] Both Lollardy and sedition were seen to challenge property as a bulwark of authority, as in the views imputed to Robert Helder of Bocking, and both refused to revere an established authority simply because it was there.

Religious dissent in late-medieval Essex was no harbinger of a revolutionary vanguard, however, despite the authorities' darkest nightmares. Historians reluctant to view the sect as a socially rebellious group point out that few Lollards whose beliefs can be examined articulated any coherent programme for restructuring society[34]; but then again, the same was true for the rebels of 1381. Lollardy did, nevertheless, spring in part from the same societal roots as civil disobedience: a stratified social structure with persistent disparity between rich and poor at village level, a volatile economy, vestigial and vexatious attempts to preserve traditional authority, and a willingness at least to contemplate an alternative vision of the world's ordering, however unattainable that vision was in practice. In many traditional societies, religion has been linked with rural revolts by uniting otherwise disparate groups under a 'mandatory system of moral values'.[35] Thomson suggested that 'Lollardy can be seen as a series of attitudes from which beliefs evolved'.[36] While it would be facile to strip popular religion of all but social and economic predispositions, in Essex it may be more accurate to say that widespread attitudes, conditioned in part by social and economic circumstances, found in Lollardy some beliefs to seize upon.

[32] Aston, 'Lollardy and sedition'. Hudson, *The premature reformation*, p. 117, emphasises that this linkage was not necessarily inevitable earlier in the heresy's history.

[33] PRO.C139.78.53 (inquest, 29 Oct 1435): '. . . apud villatam de Horndon multi lollardi congregati fuerunt cum insurrectoribus contra [?opulantitatem] & privilegem ecclesiasticam & quasi perturbatores pacem domini Regis distruerunt . . .'.

[34] Thomson, *Later Lollards*, p. 249.

[35] Bak and Benecke, 'Religion and revolt?', p. 2.

[36] Thomson, *Later Lollards*, p. 244.

Ultimately, in view of the varying degrees with which common people assimilated the formal elements of religion, it may not always be possible to draw strict demarcations between 'orthodox' and 'heretical' in this society. Indeed it may not always be necessary. One development observable throughout much of Catholic Europe in the late middle ages was reinforced both by theologically orthodox and Lollard-influenced lay piety. This development may be termed an activist stance towards management of parochial affairs, broadly defined.[37] If there was a predisposition within a broad middling range of rural people toward embryonic scepticism of secular and ecclesiastical authority as traditionally constituted, its corollary was a desire on the part of the same people for greater involvement in communal life, especially in the vacuum left by the waning of the manorial order. It would be useful to be able to pursue this point into the formal sanctions of the contemporary criminal law, but for the fifteenth century most of the relevant records at the county level, especially those of sessions of the peace, have not survived. But other channels for parochial activism were open to Essex communities.

A number of recent writers, most notably McIntosh, have observed that many communities in fifteenth-century England were redoubling their attempts to control irregular behaviour and petty disorder.[38] Through the mechanisms of the leet courts, and apparently at the instigation of the better-off husbandmen and artisans who served as jurors, constables and churchwardens, this community control was aimed against disorderly games, alehouses, and a variety of offences that fall outside 'crimes' as ordinarily construed, though in some instances statutory authority lay behind their prosecution, but that in other instances shade off into the realm of sexual or other morals charges ordinarily falling within the purview of ecclesiastical jurisdiction. Since servants, labourers, vagrants and the poor were often the offenders in these cases, in one respect such efforts can be envisaged as behavioural clashes between upper and lower social strata at the village level. Community behavioural sanctions in this period thus form part of a longer-term continuity, analogous to similar efforts both at the height of economic tensions around 1300 and in the late Tudor and early Stuart era.[39]

Efforts at community control are reflected in a scattering of cases at Essex leet courts throughout the later middle ages. Seven men

[37] Bossy, *Christianity in the West*, pp. 64–72.

[38] McIntosh, 'Local change and community control'; McIntosh, *Autonomy and community*, pp. 235–40, 244–61; Dyer, *Lords and peasants in a changing society*, pp. 358–72.

[39] Spufford, 'Puritanism and social control?'.

'continually play handball against the statute' (Great Dunmow, 1399);[40] 'William [Clerk] is a common player at "le Cards" . . . in bad example to others living there' (Birchanger, 1511).[41] At Great Dunmow in 1390, three men 'in unreasonable manner frequent the alehouse at night to the prejudice of neighbours'.[42] At Writtle in 1382, perhaps in reaction to the events of the previous year, jurors declared that 'William Reve is a common disturber of the peace, a common tavern-goer and night-watcher, and by his abusive words excites strife and dissension among people daily, because of which . . . much bloodshed and outrage come among the people'.[43] At Boreham in 1409 William Reehoed is 'a common night-walker and frequently stands under the roofs of various of the lord's tenants'.[44] In order to enforce these efforts many communities had erected stocks, cucking-stools and pillories by the fifteenth century.[45] The ultimate sanction, however, was expulsion from local households or from the community itself: within the space of five years in the early 1500s at Birchanger, two different men were ordered to remove from their homes Agnes the wife of John Crowcheman, who was a 'suspect person' and had pilfered articles from surrounding households.[46]

After perusing a large volume of Essex leet-court records it is quite

[40] ERO D/DMg M39 (Great Dunmow leet, 22 Feb 1399): '. . . utuntur ludere ad pilam manualem continue contra ordinatum statuti'. The statute against games mentioned here was probably 12 Ric. II c. 6; cf. McIntosh, 'Local change and community control', p. 232.

[41] NCO 3599 m.3 (Birchanger leet, 19 Dec 1511): '. . . est communis lusor apud le Cards infra pertinitium huius visi per diversas vices in male exemplum aliorum comorantum . . .'.

[42] ERO D/DMg M39 (Great Dunmow leet, 22 Feb 1390): '. . . modo irrationabili frequentant noctanter tabernam ad preiudicium vicinorum suorum . . .'.

[43] ERO D/DP M189 m.12v (Writtle leet, 26 May 1382): '. . . communis perturbator pacis & communis tabernator noctanterque vigilator & eciam per sua verba contumeliosa rixas & discensa in populum de die in diem excitat . . . causa quorum verborum contumeliosorum . . . maxima sanguinis effusio & contumelia sepius in populum adveniunt . . .'.

[44] PRO.SC2.171.30 (Boreham leet, 30 Jun 1409): '. . . communis noctivagans & frequentat noctanter stare subtus tecta diversorum tenentum domini . . .'.

[45] NCO 3623 m.8 (Widdington leet, 7 Nov 1499): 'le Cokkyngstole'; ERO D/DU 267/30 (Birdbrook leet, 20 Jul 1382): '. . . deficit furce collistrigii & tumberelli in preiudicium libertatis & dominij'; ERO D/DMg M40 (Great Dunmow leet, 22 Feb 1416): '. . . dominus huius manerij repararet unum collistrigium & trebechetum in mercato pro libertate ville salvanda . . .'; Furber, ed., *Essex sessions of the peace*, pp. 105–6.

[46] NCO 3598 m.6 (Birchanger leet, 19 Dec 1506): '. . . Agnes uxor Johannis Crowcheman est persona suspectiva eo quod ipsa diversos pannos lineos diversorum tenentum domini . . . [?cepit] ad gravem dampnum ipsorum tenentum . . . preceptum est Johanni Clerk predictam Agnetem ammovere extra tenementum suum . . .'; *ibid.* m.7 (Birchanger leet, 18 Dec 1507); NCO 3599 m.2 (Birchanger leet, 19 Dec 1510): 'Preceptum est Hugoni Whityngton iam firmario Rectorie de Birchanger quod ipse decetero non confortat neque in Rectoriam predictam recipiet quandam Agnetem uxorem Johannis Crowcheman personam suspectivam . . .'.

difficult to discern any definite chronology of trends over the period for these offences or attempts to combat them. Cases like this are intermittent enough to make quantitative analysis meaningless. McIntosh chooses to view them as products of economically or demographically induced stress, which she believes was increasing in the last decades of the fifteenth century.[47] But the Essex tithing data indicate no demographic resurgence in this district until the early 1500s, and moreover an undercurrent of these cases is scattered throughout the later-medieval period. At any rate it is doubtful whether such evidence is a sensitive enough barometer of economic conditions to reflect decade-by-decade changes in levels of distress.

On the other hand, while these cases doubtless reflect material interests in preserving order within communities, it would seem wrong to dismiss altogether a component of religiously motivated concern for propriety and morality among the initiatives of parish notables. Comparison is perhaps inevitable between this earlier period and the Puritan-influenced quest for order in the half-century before the English Civil War, of which Essex itself constitutes the most conspicuous example in recent historical studies.[48] In both instances, lay attitudes, informed in part by a religious framework, merged with activism in parochial affairs.

In late-medieval Essex parish notables were at the forefront in other lay initiatives into religious matters: parish guilds, almshouses and other poor-relief efforts, school foundations, miracle or mystery plays, even lay endowment of preachers' stipends.[49] An activist moral stance, coupled with a concern for social cohesion, was seldom entirely absent from these efforts. The statutes of a parish guild founded at Moreton in 1473 not only demanded compulsory church attendance from each member 'in his best clothynge in the worshipe of God' at the guild's annual observances and provided for distributing 'brede to poor peple of the same parasch', but also directed that if any member 'be at hevyness wyth any of hys bretheryne for any maner of trespas he schall noth persewyn hym in no maner of cowrte' but seek the guild alderman's aid 'for to acorde thame and set thame at reste and pes'.[50]

Similarly, the statutes of an almshouse founded at Walden in 1400 provided lodging for thirteen paupers to live in 'good rewle and clene

[47] McIntosh, 'Local change and community control'.
[48] Cf. Hunt, *The Puritan moment*, pp. 64–84, 130–55; Wrightson and Levine, *Poverty and piety*, pp. 110–85.
[49] McIntosh, *Autonomy and community*, pp. 235–40; McIntosh, 'Responses to the poor'; Hunt, *The Puritan moment*, p. 132.
[50] Curling, ed., 'The gild of All Saints', pp. 224, 227, 228, 229.

levyng, Non rebawdys [ribalds] no chyderys [chiders] drunkelew [drunkards] ne latemakerys [evilly disposed men]', and also gave short-term relief to 'ony stronge poure womman w^{t} childe or any othir pore stronge syk man or womman' passing through the town. The paupers were required to attend church to pray for their benefactors, and an endowment was provided for a chaplain 'able to rede and synge and of good name and clene levynge'.[51] Thus were combined an acknowledgement of persistent poverty, an attempt at maintenance of moral order, and an entirely orthodox desire to perform good works for the health of the benefactors' souls.

Concern with the morality of local clergy was one conspicuous area in which orthodox lay activism coincided with, and may even have been reinforced by, Lollard tendencies. Under the rubric of suppressing community nuisances, Essex leet courts occasionally punished sexually related offences: for example, at Little Dunmow in 1370 the jurors presented two men who had 'received a certain outsider, Juliana, who is a whore, to the nuisance of neighbours'.[52] But a disproportionately large number, indeed on the basis of an admittedly unsystematic scrutiny of Essex leet records the great majority, of Essex leet-court presentments that were aimed directly at sexual delicts as such concerned clergy, and these cases too are scattered throughout the later middle ages.

At South Hanningfield in 1340, 'John Gossebel chaplain holds in concubinage Elena Fairynogh against her will'.[53] At Great Waltham in May 1403 'John, vicar of Waltham, . . . entered at night the farmyard of John Wroth . . . and there copulated three times with John Brode's wife, as he himself openly said afterward'.[54] In 1441 'John, vicar of Boreham church, kept a whore in his house for four days'.[55] In 1501, 'John Grene, vicar of Little Dunmow church, visits the house of Johanna Warde, widow, at illicit, unseemly and suspect times', and he was ordered to cease doing so on pain of his forfeiting 40s. and her being expelled from the manor.[56] Special sensitivity to such situations

51 Steer, ed., 'Statutes of Saffron Walden almshouses', pp. 174, 178.

52 PRO.SC2.171.64 (Little Dunmow leet, 8 Jun 1370): '. . . receptavit quamdam Julianam extraneam que meretrix est ad nocumentum vicinorum . . .'.

53 ERO D/DP M874 (South Hanningfield leet, 25 Feb 1340): '. . . tenet in concubina Elenam Fairynogh contra voluntatem suam & contra pacem domini Regis . . .'.

54 ERO D/DTu M240 (Great Waltham leet, 22 May 1404): '. . .ad noctem intravit clausum . . . & ibidem per iij vices concubuit cum uxore Johannis Brode prout ipse manifeste inde locutus fuit postea . . .'.

55 PRO.SC2.171.33 (Boreham leet, 30 Jun 1441): '. . . custodivit infra domum suam unam meretricem per iiij dies contra pacem domini Regis . . .'.

56 PRO.DL30.58.722 (Barnston leet, 10 May 1501): '. . . occupat domum Johanne Warde vidue tempore illicite & incongruitive & susspective agito ideo preceptum est quod

may even have led to the coining of a distinctive epithet: 'Alice Tailor is a strang hoore and a prests hoore' was overheard in Walden market-place in 1496 by a deponent in a subsequent defamation suit before the London diocesan court.[57]

One must not, of course, view the more prurient cases of this sort as portraying rampant clerical immorality, but rather as reflecting a persistent contemporary concern to detect and punish such dalliances when they did occur. And such concern may stem equally from lay activism in parochial affairs, and from condemnation of immoral clergy in a Lollard-tinged atmosphere. Here too community order was at issue, since feuds between priest and parishioner could disrupt village life. Nicholas, a parochial chaplain at Roxwell, was cited by the leet court at Writtle because from Easter until the following Thursday in 1426, 'unjustly and without any lawful process' he 'refused to administer the sacraments to a certain John Laurence, because John owed two bushels of wheat to a certain William Parker, to the grave scandal of John and the great offence of all his neighbours'.[58]

One Sunday in July 1494, in the parish church of the tiny community of Beauchamp Roding, a heated exchange took place between the rector, William Kirkham, and a parishioner, James Ely, that must have been the culmination of a long series of personal clashes, and that also lends vivid insight into these conflicts between clergy and people. The vignette can be reconstructed from depositions that five other parishioners gave before the London diocesan court, probably in a defamation suit, although the substance of the case is unclear from the surviving record.[59] Each deponent gave a slightly different version of what happened that Sunday, and one or two added further details to the basic story, but the essence of the exchange is clear. Thomas Saveryng recalled that he was present in the church with other parishioners when

> . . . William, going to celebrate mass, in his priestly vestments, looked back and said to James Ely, 'Woyd owt of my chauncell thow unthryfft and goo sett wyth the sowys.'
>
> And James withdrew from the chancel and stood leaning on a certain altar of St Katherine in the church's nave, until William came to his pulpit to preach God's word to the parishioners, and among other things in his preaching he

non occupat nec ibidem remanet sub pena xl s. et sub pena Johanne extra ponendi domenium . . .'.

57 GL MS 9065 fo. 263v.

58 ERO D/DP M230 (Writtle court, 18 May 1426): '. . . iniuste & absque processu legis alicuius . . . sacramenta ecclesiastica . . . renuit ministrare . . . eo quod idem Johannes debuit cuidam Willelmo Parker ij buscellos frumenti ad grave scandelum ipsius Johannis & magnum tedium omnium vicinorum suorum . . .'.

59 GL MS 9065 fos. 215v–218.

said to James, 'Loo Serys, take no hydd of that cursyd mane that lenyth on that awter, ther shuld noo such cume to the awter.'
And James answered him, 'Fynd ye that in the Gospell of this daie?'
And then William replied, 'Goo loke thow in the boke.'[60]

Thomas Gibbes recalled the rector warning his flock

'Be ware ye all my parysshons that ye nether ete nether drynke w^{t} the seid James, for he is acursed, and be ware of such holy mene.'[61]

And another deponent said that James responded

'I deffye the[e], jurlyssh prest as thow artt, and all other as thow arte.'[62]

That this had been a longstanding clash seems clear, since Gibbes added that nearly a year and a half earlier, in February 1493, the two men had had a similar confrontation in the church:

[Kirkham] 'A woyd owt of my churche and walke among thy felows.'
[Ely] 'What felaws have I & what know yow wha felaws I have?'
[Kirkham] 'A meny of fals harlotts and theffs, as for sume of them be hadd forth to Colchestyr, and so shall thow be tymys, for I have sene as trew a face loke thorow a halter er this tyme.'[63]

Apart from the fact that circumstantial and vernacular accounts of conflicts like this one are quite rare from pre-Reformation England, several points stand out. A tinge – it can scarcely be put more strongly than that – of Lollard leaning is implied in James' derisive challenge to William to justify himself by scripture, and William's taunt to go find the passage for himself, all deponents agreeing upon this part of the story. William's sarcastic warning to beware of 'such holy men' may point the same way. The anecdote also shows the influence the clergy might try to exercise in ostracising their opponents from parish social intercourse. William's insinuation that James' 'fellows' had been brought to Colchester (that is, ended up as indicted felons, for that town was also the site of the county gaol), and that James might fare similarly, underscores this attempt to invoke parish opinion. Finally, the open insolence James displayed is perhaps the most evocative instance of casual anti-clericalism to survive from the district in this period.

It would, however, be quite wrong to leave the impression that most, or even very many, in the fifteenth-century Essex countryside were infected with such a degree of derisive scepticism, or the religious radicalism that fuelled the more noteworthy episodes of local dissent. It would be equally wrong to imply that the church, its liturgy and its

[60] *Ibid.* fo. 215v. [61] *Ibid.* fo. 217v. [62] *Ibid.* fo. 218.
[63] *Ibid.* fos. 217–217v.

clergy failed to continue to meet the spiritual needs of most ordinary lay people at the time. A number of recent writers have in fact tended to play down the volume of dissent or anti-clerical friction in rural England generally at the eve of the Reformation.[64] As Bossy observed, 'Since parishes were rarely backward in coming forward with charges against their priests, it seems reasonable to assume that in the majority of cases, where they kept silent, the priest was doing his job with fair conscientiousness, sensitivity and common sense'.[65] That is undoubtedly correct. But the fact that a relatively few fully fledged Lollard communities took root in the district may be less important than the fact that the district, to an apparently much greater degree than much of the rest of England, was receptive enough to contain them.

64 E.g. Scarisbrick, *Reformation and English people*.
65 Bossy, *Christianity in the West*, p. 66.

13

Literacy

One of the most central questions surrounding the medieval transmission of heretical and possibly political knowledge and opinions is the extent to which literacy had spread into the middling and lower orders of lay society by the fifteenth century. That access to written works, either directly by reading or indirectly through the intermediation of readers who transmitted the written word orally to the non-reading, was intimately bound up with Lollardy has of course long been recognised.[1] But the quantitative dimensions of lay literacy in this era have been quite difficult to estimate, and in the absence of detailed information on this score historians have fallen back upon certain conjectures about the relationships between economic or social developments, literacy, and nonconformist opinion.

The statements of Davis may be taken as typical of arguments of this kind.[2] Proclivities to heretical opinion, in this view, were at least partly a by-product (in economically advanced regions like Essex and East Anglia) of social changes, and specifically the presence of large numbers of clothworkers and other artisans. Such workers were geographically mobile, somewhat divorced from the old manorial regime, and, critically, more likely to have acquired at least rudimentary literacy as a practical adjunct to their occupations. 'Literate craftsmen ... had a more independent stance towards society and Church than did labourers ... The textile artisan could migrate with greater freedom than the labourer, infecting other districts with heresy ...'.[3] It has already been shown, though, that in late-medieval Essex labourers were if anything rather more mobile than craftsmen and

[1] E.g. Aston, 'Lollardy and literacy'; Hudson, *The premature reformation*, esp. pp. 180–208.

[2] Davis, 'Lollard survival and the textile industry'; cf. Tanner, ed., *Norwich heresy trials*, pp. 25–9; Aston, 'Lollardy and literacy', pp. 202–3; Thomson, *Later Lollards*, p. 125.

[3] Davis, *Heresy and reformation*, p. 2.

retailers. And although plausible, these posited connections between economic development and literacy need firmer substantiation than heretofore achieved before becoming fully convincing.

A variety of approaches has been applied to estimating the prevalence of literacy in the later middle ages. Not surprisingly, how one understands or defines 'literacy' has a strong bearing upon how one goes about measuring its extent and how high one's estimate will be.[4] Before the later fourteenth century at the earliest, historians are largely left with qualitative impressions drawn from anecdotal or other narrative evidence. Parkes' well-known essay on 'The literacy of the laity' typifies this approach, and Parkes was commendably cautious in being reluctant to draw even tentative quantitative conclusions.[5]

Recent work on the later fourteenth to early sixteenth centuries, notably that by Orme and Moran, has by contrast focused upon the expanding availability of elementary and grammar-school education. Apart from endowed schools that left records of foundation, benefaction and property endowment, however, the more ephemeral schools typical in rural areas of late-medieval England are difficult to trace, and at present there seems to be no comprehensive listing of schools of this sort in Essex.[6] Recently Moran, through painstaking scrutiny of a wide array of documentary evidence, demonstrated that the availability of educational opportunities to lay people of sub-gentry status was not only expanding in the diocese of York during the century before the Reformation but was also much wider than previously appreciated. Based upon her estimates of numbers of schools and of the pupils passing through them, she argued that as many as 15 per cent of adults, or 25 per cent of adult males, in this area of northern England had received some elementary education and, by inference, at least basic reading literacy in the vernacular and possibly Latin too, in the early sixteenth century.[7] She is thus in broad agreement with writers such as Du Boulay and Thrupp, who also argued for relatively high literacy levels at the end of the middle ages.[8]

On the other hand the work of some early-modern historians,

[4] Schofield, 'The measurement of literacy'. [5] Parkes, 'Literacy of the laity'.

[6] Orme's 1973 list contained eight Essex schools known to have existed by the mid-sixteenth century, at Chelmsford, Colchester, Earls Colne, Maldon, Pleshey, Walden, Waltham Holy Cross and Walthamstow: Orme, *English schools in the middle ages*, pp. 114, 283, 284, 300, 302, 310, 313, 314, 318, 319. The list, however, omits schools kept by religious orders and chantry schools. Orme's later work in other parts of the country indicates that his early estimates of numbers of schools generally may be conservatively low: Orme, *Education in the west of England*.

[7] Moran, *Growth of English schooling*, pp. 178–82; Moran, 'Literacy and education', pp. 14–18.

[8] Du Boulay, *Age of ambition*, p. 118; Thrupp, *Merchant class of medieval London*, pp. 155–8.

particularly Cressy, has tended to minimise the incidence of literacy among the male laity even by the middle of the sixteenth century. Cressy's estimates, based upon the ability to sign one's name (and upon the premise that reading skills were normally acquired before even such limited writing ability as this) would imply quite low literacy rates in Essex as late as the end of the 1500s. As measured by presence or absence of signatures in ecclesiastical-court depositions, in the 1580s in the diocese of London outside the City 35 per cent of yeomen and 81 per cent of husbandmen were illiterate, as were 64 per cent of tailors and 71 per cent of weavers in a more widely based sample of rural England. Women, and males of lower statuses and occupations who, after all, together comprised the majority of the adult population, were generally much closer to universal illiteracy.[9]

However one may choose to extrapolate these rates back to the later fifteenth century, they seem difficult to reconcile with the more optimistic estimates of the medieval historians who have been mentioned. In part this is doubtless due to defining literacy as the ability to sign one's name, a methodology which has attracted some criticism and which, as Moran points out, is untenable for pre-1500 England.[10] At the same time Moran's ingenious calculations, even if accepted fully, remain an indirect measure of *potential* literacy, and moreover leave uncertain the extent to which her estimated literacy rates were diffused down into the humbler ranks of society.

It is useful to bear in mind Clanchy's arguments concerning what he termed the 'literate mentality', arising from 'practical literacy' or awareness, and experience in the use, of written instruments in such contexts as legal transactions, which need not necessarily have been restricted to those who themselves could read.[11] Observing from a somewhat different vantage, Goody and Watt wrote that 'The high degree of differentiation in exposure to the literate tradition sets up a basic division which cannot exist in non-literate society: the division between the various shades of literacy and illiteracy'.[12] Essex evidence anecdotally illustrates various intermediate stages from complete illiteracy to full literacy in the modern sense. In several proof-of-age inquests, witnesses recalled the birth date of a feudal heir because, they claimed, the birth coincided with acquisition of property or other transactions, for which they retained written records. Often these

[9] Cressy, *Literacy and the social order*, pp. 144, 148, 150, 152.
[10] Moran, 'Literacy and education', pp. 8–9.
[11] Clanchy, *Memory to written record*, esp. pp. 175–201, 258–65.
[12] Goody and Watt, 'The consequences of literacy', p. 59.

people had had to seek out parish clergymen to make their records. In 1354, Thomas Wright recalled, he

> made a certain agreement with ... John Salman for making him [Wright] a new grange in the vill of Ridgewell, and for greater security on either side they made letters of obligation between the said parties, and going to seek a chaplain to make the said letters they found the chaplain baptising the aforesaid William ...[13]

In 1311 at Mayland, Ralph Nenen

> took at farm a carucate of land from John de Waleton for a term of years, and John the brother of the vicar of Mayland made and wrote his indentures in the presence of Hugh, father of the said John [the heir whose birth date was in question], that is, the third day after his birth, by the date of which he well remembers ...[14]

Many documents of this kind, especially those concerned with land transactions, would have been written in Latin, so the need to seek out a clerk to compose them need not necessarily imply illiteracy in English. Again, readers might not necessarily have been writers. Nevertheless, the practical need to deal with written instruments which one could not oneself write, and probably not read as well, is well illustrated in medieval scenarios like these.

And at any rate the reach of the written word extended well beyond the ranks of the properly literate, when readers read aloud to the non-reading, especially where religious texts were involved. Apart from the intense official concern about possession of *libri Anglici* by suspected Lollards in the wake of Oldcastle's rebellion, already discussed, other inquests into suspected heresy reinforce this image. In fact, some of the more vivid of surviving vignettes concerning the transmission of Lollard opinions deal with exactly this point. One Essex example is the case of William Sweeting, who read portions of heretical books to illiterate disciples in and around Colchester in the early years of the sixteenth century: a carpenter named James Brewster 'who, being unlettered, could neither read nor write', confessed that 'he had been five times with William Sweeting in the fields keeping

[13] PRO.C135.249.19 (inquest, 5 Sep 1375): '... predictus Thomas Wright fecit quandam convencionem cum predicto Johanne Salman ad faciendum sibi quandam grangiam novam in villa de Reddeswell & pro maiore securitate que convencionis predicte ex utraque parte habenda fecerunt quasdam literas obligatorias inter partes predictas & euntes ad querendum quendam capellanum ad faciendum literas predictas invenerunt dictum capellanum predictum Willelmum baptizantem ...'.

[14] PRO.C135.33.12 (inquest, 16 May 1332): '... ipse cepit ad firman unam carucatam terre de Johanne de Waleton ad terminum annorum & Johannes frater vicarij de Maylond fecit & scripsit indenturas suas in presencia Hugonis patris dicti Johannis ...'.

beasts, hearing him read many good things out of a certain book'.[15] A similar process of transmission took place at Lollard 'schools', the groups meeting in homes or workplaces like John Abraham's Colchester conventicle, discussed in the previous chapter.

That mode of transmission persisted after 1538, when the Crown ordered an approved English translation of the Bible placed into parish churches. William Maldon recalled that

> imedyately after dyveres poore men in the towne of Chelmysford in the county of Essex, where my father dwelled and I borne, and with him brought up, the sayd poore men bought the Newe Testament of Jesus Christ, and on sundays dyd set redinge in lower ende of the church, and many wolde floke about them to heare theyr redinge. Then I came amonge the sayd reders, to here their redyng of that glad and sweet tydyngs of the gospell ... Then thought I, I will learne to rede Englyshe, and then will I have the Newe Testament and rede ther on myself ...[16]

Clearly, then, it would require the presence of only one literate enthusiast in a household or a community for its residents to be exposed, potentially, to the written word of religion, orthodox or otherwise.

But late-medieval Essex also permits some direct measures of literacy. These come from the preambles to depositions in the London consistory courts of the later fifteenth century, which, as already shown (above, Chapter 8), usually contained notes as to whether an individual was *literatus*, *illiteratus*, or more ambiguously *aliqualiter literatus* ('somewhat literate'). It was upon one of the London consistory-court deposition books that Thrupp based her estimate of about 50 per cent literacy among male deponents in the city of London, though re-examination of this source indicates that Thrupp was insufficiently sensitive to the social selectiveness of the deponent sample.[17]

It is of course critically important to know what the curial scribes meant by *literatus*, but no straightforward answer seems possible.

[15] Aston, 'Lollardy and literacy', pp. 199–200; Foxe, *Acts and monuments* vol. iv, pp. 215–16.

[16] Nichols, ed., *Narratives of the Reformation*, p. 349. The author is grateful to Roger Schofield for this reference.

[17] Thrupp, *Merchant class of medieval London*, pp. 155–8. Thrupp tabulated 116 male deponents appearing in the consistory court between 1467 and 1476, and though she provides no precise document references this implies that her data were drawn only from GLRO DL/C/205. Virtually all her deponents (except for three labourers) were described as belonging to crafts, and so it is likely that these deponents, to a rather greater extent than the rural Essex deponents discussed below, were mainly a 'middle class' group. Thrupp also believed that *literatus* in this context meant Latin literacy, and since about 40 per cent of her sample were so described she believed English literacy was closer to 50 per cent.

Before about 1300 the term can usually be taken fairly safely to mean able to read Latin', and thus often by implication in, or at least possessing education normally expected to lead to, clerical orders. It was doubtless in this sense that the term was used at Ingatestone in 1305, when the manor court there recorded that 'Thomas Daty *literatus*' had fled the manor; in other words he had, apparently, been to school, by implication without seigneurial permission and probably to become a clerk.[18]

By the later fifteenth century, however, the term had become more ambiguous. Moran usefully distinguishes the older sense of the term, which she expresses as being 'latinate', from 'literacy' in the sense of having some proficiency at reading English and possibly some Latin also (since most evidence indicates that in late-medieval elementary schools reading English preceded the study of Latin), but implies that the term *literatus* in contemporary sources might still connote 'latinacy'.[19] But the newer ambiguity of the word was demonstrated, admittedly, a few decades later, by one deponent's response in the diocese of Lincoln in 1527: 'Asked whether he be *literatus* and whether he can read Latin and English, he says that he is *literatus* but cannot read perfectly either English or Latin, but can somewhat read here one word, there another. But he knows nothing of Latin.'[20]

In the absence of clearer evidence from the Essex deposition records themselves it seems most plausible to regard *literatus* in these records as denoting something similar to the sense used in this deposition, and thus closer to Moran's definition of 'literacy', though this means that proportions of *literati* among the deponents will probably be, if anything, a minimal estimate of literacy in English.

One further observation is pertinent to any evidence of literacy arising from ecclesiastical-court records. This is the suspicion that in certain contexts in the later middle ages there was a very real incentive for some witnesses to claim illiteracy, for ability to read English was liable to reinforce suspicions of Lollardy in the course of heresy examinations, itself an indication of how closely the two were associated in the minds of contemporary authorities. Thus it is perhaps inadvisable to take at face value a claim of inability to read in such

18 ERO D/DP M19 m.3 (Ingatestone leet, 14 Jun 1305): 'Item [chief pledges] presentant quod Thomas Daty literatus est & elongavit se extra feodum Abatisse . . .'.

19 Moran, 'Literacy and education', pp. 1 note, 3–5.

20 LAO, Lincoln Episcopal Court Book Cj/3 fo. 39v: 'Examinatus an ipse sit literatus et an scit legere latinum et anglicum [sic] dicit quod est literatus sed nescit perfecte legere nec anglicum nec latinum aliqualiter tamen scit legere hic unum verbum et ibi aliud Nichill tamen intelligit de latino . . .'. The author is extremely grateful to R. H. Helmholz for this reference.

Table 13.1. *Recorded literacy among deponents in London diocese ecclesiastical courts, 1467–97 (percentages in all cases)*

	Literatus	*Aliqualiter literatus*	*Illiteratus*
Essex			
No occupation given (N = 106)	20.8	0.9	78.3
Agriculturalists (N = 21)	9.5	4.8	85.7
Craftsmen/retailers (N = 29)	0.0	0.0	100.0
Labourers (N = 10)	0.0	0.0	100.0
Servants (N = 1)	0.0	0.0	100.0
Clergy (N = 5)	100.0	0.0	0.0
Total (N = 172)	16.9	1.2	82.0
Entire London diocese excluding city of London			
No occupation given (N = 155)	20.6	0.6	78.7
Agriculturalists (N = 27)	11.1	3.7	85.2
Craftsmen/retailers (N = 45)	6.7	0.0	93.3
Labourers (N = 11)	0.0	0.0	100.0
Servants (N = 1)	0.0	0.0	100.0
Clergy (N = 5)	100.0	0.0	0.0
Total (N = 244)	17.6	0.8	81.6

Sources: GLRO DL/C/205; GL MS 9065.

trials.[21] But it is difficult to believe that such considerations arose for many, or any, of the deponents in the matrimonial and other non-heretical proceedings in the London-diocese causes used here, where the nature of the trial was quite different; certainly nothing in these depositions would encourage such a view.

Table 13.1 presents percentages of deponents appearing in the surviving fifteenth-century consistory courts who were described as *literatus* or otherwise, by occupation. Two separate tabulations are offered: one for Essex alone, and one for the entire diocese of London outside the city (and thus comprising Essex, Middlesex and most of Hertfordshire), in order to provide a more broadly based sample from the same region.

Several of the occupational subgroups in this table may be somewhat misleading. For one thing, although as one might hope to expect all the clergy in this table were described as *literatus*, for very few of the clerks appearing as deponents in the records was any notation of this

[21] Hudson, *The premature reformation*, pp. 185–6; Aston, 'William White's followers', pp. 97–8.

characteristic actually given, the presumption in nearly all cases being apparently that the information was superfluous. On the other hand, those deponents not designated by an occupation were much more likely to be described as *literatus* than any other group (clergy excluded), so it seems clear that some type of social selectiveness not made explicit in the details given for this group marked them off from the rest, and their experience is virtually impossible to place into context.

This leaves three groups with meaningfully large sample sizes, and as already noted these were males, mostly middle-aged, and mostly rural residents. Labourers, who, though relatively few in this sample, comprised nearly one-half of the 'households' in the 1381 Essex poll-tax returns, were in this sample exclusively *illiteratus*. The 'craftsmen/retailers' subgroup in the Essex sample were also completely *illiteratus*, though elsewhere in the diocese there were one *cirurgius*, one maltman and, not surprisingly, one *scriptor* who were denoted as *literatus*. On the other hand, although about 85 per cent of the agriculturalists in this sample were also *illiteratus*, the first halting steps towards acquiring literacy that this social group had taken by the later fifteenth century are yet another index of their relative differentiation from their humbler rural contemporaries. And their experience in this regard seems comparable to, indeed relatively unchanged from, that of husbandmen in the London diocese in the middle decades of the sixteenth century, when by Cressy's estimates literacy was still on the order of only about 20 per cent.[22] Significant gains for tradesmen and craftsmen would have had to await the proportionately more dramatic (because starting at a rather higher level) decline of illiteracy which Cressy has charted for the middle and later decades of the 1500s.[23] In fact, even though the two sets of estimates are based upon quite different empirical bases, the fifteenth-century Essex data seem to fit quite well with Cressy's projections of a half-century or so later, when some intervening minor improvement in literacy for all ranks is allowed for.

In sum, although the exact meaning of the terminology may remain slightly unclear and these figures may conceivably understate English reading literacy, this rare, direct evidence for literacy levels appears to validate the early-modernists' more pessimistic estimates of the growth of English literacy at the eve of the Reformation. Only agriculturalists – no more than one-quarter of Essex rural society at that time – register any indication in these sources of meaningful literacy levels. As the anecdotal Essex evidence implies, this minimal

22 Cressy, *Literacy and the social order*, p. 153.
23 *Ibid.*, pp. 149–57.

literacy need not have precluded what may be termed 'document-awareness' on the part of a somewhat larger proportion of local rural dwellers, who needed and used records of land transfers and agreements with craftsmen. And this should also not be taken to mean that no artisans or labourers whatsoever in the region were capable of reading – the Lollardy evidence of course provides evidence to the contrary – but rather that, on the basis of this sample at any rate, these social groups lagged significantly behind agriculturalists in educational accomplishment.

And it is striking that, while it would be difficult in the light of these data to continue to view craftsmen, retailers and clothworkers as the persons *best equipped* in late-medieval Essex to be the primary agents in the dissemination of written heretical doctrine, it is none the less these occupational and social groups that seemingly formed the core of the heretical movement. Such individuals continued to be a rich source for new recruits to unorthodoxy despite, rather than because of, disparities of literacy attainment. But this need not be surprising because, in view of the modes of transmission of the written word outside the ranks of the literate which have been shown to have existed, it need have taken only a proportionately insignificant number of literate artisans to transmit heretical attitudes and doctrine. The linkages between social change and industrial or commercial development, literacy and unorthodoxy are less direct than they have conventionally been depicted.

PART VII

Synthesis

Surveying its immediate prologue from the vantage point of their own period, modern historians of early-modern England have often elaborated a presumptive paradigm of the corporate village community of the middle ages. In sketching this picture they draw in part upon the writings of medievalists, but they are also concerned with the motive forces of economic and social change that pervade the Tudor and Stuart centuries. Retrospectively viewed in this way, corporate communities with internal cohesion and little in the way of social or cultural differentiation gave way, between 1500 and 1750, to a changed rural social order. Pressure of expanding population during the long sixteenth century drove irrevocable economic wedges between layers of rural society. The English Reformation destroyed a syncretic medieval popular religion, and then Puritanism effected a further widening of culture and ethos between the godly and the multitude, riven further still as the soaring literacy of the former (at least among males) consigned the latter to a more sharply delineated inferior cultural status. A capitalist market economy promoted economic individualism, while the spreading tentacles of the early-modern state quashed local autonomy but afforded to parish notables new avenues of social control.[1]

Such is the view that some historians have sketched when looking backward from the early-modern world. The view backward from that world is far from easy to comprehend. The fundamental nature of primary documentation for English local society changed enormously from the late-medieval to the early-modern period, a fact that conspires to raise correspondingly profound methodological issues. For

[1] Wrightson, 'Aspects of social differentiation', and Smith, '"Modernization" and the corporate medieval village community', are important statements of these presumptive transformations.

only comparatively few of the individual components of rural social structure are the sources, methods and analyses of the preceding chapters capable of yielding anything approximating watertight answers; nor, in line with the methodology of social science, are they strictly intended to be read as such. What is much clearer is the unanimity of direction in which the remarkable, and remarkably consistent, record of local social structure in Essex points. In this corner of England the world that fifteenth-century countryfolk knew as theirs was not so very alien from the world familiar to their descendants of one or two hundred years later.

Within the frame of reference for 'social structure', as these pages have parsed the phrase, demographic experience lay at the core of that late-medieval world. Geographical mobility in turn stands out as the least ambiguously documented component of the local demographic system, for this was a world in which only a relatively small minority passed their lives in one place even before 1350. The one-quarter or so of middle-aged male deponents of middling rank in ecclesiastical-court proceedings who still lived in their parish of birth corresponds strikingly closely to the one-quarter or so of locals with significant land endowments in contemporary rentals. For people without such ties to home, it was wage-earning opportunities that shaped the trajectory of mobility over the course of their life cycles. And in terms both of overall mobility and of its occupation-, status- and age-specific nature, fifteenth-century Essex was virtually indistinguishable from early-modern East Anglia.

Constraints of evidence upon other features of late-medieval demography are more severe; much still needs to be recovered of the specific variables of population processes in the pre-parish-register era. There is in fact a basic unanimity within the Essex tithing series, for a wide range of community sizes and types, concerning the aggregate outline of population change and the late-medieval demographic depression. Some features of the patterns these datasets outline deviate little from historians' established consensus. Others do: the local onset of population decline before the Black Death itself, for instance, or the delayed recovery commencing only in the second or third decade of the sixteenth century, the latter meshing very well with early parish-register data. And the more roundabout measures of mortality and fertility available from the district suggest that late-medieval population depression resulted from both fairly high mortality and fairly low fertility, both however resting comfortably within the same general order as England's early-modern experience.

What is more important here is not the absolute variables of population processes, whose derivation will probably always be arguable for this period, but rather the degree to which they add up to a demographic system of recognisable internal logic that is familiar from the post-medieval vantage. The respective estimates of mortality, fertility and nuptiality derived here from quite different bodies of evidence are consistent with one another, and with demographic equilibrium. But even more profoundly, they paint a coherent picture of the means by which local demography and local economy interacted with and mutually reinforced one another. Marriage and household formation, migration and settlement, all varied along lines cut by the occupational or status profile of local society: the means by which persons of differing circumstances fitted themselves into the interstices of the local economy resulted in different timing and incidence of nuptiality and migration. The peculiarities of the life cycles and migration patterns of servants and labourers resulted in settlement later in life, and later or less inevitable marriage. For those in the minority, with significant landholdings, the timing and incidence of these events were correspondingly different.

In short, all these features of local demography and the culture of family formation that they imply were both part cause and part consequence of the economy with which they coexisted. Within the broader perspective of comparative preindustrial economies, wage-labour markets of sizeable proportions tend to be associated with mobile populations, most of whose children 'are expected to leave home, accumulate their own wealth, choose their own marriage partners, and locate and occupy their own economic niche',[2] and thus a distinctly non-familistic ideology of family formation. New households come into being in tune with the tempo of living standards and expectations of future opportunity. Such, unambiguously, was the logic of the early-modern English demographic system and its dilatory homeostasis, its variant upon the Malthusian preventive check. Such, too, was that of the late-medieval Essex world, when the shape of landholding profiles and the structure of labour demand and its superficially paradoxical implications for labourers' incomes are taken into account.

In this respect the most salient features of the district's local economy were its predominance of wage-earners and the existence of an industrial sector, albeit of modest scale and imperfectly proletarianised but driven in part by export demand. All these features of local economic environment comprised a close corollary of the district's

[2] Schofield, 'Family structure and economic growth', p. 285; the arguments of this paragraph draw heavily from Schofield's remarks.

social structure. Each, in effect, presupposed the other. And although the origins of such a demographic regime are bound to remain a debating point, these reflections suggest one means of making sense of the pre-Black Death population decline. A densely populated and economically stratified local population, beginning a gradual, decades-long retreat from an earlier or more universal nuptiality pattern, would be consistent with the logic of the district's later demographic system and with observed decline in the second quarter of the 1300s. Though plausible and consistent with subsequent patterns, in the absence of earlier evidence such a scenario can only remain conjectural at this point.

If the district's record suggests differential demographic experiences cutting along occupational or status lines within local society, less clear-cut hints point to cultural heterogeneity also. Local literacy evidence and patterns of rural housing, each in its own modest way, suggest as much. In both of these cultural contexts the persistent dominance of the few more land-rich agriculturalists, the district's proto-yeomanry, by the decades around 1500 had already taken their first steps toward the more definitive distancing from the multitude that the sixteenth century would later exacerbate. To the extent that one can trust available data for participants in rural revolts and religious nonconformity, this tendency towards cultural heterogeneity applies here too. Most of these participants sprang, apparently, from the middling band of agriculturalists and craftsmen, in the central range of a highly stratified local society: neither, that is, from the mass of the rootless nor from those who most benefitted from the conditions of the post-Black Death economy.

Those who filled the upper ranks of this middling band, including village-level officialdom, simultaneously provided conspicuous leadership and organisational expertise for civil disorder and exercised measures of communal control against their inferiors. Religious nonconformist tendencies, which for many need not have taken on the fully articulated Lollard cosmological view, and precocious political consciousness helped to reinforce their motivations. Participation in civil unrest, however, sprang from many bases. The submerging of strictly anti-seigneurial animus among a welter of other causes is unambiguous. But the ground-level sociology of mass movements in the district was such that in no large-scale revolt, and perhaps in few episodes of more modest scale, did one simple rubric of protest express the agendas or aspirations of all those drawn into violence. In that sense, too, it is difficult to perceive any idealised, organic community of an undifferentiated rural past.

In all these ways, northern and central Essex fits only very uncomfortably into the matrix of synthetic cyclical or linear transition from the medieval to the early-modern world. Demographic change between, say, 1300 and 1650 was cyclical in the aggregate, but the normative rules of individual demographic behaviour persisted broadly unchanged across the medieval/early-modern divide. And although in some respects their pattern is less clearly capable of being delineated, and although they fluctuated in a long-term cyclical fashion, absolute measures of demographic rates remained recognisably within the same order of magnitude. Economic and cultural differentiation, even if in some cases in embryonic form during this earlier period, were functionally operative then as later. Religious ties and seigneurial or other dependencies were more discontinuous, but the ways rural people acted upon them were less so.

Essex was not England, and this study has been at pains to point out its peculiarities: its population density, its economic development, its enduring landscape. It is for a new generation of regional studies of social structures, and for a new paradigm of research, to situate the district's experience within a national context. But one should perhaps not make too much of its peculiarity either. After all it was this world, the world that the Walthamstow labourer Richard Gamone knew as his own in 1502, that lasted.

APPENDIX A

The fourteenth-century poll taxes

The foregoing study of late-medieval Essex has drawn heavily and in a number of different ways upon data from the later-fourteenth-century poll-tax returns. These sources pose large obstacles to anyone attempting to see through them some basic, systematic measures of post-Black Death society, economy and demography. A definitive study of all the issues that these sources pose has yet to be written. Nevertheless, the data are by no means entirely impervious to systematic analysis of broad, aggregate patterns, especially when taken at a county-wide level. But any such analysis must take into account a number of factors concerning the collection of these taxes, and particularly the tendencies of relative underenumeration apparent in their returns.

The three successive Parliamentary grants of poll taxes – in 1377, 1379 and 1380–1 – represented an innovative though short-lived experiment in English fiscal policy, compelled by the need to raise new revenues in the face of renewed threat of war with France.[1] In place of the traditional 'lay subsidy', a tax of fixed percentage upon moveable goods, the new tax was to be collected on a *per capita* basis, greatly widening the net of revenue collection by extending it to persons who would have been too poor to pay the older-style subsidy. The first collection, in 1377, was to be levied at a flat rate of 4d. per head upon all males and females aged 14 and older who were neither clerics nor genuinely impoverished. The two later collections, by contrast, were to be paid on a graduated scale (varying by rank or wealth) by lay people aged 16 (in 1379) or 15 (in 1380–1) years and older, with the poor again exempt.

[1] The discussion in the following three paragraphs is based mainly upon Fenwick, 'The English poll taxes'; Beresford, *Lay subsidies and poll taxes*; Poos, 'Population and resources', p. 139–58; Hilton, 'Some social and economic evidence'; Fryde, 'English Parliament and the peasants' revolt'.

The exact form in which local collections were recorded for each successive taxation varied considerably from county to county, and in some cases from hundred to hundred or even community to community, doubtless as a result of policies followed at local levels whose nature can be inferred only from the returns themselves. For most counties the local returns from 1377 provide only a total number of persons paying the tax in each respective vill or township (the most basic level of collection). On the other hand, enrolled accounts compiled by the central Exchequer provide county totals. For the latter two collections, however (and for a few 1377 collections also, such as those from Rutland and Northumberland and some towns, including York and Colchester), the returns took the form of lists of taxpayers' names in each vill. Occasionally these nominative listings furnish occupational or status designations and rudimentary 'household' information as well, in the form, to take a random example from Little Canfield (Essex) in 1381:

> John Raven, free tenant
> Cecilia his wife
> Agnes his daughter
> John Broun his servant[2]

Again, the degree of inclusion of such information as this and the nature of the terminology used are especially variable from place to place. Further details, such as notations of widowhood, are so sporadically given in many counties' returns as to provide no firm basis for systematic study. Another important variation in the available evidence is survival: for no county does the entire complement of returns from every individual vill survive for any given collection, let alone all three.

The most basic use to which historians have put this evidence is for estimating the total resident population of individual communities or larger areas.[3] For this purpose the 1377 returns have been regarded as by far the most reliable where they survive, because (as shown above, Chapter 7) the later collections generally touched demonstrably many fewer taxpayers. Indeed, what was clearly perceived by many as heavy-handed attempts to wring more revenue after the initial collec-

[2] PRO.E179.107.49 m.9:
'Johannes Raven liber tenens
Cecilia uxor eius
Agnes filia dicti Johannis
Johannes Broun serviens eius'

[3] E.g. Baker, 'Changes in the later middle ages', pp. 190–2.

tion of the third poll tax in Essex are generally agreed to have been the immediate cause of the 1381 revolt.[4]

The major issue, for historians considering the 1377 returns for this purpose, is the degree of 'evasion' that the collectors encountered. Russell concluded that evasion was no greater than 5 per cent of liable taxpayers, a figure Hatcher termed 'derisory', while Postan guessed it was closer to 25 per cent.[5] In view of the fact that in five Essex communities, total numbers of poll-tax payers in 1377 fall quite close to what one would expect from contemporary tithing data (above, Chapter 5), a figure rather closer to Russell's than Postan's does seem plausible for the Essex returns; with present evidence it is scarcely possible to be more precise than that. But a more fundamental issue, affecting interpretation of the returns from all three collections, is not so much the degree of underenumeration but the systematic biases evident in the inclusion or exclusion of certain groups on the basis of sex, marital status, and occupation or social status.

In her recent exhaustive study of all the surviving returns for the three poll-tax collections, Fenwick has persuasively argued that in certain critical respects what historians have taken to be demographic deficiencies in the returns – that is, 'evasions' by people liable to pay – can to a large extent be viewed as 'exclusions' of some categories of persons from liability that were quite legitimate under the terms of the tax collectors' briefs.[6] In particular she pointed out that the nature of 'poverty', for which exemption from the tax was granted, and which most historians have chosen to equate with genuine, open begging or absolute indigence, should be reconsidered in light of the taxation documents' own language and contemporary readings of their wording. This is especially true for 1380–1, when the Exchequer's writs and enrolled accounts spoke of *pauperi et mendicantes* ('poor and beggars'). Since it was the subcollectors in each township who were immediately responsible for assessing and collecting the tax from other members of their own communities, it was their perceptions which carried most weight in determining who were the exempt 'poor'. And there is no reason to regard these 'poor' as being restricted only to 'open beggars'. Rather, the term can be read more widely as those regarded by the subcollectors as the members of their communities from whom it would have been unjust to require payment.

This helps to make explicable some of the more obvious ways in

[4] See above, Chapter 11.

[5] Russell, *British medieval population*, pp. 124–30; Hatcher, *Plague, population and the English economy*, p. 14; Postan, *The medieval economy and society*, p. 29.

[6] Fenwick, 'The English poll taxes', esp. pp. 167–78.

which the raw poll-tax data deviate from what would under any reasonable set of expectations be the actual lay populations aged 15 and older in 1381. Most obviously, it has been generally agreed that servants, labourers and cottagers or smallholders are less numerous in these records in relation to more substantial agriculturalists or artisans than was actually the case in rural English society.[7] Even more fundamentally, one feature widely commented upon by those who have studied the tax listings is their underenumeration of single females: sex ratios (100 × [number of males/number of females]) in the lists for some counties exceed 110 or even 120, with individual vills' returns at times exceeding 200.

But single women, Fenwick argued, were also more likely to have been poor than married couples or single men, and so at least some of this shortfall of females may be due to exemptions by township subcollectors. At the same time it was doubtless more difficult for the subcollectors to be certain that an adolescent female had reached the age of 14 or 15, the minimum age liable for payment, than was the case with adolescent males, who were subject to compulsory tithing membership at the age of 12. Similarly, poverty was more likely to have been the experience of single persons who had not managed to acquire the resources necessary for foundation of independent households, so one might *a priori* expect that the percentage of persons recorded as married in the listings would be if anything an overestimate of the true proportions in English society at that time.

It is necessary to consider more closely the occupation- or status-specific tendencies toward exclusion which the collections of these taxes are known to have had, and then the probable connections between these tendencies and more general nuptiality patterns. That the later poll-tax collections in England generally were most likely to exclude the lowest statuses or economic levels of society is clear from the fact that in some counties where second tax collections (that is, from persons who previously had not paid) were made after revenues from the first had been found to be seriously deficient, surviving returns from these later collections list predominantly labourers and servants.

In one such case, that of Gloucestershire, Hilton has shown that servants were underenumerated by as much as 100 per cent in some vills during the first collection in 1381.[8] In seven vills in Leicestershire for which both first- and second-collection returns survive from the

[7] Hilton, 'Some social and economic evidence', pp. 120–1; Hilton, *The English peasantry in the later middle ages*, pp. 31–3.

[8] Hilton, *The English peasantry in the later middle ages*, p. 32.

same year, the proportion of servants among all taxpayers rose from 15.5 per cent (first collection) to 24.8 per cent (combined data from both first and second collections); labourers rose from 3.0 to 27.4 per cent, while agriculturalists fell from 54.0 to 28.3 per cent.[9]

Unfortunately no such direct evidence is available for the Essex tax returns. In its absence, though, there seems no reason to doubt that these 'exclusions' in Essex were also composed largely of servants – almost by definition nearly universally single, and appearing in rather small numbers in the 1381 Essex returns – and labourers. In short, the sex-specific and occupation- or status-specific nature of systematic underenumeration in these records constitutes their most serious shortcoming. But it is a shortcoming that, by its very nature, can be recognised and to some degree accounted for, so long as large aggregative samples are analysed for broad tendencies rather than precise calibrations.

In a similar sense, at various points this study has referred to estimates of the total resident populations of Essex communities, or other aspects of their age and sex structures, on the basis of the 1377 returns (see especially Chapters 2 and 7). It should be emphasised that these estimates are presented only as rough approximations, and must not be taken to imply a spurious precision. In particular, estimates like these for individual communities, as opposed to entire hundreds or larger aggregations, are order-of-magnitude measures only. These estimates have been based upon Princeton Model West life tables.[10] The Princeton tables are derived from a variety of historical contexts, and (among other things) they include projections of relative proportions within a base population that represent different sex and age groups. Model West, one of four models in the Princeton tables, is used here because it appears to fit most closely the characteristics of infant and child mortality (the most critical factor in deriving proportions of under-14s to total population) observable in the earliest English parish registers, though it may in fact result in a modest underestimate of the proportion of those aged less than 14 years to total population.[11]

[9] Preliminary calculation from PRO.E179.133.35; cf. Poos, 'Population and resources', p. 150n. A much more systematic assessment of first-collection exclusion tendencies will be possible when the Fenwick/Smith poll-tax database is completely assembled and analysed.

[10] Coale and Demeny, *Regional model life tables*.

[11] Princeton Model West fits age-ranges above 10 years reasonably well in the earliest English parish-register reconstitution data, those of the later sixteenth century, but earlier age-ranges are better approximated by Princeton Model North tables at lower mortality rates: Schofield and Wrigley, 'Infant and child mortality in Tudor–Stuart England', esp. p. 95n. There is, of course, no empirical basis for believing that

These tables enable one to take a number that purports to be a population's males and females aged 14+ (as the 1377 poll-tax returns purport to do) and inflate to a total population reflecting all ages. The pertinent inflation factor within the Model West tables is mainly a function of two demographic variables. One is life expectancy. Wherever this study estimates total residents from 1377 poll-tax payers, a range of extreme values is given, based upon extreme assumptions of life expectancy at birth (e_0): these are Princeton mortality levels 1 and 8, corresponding to female e_0 under zero population growth of 20.0 and 37.5 years respectively, or in other words mortality experiences ranging from much worse than, to roughly equivalent to, England's national levels in the sixteenth century.[12] The Princeton life tables also make it necessary to estimate underlying population growth rates relevant to a given situation: here, based upon Essex tithing series (see Chapter 5), growth of −0.5 per cent per annum is assumed for estimates of population in 1377. On the basis of Princeton tables the total number of 1377 poll-tax payers should thus be multiplied by 1.323 and 1.454 (the ratios in Model West tables of all ages to ages 14+, both sexes), for a corresponding range of total population estimates. Occasionally a similar kind of estimate for total resident population has been made in the preceding pages (e.g. Chapter 2) on the basis of tithing data, representing resident males aged 12+. Model West has been used in the same fashion here also, with appropriate growth rates presumed (for the fifteenth century, 0.0 per cent per annum).

Inevitably, these are approximations only. Not only do they omit (as the poll-taxes and tithings themselves did) clergy,[13] they are also deficient in the case of the poll taxes by a further factor – unknown but, at an informed conjecture, at least 5 or 10 per cent, due to the patterns of poll-tax underenumeration already discussed. As used here these estimates mostly aspire to no more than illustrative impressions of relative community size, and where these further shortcomings pose particular interpretative dilemmas, their implications are explored in the chapters above via alternative extreme scenarios.

later-medieval Essex was identical in this respect, but this is the earliest English situation capable of illustrating the exact age structure of mortality.

12 Wrigley and Schofield, *Population history of England*, p. 528.

13 Omission of clergy is unlikely to distort these estimates greatly. The 1381 clerical poll tax (whose definitive analysis awaits further research) netted only 394 taxpaying clergy in Essex: Russell, *British medieval population*, p. 136.

APPENDIX B

Time-series of economic data

At various points in this study it has been necessary to refer to time-series data for economic trends over the later fourteenth and fifteenth centuries. Thus Chapter 2 presents data for land farms (cash rents per acre of arable land let to tenants for terms of years) and for grain prices (sale price per quarter – eight bushels – of wheat and barley). Chapter 10 presents similar series for per-diem cash wages of carpenters and labourers. The purpose of this appendix is to discuss further the sources for these data and the conventions that have been adopted for their selection and compilation.

These data come from the account rolls of various manors within the north-central district of Essex. Manorial accounts have long served as the most important source for price, wage and rent data from medieval England, and a substantial literature is available on the subject.[1] These accounts recorded, among many other things, sales of grain raised on the manorial lord's own 'demesne' land, wages paid to workers of many different varieties who were hired by the lord's officials for agricultural or other work, and rent or lease payments (often itemised) for land and other types of property that tenants held. The strengths of these sources are well known. They are a relatively abundant and accessible source for economic data compiled on an annual basis over a very long period, from the later thirteenth century to (in some cases, at least) the end of the middle ages.

The drawbacks inherent in these data are also familiar to students of medieval English agrarian history. The wages they recorded for occasional hiring of skilled and unskilled workers pertain to a very specific employment context: hiring workers by manorial officials,

[1] For this topic in general, see Harvey, *Manorial records*, pp. 25–41. Studies of wages and prices from these records include Beveridge, 'Westminster wages'; Thorold Rogers, *History of agriculture and prices*; Farmer, 'Crop yields, prices and wages'.

who competed in a labour market with other employers and who had their own particular configuration of labour needs that may have been distinct from those of the demand side of that market at large. The grain prices recorded in these accounts are prices paid to producers rather than, necessarily, those paid by ultimate consumers; they are, in effect, possibly closer to 'wholesale' than 'retail' prices. And for both wages and grain prices, data tend to become quite sparse after 1400, when agricultural production on lords' demesne lands was being phased out at most manors in favour of leasing that land to tenants. And so from thenceforth manorial accounts simply had no grain sales, and less frequent and more restricted types of hiring, to record.

The time-series data in question come from the accounts of eight manors plus three other groups of estates in the district. The manors were those of Birdbrook, Bocking, Borley, Claret Hall in Ashen, Crondon in Stock, Felsted, Lindsell and Moulsham, plus collected manors from the estates of the Bohun family, Canterbury Cathedral Priory and Colne Priory.[2] Archival references are given in the Bibliography, below. These account-roll series have been combined to produce an aggregated dataset for the district at large. For example, for each year in the series (taking the Michaelmas-to-Michaelmas accounting year 1385/6 as 1385),[3] all grain sales recorded in all surviving accounts for that year were summed, and aggregated sales revenue was divided by aggregated sales volume to produce an index of price per unit for the year in question.

Traditionally, agrarian historians have compiled such data for individual manors or lordships. But most of these Essex account-roll series are highly discontinuous, due to irregular document survival, and also because not every surviving account contains grain sales, hiring data, or land farms. Aggregating the series, as has been done here, thus makes it possible to construct a more continuous dataset over time, and one that is broadly based among different communities

[2] In the case of Claret Hall, the Colne Priory estates, Crondon, Lindsell and Moulsham, the account rolls included in the dataset represent all the surviving, legible rolls for the manors in question. In the cases of Bocking, Borley, Felsted and the Bohun and Canterbury estates, included in the present dataset are only a random sample of accounts from the surviving series. In the case of Birdbrook, a random sample was taken of accounts before 1375/6, then every account roll after that was searched for usable data. The complete dataset represents data from 249 individual account rolls.

[3] This convention was chosen because it was the harvest of 1385 that chiefly determined price levels of grain sold throughout the accounting year 1385/6. The convention adopted here is consistent with Beveridge's practice but not with Titow's, with Phelps-Brown and Hopkins', or with Wrigley and Schofield's: Titow, *Winchester yields*, p. 35; Wrigley and Schofield, *Population history of England*, p. 641.

throughout the district. Such a procedure does have one potential drawback, however. The index price for a unit of grain, for instance, may represent the weighted mean of a different collection of manors in each successive year, because of the highly discontinuous nature of the data from most individual manors over time. In fact, for any given year in the later 1300s, the aggregate price index typically represents data from no more than three or four manors or estates, and in the early 1400s no more than one or two. If it were the case that any given manor's grain sales consistently fetched significantly higher prices than those at other manors, for whatever reason, then conceivably the year-on-year fluctuations in the aggregated price index as calculated here might be partly a reflection of that manor's intermittent inclusion in or exclusion from the index. Ideally one should be able to test for consistent differences like this between manors. But in practice, with such discontinuous individual series and with the wide year-on-year fluctuations inherent in pre-modern grain prices especially, it is doubtful that any such test could be contrived that would be meaningful. All one can do here is note that no consistently 'rogue' series are evident within the dataset at large.

Within each category of data aggregated in this way, it has been necessary to adopt strict criteria in order to ensure as much as possible that the resulting series consistently measure the same phenomena between manors and over time. These criteria can be summarised as follows.

Land farms

Data are taken only from sections of accounts headed *firme terre* or the like. This dataset also includes only farms expressed in cash rents for a specific number of acres of *terra* or arable land (i.e. not simply a 'croft' or similar unspecified area, and not meadow or pasture), and excludes any property described as including houses or other buildings. Farm data here pertain only to the annual cash rent, and so exclude the entry fine that was usually paid when a tenant took up the property and that was seldom itemised separately in the account as such. For any given year the aggregate index is the total sum of cash farms recorded, divided by the total number of acres involved, that meet these criteria in all the surviving account rolls for that year.

These data are the most variable of the three categories aggregated here at the level of the individual property, as would be expected since landholdings doubtless varied greatly in productivity or desirability. On the other hand, once initiated, a lease of this sort often persisted for a number of years and can be observed over a series of accounts, even if no other description (a tenement-name or former tenant's name, for example) is given in addition to its simple acreage and farm rate. For this reason, then, the aggregated series over the medium to long term contains the least pronounced year-on-year fluctuations, comprising as it does a stable core of properties, each persisting many years during the course of the dataset. Moreover, for the same reason the resulting index tracks a measure that in any given year represents not the marginal rate at which new leases were being agreed in that year, but rather an amalgam of rates from a number of leases current in that year, some more and some less recently initiated.

Grain prices

Data are taken from all sales of wheat and barley expressed in tangible units of volume and sales proceeds. For any given year the aggregate index is the total sale proceeds, divided by the volume of sales, of wheat and barley in all surviving account rolls for that year. Superficially this is straightforward. In practice, any manor's grain sales data for a given year are a composite of different sales made at various times within the year, often for different prices in successive months, and the seasonal configuration of sales probably reflected that manor's particular considerations of cash-flow needs and marketing strategy. At Birdbrook in 1395/6, ten quarters of barley were sold in November at 4s. per quarter, ten more quarters in February at 4s. 8d., two and a half quarters 'afterward' at the same price, and so forth.[4] But this is only seldom spelled out fully in the accounts, which usually give one simple total for all sales over the accounting year. As another complication potentially affecting the price-index data, demesne grain diverted to consumption by the manorial lord or lady's household was entered into accounts as notional sales, though there seems no reason to suspect that the notional sums recorded for these 'sales' varied significantly from prevailing market prices per volume.[5] And so the aggregated index figure for grain price for all manors in each year is an especially heterogenous figure. Nevertheless, its extreme variability on a year-on-year basis is chiefly ascribable to

[4] WAM 25491: '... x quarteria ordei vendita ... mense Novembris ... x quarteria ordei postea vendita ... mense Februarii ... ij quarteria iiij buscelli ordei postea vendita ...'.

[5] E.g. PRO.SC6.838.22 (Claret Hall account, 1347/8): '... xx quarteria frumenti vendita ad expensa hospitie domine ... precio quarterij viijs. ... xviij quarteria ordei vendita dicte hospitie ... precio quarterij vs. ... ij quarteria iij buscelli & dimidius ordei vendita in Mercato ... precio quarterij vs. iiijd. ...'.

variability inherent in the period's grain-price behaviour, stemming from harvest fluctuations.

Wage rates

Data are taken from all itemised hirings of carpenters and of labourers that were recorded with number of days worked and wages earned. No data are included from hirings for which meals explicitly represented part of the worker's payment.[6] It occasionally happened, especially in the period of escalating wages after 1350, that the reeve or other manorial official reported having hired and paid workers at a certain wage rate, but auditors subsequently disallowed this expenditure (on the grounds that the wages paid were too high) and altered the account to reduce the recorded payments; in such cases the reeve would have been responsible for making up the difference out of his own pocket.[7] In instances where such a thing is apparent in the account roll, the dataset includes the higher wage rate, because that is the more realistic figure for actual earnings.

Identifying carpenters' wages in the accounts is fairly straightforward. In most cases they are actually called *carpentarii* in the documents, whether they are named or not. In other instances the nature of the tasks they performed makes their trade clear. Carpenters whose employment was recorded in manorial accounts were hired typically to build or repair buildings, mills, or agricultural equipment belonging to the manor. The dataset omits cases where a carpenter's wages and those of his assistant or apprentice cannot be separated.[8]

Criteria demarcating labourers' inclusion in the dataset are rather less easily summarised. The data include only male labourers, because female labourers crop up exceedingly rarely in these sources. Harvest workers are not included here, because wages in that season were higher than at other times of the year (see above, Chapter 10) and so an index comprising shifting proportions of harvest and non-harvest

[6] E.g. PRO.SC6.838.23 (Claret Hall account, 1348/9): '. . . in xlvj hominibus & dimidio conductis ad metendum garbas per j diem quolibet capiente per diem ad mensam vd. – xixs.iiijd. ob.'.

[7] E.g. PRO.SC6.838.30 (Claret Hall account, 1357/8): '. . . In stipendio j carpentarij per iiij dies facientis stothes & chencron' & illa imponentis in domum feni & straminis xijd. capiendo per diem iijd. [crossed out: xvjd. capiendo per diem iiijd.]'.

[8] Included, however, are cases where these wages are kept separate, e.g. PRO.SC6.839.9 (Claret Hall account, 1374/5): '. . . In stipendio Johannis Nichel carpentarij per iij septimanias emendentis tibias dagshoos & le Fullyngstoks molendini fullonici ibidem vijs. vd. per diem vd. Et in stipendio Roberti Heg' per x dies auxilientis eidem opere iijs. iiijd. per diem iiijd. Et in stipendio unius apprentici dicti Roberti per vj dies auxilientis eidem opere xviijd. per diem iijd.'. Here, only the wages of the carpenter John Nichel are included in the dataset.

work would be inconsistent. Nor are tasks included, such as threshing, that were usually recorded on a piece-work payment basis. At times labourers are identified by that term in the accounts.[9] But the dataset also includes hirings of men, without the term *laborarius* appended, for unskilled or semiskilled work, most typically digging,[10] shovelling manure,[11] or carrying goods.[12] Cases where a man was hired along with his horse, cart or wagon are omitted, since his payment may well have included an increment representing the use of his equipment. As it turns out, despite the inevitably somewhat miscellaneous nature of the hirings included as those of 'labourers' in the dataset, the rather narrow band within which *per-diem* wage rates fluctuate in this series between different manors in the district, and over the short term, encourages confidence that these data do represent realistically the wage rates of the least skilled Essex labourers during the period.

[9] PRO.DL29.43.828 (Bohun manors, Great Waltham account, 1442/3): '... Et in stipendio unius laborari per unum diem evacuantis terram fundi subtus gruncillas grangie & stabuli manerj ad locum aptum ibidem erga novam gruncillacionem ... ut neccesse erat iijd.'.

[10] E.g. PRO.SC6.839.4 (Claret Hall account, 1363/4): '... In stipendio j hominis per j diem fodientis argillam pro opere molendini iij d.'.

[11] E.g. PRO.SC6.842.7 (Felsted account, 1423/4): '... abiecentes fimos ab hostiis & muris stabularum ...'.

[12] E.g. PRO.SC6.839.3 (Claret Hall account, 1362/3): '... In stipendio j hominis per iij dies euntis ad cariandum ... ixd. per diem iijd.'.

APPENDIX C

Essex fulling mills

This appendix summarises documentary references to the Essex fulling mills known to have been in existence between the later thirteenth and early sixteenth centuries and mapped and discussed in Chapter 3. It makes no pretence at being comprehensive. In particular, because of the sporadic nature of some of the sources involved (such as inquisitions post mortem) and the sporadic survival of references to mills in others (such as manorial court rolls and accounts), one must not presume that the earliest recorded reference to any single mill coincided at all with its construction, nor that one isolated reference, or even two references separated by many years, imply that a given mill was continually in operation throughout the period. The author here gratefully acknowledges references to fulling mills in Britnell, *Growth and decline in Colchester*, pp. 14, 76, 157, 185, 229, from which several of these references were taken.

Ashen (manor of Claret Hall): 1391/2 [PRO.SC6.839.14], 1398/9 [PRO.SC6.839.15], manorial accounts.

West Bergholt: 1445 [*Essex feet of fines* vol. iv, p. 35]; 1472 [PRO.C140.41.34], inquisition post mortem extent; *circa* 1500 (Britnell, *Growth and decline in Colchester*, p. 185).

Birdbrook: 1344/5 [WAM 25441] to 1360/1 [WAM 25456], manorial accounts (fulling mill noted as 'otiosum et dirructum' in latter account); 1388/9 [WAM 25484] to 1434/5 [WAM 25508], recorded as at farm in manorial accounts; noted as 'totaliter devastatum' in 1443/4 [WAM 25516], manorial account; not mentioned again in surviving account rolls into second decade of sixteenth century.

Bocking: 1303 [BL MS Cotton Galba E.iv fo. 106], account for construction of new mill by prior of Christ Church, Canterbury; 1309 [BL MS Harley 1006 fo. 2], manorial extent; 1342/3 to 1457/8 [CALC beadles' rolls, Bocking] and to 1526/7 [CALC miscellaneous accounts vol. 15 fo. 31v], farms of and repairs to fulling mill recorded in intermittently surviving manorial accounts.

Boreham: 1315 [PRO.C134.34.4], inquisition post mortem extent; 1437 [PRO.SC2.171.32], manorial court roll: ' . . . Et preceptum est ballivo distringere contra proximam curiam terram tenentum medietatis unius molendini aquatici aliter nuncupati a fullyngmelle & unius parcelli prati . . . que tenentur de domino huius manerij per medietatem unius feodi militis . . . '.

Coggeshall: 1305 [PRO.C133.117.15], inquisition post mortem extent.

Colchester: *circa* 1350–1400 [Britnell, *Growth and decline in Colchester*, p. 76], three or four mills in operation; 1466 [PRO.C140.21.41], inquisition post mortem extent; 1490 [Britnell, *Growth and decline in Colchester*, p. 229], a new mill constructed.

Dedham: 1388 [*Calendar of inquisitions miscellaneous* vol. v, p. 133], inquisition.

Feering: 1361 [WAM 25677], manorial account.

Felsted: 1392/3 [ERO D/DSp M37], 1399/1400 [ERO D/DSp M38], 1424/5 [PRO.SC6.842.7], manorial accounts.

Finchingfield: 1300 [PRO.C133.93.9], inquisition post mortem extent.

Fordham: 1414/15 [BL Egerton Roll 2181], manorial account.

Foxearth: 1360 [PRO.C135.150.18], inquisition post mortem extent.

Halstead: 1339 [PRO.C135.60.9], inquisition post mortem extent.

Hatfield Peverel: 1337 [PRO.C135.51.11], inquisition post mortem extent.

Great or Little Horksley: 1476 [PRO.C140.53.41], inquisition post mortem extent.

Lawford: 1287 [PRO.C133.47.8], inquisition post mortem extent.

Manningtree: 1309 [PRO.C146.906], charter.

Little Maplestead: *circa* 1275 [Gervers, ed., *Cartulary of St John*, p. 385], charter. Professor Gervers (personal communication) suggests that this mill may have lain within Halstead township.

Stanstead Mountfichet: 1414/15 [BL Egerton Roll 2181], manorial account.

Stebbing: 1422/3 [BL Add. Roll 65958], manorial rental.

Ulting: 1518 [ERO D/ACR 2/83], will.

Great Waltham: 1336 [PRO.C135.48.2], inquisition post mortem extent; 1402/3 [BL Egerton Roll 2182], manorial account; 1442/3 [PRO.DL29.43.828], manorial account.

Wethersfield: 1319 [PRO.C134.63.27], inquisition post mortem extent.

Witham: 1307 [PRO.E142.1.10]; 1309 [Gervers, ed., *Cartulary of St John*, p. 52], charter.

Woodham Walter: 1328 [PRO.C135.12], inquisition post mortem extent.

Wrabness: 1383 [Fisher, *Medieval farming glossary*, p. 15], manorial court roll.

Writtle: 1406 [ERO D/DP M209 m.4v], manorial court roll.

Bibliography

I MANUSCRIPT SOURCES

The following section lists only the most important or most frequently cited manuscripts or classes of documentary sources used in this study. Manuscripts are listed here under type of source. Within the first three subheadings (containing manorial records), sources are listed by manor. In the case of manorial court rolls and accounts, dates provided here indicate the periods within which records have been cited or otherwise referred to for this study. These dates should not be taken to imply either that the records in question survive continuously throughout the years cited, or that the extant record series are limited only to those years.

A Essex manorial court rolls

PRO.DL30.58.717–22	Barnston: 1395–1501
ERO D/DU M565/1–4	Berden: 1334–90
NCO 3595–9	Birchanger (Priors Hall): 1391–1555
ERO D/DU 267/29–31, 85–7; WAM 25567–70	Birdbrook: 1293–1454
ERO D/DK M108; D/DHt M92–7	Blackmore (Finegreth Hall): 1327–1508
CALC U15.11.1–13	Bocking: 1382–90
PRO.SC2.171.25, 27, 30, 32–3	Boreham (Boreham Hall): 1348–1456
BL Add. Roll 19108	Little Canfield: 1400–12
ERO D/DMg M39–42	Great Dunmow: 1387–1509
PRO.SC2.171.64	Little Dunmow: 1328–77
PRO.DL30.63.750 – DL30.72.891	High Easter: 1266–1520
ERO D/DCw M97–101	Fyfield: 1386–1441
ERO D/DP M874–7	South Hanningfield: 1339–1508
ERO D/DGe M251; ERO D/DK M1; BL Add. Roll 28555	Hatfield Broadoak: 1315–1459
PRO.SC2.173.6	Hordon on the Hill and Seaborough Hall: 1335–57
ERO D/DP M15–54	Ingatestone: 1305–1471

Bodl. Essex Rolls 8	Little Leighs: 1285–1318
NCO 3655–9	Lindsell (Priors Hall): 1363–1508
Bodl. MS Ch. Essex 1187	Pentlow: 1354
UCO Pyx G–H	Margaret Roding: 1318–1598
BL Add. Rolls 65926, 65929, 65933, 65936–7; BL Add. MS 40632A; PRO.DL30.77.979; PRO.SC2.173.89	Stebbing: 1409–1543
NCO 3697–3700	Takeley (St Valery's or Warish Hall): 1356–1508
JRL Tey Magna rolls 1–6	Great Tey: 1399–1557
PRO.DL30.63.750 – DL30.68.850; ERO D/DTu M239–42; ERO D/DHh M151	Great Waltham (Walthambury): 1265–1528
ERO D/DTu M257–9	Great Waltham (Chatham Hall): 1308–1465
NCO 3620–4	Widdington (Priors Hall): 1391–1546
ERO D/DBw M98–100	Witham and Cressing: 1326–1442
ERO D/DP M189–295	Writtle: 1382–1492

B *Essex manorial accounts*

PRO.SC6.838.6–13, 16–18, 20–25, 29–30; PRO.SC6.839.1–4, 6–10, 12–15	Ashen (Claret Hall): 1323/4–1398/9
WAM 25406–8, 25431–2, 25434, 25436–8, 25440–1, 25443–5, 25447, 25449, 25454–6, 25458–9, 25461, 25463, 25465, 25469, 25471–25566	Birdbrook: 1301/2–1515/16
CALC beadles' rolls; CALC Misc. Accts. 6	Bocking: 1336/7–1478/9
BL Egerton Rolls 2181–2; PRO.DL29.42.820, 826, 828, 829	Bohun estates: 1402/3–1454/5
CALC beadles' rolls; CALC misc. accts. 6, 12, 13	Borley: 1331/2–1521/2
CALC misc. accts. 6, 12, 13	Canterbury estates: 1479/80–1521/2
ERO D/DPr 13–14, 17–18	Colne Priory estates: 1374/5–1441/2
ERO D/DSp M38–9; PRO.SC6.842.7	Felsted: 1400/1–1423/4
NCO 9185	Lindsell (Priors Hall): 1475/6
ERO D/DM M69–83, 118, 131, 133, 140; ERO D/DGe M87	Moulsham: 1338/9–1471/2
ERO D/DP M806–31	Stock (Crondon Hall): 1342/3–1454/5

C *Essex manorial rentals*

PRO.DL43.2.5	Barnston: 1435
BL MS Harley 1006	Canterbury estates: 1308–9
PRO.DL43.2.32	High Easter: 1328
PRO.SC11.188	Felsted: 1367
ERO D/DCw M158/1	Felsted: 1576
ERO D/DBa M3	Hatfield Broadoak: *circa* 1450

PRO.DL43.3.8	Great Leighs: *circa* 1400
ERO D/DP M1411	Margaretting (Fristling Hall): 1340
PRO.SC12.7.44	Matching (Housham Hall): 1288
BL Add. Roll 66041	Stebbing: 1294
BL Add. Roll 65957	Stebbing: 1383
BL Add. Roll 65958	Stebbing: 1422
BL Add. Roll 66046	Stebbing: 1444
BL Add. Roll 66054	Stebbing: 1487
ERO D/DHu M58	Thaxted: 1393
BL Cotton Ch. XIII.5	Great Waltham: 1328

D *Ecclesiastical records*

GL MS 9065	diocese of London, depositions: 1489–97
GL MS 9065B	diocese of London, depositions: 1488
GLRO DL/C/205	diocese of London, depositions: 1467–76
CALC X.10.1	diocese of Canterbury, depositions: 1410–21
SJCC D57.170	diocese of Rochester, consistory court: 1363–4
LPL reg. Arundel	register of Thomas Arundel, Archbishop of Canterbury: 1396–7, 1399–1414
WRO D1/2/9	register of Robert Nevill, bishop of Salisbury: 1427–38
ERO D/DBy Q12	Walden churchwardens' account, 1439–88

E *Royal-court records*

PRO.KB145.3.6.1; PRO.KB9.166.2	inquests into revolt: 1381
PRO.JUST2.36.3	King's Bench indictments, Essex: 1380
PRO.KB9.25	King's Bench indictments, Essex: 1389
PRO.KB9.204.1	inquests into Lollards and Oldcastle's rebellion: 1414
PRO.KB9.268	inquests into Cade's rebellion: 1451
PRO.KB27.-	King's Bench, plea roll series
PRO.CP40.-	Common Pleas, plea roll series
PRO.JUST2.35.5	coroner's inquests, Essex: 1370–5

F *Taxation returns*

PRO.E179.107.46–8, 50–3, 55–8	poll-tax returns, Essex: 1377
PRO.E179.107.49, 59–60, 63–5, 67–9, 75; E179.123.44; E179.240.308	poll-tax returns, Essex: 1381

PRO.E101.342.9	aulnage accounts, Essex: 1395–7
PRO.E101.342.13	aulnage accounts, Essex: 1398–9
PRO.E101.343.4	aulnage accounts, Essex: 1467–8
PRO.E179.108.151, 154, 161	lay subsidy, Essex (Chelmsford, Witham, Dunmow Hundreds): 1524

G Miscellaneous manuscript sources

PRO.C133–C141	inquisitions post mortem, reigns of Edward I – Richard III
PRO.E137.11.2	estreat roll of fines imposed under Statute of Labourers, Essex: 1352
ERO D/DCm Z 18/5	partition of lands and buildings, Witham: 1359
WAM 28079	bond for recovery of fugitive serf, Birdbrook: 1378
PRO.SC8.10737	petition by Hatfield Broadoak Priory to royal council: 1378
BL Add. Ch. 28604	bond for arbitration between Hatfield Broadoak Priory and parishioners: 1378
Bodl. MS Top. Essex b.5 (R)	precedent-roll of serfdom-related cases, Waltham Abbey manors: later fourteenth century
BL Add. Roll 66051	farmer's account, Stebbing (Porter's Hall): 1483/4

II PRINTED PRIMARY SOURCES

Bracton, H., *On the laws and customs of England*, ed. G. E. Woodbine, tr. S. E. Thorne, 5 vols. (Cambridge, MA, 1968–77).

British Parliamentary papers: 1851 census, Great Britain, vol. 6, *Population* (reprinted, Shannon, 1970).

Calendar of close rolls (London, 1892–).

Calendar of inquisitions miscellaneous (London, 1916–).

Calendar of patent rolls (London, 1891–).

Chibnall, M., ed., *Charters and custumals of the Abbey of Holy Trinity Caen* (Oxford, 1982).

Curling, T. H., ed., 'The gild of All Saints, Moreton', *Transactions of the Essex Archaeological Society* new series xi (1910), 223–9.

Dewindt, E. B., ed., *The Liber Gersumarum of Ramsey Abbey* (Toronto, 1976).

Emmison, F. G., ed., *Wills at Chelmsford*, vol. i, British Record Society 78 (1958).

Essex feet of fines, ed. R. G. Kirk *et al.*, 4 vols. (Colchester, 1899–1964).

Fitch, M., ed., *Index to testamentary records in the Commissary Court of London*, vols. i–ii, British Record Society 82, 86 (London, 1969, 1974).

Flenley, R., ed., *Six town chronicles of England* (Oxford, 1911).

Fowler, R. C., ed., *Registrum Simonis de Sudbiria diocesis Londoniensis AD 1362–1375*, Canterbury and York Society 34, 38 (1927, 1938).

Foxe, J., *Acts and monuments*, ed. S. R. Cattley and G. Townsend, 8 vols. (reprinted, New York, 1965).
Friedberg, E. A., ed., *Corpus Juris Canonici*, 2 vols. (2nd edn, Graz, 1959).
Furber, E. C., ed., *Essex sessions of the peace 1351, 1377–1379*, Essex Archaeological Society occasional publications 3 (1953).
Gervers, M., ed., *The cartulary of the Knights of St John of Jerusalem in England* (Oxford, 1982).
Glasscock, R. E., ed., *The lay subsidy of 1334* (London, 1975).
Harriss, G. L. and M. A., eds., 'John Benet's chronicle for the years 1400 to 1462', *Camden Miscellany*, Camden Society 4th series 9 (1972), 151–233.
Harvey, P. D. A., ed., *Manorial records of Cuxham, Oxfordshire, circa 1200–1359*, Oxfordshire Record Society 1 (1976).
Jacob, E. F., ed., *The register of Henry Chichele, Archbishop of Canterbury, 1414–1443*, 4 vols. (Oxford, 1938–47).
Maitland, F. W., ed., *The court baron*, Selden Society iv (1890).
Myrc, J., *Instructions for parish priests*, ed. E. Peacock, Early English Text Society, original series 31 (1868).
Nichols, J. G. ed., *Narratives of the Reformation, chiefly from the manuscripts of John Foxe the martyrologist*, Camden Society 77 (1859).
Norden, J., *Speculum Britanniae pars: An historical and chorographical description of the county of Essex*, ed. H. Ellis, Camden Society 9 (1840).
Oschinsky, D., ed., *Walter of Henley and other treatises on estate management and accounting* (Oxford, 1971).
Powicke, F. M. and C. R. Cheney, eds., *Council and synods, with other documents relating to the English church*, 2 vols. (Oxford, 1964).
Riley, H. T., ed., *Annales monasterii S. Albani a Johanne Amundesham monacho* (London, 1870).
Robbins, R. H., ed., *Secular lyrics of the xivth and xvth centuries* (2nd edn, Oxford, 1955).
Rotuli Parliamentorum, 6 vols. (n.p., n.d.).
Rumble, A., ed., *Domesday Book 32: Essex* (Chichester, 1983).
Statutes of the realm (London, 1810–28).
Steer, F. W., ed., 'The statutes of Saffron Walden almshouses', *Transactions of the Essex Archaeological Society* new series xxv (1958), 161–221.
Tanner, N. P., ed., *Heresy trials in the diocese of Norwich 1428–31*, Camden Society 4th series 20 (1977).
Thomas, A. H. and I. D. Thornley, eds., *The Great Chronicle of London* (London, 1938).
Thompson, E. M., ed., *Chronicon Adae de Usk* (2nd edn, London, 1904).
Williams, B., ed., *Chronique de la traison et mort de Richard Deux Roy Dengleterre* (London, 1846).
Wood, A. C., ed., *Registrum Simonis Langham Cantuariensis Archiepiscopi*, Canterbury and York Society 53 (1956).

III SECONDARY SOURCES

Allen, R. H. and R. G. Sturdy, 'The environmental background', in D. G. Buckley, ed., *Archaeology in Essex to AD 1500*, Council for British Archaeology Research Report 34 (1980), 1–7.

Aston, M., *Lollards and reformers: Images and literacy in late medieval religion* (London, 1984).

'Lollardy and literacy', in M. Aston, *Lollards and reformers*, 193–218.

'Lollardy and sedition, 1381–1431', in M. Aston, *Lollards and reformers*, 1–48.

'William White's Lollard followers', in M. Aston, *Lollards and reformers*, 71–100.

Aston, T. H. and C. H. E. Philpin, eds., *The Brenner debate: Agrarian class structure and economic development in pre-industrial Europe* (Cambridge, 1985).

Ault, W. O., 'Open-field husbandry and the village community: A study of agrarian by-laws in medieval England', *Transactions of the American Philosophical Society* new series 55 (1965), 5–102.

Bak, J. M. and G. Benecke, 'Religion and revolt?', in J. M. Bak and G. Benecke, eds., *Religion and rural revolt* (Manchester, 1984), 2–13.

Baker, A. R. H., 'Changes in the later middle ages', in H. C. Darby, ed., *A new historical geography of England before 1600* (Cambridge, 1976), 186–247.

Bennett, J. M., 'Medieval peasant marriage: An examination of marriage license fines in the *Liber Gersumarum*', in J. A. Raftis, ed., *Pathways to medieval peasants* (Toronto, 1981), 193–246.

'The tie that binds: Peasant marriages and families in late medieval England', *Journal of Interdisciplinary History* xv (1984), 111–29.

'The village ale-wife: Women and brewing in fourteenth-century England', in B. A. Hanawalt, ed., *Women and work in preindustrial Europe* (Bloomington, 1986), 20–36.

Women in the medieval English countryside: Gender and household in Brigstock before the plague (Oxford, 1987).

Beresford, M. W., *Lay subsidies and poll taxes* (Canterbury, 1963).

Beveridge, W. H., 'Westminster wages in the manorial era', *Economic History Review* 2nd ser. viii (1955), 18–35.

Biller, P. P. A., 'Birth-control in the West in the thirteenth and early fourteenth centuries', *Past and Present* 94 (1982), 3–26.

Bindoff, S. T., ed., *The House of Commons 1509–1558*, vol. i (London, 1982).

Biraben, J.-N., 'Current medical and epidemiological views on plague', *The plague reconsidered* (*Local Population Studies* supplement, 1977), 25–36.

Bolton, J. L., *The medieval English economy 1150–1500* (London, 1980).

Bongaarts, J., 'Why high birth rates are so low', *Population and Development Review* 1 (1975), 289–96.

Bossy, J., *Christianity in the West 1400–1700* (Oxford, 1985).

Boulton, J., *Neighbourhood and society: A London suburb in the seventeenth century* (Cambridge, 1987).

Bradley, L., 'Some medical aspects of plague', *The plague reconsidered* (*Local Population Studies* supplement, 1977), 11–24.

Bridbury, A. R., *Economic growth: England in the later middle ages* (2nd edn, Hassocks, 1975).

Medieval English clothmaking: An economic survey (London, 1982).

Britnell, R. H., 'The making of Witham', *History Studies* 1 (1968), 13–21.

'Agricultural technology and the margin of cultivation in the fourteenth century', *Economic History Review* 2nd series xxx (1977), 53–66.

'Essex markets before 1350', *Essex Archaeology and History* 13 (1981), 15–21.

'The proliferation of markets in England 1200–1349', *Economic History Review* 2nd series xxxiv (1981), 209–21.

'Agriculture in a region of ancient enclosure, 1185–1500', *Nottingham Medieval Studies* xxvii (1983), 37–55.

Growth and decline in Colchester, 1300–1525 (Cambridge, 1986).

'Utilisation of the land in East Anglia, 1350–1500', in E. Miller, ed., *The Agrarian History of England and Wales*, vol. iii (Forthcoming).

Britton, E., *The community of the vill: A study in the history of the family and village life in fourteenth-century England* (Toronto, 1977).

Brooks, N., 'The organization and achievements of the peasants of Kent and Essex in 1381', in H. Mayr-Harting and R. I. Moore, eds., *Studies in medieval history presented to R. H. C. Davis* (London, 1985), 247–70.

Brown, A., 'London and north-west Kent in the later middle ages: The development of a land market', *Archaeologia Cantiana* 92 (1976), 145–55.

Brown, R. J., *English farmhouses* (London, 1985).

Cam, H. M., *The hundred and the hundred rolls* (2nd edn, London, 1963).

Campbell, B. M. S., 'Population change and the genesis of commonfields on a Norfolk manor', *Economic History Review* 2nd series xxxiii (1980), 174–92.

'Arable productivity in medieval England: Some evidence from Norfolk', *Journal of Economic History* 43 (1983), 379–404.

'The complexity of manorial structure in medieval Norfolk: A case study', *Norfolk Archaeology* xxxix (1986), 225–61.

Carrick, D. J. E. L., P. M. Richards and M. C. Wadhams, 'Historic building surveys', *Essex Archaeology and History* 12 (1980), 86–93.

Carus-Wilson, E. M., 'The aulnage accounts: A criticism', in E. M. Carus-Wilson, *Medieval merchant venturers: Collected studies* (London, 1954), 279–91.

'An industrial revolution of the thirteenth century', in E. M. Carus-Wilson, ed., *Essays in economic history*, vol. i (London, 1954), 41–60.

Chambers, J. D., *Population, economy and society in pre-industrial England*, (Oxford, 1972).

Clanchy, M. T., *From memory to written record: England 1066–1307* (London, 1979).

Clark, A., 'Tithing lists from Essex, 1329–1343', *English Historical Review* xix (1904), 715–19.

Clark, E., 'Debt litigation in a late medieval English vill', in J. A. Raftis, ed., *Pathways to medieval peasants* (Toronto 1981), 247–79.

'Some aspects of social security in medieval England', *Journal of Family History* 7 (1982), 307–20.

'Medieval labor law and English local courts', *American Journal of Legal History* xxvii (1983), 330–53.

'The decision to marry in thirteenth- and early fourteenth-century Norfolk', *Mediaeval Studies* xlix (1987), 496–516.

Clark, P., 'Migration in England during the late seventeenth and early eighteenth centuries', *Past and Present* 83 (1979), 57–90.

The English alehouse: A social history 1200–1830 (London, 1983).

Clarke, H., *The archaeology of medieval England* (London, 1984).

Clarkson, L. A., *Proto-industrialization: The first phase of industrialization?* (London, 1985).

Coale, A. J. and P. Demeny, *Regional model life tables and stable populations* (2nd edn, New York, 1983).

Cohn, N., *The pursuit of the millennium: Revolutionary millenarians and mystical anarchists of the middle ages* (2nd edn, Oxford, 1970).
Coleman, J., *English literature in history 1350–1400: Medieval readers and writers* (London, 1981).
Copinger, W. A., *The manors of Suffolk: Notes on their history and devolution*, 7 vols. (London, 1905–11).
Cornwall, J. C. K., *Wealth and society in early sixteenth century England*, (London, 1988).
Cressy, D., *Literacy and the social order: Reading and writing in Tudor and Stuart England* (Cambridge, 1980).
Cromarty, D., *The fields of Saffron Walden in 1400* (Chelmsford, 1966).
Cross, C., *Church and people 1450–1660: The triumph of the laity in the English church* (Atlantic Highlands, NJ, 1976).
Crowley, D. A., 'The later history of frankpledge', *Bulletin of the Institute of Historical Research* xlviii (1975), 1–15.
Czap, P., 'Marriage and the peasant joint family', in D. L. Ransel, ed., *The family in imperial Russia: New lines of historical research* (Urbana, 1978), 103–23.
Darby, H. C., R. E. Glasscock, J. Sheail and G. R. Versey, 'The changing geographical distribution of wealth in England: 1086–1334–1525', *Journal of Historical Geography* 5 (1979), 247–62.
Davis, J. F., 'Lollard survival and the textile industry in the south-east of England', *Studies in Church History* 3 (1966), 191–201.
Heresy and reformation in the south east of England 1520–1559 (London, 1983).
Derouet, B., 'Une démographie sociale différentielle: Clés pour un système auto-régulateur des populations rurales d'ancien régime', *Annales: Economies, Sociétés, Civilisations*, 35 (1980), 3–41.
Dickens, A. G., *The English Reformation* (London, 1964).
Dobson, M., '"Marsh fever": The geography of malaria in England', *Journal of Historical Geography* 6 (1980), 357–89.
Dobson, R. B., ed., *The peasants' revolt of 1381* (2nd edn, London, 1983).
Donahue, C., 'Proof by witnesses in the church courts of medieval England: An imperfect reception of the learned law', in M. S. Arnold, T. A. Green, S. A. Scully and S. D. White, eds., *On the laws and customs of medieval England: Essays in honor of Samuel E. Thorne* (Chapel Hill, 1981), 127–58.
'The canon law on the formation of marriage and social practice in the later middle ages', *Journal of Family History* 8 (1983), 144–58.
Drake, M., *Historical demography: Problems and projects* (Milton Keynes, 1974).
Drury, P. J., *Excavations at Little Waltham 1970–71*, Council for British Archaeology Research Report 26 (1978).
Du Boulay, F. R. H., *An age of ambition: English society in the late middle ages* (New York, 1970).
Dyer, C. C., *Lords and peasants in a changing society: The estates of the Bishopric of Worcester, 680–1540* (Cambridge, 1980).
Warwickshire farming 1349–c.1520: Preparations for agricultural revolution, Dugdale Society Occasional Paper 27 (1981).
'The social and economic background to the rural revolt of 1381', in R. H. Hilton and T. H. Aston, eds., *The English rising of 1381* (Cambridge, 1984), 9–42.

'English peasant buildings in the later middle ages (1200–1500)', *Medieval Archaeology* xxx (1986), 19–45.
Standards of living in the later middle ages (Cambridge, 1989).
Edwards, A. C. and K. C. Newton, *The Walkers of Hanningfield: Surveyors and mapmakers extraordinary* (London, 1984).
Everitt, A., 'Farm labourers', in J. Thirsk, ed., *Agrarian history of England and Wales*, 396–465.
'The marketing of agricultural produce', in J. Thirsk, ed., *Agrarian history of England and Wales*, 466–592.
Faith, R. J., 'Seigneurial control of women's marriage', *Past and Present* 99 (1983), 133–48.
Farmer, D. L., 'Crop yields, prices and wages in medieval England', *Studies in Medieval and Renaissance History* vii (1983), 117–55.
Fenwick, C. C., 'The English poll taxes of 1377, 1379, and 1381: A critical examination of the returns' (unpublished University of London Ph.D. dissertation, 1983).
Field, R. K., 'Worcestershire peasant buildings, household goods and farming equipment in the later middle ages', *Medieval Archaeology* ix (1965), 105–45.
Fisher, J. L., 'The Black Death in Essex', *Essex Review* lii (1943), 13–20.
A medieval farming glossary of Latin and English words, taken mainly from Essex records (London, 1968).
Fletcher, A., *Tudor rebellions* (2nd edn, London, 1973).
Forrester, H., *The timber-framed houses of Essex* (3rd edn, London, 1976).
Fryde, E. B., 'The English Parliament and the peasants' revolt of 1381', in *Liber memorialis Georges de Lagarde*, studies presented to the International Commission for the History of Representative and Parliamentary Institutions, 1968 (Louvain, 1970), 75–88.
Gasquet, F. A., *Parish life in medieval England* (London, 1936).
Gattrell, P., 'Historians and peasants: Studies of medieval English society in a Russian context', *Past and Present* 96 (1982), 22–50.
Gibson, A. V. B., 'Some small un-jettied medieval houses in Essex', *Essex Journal* 9 (1974), 22–31.
Glasscock, R. E., 'England *circa* 1334', in H. C. Darby, ed., *A new historical geography of England before 1600* (Cambridge, 1976), 136–85.
Glennie, P., 'In search of agrarian capitalism: Manorial land markets and the acquision of land in the Lea Valley *c.* 1450–*c.*1560', *Continuity and Change* 3 (1988), 11–40.
Goldberg, P. J. P., 'Marriage, migration, servanthood and life-cycle in Yorkshire towns of the later middle ages: Some York cause paper evidence', *Continuity and Change* 1 (1986), 141–69.
Goodman, A., 'The countess and the rebels: Essex and a crisis in English society', *Transactions of the Essex Archaeological Society* 3rd series ii (1970), 267–79.
Goody, J. and I. Watt, 'The consequences of literacy', in J. Goody, ed., *Literacy in traditional societies* (Cambridge, 1968), 27–68.
Gottfried, R. S., *Epidemic disease in fifteenth century England: The medical response and the demographic consequences* (Leicester, 1978).
Griffiths, R. A., *The reign of King Henry VI: The exercise of royal authority, 1422–1461* (Berkeley, 1981).

Hajnal, J., 'European marriage patterns in perspective', in D. V. Glass and D. E. C. Eversley, eds., *Population in history: Essays in historical demography* (London, 1965), 101–43.
'Two kinds of pre-industrial household formation system', in R. Wall, ed., *Family forms in historic Europe* (Cambridge, 1983), 1–64.
Hallam, H. E., *Settlement and society: A study of the early agrarian history of south Lincolnshire* (Cambridge, 1965).
Rural England 1066–1348 (London, 1981).
'Age at first marriage and age at death in the Lincolnshire Fenland, 1252–1478', *Population Studies* 39 (1985), 55–69.
Hanawalt, B. A., *The ties that bound: Peasant families in medieval England* (Oxford, 1986).
Harvey, B., *Westminster Abbey and its estates in the middle ages* (Oxford, 1977).
Harvey, P. D. A., *Manorial records*, British Records Association, Archives and the User, 5 (1984).
ed., *The peasant land market in medieval England* (Oxford, 1984).
Hassell Smith, A., 'Labourers in late sixteenth-century England: A case study from north Norfolk (Part 1)', *Continuity and Change* 4 (1989), 11–52.
Hatcher, J., *Plague, population and the English economy 1348–1530* (London, 1977).
'Mortality in the fifteenth century: Some new evidence', *Economic History Review* 2nd ser. xxxix (1986), 19–38.
Heath, P., *The English clergy on the eve of the Reformation* (London, 1969).
Helmholz, R. H., *Marriage litigation in medieval England* (Cambridge, 1974).
Herlihy, D. and C. Klapisch-Zuber, *Tuscans and their families: A study of the Florentine catasto of 1427* (New Haven, 1985).
Hewett, C. A., *The development of English carpentry 1200–1700: An Essex study* (Newton Abbot, 1969).
'A medieval timber kitchen at Little Braxted, Essex', *Medieval Archaeology* xvii (1973), 132–4.
'The smaller medieval house in Essex', *Archaeological Journal* 30 (1973), 172–82.
'Aisled timber halls and related buildings, chiefly in Essex', *Transactions of the Ancient Monument Society* new series 21 (1976), 45–99.
English historic carpentry (London, 1980).
Hill, C., 'From Lollards to Levellers', in J. M. Bak and G. Benecke, eds., *Religion and rural revolt* (Manchester, 1984), 86–103.
Hilton, R. H., *Bond men made free: Medieval peasant movements and the English rising of 1381* (New York, 1973).
'Peasant society, peasant movements and feudalism in medieval Europe', in H. A. Landsberger, ed., *Rural protest: Peasant movements and social change* (London, 1974), 67–94.
'Some social and economic evidence in late medieval English tax returns', in S. Herbst, ed., *Spoleczenstwo gospodarka kultura: Studia ofiarowane Marianowi Malowistowi* (Warsaw, 1974), 111–28.
The English peasantry in the later middle ages: The Ford Lectures for 1973 and related studies (Oxford, 1975).
ed., *The transition from feudalism to capitalism* (London, 1976).
'Freedom and villeinage in England', in R. H. Hilton, ed., *Peasants, knights and heretics: Studies in medieval English social history* (Cambridge, 1976), 174–91.

'Reasons for inequality among medieval peasants', *Journal of Peasant Studies* 5 (1978), 271–84.
'Individualism and the English peasantry', *New Left Review* 120 (1980), 109–11.
The decline of serfdom in medieval England (2nd edn, London, 1983).
A medieval society: The West Midlands at the end of the thirteenth century (reissued, Cambridge, 1983).
'Small town society in England before the Black Death', *Past and Present* 105 (1984), 53–78.
'Medieval market towns and simple commodity production', *Past and Present* 109 (1985), 3–23.

Holt, R., *The mills of medieval England* (Oxford, 1988).

Homans, G. C., *English villagers of the thirteenth century* (reissued, New York, 1960).

Houlbrooke, R. A., *Church courts and the people during the English Reformation 1520–1570* (Oxford, 1979).

Houston, R. A. and K. D. M. Snell, 'Proto-industrialization? Cottage industry, social change, and industrial revolution', *Historical Journal* 27 (1984), 473–92.

Hudson, A., *Lollards and their books* (London, 1985).
'The examination of Lollards', in A. Hudson, *Lollards and their books*, 125–40.
'Some aspects of Lollard book production', in A. Hudson, *Lollards and their books*, 181–92.
'A Lollard compilation and the dissemination of Wycliffite thought', in A. Hudson, *Lollards and their books*, 13–30.
'A Lollard mass', in A. Hudson, *Lollards and their books*, 111–24.
The premature reformation: Wycliffite texts and Lollard history (Oxford, 1988).

Hunnisett, R. F., 'The reliability of inquisitions as historical evidence', in D. A. Bollough and R. L. Storey, eds., *The study of medieval records* (Oxford, 1971), 206–35.

Hunt, W., *The Puritan moment: The coming of revolution in an English county* (Cambridge, MA, 1983).

Jones, A., 'Land measurement in England, 1150–1350', *Agricultural History Review* 27 (1979), 10–28.

Ker, N. R., 'More manuscripts from Essex monastic libraries, with notes on manuscripts connected with Essex parish churches', *Transactions of the Essex Archaeological Society* new series xxiii (1945), 298–310.

Kershaw, I., 'The great famine and agrarian crisis in England 1315–1322', in R. H. Hilton, ed., *Peasants, knights and heretics: Studies in medieval English social history* (Cambridge, 1976), 85–132.

Kightly, C., 'The early Lollards: A survey of popular Lollard activity in England, 1382–1428', (unpublished University of York Ph.D. dissertation, 1975).

Knodel, J., 'Demographic transitions in German villages', in A. J. Coale and S. C. Watkins, eds., *The decline of fertility in Europe* (Princeton, 1986), 337–89.

Kosminsky, E. A., *Studies in the agrarian history of England in the thirteenth century* (Oxford, 1956).

Kriedte, P., H. Medick and J. Schlumbohm, *Industrialization before industrialization: Rural industry in the genesis of capitalism*, tr. B. Schempp (Cambridge, 1981).

Kussmaul, A. S., 'The ambiguous mobility of farm servants', *Economic History Review*, 2nd series xxxiv (1981), 222–35.
Servants in husbandry in early modern England (Cambridge, 1981).
Laslett, P., ed., *Household and family in past time* (Cambridge, 1972).
'Parental deprivation in the past: A note on orphans and stepparenthood in English history', in P. Laslett, *Family life and illicit love in earlier generations* (Cambridge, 1977), 160–73.
'Clayworth and Cogenhoe', in P. Laslett, *Family life and illicit love in earlier generations* (Cambridge, 1977), 50–101.
'Demographic and microstructural history in relation to human adaptation: Reflections on newly established evidence', in D. J. Ortner, ed., *How humans adapt: A biocultural odyssey* (Washington, 1983), 343–70.
Le Roy Ladurie, E., *Montaillou: The promised land of error*, tr. B. Bray (New York, 1979).
Lee, R., 'Population homeostasis and English demographic history', in R. I. Rotberg and T. K. Rabb, eds., *Population and history: From the traditional to the modern world* (Cambridge, 1986), 75–100.
Lesthaeghe, R., 'On the social control of human reproduction', *Population and Development Review* 6 (1980), 527–48.
Levine, D., 'Production, reproduction and the proletarian family in England, 1500–1851', in D. Levine, ed., *Proletarianization and family history* (New York, 1984), 87–127.
Reproducing families: The political economy of English population history (Cambridge, 1987).
Liddell, W. H. and R. G. E. Wood, eds., *Essex and the peasants' revolt* (Chelmsford, 1981).
eds., *Essex and the great revolt of 1381* (Chelmsford, 1982).
Lindert, P. H., 'English population, wages, and prices: 1541–1913', in R. I. Rotberg and T. K. Rabb, eds., *Population and history: From the traditional to the modern world* (Cambridge, 1986), 49–74.
Loschky, D. 'Seven centuries of real income per wage earner reconsidered', *Economica* 47 (1980), 459–65.
McCloskey, D. N., *Econometric history* (London, 1987).
Macfarlane, A., *The origins of English individualism: The family, property and social transition* (Oxford, 1978).
McFarlane, K. B., *Wycliffe and English non-conformity* (Harmondsworth, 1972).
McIntosh, M. K., 'Land, tenure and population in the royal manor of Havering, Essex, 1251–1352/3', *Economic History Review* 2nd series xxxiii (1980), 17–31.
Autonomy and community: The royal manor of Havering, 1200–1500 (Cambridge, 1986).
'Local change and community control in England, 1465–1500', *Huntington Library Quarterly* 49 (1986), 219–42.
'Local responses to the poor in late medieval and Tudor England', *Continuity and Change* 3 (1988), 209–46.
Manning, R. B., *Village revolts: Social protest and popular disturbances in England 1509–1640* (Oxford, 1988).
Martin, J. E., *Feudalism to capitalism: Peasant and landlord in English agrarian development* (London, 1983).
Mate, M., 'Labour and labour services on the estates of Canterbury Cathedral Priory in the fourteenth century', *Southern History* 7 (1985), 55–67.

'Medieval agrarian practices: The determining factors?', *Agricultural History Review* 33 (1985), 22–31.

'The estates of Canterbury Cathedral Priory before the Black Death 1315–1348', *Studies in Medieval and Renaissance History* new series viii (1986), 3–30.

'Pastoral farming in south-east England in the fifteenth century', *Economic History Review* 2nd series xl (1987), 523–36.

Medick, H., 'The proto-industrial family economy: The structural function of household and family during the transition from peasant to industrial capitalism', *Social History* 1 (1976), 291–315.

Middleton, C., 'The sexual division of labour in feudal England', *New Left Review*, 113–14 (1979), 147–68.

Miller, E. and J. Hatcher, *Medieval England: Rural society and economic change 1086–1348* (London, 1978).

Minet, W., 'The Capells at Rayne 1486–1622', *Transactions of the Essex Archaeological Society* new series ix (1906), 243–72.

Moran, J. H., 'Literacy and education in northern England 1350–1550: A methodological enquiry', *Northern History* 17 (1981), 1–23.

The growth of English schooling 1340–1548: Learning, literacy and laicization in pre-reformation York diocese (Princeton, 1985).

Morant, P., *The history and antiquities of the county of Essex*, 2 vols. (2nd edn, London, 1978).

Morgan, K. O., *The Oxford history of Britain*, (Oxford, 1988).

Morris, W. A., *The frankpledge system* (Cambridge, MA, 1910).

Netting, R. M., R. R. Wilk and E. J. Arnould, eds., *Households: Comparative and historical studies of the domestic group* (Berkeley, 1984).

Newton, K. C., *Thaxted in the fourteenth century* (Chelmsford, 1960).

'A source for medieval population statistics', *Journal of the Society of Archivists* iii (1969), 543–6.

The manor of Writtle: The development of a royal manor in Essex, 1086–1500 (Chichester, 1970).

Newton, K. C. and M. K. McIntosh, 'Leet jurisdiction in Essex manor courts during the Elizabethan period', *Essex Archaeology and History* 3rd ser. 13 (1981), 3–14.

North, T., 'Legerwite in the thirteenth and fourteenth centuries', *Past and Present* 111 (1986), 3–16.

Oman, C., *The great revolt of 1381* (reprinted, New York, 1968).

Oosterveen, K., R. M. Smith and S. Stewart, 'Family reconstitution and the study of bastardy: Evidence from certain English parishes', in P. Laslett, K. Oosterveen and R. M. Smith, eds., *Bastardy and its comparative history* (London, 1980), 86–140.

Orme, N., *English schools in the middle ages* (London, 1973).

Education in the west of England, 1066–1548 (Exeter, 1976).

Outhwaite, R. B., 'Age at marriage in England from the late seventeenth to the nineteenth century', *Transactions of the Royal Historical Society* 5th series 23 (1973), 55–70.

Padfield, A., 'The development of two mediaeval houses', *Historic Buildings in Essex* 1 (1984), 2–5.

Palliser, D. M. and A. C. Pinnock, 'The markets of medieval Staffordshire', *North Staffordshire Journal of Field Studies* 11 (1971), 49–63.

Parkes, M. B., 'The literacy of the laity', in D. Daiches and A. Thorlby, eds., *Literature and western civilization: The mediaeval world* (London, 1973), 555–77.

Patten, J., 'Village and town: An occupational study', *Agricultural History Review* 20 (1972), 1–16.

Payer, P. J., *Sex and the penitentials: The development of a sexual code 550–1150* (Toronto, 1984).

Pelham, R. A., 'The distribution of early fulling mills in England and Wales', *Geography* xxix (1944), 52–6.

Fulling mills: A study in the application of water power to the woollen industry, Society for the Protection of Ancient Buildings, Wind and Watermill Section, 5 (1958).

Penn, S. A. C., 'Female wage-earners in late fourteenth-century England', *Agricultural History Review* 35 (1987), 1–14.

Pevsner, N., *The buildings of England: Essex* (2nd edn, Harmondsworth, 1965).

Phelps Brown, H. and S. V. Hopkins, *A perspective of wages and prices* (London, 1981).

Phythian Adams, C., *Desolation of a city: Coventry and the urban crisis of the late middle ages* (Cambridge, 1979).

Pollock, F. and F. W. Maitland, *The history of English law before the time of Edward I*, 2 vols. (2nd edn, Cambridge, 1968).

Poos, L. R. 'Plague mortality and demographic depression in later medieval England', *Yale Journal of Biology and Medicine* 54 (1981), 227–34.

'The social context of Statute of Labourers enforcement', *Law and History Review* 1 (1983), 27–52.

'Population and resources in two fourteenth-century Essex communities: Great Waltham and High Easter 1327–1389' (unpublished University of Cambridge Ph.D. dissertation, 1984).

'The rural population of Essex in the later middle ages', *Economic History Review* 2nd ser. xxxviii (1985), 515–30.

'Population turnover in medieval Essex', in L. Bonfield, R. M. Smith and K. Wrightson, eds., *The world we have gained: Histories of population and social structure* (Oxford, 1986), 1–22.

Poos, L. R. and L. Bonfield, 'Law and individualism in medieval England', *Social History* 11 (1986), 287–301.

Poos, L. R. and R. M. Smith, '"Legal windows onto historical populations?" Recent research on demography and the manor court in medieval England', *Law and History Review* 2 (1984), 128–52.

'"Shades still on the window": A reply to Zvi Razi', *Law and History Review* 3 (1985), 409–29.

Postan, M. M., *The famulus: The estate labourer in the xiith and xiiith centuries, Economic History Review* supplement 2 (1954).

The medieval economy and society: An economic history of Britain 1100–1500 (London, 1972).

'Some agrarian evidence of a declining population in the later middle ages', in M. M. Postan, *Essays on medieval agriculture and general problems of the medieval economy* (Cambridge, 1973), 186–213.

Postan, M. M. and J. Titow, 'Heriots and prices on Winchester manors', in M. M. Postan, *Essays on medieval agriculture*, 150–85.

Powell, Edgar, *The rising in East Anglia in 1381* (Cambridge, 1896).

Powell, Edward, 'The restoration of law and order', in G. L. Harriss, ed., *Henry V: The practice of kingship* (Oxford, 1985), 53–74.

Power, E., *The Paycockes of Coggeshall* (London, 1930).

Prescott, A. J., 'London in the peasants' revolt: A portrait gallery', *London Journal* 7 (1981), 125–43.

'Essex rebel bands in London', in W. H. Liddell and R. G. E. Wood, eds., *Essex and the great revolt of 1381* (Chelmsford, 1982), 55–66.

'Judicial records of the rising of 1381' (unpublished University of London Ph.D. dissertation, 1984).

Putnam, B. H., *The enforcement of the statutes of labourers during the first decade after the Black Death, 1349–1359* (reprinted, New York, 1970).

Rackham, O., 'The medieval landscape of Essex', in D. G. Buckley, ed., *Archaeology in Essex to AD 1500*, Council for British Archaeology Research Report 34 (1980), 103–7.

Raftis, J. A., *Tenure and mobility: Studies in the social history of the mediaeval English village* (Toronto, 1964).

Assart data and land values: Two studies in the East Midlands 1200–1350 (Toronto, 1974).

Rappaport, S., *Worlds within worlds: Structures of life in sixteenth-century London* (Cambridge, 1989).

Ravensdale, J., 'Population changes and the transfer of customary land on a Cambridgeshire manor in the fourteenth century', in R. M. Smith, ed., *Land, kinship and life-cycle* (Cambridge, 1984), 197–226.

Razi, Z., *Life, marriage and death in a medieval parish: Economy, society and demography in Halesowen 1270–1400* (Cambridge, 1980).

'Family, land and the village community in later medieval England', *Past and Present* 93 (1981), 3–36.

'The use of manorial court rolls in demographic analysis: A reconsideration', *Law and History Review* 3 (1985), 191–200.

'The demographic transparency of manorial court rolls', *Law and History Review* 5 (1987), 523–36.

Reaney, P. H., *The place-names of Essex*, English Place-Name Society xii (1935).

Richmond, C. F., 'Fauconberg's Kentish rising of May 1471', *English Historical Review* lxxxv (1970), 673–92.

Ritchie, N., 'Labour conditions in Essex in the reign of Richard II', in E. M. Carus-Wilson, ed., *Essays in economic history* (London, 1962), vol. ii, 91–111.

Rodwell, W., 'Relict landscapes in Essex', in H. C. Bowen and P. J. Fowler, eds., *Early land allotment in the British Isles*, British Archaeological Reports 48 (1978), 89–98.

Ross, C., *Edward IV* (Berkeley, 1974).

Russell, J. C., *British medieval population* (Albuquerque, 1948).

The control of late ancient and medieval population (Philadelphia, 1985).

Scarisbrick, J. J., *The Reformation and the English people* (Oxford, 1984).

Schofield, R. S., 'The measurement of literacy in pre-industrial England', in J. Goody, ed., *Literacy in traditional societies* (Cambridge, 1968), 311–25.

'Age-specific mobility in an eighteenth century rural English parish', *Annales de Démographie Historique* 27 (1972), 261–74.

'The relationship between demographic structure and environment in pre-industrial Western Europe', in W. Conze, ed., *Sozialgeschichte der Familie in der Neuzeit Europas* (Stuttgart, 1976), 147–60.

'English marriage patterns revisited', *Journal of Family History* 10 (1985), 2–20.

'Did the mothers really die? Three centuries of maternal mortality in "the world we have lost"', in L. Bonfield, R. M. Smith and K. Wrightson, eds., *The world we have gained: Histories of population and social structure* (Oxford, 1986), 231–60.

'Taxation and the political limits of the Tudor state', in C. Cross, D. Loades and J. J. Scarisbrick, eds., *Law and government under the Tudors: Essays presented to Sir Geoffrey Elton, Regius Professor of Modern History at the University of Cambridge on the occasion of his retirement* (Cambridge, 1988), 227–55.

'Family structure, demographic behaviour, and economic growth', in J. Walter and R. S. Schofield, eds., *Famine, disease and the social order in early modern society* (Cambridge, 1989), 279–304.

Schofield, R. S. and E. A. Wrigley, 'Infant and child mortality in the late Tudor and early Stuart period', in C. Webster, ed., *Health, medicine and mortality in the sixteenth century* (Cambridge, 1979), 61–96.

Searle, E., 'Seigneurial control of women's marriage: The antecedents and function of merchet in England', *Past and Present* 82 (1979), 3–43.

Sheail, J., 'The regional distribution of wealth in England as indicated by the lay subsidy returns of 1524/25' (unpublished University of London Ph.D. dissertation, 1968).

Sheehan, M. M., 'The formation and stability of marriage in fourteenth-century England: Evidence of an Ely register', *Mediaeval Studies* xxxiii (1971), 228–63.

'Choice of marriage partner in the middle ages: The development and mode of application of a theory of marriage', *Studies in Medieval and Renaissance History* new series 1 (1978), 3–33.

Shryock, H. S., J. S. Siegel *et al.*, *The methods and materials of demography* (London, 1976).

Smith, R. M., 'Kin and neighbours in a thirteenth century Suffolk community', *Journal of Family History* 4 (1979), 219–56.

'Some reflections on the evidence for the origins of the "European marriage pattern" in England', in C. Harris, ed., *The sociology of the family: New directions for Britain, Sociological Review* monograph 28 (1979), 74–112.

'Fertility, economy, and household formation in England over three centuries', *Population and Development Review* 7 (1981), 595–622.

'The people of Tuscany and their families in the fifteenth century: Medieval or Mediterranean?', *Journal of Family History* 6 (1981), 107–28.

'Rooms, relatives and residential arrangements: Some evidence in manor court rolls 1250–1500', Medieval Village Research Group, *Annual Report* 30 (1982), 34–5.

'Hypothèses sur la nuptialité en Angleterre aux xiiie–xive siècles', *Annales: Economies, Sociétés, Civilisations* 38 (1983), 107–36.

'Some thoughts on "hereditary" and "proprietary" rights in land under customary law in thirteenth and early fourteenth century England', *Law and History Review* 1 (1983), 95–128.

ed., *Land, kinship and life-cycle* (Cambridge, 1984).

'Some issues concerning families and their property in rural England 1250–1800', in R. M. Smith, ed., *Land, kinship and life-cycle*, 1–86.

'"Modernization" and the corporate medieval village community in England: Some sceptical reflections', in A. R. H. Baker and D. Gregory, eds., *Explorations in historical geography* (Cambridge, 1984), 140–79.

'Marriage processes in the English past: Some continuities', in L. Bonfield, R. M. Smith and K. Wrightson, eds., *The world we have gained: Histories of population and social structure* (Oxford, 1986), 43–99.

'Human resources', in A. Astill and A. Grant, eds., *The countryside of medieval England* (Oxford, 1988), 188–212.

Souden, D., 'Pre-industrial English local migration fields' (unpublished University of Cambridge Ph.D. dissertation, 1981).

Sparvel-Bayly, J. A., 'Essex in insurrection, 1381', *Transactions of the Essex Archaeological Society* new series i (1878), 205–19.

Spufford, M., 'Puritanism and social control?', in A. Fletcher and J. Stevenson, eds., *Order and disorder in early-modern England* (Cambridge, 1985).

Thirsk, J., 'Industries in the countryside', in F. J. Fisher, ed., *Essays in the economic and social history of Tudor and Stuart England* (Cambridge, 1961), 70–85.

ed., *The agrarian history of England and Wales*, vol. iv, *1500–1640* (Cambridge, 1967).

'The farming regions of England', in J. Thirsk, ed., *Agrarian history of England and Wales*, 1–112.

Thomas, K., *Religion and the decline of magic: Studies in popular beliefs in sixteenth and seventeenth-century England* (Harmondsworth, 1973).

'Age and authority in early modern England', *Proceedings of the British Academy* lxii (1976), 205–48.

Thomson, J. A. F., *The later Lollards 1414–1520* (Oxford, 1965).

Thorold Rogers, J. E., *A history of agriculture and prices in England 1259–1793*, 7 vols. (Oxford, 1866–1902).

Thrupp, S. L., *The merchant class of medieval London 1300–1500* (Chicago, 1948).

'The problem of replacement-rates in late medieval England', *Economic History Review* 2nd series xiv (1965), 113–28.

Tilly, C., 'Demographic origins of the European proletariat', in D. Levine, ed., *Proletarianization and family history* (New York, 1984), 1–85.

Titow, J. Z., 'Some evidence of the thirteenth century population increase', *Economic History Review* 2nd ser. xiv (1961), 231–51.

'Some differences between manors and their effects on the condition of the peasant in the thirteenth century', *Agricultural History Review* 10 (1962), 1–13.

English rural society 1200–1350 (London, 1969).

Winchester yields: A study in medieval agricultural productivity (Cambridge, 1972).

Unwin, T., 'Rural marketing in medieval Nottinghamshire', *Journal of Historical Geography* 7 (1981), 231–51.

Victoria County History of Essex (1903–).

von Arx, W., 'The churching of women after childbirth: History and significance', *Concilium* 112 (1979), 63–72.

Wadhams, M. C., 'Historic building surveys', *Essex Archaeology and History* 11 (1979), 78–89.

Walker, S. S., 'Proof of age of feudal heirs in medieval England', *Mediaeval Studies* xxxv (1973), 306–23.

Wall, R., 'The age at leaving home', *Journal of Family History* 3 (1978), 181–201.
'Regional and temporal variations in English household structure from 1650', in J. Hobcroft and P. Rees, eds., *Regional demographic development* (London, 1979), 89–113.
Wareing, J., 'Changes in the geographical distribution of the recruitment of apprentices to the London companies 1486–1750', *Journal of Historical Geography* 6 (1980), 241–9.
Watts, S., 'Demographic facts as experienced by a group of families in eighteenth-century Shifnal, Shropshire', *Local Population Studies* 32 (1984), 34–43.
Weir, D. R., 'Rather never than late: Celibacy and age at marriage in English cohort fertility', *Journal of Family History* 9 (1984), 340–54.
White, S. D. and R. T. Vann, 'The invention of English individualism: Alan Macfarlane and the modernization of pre-modern England', *Social History* 8 (1983), 345–63.
Williamson, T. M., 'The Roman countryside: Settlement and agriculture in N. W. Essex', *Britannia* xv (1984), 225–30.
Wood, R. G. E., 'Essex manorial records and the revolt', in W. H. Liddell and R. G. E. Wood, eds., *Essex and the great revolt of 1381* (Chelmsford, 1982), 67–84.
Wrightson, K., 'Aspects of social differentiation in rural England, *c.* 1580–1660', *Journal of Peasant Studies* 5 (1977), 33–47.
Wrightson, K. and D. Levine, *Poverty and piety in an English village: Terling, 1525–1700* (New York, 1979).
Wrigley, E. A., 'The means to marry', *Quarterly Journal of Social Affairs* 1 (1985), 271–80.
Wrigley, E. A. and R. S. Schofield, *The population history of England 1541–1871: A reconstruction* (London, 1981).
'English population history from family reconstitution: Summary results 1600–1799', *Population Studies* 37 (1983), 157–84.
Wunderli, R. M., *London church courts and society on the eve of the reformation* (Cambridge, MA, 1981).

Index

Note: Except for London, all place-names indexed here are in Essex unless otherwise specified.

Cambridge Studies in Population, Economy and Society in Past Time 18

1 *Land, kinship and life-cycle* edited by RICHARD M. SMITH
2 *Annals of the labouring poor: social change and agrarian England 1660–1900* K. D. M. SNELL*
3 *Migration in a mature economy: emigration and internal migration in England and Wales 1861–1900* DUDLEY BAINES
4 *Scottish literacy and the Scotttish identity: illiteracy and society in Scotland and Northern England 1600–1800* R. A. HOUSTON
5 *Neighbourhood and society: a London suburb in the seventeenth century* JEREMY BOULTON
6 *Demographic behavior in the past: a study of fourteen German village populations in the eighteenth and nineteenth centuries* JOHN E. KNODEL
7 *Worlds within worlds: structures of life in sixteenth-century London* STEVE RAPPAPORT
8 *Upland communities: environment, population and social structure in the Alps since the sixteenth century* PIER PAOLO VIAZZO
9 *Height, health and history: nutritional status in the United Kingdom 1538–1840* RODERICK FLOUD, KENNETH WACHTER and ANNABEL GREGORY
10 *Famine, disease and the social order in early modern society* edited by JOHN WALTER and ROGER SCHOFIELD*
11 *A general view of the rural economy of England, 1538–1840* ANN KUSSMAUL
12 *Town and country in pre-industrial Spain: Cuenca 1540–1870* DAVID REHER
13 *A stagnating metropolis: the economy and demography of Stockholm 1750–1850* JOHAN SODERBERG, ULF JONSSEN and CHRISTER PERSSON
14 *Population and Nutrition: an essay on European demographic history* MASSIMO LIVI-BACCI*
15 *Istanbul households: marriage, family and fertility 1880–1940* ALAN DUBEN and CEM BEHAR
16 *A community transformed: the manor and liberty of Havering-atte-Bower 1500–1620* MARJORIE KENISTON MCINTOSH
17 *Friends in life and death: the British and Irish Quakers in the demographic transition* RICHARD T. VANN and DAVID EVERSLEY
18 *A rural society after the Black Death: Essex 1350–1525* L. R. POOS

Titles available in paperback are marked with an asterisk

Printed in the United Kingdom
by Lightning Source UK Ltd.
134672UK00002BB/43-45/A